"NO ONE CAN
HURT HIM
ANYMORE"

"NO ONE CAN HURT HIM ANYMORE"

CAROL J. ROTHGEB
AND
SCOTT H. CUPP

PINNACLE BOOKS
Kensington Publishing Corp.
http://www.kensingtonbooks.com

Acknowledgments

First of all, I would like to thank my editor of *Hometown Killer*, Gary Goldstein, for recommending me to Miles Lott, the editor of *"No One Can Hurt Him Anymore"*—and for his confidence in me—making it possible for me to be a part of this project.

And Scott Cupp—not only for being a joy to work with but, more important, for everything he's done in his career to bring justice to those who would do harm to the youngest and most vulnerable in our society.

My love and gratitude to my children—Jeanne, David, and Dana. Once again, I had their unwavering support, love, and encouragement.

And, as always, my love to my granddaughters—Mallory, Chelsea, Miranda, and Sarah. My hope is that they will know that their dreams can come true.

Most of all, I want to thank with all my heart F. Peter "Pete" Dixon, retired homicide prosecutor, for supporting me, encouraging me, and loving me through this difficult project. If it hadn't been for his guidance and honesty, I don't know if I would have made it. He is truly *The Wind Beneath My Wings*.
—Carol J. Rothgeb

To my brother, George, the smartest and bravest man I know.

For my children—Kaitlin, Elizabeth, and Scotty—and the wonderful future that awaits them.

I want to specifically acknowledge three people: Judge Joe Marx, without whom the cases would never have been won; State Attorney Barry Krischer, who supported me before the filing of the charges, during the time it took to get the cases tried, and has supported me as this book made its way to print. This case is also a testament to the fine police work of the men and women of the Palm Beach County Sheriff's Office, which was exemplified by the hard work, dedication, and persistence of lead detective Michael Waites.
—Scott H. Cupp

PROLOGUE

His name was A.J.

He loved Ninja Turtles and Steven Seagal movies.

He was ten years old and small for his age. He had tousled brown hair, watchful brown eyes, and a look of perpetual apology on his baby face, as if everything he did—or thought—required one. A.J. had a sixth sense about anger and aggression. He could see it in the twitch of an eye or the tilt of a head. He had mastered "body language." He had endured. Scars—psychological and physical—were his constant companions.

This was as happy and secure as it ever got for A.J.: He was walking his dog. To be sure, the animal was truly a mutt, but no ordinary dog—not to A.J. The peaceful look on his face revealed that they had a bond. Neither of them had anywhere else to look to for friendship—much less love.

In truth, the dog had it better.

It was 1:30 in the morning and cool outside—almost cold. A.J. wore a stained T-shirt and pants a size too small. He laughed out loud as he tried to keep up with the dog.

The neighborhood was veiled in darkness, but A.J. wasn't afraid. At least, not of walking his dog at such strange hours. Going back home—that's what he feared more than anything.

The dog took him full circle around the neighborhood and they finally ended up in front of their residence—nearly indistinguishable in the row of look-alike houses. The dog stopped, sharing A.J.'s reluctance.

Maybe if he used the patio door, they wouldn't notice him coming in. . . .

CHAPTER 1

No more pain . . . no more humiliation . . . no more fear . . . it was finally over. No one could ever hurt him again. In the cold, still water, in the middle of the spring night, he had finally found peace.

David Schwarz struggled to wake up enough to understand what his wife was saying to him—and why she was shaking him. After a moment, he realized that Jessica was telling him that his ten-year-old son, A.J., was missing. Now wide-awake and alarmed, he stumbled to the kitchen, with his wife right behind him—insisting that she had already looked everywhere and he was nowhere to be found.

As he passed by the patio door—still trying to comprehend what was happening—he glanced outside and noticed that the ladder was hanging on the side of their aboveground swimming pool. Could it be? Was it possible that A.J. had gone swimming? At this hour? It was barely daylight—the sun had just come up.

David rushed to the side of the pool, which was located about five feet from the patio door, and saw the boy under the water about halfway down. But something was terribly wrong. He quickly jumped into the pool and lifted his son out of the water.

It was heartbreakingly obvious that A.J. was dead. David shouted at Jessica to call 911, and then gently laid his son's cold, stiff body on the ground. Disbelieving—and stunned—

he went into the house to get a sheet to cover him. Then he sat down in a chair at the patio table—a few feet from his son's body—to wait.

The beautiful Sunday morning of May 2, 1993, was clear and dry with the promise of becoming very hot, with the temperature already in the low seventies. Within minutes of the 911 call, sirens screamed in the distance as paramedics and law enforcement officials approached the area from different directions. Their destination was a residence on Triphammer Road in the Concept Homes Development, a low-to-medium-income neighborhood near Lantana, Florida.

As soon as the officers from the Palm Beach Sheriff's Office (PBSO)—who were working the graveyard shift—arrived, they cordoned off the ranch-style house with yellow crime-scene tape. Neighbors started filtering out of their homes—some still in their nightclothes—trying to find out what had happened.

Corporal Bobbie Hopper, the responding officer, walked around the house and entered the backyard through a wooden gate located on the west side of the house. A six-foot-high privacy fence surrounded the entire area.

The octagon-shaped swimming pool was centered in—and completely dominated—the small yard. It was no more than four feet deep and there was a white plastic ladder on the outside of the pool and another on the inside.

The victim was lying on the grass under a flowered bedsheet next to the north side of the pool. When the officer removed the sheet, she saw that the young boy was on his back and was naked.

His right arm was bent at the elbow and lying across his chest, and his left arm was bent at the elbow near his side—his forearm outstretched. The tips of his fingers on both hands were bent inward, not quite—but almost—balled into fists, therefore suggesting a struggle might have taken place.

Both his legs were bent at the knees and the heels of both feet rested on the ground with his toes pointed upward.

And he was covered with bruises. They were everywhere, on his arms, his legs, his neck, and his face. A deep abrasion scored the right side of his nose. Another feathered away from his mouth. The underside of his chin was clearly bruised. The neck, chest, and abdomen were nicked and abraded. A patchwork of bruises ran down his hips and his legs.

Oddly enough, there was a blue-and-green-colored stain—along with some sparkles in his hair—on the left side of his hairline.

Detective Michael Waites was awakened by the shrill ringing of the telephone at 6:25 that morning. The police dispatcher on the other end of the line requested that he respond to an apparent drowning. After being informed that the victim was a child, he was in his car and on the road within minutes.

Sergeant Ken Deischer, of the PBSO's Homicide Unit, met him in front of the house and briefed him: The victim was a ten-year-old white male. He had been discovered floating facedown in an aboveground swimming pool in the backyard. Nude. And covered with bruises.

Michael Waites would be the lead investigator. He had been a homicide detective since 1987 and a member of the SWAT team since 1985. Quiet, easygoing, and thorough, he listened more than he spoke.

Several detectives, including Jimmy Restivo and Chris Calloway, were en route to conduct a canvass of the neighborhood. They could only hope that if there had been child abuse—or anything suspicious—that the neighbors would be willing to talk to the investigators.

Deischer and Waites circled around to the backyard and Waites examined the body. He anticipated that the cause of death was drowning. The manner of death, on the other hand—

whether it was from natural causes, suicide, accident, or homicide—was something he hoped the medical examiner would be able to determine.

Corporal Hopper provided him with the victim's name and date of birth: Andrew J. Schwarz, born April 24, 1983. She added, "But everyone called him A.J. He lives . . . lived here with his father, stepmother, and two stepsisters." They would later learn that the older one was A.J.'s stepsister and the younger one was actually his half sister.

Waites entered the house through the patio door that led into the extremely cluttered kitchen. Among other things, there were empty beer cans everywhere.

David Schwarz, a big man with an untamed beard and a look of disbelief and shock on his face, was seated at the kitchen table. It was easy to see why everyone—as the detective would later learn—called him "Bear."

Waites introduced himself and immediately began assessing the father's state of mind, searching for signs of shock: the onset of grief, anger, and loss.

David, struggling to speak, said that A.J. went to bed around 9:00 the night before and was fine. He said that he had stayed up, watching TV, until around midnight—maybe 12:30—and that Jessica had gone to bed sometime prior to that. Before he went to bed, he had checked on the kids. All three of them were sound asleep in their bedrooms—including A.J.

The next thing he remembered was his wife waking him up with the news that A.J. was missing. She informed him that A.J. wasn't in his bedroom or anywhere else in the house.

Waites asked him what time that was and Bear said it was around 6:00—maybe a little after. He went on to say that he was standing in the kitchen when he noticed that the ladder was in the pool, and he remembered removing the ladder from the pool late the previous evening. When he stepped into the backyard to investigate, he saw his son's body in the pool.

David Schwarz was seriously shaken. He could have been

acting, but Waites didn't think so. The detective asked what A.J. had been wearing when he went to bed, and Bear replied, "Ninja Turtle sweatpants and a T-shirt."

And now he was naked next to the swimming pool.

Waites asked David Schwarz to sign a "consent to search" for the house and curtilage and he agreed.

When Detective Doreen Schoenstein, of the Crime Scene Unit, returned to her vehicle to obtain the items necessary for the investigation and the search, she noticed that several of the neighbors who had gathered outside their homes were very upset and speaking in hostile tones about Jessica and David Schwarz.

When Schoenstein went into the house, Detective Waites told her that he was attempting to speak with A.J.'s step-mother. Due to the suspicious circumstances surrounding the child's death, Jessica and David had been kept separated until they could be questioned.

Hopper and Schoenstein accompanied Detective Waites to the other side of the house and found Jessica, along with her daughters, in the younger girl's bedroom. It was a cheerful room with posters and pictures on the walls and cluttered with dolls and toys.

When Hopper knocked on the open door, Jessica was stretched out on the bed and looked ill when they entered the room. Waites wondered silently if she was hungover and made a mental note to inquire about the couple's drinking habits.

Jessica Schwarz was a heavyset woman—5' 2" tall and weighing 175 pounds. Her state of mind was not as easy to read as her husband's. She appeared to be dazed and the first thing she said was that she couldn't believe this was happening. The next was that she felt sick to her stomach.

Detective Waites asked for some time alone with her and Hopper took Jessica's two daughters, four-year-old Jackie Schwarz and ten-year-old Lauren Cross, to another bedroom.

Schoenstein left the room to continue her investigation. First she went to the backyard to examine the pool and found that the water was fairly clean—except for a few leaves in the bottom—and cold to the touch. After collecting a water sample, she returned to the house through the patio door. She examined and photographed the sliding door and noticed that the lock was broken. She determined that the Schwarzes were in the habit of securing the door by placing an old cane in the track.

David Schwarz told her he couldn't remember whether the sliding door was open or not, prior to finding A.J.'s body.

Her next stop was A.J.'s bedroom: a dungeonlike room on the northeast corner of the house, directly off the kitchen, and attached to the garage. There was no doorknob. Instead, there was a piece of cloth—or rag—pulled through the knob hole and tied. And a lock—on the outside of the door.

On the inside of the door was a note from A.J.'s teacher—a progress report dated "4-2-93" that indicated that he and his teacher had had a very good day.

"Bleak" was the word that came to mind when she entered A.J.'s room. There was a simple twin bed along one wall and, on the opposite wall, a dresser that appeared to be used for storage with boxes—marked "Christmas decorations"—stacked on top of it. The window covering was a floral sheet, and there was a door leading to the attached garage.

And, on a desk, there was a piece of notebook paper with a child's handwriting on it. "I have a big stupid mouth, I don't know when to shut up" was written over and over again.

Black trash bags filled with clothing were on the floor, and several socks were scattered around.

Poorly lit. The room smelled of stale urine. There were no posters on the walls. No photographs. No Nintendo. No stereo or radio. No books. On a bookcase under the window, there were a few toy action figures and toy cars. In the center of the room—on the floor—were a turquoise sleeping bag, a dark T-shirt, and a pair of Ninja Turtle sweatpants. And inside the pants, a pair of boy's underwear.

The clothes A.J. had worn to bed the night before.

On a small table, Schoenstein found two bottles of Easter-egg coloring—blue and green—but both of them were empty.

When she went back through the kitchen and entered the living room, she saw several pictures of the girls displayed, but did not see any photographs—not even one—of A.J. anywhere in the room. Or anywhere else in the house.

Next she went to Lauren's room and—like Jackie's—it was bright and cheerful with pictures and posters on the walls and dolls and toys scattered around. A color television. A Nintendo game. And a stereo system.

Meanwhile, after everyone else had left the room, Waites asked Jessica, "How was it that you found out that A.J. was missing?"

"I just woke up out of the blue. I never wake up that early on a Sunday. But I was thirsty. So I went to the kitchen for a drink of water and there was A.J.'s door open. I mean, he always sleeps with it closed, so I looked in his room and he wasn't there. I even looked under the bed. Uh-uh. I checked everywhere, in the garage—in the bathroom—in the family room—everywhere. . . . When I couldn't find him, I figured I better wake up Bear. And he found him in the pool a couple of minutes later."

Without prompting, she began to describe the abuse that A.J. had suffered at the hands of his natural mother, Ilene Logan (who had—after her divorce from David Schwarz—married and then divorced a man named Timothy Logan). It was that abusive situation, Jessica told him, that led to A.J.'s placement with her and Bear.

If Jessica had seemed upset when Waites first came into the room, she didn't now. She appeared agitated and aggressive, but not overwhelmed with the grief or disbelief that Bear had demonstrated.

She went on to tell him that A.J. had been treated for hyperactivity—and also received therapy for the past abuse—at South County Mental Health. He also had spent six weeks at the mental institution, located in Vero Beach, the previous year. She explained that he had presently been "in between counselors."

Detective Waites later informed Doreen Schoenstein that

A.J. had been under the care of a psychiatrist and had been in protective custody. He had also been taking a medication known as imipramine, a drug used to relieve symptoms of depression.

Jessica had told him that she was the one who personally administered the medication to A.J., but now she couldn't find it. Nor could she find it the day before. She claimed she did not know "what happened to it."

Schoenstein searched the residence, but she was unsuccessful in locating the medication.

It was after 8:00 when Waites returned to the backyard. Before the body was removed, he studied it again. What about an errant dive into the pool? Could A.J. have gone for a swim and knocked himself out? He examined A.J.'s forehead, looking for the full bruising that is consistent with such a hypothesis, and couldn't detect it.

Could A.J. have gone swimming, cramped up, and gone under? Possible, but the pool wasn't that deep. As he looked from the body to the pool, he realized that A.J. was tall enough to stand up, no matter how severe the cramps. That led to another question: do ten-year-old boys go swimming naked?

As he looked at A.J.'s face, he wondered if the boy could have inexplicably decided to go snorkeling in the middle of the night. Gotten up, taken off his Ninja Turtle pants, gone outside, and put the ladder up next to the pool? Could he have taken in water through the snorkel, panicked, and wrenched off the mask with enough force to cause such lacerations and bruising? Not likely. Still, he walked back to the swimming pool and searched the bottom. There was a mask, but no snorkel.

Could he have been electrocuted? Doubtful, given the condition of the body, but he made a note to check any electrical problems around the house. Could he have been climbing the ladder, slipped, and hit his head against the wood railing that framed the pool? That was a real possibility, but it didn't explain the abrasions on his neck and shoulders—or the bruises on his chest and legs.

No one from the medical examiner's office had arrived

and Waites was informed that they wouldn't be coming. Forensic investigator Doug Jenkins had been contacted and he advised that he would not respond to the scene, but would send Professional Removal Service (a body removal service contracted by the county) to transport the corpse to the Palm Beach County Medical Examiner's Office.

The attendants, David Grant and Don Scott, finally arrived at 8:35 and—after checking for signs of recent trauma—removed the body. An autopsy was scheduled for the next afternoon; Detective Waites would be there.

An extraordinary scene had developed in front of the house. Besides the official vehicles, investigators, and neighbors, members of the press and curiosity seekers now had converged. The detectives who had been conducting the neighborhood canvass began to check in.

Jimmy Restivo—a huge, burly man—was a transplant from New York, and his twenty-two years with NYPD had done as much to solidify his cynicism as it did to sharpen his skills. He consulted the scribbles on his notepad and said, in his heavy New York accent, "Wait'll you hear this. The kid was out walking his dog at one-thirty last night. One-thirty this morning! Guy next door saw him. Name's Ron Pincus Junior. He's pulling in from work and here's A.J. wandering the streets with his dog."

Waites looked at Restivo. "He sure it was one-thirty?"

"Positive. He'd just gotten off work."

Waites responded, "Mr. Schwarz says the boy was sound asleep when he went to bed at twelve-thirty."

Restivo shook his head. "Uh-uh. That doesn't fit either. Pincus says he noticed a light on in the Schwarz living room and the TV on. Same time—one-thirty.

"Two weeks ago, Pincus overheard the stepmom shouting at the kid that if he 'doesn't straighten up,' she's going to 'tie him up and run him over.' Heard her say she hates him. Pincus says it goes on all the time. Guess what the stepmom calls the kid? She calls him 'Jeffrey Dahmer.' You believe that?"

Another detective added: "She's been heard calling Andrew everything from a 'stupid loudmouth' and a 'slut' to a 'piece of shit' and a 'bitch.' "

"You've got names and addresses on all these people?" Waites asked.

"Every one."

Chris Calloway, of the Special Investigations Unit, dealt—on a daily basis—with sex crimes, child abuse, and neglect. He had at least a dozen pages of notes to follow up on, all of them indicating that Andrew Schwarz had been subjected to physical and emotional abuse for years—up to and including the day before his death.

Waites asked, "Was HRS ever involved?" HRS—Health and Rehabilitative Services—is Florida's version of social services, and their handling of child abuse cases had been under intense scrutiny for almost a year.

Calloway replied, "They were regular visitors. The last time was when A.J. showed up at a neighbor's house with a broken nose and two black eyes. Very suspicious.

"The story was that A.J. had cracked his face against the handlebars of his sister's bike. This neighbor, an Eileen Callahan, doesn't believe it. She thinks Jessica threatened the kid to get him to tell that story and to stick with it.

"I talked to him myself. If someone hit him, he wouldn't say."

Detective Waites requested that David and Jessica Schwarz, along with Jackie and Lauren, come to the sheriff's office to be interviewed. Detective Calloway would conduct a joint investigation into the allegations of the abuse.

The investigation into his death—and life—would reveal that by no stretch of anyone's imagination had A.J. Schwarz lived anything even close to a happy life—or even a normal one.

CHAPTER 2

Please, for the kids' sakes, give them both to us and I promise we will comply with everything you want us to do. Give them a break, and David and myself a chance to prove we can make a difference and change their lives for the best.

—Jessica Schwarz

Andrew J. "A.J." Schwarz was born to David Schwarz and his first wife, Ilene, on April 24, 1983. Ten years and eight days later he was dead.

When David met Ilene Spence in 1980, she already had a baby girl named Patsy. There was no father's name listed on Patsy's birth certificate, only the notation that he had "left before she was born." Therefore, her last name was Spence—her mother's maiden name. David and Ilene were married in 1982 and their son was born the following year.

According to David, Ilene kept the children—and the apartment—clean. But after she "kicked him out" and they were divorced in 1986, she "worked nights as a stripper, had many lovers, and abused drugs and alcohol."

He saw A.J. and Patsy every weekend. Even though Patsy was not his own child, he loved her and did not want to separate the two children.

David lived alone for a short time until he met Jessica. A

former truck driver, traveling from New York City to Miami, she had sold her truck and moved to Florida.

A.J. was three years old when he first visited with both Jessica and David. Jessica would later say that the children were "malnourished, dirty, and dressed poorly." She also claimed that A.J. could not talk, was shy or frightened, that he would hide his face, and was totally inarticulate. She also said that he did not use tableware and acted like a sick animal.

David's words were similar: The children were "kept poorly, dirty, thin, and ragged." The children told him that Ilene's lovers had beaten them.

In 1987, A.J. became ill and was hospitalized. HRS was called in because A.J. had bruises on his back and claimed he had been beaten "with a stick."

Shortly after that, Ilene, along with the children, disappeared, and David did not see them again until November 1989, when he—by chance—met them on the street. They again disappeared and he did not see them until HRS called him in 1990.

At the initial HRS medical exam, A.J. was diagnosed as hyperactive. He also could not hear well, suffered from asthma, and his front teeth were rotten. He was a mess.

Jessica and David were given temporary custody of the children—although they remained under protective custody of the state. Both of them were sickly when they arrived and had lice and ringworm.

Jessica had sent a letter to HRS, which read in part:

Please, for the kids' sakes, give them both to us and I promise we will comply with everything you want us to do. Give them a break, and David and myself a chance to prove we can make a difference and change their lives for the best.

Shortly before noon on Sunday, May 2, Michael Waites interviewed thirty-six-year old David Schwarz at the sheriff's office. Still quite distraught, his voice echoed the genuine disbelief and shock that he was feeling:

Waites: I just need to—real quickly—go over what happened this morning. Start with dinnertime last night—how A.J. was acting up until he goes to bed.

David: He was fine. He ate dinner with everybody else. No, he ate in his room. Uh, chicken—just like everybody else. Fine. Offered to do the dishes. So he did the dishes. Fine. Girls were in playin' Nintendo. And, uh, he finished up the kitchen. Did some schoolwork in his room. 'Cause he hadn't been to school—he hadn't been feelin' good. And around nine o'clock or so, he came in and said "good night." Went to the bathroom and went to bed. I watched TV until about midnight. Checked on all the kids and I went to bed. This morning the wife said, "A.J.'s gone." I said, "What?" The door was open. The garage door was locked. Front door was locked. She was looking in the backyard. I looked in the backyard. Saw him in the pool. I noticed the ladder was up on the pool.

Waites: Uh-huh.

David: Ladder was up. I said, "Oh, shit!" I looked in and there he was. Jumped in and carried him out. Arm was stiff. . . . I told the wife, "911." Came in while she was on the phone and I said, "He's stiff. I don't think there's any way they're gonna revive him. Paramedics came. I covered him with a sheet. That's the extent . . .

Waites (after a slight pause): You were saying earlier that there had been some problems with the neighbors?

David: From what my wife's been sayin' . . . I have, myself, no problems with the neighbors. I'm not there during the week. I work twelve, thirteen hours a day. I come home. I eat there and I'm in the house. Just from what the wife says . . . I mean . . . I don't have any problems myself with any of the neighbors.

Waites: Have the neighbors ever called HRS or anything like that?

David: Someone has.

Waites: In the past?

David: Yeah. They don't tell us who does it. I forget how many times, but it's been cleared each time.

Waites: Uh-huh. Okay.

David: With no problems.

Waites continued after a long silence: And when—either you or your wife—aren't out by the pool . . . the ladder's normally kept away from the pool, so that your kids or neighborhood kids don't get into it?

David: Right. The ladder's only put up when they're going in to swim. That was our thought for safety—along with the fence. The ladder was kept on the ground against the house till we got this puppy and he likes to chew things. So we put it up on that table.

Waites: The door that was open that you talked about—that was his bedroom door?

David: Yes.

Waites: He normally sleeps with that closed?

David: Yeah. The kids do sleep with their doors closed, because I like to watch TV at night and Jessica gets up once in a while to get something to eat. And this way, they don't get bothered. The dogs can't go in their rooms. The dogs sleep with us in our room.

Waites: One of the neighbors told one of the detectives standing out there that they saw A.J. out walking the dog—after midnight last night. Is that any way possible? I mean, you just said the dogs sleep with you.

David: Yeah. The dogs weren't out after midnight.

Waites: Okay. That's just what one of them said as one of the detectives was walking to his car and it kind of struck me as odd because I can't see—

David: What? We don't walk the dogs.

Waites: I'm just telling you what someone said. I'm just trying to make sure I've got everything cleared up.

David (exclaiming): Lord Almighty!

Waites: I mean, once you're in at night—unless the dogs wake you up—they're in with you, right?

David: If they wake me up, I put them out the back.

Waites: The back? Okay.

David: Once in a while, the girls would walk them around the block.

Waites: Uh-huh. But that's going to be daylight hours—it's not going to be after midnight. . . .

David (distressed): Yeah! Good God! I'm gonna be sick. He was not out walking the dog after midnight!

(The detective waited several moments before continuing the questioning, allowing David to regain his composure.)

Waites: The problems that your wife had with the neighbors . . . ?

David: Uh-huh.

Waites: And I realize again that you're not home during the day with the hours that you're putting in working. Do you think it could have been—normally, she talks kind of in a loud voice . . . ?

David: Yeah.

Waites: Well, I don't have a problem with that. Did you ever think, like, if she may have been just yelling at one of the kids or something—just with her being naturally loud-natured—that they may have misinterpreted it? That it may have resulted in HRS being called? Or people may have seen her out yelling at the kids not to do something and just thought something else?

David: She doesn't yell unless she's out the back door or in the house. She doesn't go out front yelling.

Waites: Okay.

David: But, yeah, she does raise her voice. I raise my voice. The neighbors raise their voice.

Waites: It's normal? Well, normal to kids.

David: Yeah. Well, Jessica has a loud voice to begin with.

Waites: But there was never anything that someone might consider excessive punishment? That's ever gone on?

David: All right, on Thursdays, A.J. would get up early and go out and collect cans. And someone thought that was punishment.

Waites: Because he went out and collected cans?

David: Yeah.

Waites: Would he do this before school?

David: Yeah. And HRS came and asked about this shit. Punishment? Punishment is taking away the TV; not letting him go in the pool.

Waites: HRS just came out because someone called and said you had your kid out collecting cans on Thursdays?

David: No, they didn't come out for that. The guardian ad litem brought that up—that someone called him on it.

Waites: Did he say if there was anything else said other than just out picking up cans or . . . ?

David: Yeah. They (HRS) come over, woke all the kids up, looked at their bodies . . . nothing—nowhere. They get spanked—of course.

Waites: Yeah.

David: We can't do much more than that because they can call on us. The kids themselves can call on us.

Waites: Yeah. True.

David: I mean, excessive punishment would be grounding—can't go out and play. That may be excessive.

Waites: But nothing excessive, as far as physical? I mean, I agree with you. A slap across the butt is a slap across the butt. Every once in a while a kid's going to get one.

David: I've used my belt on them a few times.

Waites: Now . . . and again. . . . I mean, I was raised that way, you know?

David: I was too. But you can't do that—well, you're not supposed to do that nowadays.

Waites: It's not like you're standing over them—over one of the kids and hitting on them for five or six minutes. I mean—

David: They'd be in the hospital if I did that.

Waites: Exactly.

David: I'm not a little guy.

Waites: The cans—he just liked collecting them? Is there any particular reason that he told the guardian when they asked him about it?

David: Just collecting them for Mommy (Jessica), that's all. He might've said something. He's—he was a little A.D.D. His mama (Ilene) hit him in the head with a frying pan—deaf in one ear. Had him carrying drugs and stuff—and he was molested. So he's—was not completely straight in his head. He'd give you the shirt off his back—he was a good kid.

Waites: If somebody asked him—saw him one morning and asked A.J., "Why are you out collecting cans?" would he make up something? Exaggerate something?

David: More than likely. I can't say. The neighbors came over and said some stuff he said and then he denies it. He'd tell a lie quicker than the truth—that's for sure.

Waites: But that all relates back to the stuff he went through with his natural mother?

David: I'm sure of it. It has to. One thing we did expound on with the kids—tell us the truth. He just had a very hard time doing that.

Waites: Was he a fairly good swimmer?

David: Yeah. From what I seen . . . in the pool . . . at the beach. . . .

Waites: Your wife told me he's been going to counseling and had a guardian and so forth for some period. And, I guess, he even was when he was still in Fort Lauderdale, before he came up to live with you—from the problems that he'd had down there.

David: Right.

Waites: Do you think this all could have resulted just in finally being too much pressure from all that?

David: I don't know. The psychiatrists have all said that he's got a lot of hurt inside. And I don't know. I can't say. I have no idea. Like I said, he wasn't depressed or nothing that I saw, in the last couple days. So I don't know what happened. I don't know what happened. Wife woke me up—found him in the pool. I can only speculate. I don't know. The water was awful cold.

That afternoon, HRS workers removed A.J.'s stepsister, Lauren, and half sister, Jackie, from the Schwarz home and put them in protective custody. They were placed in the home of their grandparents—Jessica's mother and father.

Records showed that sheriff's deputies had been called to the Triphammer Road residence fourteen times since May 1990—for such incidents as battery, petty theft, and "neighbor trouble."

In June 1991, deputies arrived at the house—after being called about a fight—and found Jessica Schwarz being pinned down in their driveway by her husband. David Schwarz explained that she had been drinking at a neighbor's house and when he tried to take her home, she started hitting him, then broke the windshield on his car.

Jessica informed the deputies that if they did not take her away, there would be more fighting. She was arrested, pleaded guilty to battery, and was sentenced to time served.

On Monday, there was a guidance counselor and a school psychologist present at Indian Pines Elementary School to help students deal with their feelings about their classmate's sudden and tragic death.

That morning, Detective Restivo studied his notes from the interviews with David and Jessica's neighbors. It was all too clear that there was something terribly wrong in the Schwarz home.

First he had interviewed Eileen Callahan, the neighbor who had told him that A.J. was severely abused—to the point that she had called HRS and made a complaint. She had seen

A.J. with two black eyes and what appeared to be a broken nose. Even though he told everyone who asked him that he had fallen off his bicycle, Callahan had found that hard to believe, since the child was never seen riding a bicycle.

In fact, it seemed that A.J. wasn't allowed to play at all, and was "constantly cleaning the garage" and had even been seen washing his father's truck—with a toothbrush.

Callahan also told the detective that every Thursday morning for the last couple of months—between 5:00 and 6:00— she saw A.J. collecting aluminum cans from the garbage in front of each residence on the street. She further claimed that this was a provision (community service) for a probation of some type that was imposed on Jessica Schwarz— but she wasn't sure what the charges had been.

Another neighbor, Jim Ebenhack, had also seen A.J. collecting cans very early on Thursday mornings and taking them back to his house. He also told Restivo that the stepmother was constantly verbally abusing the child, including—but not limited to—calling him "a useless piece of shit."

Louis Steinhauer—yet another neighbor—had seen the boy's black eyes and possibly broken nose. A.J. was in the company of his sister Jackie when Steinhauer asked what had happened. Jackie turned to A.J. and warned, "Remember what Mom told you to say!" A.J. replied, "Yes. I fell off my bike."

Although the parents drove Lauren to school, Steinhauer stated that A.J. was made to walk. He had actually seen the parents drive away with the girls in the car while A.J. started walking to school.

About two weeks earlier, Jessica had gone to school, taken A.J. out, and brought him home where "she beat him because he forgot to feed the cat."

The weekend before his death, A.J. was seen walking back and forth, in the front yard of his house, saying, "I'm no good; I'm a liar." Steinhauer said he could hear the stepmother and father from inside the dwelling, shouting, "Can't hear you!" And A.J. would then scream the words even louder.

He had also seen the young boy being made to edge the lawn with regular household scissors.

As Detective Restivo was canvassing the neighborhood, a thirteen-year-old girl approached him and asked if she could speak with him. Jamie Falk explained that she was a friend of A.J.'s sister Patsy. She told the detective that Jessica was "always mean to A.J. and would not let him play." One day when she was over there—a very hot day—Jessica made A.J. go to his room, where there was no air conditioner—with the windows closed. She made him stay there for hours at a time.

That same day, Michael Waites contacted South County Mental Health and verified that the victim, Andrew Schwarz, had indeed been treated there.

At 12:30 that afternoon, Waites, along with Detective Calloway and Sergeant Deischer, met with several members of the Florida Department of Health and Rehabilitative Services. Terry Neuenhaus, Sandra Owen, Sandy Warren, Richard Lyles, and Jim Koubla met with the investigators at the PBSO Crimes Against Persons Unit.

On May 19, 1992, the reports indicated that Jessica Schwarz had been the subject of an HRS investigation involving crack cocaine use, sale of crack cocaine, and physical abuse on Andrew Schwarz. The case was closed by HRS without classification. Detective Ole Olsen, of the PBSO, had also investigated the charges, which were determined to be "unfounded."

On January 25, 1993, Jessica Schwarz was again investigated by HRS and the PBSO because of the injuries Andrew Schwarz had suffered to his nose, which caused both of his eyes to swell. It was feared that Jessica Schwarz had broken the child's nose. HRS closed the investigation without classification. Detective Chris Calloway had closed the criminal investigation as "unfounded."

HRS had ordered a psychological evaluation for both Jessica and Andrew Schwarz at the conclusion of their investigation.

* * *

At 3:30 in the afternoon, Detectives Waites and Schoenstein were in attendance as Dr. James Benz, the chief medical examiner for Palm Beach County, performed the autopsy on Andrew Schwarz.

On A.J.'s head, Dr. Benz found a large area—about 5 inches long and 1¾ inches wide—covered with "a bluish-green dye containing glitter." And he found recent mild scratches behind each of his ears and a long recent abrasion on the right side of his nose, mild recent abrasions on the inside of his upper lip, the corner of his mouth, and his face. There were recent abrasions on his right elbow, a recent scratch on his left forearm.

He found multiple old, discolored bruises under his chin, on his torso, on his buttocks, and on his thigh. He also observed brown, yellow, and purple bruises of various sizes and age on almost every part of A.J.'s body.

Dr. Benz's opinion was that the cause of death for Andrew Schwarz was the result of drowning—the manner of death undetermined.

CHAPTER 3

The next thing I saw was David carrying him out and then I went to the bathroom and threw up.

—Jessica Schwarz

Scott H. Cupp, of the state attorney's office, chief of the Crimes Against Children Unit, was assigned to oversee the legal aspects during the investigation of Andrew Schwarz's death. Michael Waites met with him on Tuesday, May 4, to review what they had learned to date and to request subpoenas for various medical records.

Cupp, originally from Pittsburgh, Pennsylvania, was the youngest of three children in a middle-class family. His father was a production planning engineer for U.S. Steel and his mother was a housewife. Before deciding, at the age of twenty-four, to go back to school, Cupp drove a cab, worked in a steel mill, sold cars and insurance.

Having already decided he wanted to be a lawyer, he enrolled at Duquesne University and—much to his father's disappointment—majored in English instead of one of the sciences.

After graduating from Western New England College School of Law in Springfield, Massachusetts, he promptly moved to Florida, where he became a prosecutor with the state attorney's office in Fort Myers.

Prior to arriving in West Palm Beach in January 1993,

Cupp was prosecuting child abuse and adult sex crimes in Florida's Third Circuit. The Third Circuit consists of seven counties—Suwanee, Columbia, Lafayette, Madison, Hamilton, Dixie, and Taylor. The area is sparsely populated and beautiful. The towns of Live Oak, Lake City, Madison, Jasper, Mayo, Cross City, and Perry are reminiscent of the Old South.

The Third Circuit boasted some of the finest prosecutors that Cupp had ever met. State attorney Jerry Blair and ASA Bob Dekle had tried and convicted Theodore Bundy. And, although Bundy was convicted of other homicides—committed in other jurisdictions—his death warrant was carried out for the Third Circuit conviction for the murder of twelve-year-old Kimberly Leach.

The Third Circuit was where Cupp "cut his teeth," prosecuting crimes against children, and it was an eye-opening and rewarding 3½-year experience.

Cupp listened to Detective Waites's audiotaped interview with Jessica Schwarz, conducted in an interrogation room at the sheriff's office at 10:50 the previous Sunday morning, May 2—immediately before the detective had questioned David Schwarz.

Cupp would have given anything for a video accompaniment, but he was forced to rely on his imagination. Maybe that was for the best. He listened to the voice—the inflections—the tonality. He pictured her posture—her expressions—her body language.

On the tape, Waites asked her about the previous night. About A.J.'s routine. About his state of mind.

Jessica: He was acting fine. He . . . he ate all his dinner. Ate everything. He was talking. As a matter of fact, he was singing. I don't remember why. He was fine.
Waites: What did he do throughout the evening?
Jessica: Umm . . . he was reading a book and brought it in and asked me what a word was and I told him. He was out in the living room with the girls. They were doing their hair. And that's about it. I mean, then he . . .

everybody . . . the kids went to the bathroom, brushed their teeth, and went to bed.

Waites: Okay, what time would A.J. normally go to bed?

Jessica: On a Saturday, normally between nine and ten, but last night it was closer to nine than ten. They all went to bed at the same time last night.

Waites: Do you remember what A.J. was wearing when he went to bed?

Jessica: Ninja Turtle pants and uh . . . uh, a T-shirt . . . a dark T-shirt.

Waites: Did you see him after he went to bed? Did he wake back up at all before you went to bed?

Jessica (hesitantly): I fell asleep watching *Bonanza* and, uh . . . and I didn't wake up until I got up to . . . uh . . . I was going to have a piece of cheese and I was thirsty and he usually shuts his door when he goes to bed and it was opened. . . .

Waites (patiently): Okay.

Jessica: And I called him, and there was no answer.

Waites: Then what happened after that?

Jessica (answering with more confidence): I searched the house and the garage, and then I woke my husband up.

Waites: And after you woke your husband up?

Jessica: Well, he wasn't really awake, you know; I got him out of a sound sleep. And he sees A.J. in the pool and says, "Oh, my God," and jumped in the pool.

Waites: Uh-huh.

Jessica: I didn't look. . . . I . . . I caught a . . . I don't know where he was in the pool or what position or anything. I didn't get that close.

Waites: Hmmm.

Cupp thought it was an interesting answer. A qualification that wasn't necessary. Why would she do that?

Jessica: The next thing I saw was David carrying him out and then I went to the bathroom and threw up.

(Waites then took her through the rules of the pool, when the kids were allowed to swim and when they weren't. Were they allowed to swim naked? Were they allowed to dive?)

Waites: When A.J. was found, he didn't have any clothing. Had he ever before gone in the pool without clothing?

Jessica: Yes. They all had.

Waites (surprised): They had?

Jessica: Yeah.

Waites: So that's nothing that would be . . .

Jessica: Well, it wasn't a practice. . . . They made a game out of it and, you know, they got thrown in with their clothes on. And I've turned around and—all of a sudden—their clothes were off—bathing suits were off—and . . . I mean, it wasn't a habit, but they made a game out of it a few times.

Waites shifted gears and asked her about the counseling A.J. was receiving, about his guardian ad litem, and about the intervention of the Department of Health and Rehabilitative Services.

In the guardian ad litem program, the court assigns guardians to individual children who—for whatever reason—have their young lives brought before a judge. Divorce, abuse, delinquency, the distribution of a trust—many matters can lead to the need for a guardian. The guardian was to work for one overriding concern: the best interest of the child.

Cupp was intrigued by the way Jessica answered the questions: the incessant rambling as she jumped from one thought to the other, as if every question were an attack. The lack of sorrow—it was absent from her words and indiscernible in her voice—and the defense mechanisms as she fended off questions about A.J.'s numerous interactions with psychologists and social workers.

Waites: You told me earlier that A.J. was in counseling. And that was at South County in Delray?

Jessica: Yeah.

Waites: How often would the guardian [ad litem] come?

Jessica: Every two weeks and he'd call a lot and he'd stop by. He came over and gave all the kids Easter baskets.

Waites: How did it come about? The guardian ad litem?

Jessica: He was court-appointed. To follow up on, uh, how he was doing in school. To talk to him—how he was, um, how he was at home, how he was at school—if he had any problems. I mean, he'd take him out for walks, you know, just. . . . He talked to us, but it was mainly A.J.

Waites: You also said earlier that HRS had been out to the house before—is that associated with the guardian?

Jessica: Yes, the social worker would talk to the guardian. The social worker would come and check on the kids— A.J.—and talk to us. And she was trying to help him be back on Medicaid because we couldn't afford the counseling.

Waites: How long has A.J. been going to counseling?

Jessica: Over a year, but his counselor went on to a different job—so they were short a counselor—so he hadn't been in a couple of weeks. But two weeks ago, he went to the psychiatrist and he said he would call this week coming up—with, hopefully, they would have hired another counselor.

Waites: Okay. The psychiatrist—is that down in Delray? South County?

Jessica: There's only one down there, yeah, that takes care of all of them.

Waites: Have there been problems in school?

Jessica: Not that I . . . no.

Cupp sensed that she wanted to answer quickly, but her voice suggested she knew that straight-out lying wasn't a good idea.

Jessica: A.J. had problems on and off.

Waites (encouraging her): Uh-huh.

Jessica: Now, um, I'm going to tell you that for a long time I didn't get along with his teacher. Then we all had a meeting.

Cupp made a mental note to have Waites contact A.J.'s teacher as soon as possible.

Jessica (continuing): The guardian, the teacher, me, David, HRS, and we came to a very good understanding. What was happening was that A.J. was leaving for school at seven-thirty and not getting there until eight-thirty. And nobody told me right off the bat—like it wasn't important that I know. They waited till, like, report card day to write it [up], and I had no idea. And then, um, we set up [this meeting]. He was eating his snack on the way to school. I finally got a note home saying, "Please send him with a snack," and I wrote a note back saying, "I do send him with a snack—every day." And he had his name on the board a couple of times . . . nothing . . . nothing serious, and his grades were okay.

The words rolled off her tongue. Cupp had to remind himself that this was a woman whose stepson had been found dead less than five hours ago.

Jessica: He could concentrate. . . . I mean, he could hold his concentration long enough to get his grades, study. . . . [They were] a little up and down, but nothing . . . so the teacher and I were writing notes back and forth five days a week. I would write [her]. . . . She would write a note on Monday, seal it in an envelope, and [have him] bring it to me. A.J. didn't like that.

Jessica didn't want to let go of school and snacks, but Waites finally diverted her when he asked about A.J.'s guardian ad litem, a gentleman named Richard Zimmern.

Richard Zimmern was a retired pediatrician, who was originally from Stamford, Connecticut. He left his practice in 1989, after thirty-five years, and retired to Florida. He volunteered time to the guardian ad litem program in Palm Beach County. A.J. was fortunate to have the doctor assigned to him during the summer of 1992—for the last eleven months of his short life.

> Jessica: A.J. came [to us] equipped with a guardian ad litem. He had one in Fort Lauderdale because—
> Waites: Oh, okay.
> Jessica (adding quickly): That's where it all started.

Scott Cupp was still listening for the smallest morsel of grief, and wondered if what came next passed for it.

> Jessica: I don't believe we're sitting here talking about him [in] the past [tense]. Um, anyway, everything started in Fort Lauderdale.

Cupp tried to judge the quality of the brief reference to A.J.'s passing. He wanted to give the woman the benefit of the doubt.

> Waites: Okay. What type of problems had there been in Fort Lauderdale?
> Jessica: Sex. He was sexually abused, physically abused, mentally abused. . . . Um, the mother was—she had both of her kids dealing crack. She'd stuff their pockets and tell them where to go and she trained them to lie. A.J. could lie just like his mother. He could look you right in the eye and lie, and swear to God on it, and cry on it, and insist on it. And it was like trying to deprogram somebody. And her husband—her second husband— is in jail for the sexual abuse. I don't know why she never went—but she got out of it.
> Waites: This is A.J.'s natural mother?

Jessica: Right.

(Waites told her about the interviews conducted that morning with some of her neighbors and asked if there were any problems that could have been misinterpreted by anyone.)

Jessica (exasperated): If I was gonna do something that shouldn't have been seen, I would have done it in the house, I guess.

After a while, she admitted—almost proudly—that, yes, she sure was loud and, yeah, pretty much always yelling at someone or another. But other than that, well, no, she couldn't think of anything.

Waites rephrased his question, wanting to make certain that Jessica had the opportunity to admit that maybe her behavior, on occasion, might be the kind that a neighbor could possibly misunderstand.

Cupp could almost see her shrugging.

Jessica: Right now, I really don't think so.

Jessica may have been crude and loud, but she wasn't—Cupp decided—dumb. She made certain that Waites was aware that she and David had inherited damaged goods three years earlier.

According to Jessica, when A.J. came to live with them, he was hyper, abused, inattentive, mischievous, untrustworthy, and conniving.

But none of that went very far toward explaining why A.J. was dead. Or perhaps it did.

"What about chores?" Waites asked. "I mean, was he made to, like, say, do the yard or . . . ?"

Jessica answered eagerly, "Yeah, he did the yard. Last time, we all did the yard. Time before that the lawn mower broke. He did trim—trimmed the garden."

Cupp listened closely, remembering the neighbors' comments about A.J. trimming the lawn with scissors.

Jessica continued, "David would borrow somebody's lawn mower, you know. The grass wasn't that, well . . . We've only been doing the lawn for . . . A.J. would do the garden. The girls did the back garden until the dogs ripped them up, and…"

Rambling, dodging, searching. Scott Cupp knew that Waites was waiting her out.

Eventually, knowing better, Waites asked, "As far as the trim, it's something he would do with a weed-eater?"

Jessica: Yeah.
Waites: Or a small pair of hand shears or . . . ?

Cupp leaned closer to the tape recorder.

Jessica: Okay, he'd start out with the weed-eater, and he'd run around the yard with the weed-eater for maybe ten minutes; then he'd put it away, and none of it was done. So then he'd go out with the clippers, and it still wasn't done. And then one time, he went out there and weed-eated the whole backyard to where there was no grass. I mean, no grass. The trim wasn't done, but the yard was all whacked down, and he was very proud of that. He . . . he . . . he [said], "Look what I did! Look what I did!" And I looked and there was nothing but dirt.

Cupp had listened to hundreds of witness interviews and conducted a hundred more himself. Guilty parties, invariably, shared a common trait. Either they don't say a word, or the words just roll off their tongues—out of control. Jessica was a poster child for the latter. Guilty of what was the question.

Waites: Was he fairly well coordinated? Accident prone?
Jessica: No, he was . . . He'd trip over his own feet a couple of times a day, but nothing serious. I mean—
Waites (prodding): "I mean" . . .?
Jessica: Oh . . . I got called on child abuse two months

ago because I was in the house—Jackie and him were outside. He was putting Jackie's bike away, and he must have tried to ride it, and he smashed his nose into the handlebars. When he came into the house, there was no bruises. There was no blood, but his nose was growing. And it sounds horrible right now, but I laughed because his nose was growing right in front of my face. And I gave him some ice, and it was fine. I said, "Does it hurt?" And he said, "No." And he went on playing.

Waites: Okay.

Jessica: And then the next day when he woke up . . . well, I woke him up for school . . . and when I went into his room . . . when I shook him a little and he turned over, his eyes were black. His nose was black and blue, and I had to wash his eyes out to open them. I mean they were swollen shut—just about. So I kept him home from school. We went to JFK (hospital). I couldn't even park in the parking lot—I had to park on the side street. That's how busy this place was. So I spoke to a doctor and I said, "Here's what happened. Here's the child. If I sit here and wait for five hours, are you gonna do anything?" He went, "No, just take an X ray." So I took him home. Took him to the doctor. The doctor set up the X ray. He got an X ray taken, and that was it. Put ice on it. And that was it.

Waites: Had you ever noticed any bruises that—

Jessica: He showed me a few bruises on his legs and his arms.

Waites: I mean, things that wouldn't be normal for a ten-year-old? Like, if he'd fallen off the bike or fallen on the playground or, you know, maybe look like he'd been in a fight with another kid or . . . ?

(Jessica answered that she had only seen him fighting once, on the way home from school, and that he had had a few bruises on him.)

Jessica: I think the last time I saw that boy naked was well over a year ago. Um, he showed me one or two bruises. He'd get them here on his legs. He showed me a wicked one on his leg once, and I . . . I said, "How'd that happen?" He said, "I don't know."

Waites: But, I mean, like on the forearms and maybe the chin area, the knee area? Those type bruises.

Jessica: And his thigh, you know; when he was wearing shorts, I saw it.

Waites: The front part of the thigh? The back part of the thigh?

Jessica: The side.

Waites: Okay. You were telling me you found him in the garage a couple of weeks ago?

Jessica: Last week.

Waites: Last week?

Jessica: Yeah, he was making noise in the garage and hit himself in the head with the cane. I had a cane left over from my knee surgery.

Waites: He was hitting himself on the top of the head or—

Jessica: Just banging.

Waites: All over?

Jessica: Yeah, he was just . . . and I've never seen that behavior on him before, so I guess I should have smartened up right then. (She paused and continued after a moment.) I noticed he didn't get angry when he should have. He didn't talk. He didn't know he was allowed to get angry. I told him, "If you have a problem with me, or the girls, or at school, or kids, let us know. And if you have to yell, you have to yell." He was never allowed to do that.

Scott Cupp made a note to have Waites talk to the natural mother as soon as possible, even though he was sure the detective already had that on his agenda.

Waites: How was A.J.'s attendance at school?

Jessica: On and off. When he first came, it was bad—

then it got good. Then he got bad again. He kept getting earaches. And he's so skinny that when you gave him medicine, he'd get sick. So we went to the doctor's a lot of times and then you get him home, give him the medicine, and he'd throw up. And then he never got a temperature of hundred and one—it was always a hundred and three. It was either normal or very high.
(After they discussed several of A.J.'s friends, Waites brought the interview back to the neighbors.)
Waites (as if it were the first time): Have you ever had any problems with your neighbors?
Jessica (sounding surprised): Oh . . .
Waites: Have they ever called HRS or anything like that?

Cupp had battled long and hard with Health and Rehabilitative Services over the years. They were notorious for letting cases slip through the cracks. And A.J.'s was most assuredly shaping up to be one of those.

Jessica: Yes, uh, one time they came to the house. First time . . .

Cupp noticed that she immediately contradicted herself.

Jessica: A.J.'s mother used to call HRS. Patsy, her daughter, she used to call HRS even from Fort Lauderdale. I mean, I was on the abuse line so much it was ridiculous. And they'd come out every time. It started when Jackie was still in diapers. They checked all the kids, and they'd keep the investigation going for a while; then they'd drop it, and then it would happen again.
(Jessica nonchalantly referred—once again— to the broken nose and black eyes that A.J. had suffered.) The last time, it was with the nose. Somebody said I did it to him, so they came. A cop with a gun and the HRS

investigators took Jackie away—I mean fast—into A.J.'s
room and talked to her and looked at her. But Lauren
wouldn't go. She was pissed. Very pissed, asking why
we always have to go through this. She wouldn't talk
to anybody. She just sat there and said, "I'm not going
to talk to anybody. You have no right to come into my
house and talk to me, and I'm not saying a word." So
she was just pissed off.

Cupp wondered if Waites could hear the distinct difference in the attitude and tone she exhibited toward her two
girls, Lauren and Jackie. Cupp heard pride, affection, and involvement. As Jessica rambled, Cupp tried to put words to
her feelings about A.J. Even though A.J. was dead, all Cupp
could hear was irritation, exasperation, and a general feeling
of distaste and disapproval. He wondered if he was being too
cynical or judgmental.

Jessica: She was very pissed off. She said to A.J.,
"Why does this always happen? Why do we always
have to go through this?"

Cupp could hear just how much Jessica liked the fact that
her ten-year-old daughter was "pissed" at the cops and the
HRS investigators.

Jessica: And Jackie just babbled everything to the cop.
I mean, she just yapped her mouth off. . . .

Cupp listened to this part again. A complete reversal of
feeling. Here she was angry and disgusted with her younger
daughter for "babbling everything" to the investigator, as if
she were betraying her mom with every word. Now he
couldn't wait to watch the videotape that Detective Calloway
had made of Jessica alone with her daughters in the police
interview room. All Calloway had told him about the tape
was, "You've got to watch it. Amazing."

Jessica continued—without prompting from Waites—to talk about the incident involving A.J.'s broken nose. By all accounts, including his own, A.J. had fallen against the handlebars of Jackie's bicycle. None of the neighbors seemed to believe it. A.J.'s guardian ad litem didn't believe it.

Jessica (ranting): They (the HRS investigator and the detective) brought A.J. into the garage and made him show them how it happened, because I didn't even see. . . . His hair was longer then, and he had a bruise here, under his bangs. I didn't even see it. And the cop, you know, said to the HRS people, "Let's go. He did it. He did it. She didn't do it." So then I got called in to talk to HRS. They said it was a neighbor who called them. And a girlfriend of mine who lives over on the next block, she said HRS had called her about me. And I said to her, "I'm so sick of HRS! You tell them— the next time they call you—that I watched *Silence of the Lambs*, and that I'm that crazy doctor, that crazy man that eats people. You tell them that I'm eating my children because I'm so sick of all the accusations. It's ridiculous." And she . . . it was . . . you know . . .

Jessica hesitated, as if suddenly becoming aware of what she had just said. All Waites said was "Yeah." He was leading her.

Jessica gushed something about A.J.'s half sister, Patsy, and his natural mother, Ilene, and how "that family is whacked." Then she ran out of steam.

Waites gave her one last chance, asking, "Okay, is there anything else you can think of right now?"

Scott Cupp wasn't expecting anything worthwhile, and he was sure Waites wasn't either. They were both surprised.

Jessica mumbled, "No. When we do . . . when we do find out about A.J. . . . all I know . . . oh, all I know is, it's gonna be a zoo at my house, and I know I'm gonna react. I know I'm gonna end up in jail for hitting somebody."

"Damn!" Scott listened to a stretch of silence and tried to picture the expression on Waites's face. Eventually he heard him say, "Well, let's conclude the interview at this time."

Cupp rewound the tape, staring at the spools as they spun around. Now the work started.

CHAPTER 4

I believe Jessica probably did throw up, but the cause wasn't remorse—it was the combination of committing murder with her bare hands on a belly full of beer, and then having half of PBSO pouring through her house on a Sunday morning when she's usually sleeping it off.

—Scott Cupp

After the initial investigation on Sunday morning, the whole Schwarz family—David, Jessica, Lauren, and Jackie—had been asked to come to the sheriff's office to be interviewed. While Detective Waites conducted his interview with Jessica, Detective Calloway took Lauren to a room in the Juvenile Unit to wait while he questioned Jackie.

Jackie was two months shy of being five years old and had long, dark hair pulled back in a ponytail that reached past her waist. Calloway gently told her that maybe she could answer some questions for him about what had happened earlier in the day. The little girl told him that she "didn't know any questions," and that she "only knew her ABC's."

He then spoke briefly with her about telling the truth and telling a lie. It was apparent to him that she knew the difference between the two.

Jackie revealed that A.J. had been grounded the day before his death. So while the rest of the family attended Sunfest, an annual celebration held in nearby West Palm Beach, A.J. spent the day confined to his home. When Calloway quizzed Jackie about why A.J. had been grounded, she said that he had been playing with some green dye or paint near the family's dryer.

When Jessica found some of the dye on the dryer, Jackie said her mother became "very mad." Jessica had poured the dye over A.J.'s head, and then she "spanked him with a strap."

According to Jackie, both her mother and her father spanked A.J. a lot—with a strap and a belt.

Later in the interview, Jackie told the detective that earlier that morning she heard a splash in the swimming pool that woke her up. She went outside to the pool, climbed up the ladder, and saw A.J. in the pool underneath the water. Upon further questioning about this story, it became clear to Calloway that she was not telling the truth. He noticed many inconsistencies in her story, and when he pointed them out to her, she admitted that it wasn't true. When he asked her why, she replied, "Because I have to lie." Again he asked her why, and she replied, "Somebody doesn't get in jail."

He then asked Jackie to just tell him what really happened. Crying, she told him, "I'm going to get in trouble. I just don't want anybody to get hurt."

He tried to soothe her and told her that nobody would get hurt. She said, "Somebody already did get hurt."

When he asked her who had gotten hurt, she replied, "My brother."

He learned that Jackie had no idea how A.J. had gotten into the pool, and when he tried to question her further about her brother, she stated, "I'm going to run away."

From time to time, during the course of the interview, Calloway noticed that Jackie was looking behind him and laughing. When he turned to see what she was laughing at, he heard footsteps running away from the interview room. He got up and looked out the window and saw Lauren running down the hall, back to the waiting room, where he had stationed her prior to his interview with Jackie. Lauren had been watching her little sister as she was being questioned.

He asked Jackie if her mother had told her what to tell him—in reference to the fabricated story she had told him earlier. She said, "Yes." He asked her exactly what her mother had told her to tell him, and she replied, "The whole story I just told you."

The detective said, "But that's not the truth, is it?"

She said, "Yes."

It was obvious to Calloway that the child was confused as to what exactly she was supposed to tell him in reference to the questions he was asking her regarding A.J. He asked her if she was afraid of something and she said yes. When he asked what she was afraid of, she replied, "A.J. died."

After he concluded his interview with Jackie, Calloway attempted to question ten-year-old Lauren. It was quite apparent that she did not want to speak to him about A.J.'s death. She did admit, however, that her mother poured green dye over A.J.'s head, the day before he died, because he had been playing with the dye around the dryer.

She refused to answer any of the other questions that he asked.

When Detective Waites finished questioning Jessica, she was allowed to join the girls until his interview with David Schwarz was completed. Detective Calloway watched the reunion from the television room located directly across the hall from the interview room. He turned the television set on and it activated the camera located in the room where Jessica and her two daughters were waiting.

Jessica sat in a hardback chair in the center of the room, with her sunglasses propped gingerly on top of her head. Lauren, pouting and irritable, was seated off camera during most of the tape.

Jackie was anxious and clearly confused. She paced. Her mother wanted to know what they had told the police. It was obvious that Jackie knew she was in trouble—even before she told her mom that she had told the police about A.J. being grounded and the green dye and the spanking.

As she listened, Jessica became furious. She jumped out of her chair, grabbed Jackie roughly by the shoulders, and lifted her off the ground. She held her face-to-face with her and snapped, "Do you want Mommy to go to jail?"

Shaking, Jackie said, "No."

Jessica was livid. "If you tell these people anything, Mama's gonna go to jail. Now, what did you tell them?"

Tears welled up in Jackie's eyes. Jessica shook her, and said, "I'll never see you again."

Upon hearing that, Jackie started sobbing.

Referring to the green dye and the spanking, Jessica asked, "Why did you tell them that?"

Jackie didn't answer.

Jessica insisted, "You can't tell these people anything. Okay?"

Through her tears, Jackie replied, "I'm not going to say anything else."

Jessica's face was only inches away from her daughter's: "Just say, 'I don't know. I don't know.'"

Finally Jessica released her daughter and returned to the chair. She said impatiently, "Jackie, they can throw me in jail."

Jackie exclaimed, "I don't want you to go to jail!"

Jessica, playing on the child's fears, asked, "Do you want me to go to jail?"

Jackie paced nervously. "No. I just don't want A.J. to die."

Jessica, as cold as ice, answered, "Well, he did."

A few minutes later, Jackie told her mother, "I had to tell him a lie."

Jessica responded, "Oh, God, my own daughter's going to put me in jail!"

Lauren told her mother that she had been standing on the other side of the window while the detective was interviewing Jackie, and that she had heard Jackie telling him things.

Jessica said to Jackie, "You got a big mouth. You don't talk to anybody anymore. You just say, 'I don't know.' "

Lauren added, "I was telling him lies, and he said, 'Your sister has a whole different story.' "

Jessica replied flippantly, "So? She's four—you're ten."

Investigators would later learn that Jessica Schwarz had been fired from her job—as a day care worker—the previous March. Her employer had been so intimidated by Jessica's temper that she had called the sheriff's office to have a deputy present while she gave Jessica the news.

Scott Cupp's initial involvement with A.J.'s death came with an impromptu meeting at the PBSO with Detectives Waites and Deischer, along with their lieutenant Steve Newell. Waites reported to them that Dr. Benz expressed reluctance—during the postmortem—to classify A.J.'s death as a homicide. They decided there should be a meeting with Benz at the medical examiner's office.

The purpose was to find out what questions he needed answered and to find out what they needed to do—from an investigative standpoint—in order to make him comfortable classifying A.J.'s death as a homicide.

It was decided that Scott Cupp, Lieutenant Newell, and Detectives Waites, Deischer, Calloway, and Restivo would meet with the medical examiner. Additionally, Cupp suggested that they have Dr. Philip Colaizzo there. He was the medical director of the Child Protection Team (CPT). CPT was an entity established by Florida law to assist the Department of Health and Rehabilitative Services in carrying out their responsibilities in investigating reported cases of child abuse and neglect.

The team included a medical director who performed examinations on children who had been physically and sexually battered and rendered opinions in court. A psychologist conducted interviews and evaluations of children and their caregivers. There was a host of others with specialized training who conducted forensic interviews with children. The interviews were videotaped. The purpose of the interview was to document and record exactly what had happened to a child. The information was then available for law enforcement, HRS, the state attorney, and, ultimately, a criminal and/or dependency court proceeding.

Having Dr. Colaizzo present turned out to be disastrous. Dr. Benz seemed to be offended by his mere presence. Their purpose, in gathering all these people together, was to show Benz that they were willing to do whatever he suggested needed to be done as to follow-up, and also to show him respect. But he apparently decided he was being pressured and second-guessed.

Dr. Colaizzo asked him a few medical questions, which was the beginning of the end. Benz's responses to Colaizzo's questions were—at the very least—condescending.

The net result of the meeting was that Benz—clearly—was going to be headstrong in his decision to classify A.J.'s manner of death as "undetermined."

To say that Cupp was disheartened would be an understatement, but it quickly gave way to an overwhelming sense of determination.

Attempting to prosecute someone for homicide, without first having a medical examiner's opinion that there was one, is next to impossible. Benz was highly qualified as the chief medical examiner in Palm Beach County and was held in high esteem among his peers throughout North America. Cupp was well aware of situations in which prosecutors had obtained second opinions from other medical examiners in difficult cases—but it was always to confirm the initial findings.

Cupp was faced with the task of finding someone to perform a full second autopsy and hope the result would be different. He knew that it would be next to impossible. Even if it could be accomplished—in order to convict Jessica Schwarz of killing A.J.—he would have to cross-examine Dr. Benz, who would surely be the defense's star witness.

A.J.'s death occurred just four months after Cupp's boss, Barry Krischer, took office for his first term as state attorney for the Fifteenth Judicial Circuit of Florida—in and for Palm Beach County. Krischer hired Cupp to come in with him in January when he took office, specifically to run the Crimes Against Children (CAC) Unit.

There were those outside the state attorney's office that questioned the wisdom of pursuing the case. That was not surprising. What was startling was that many within the office thought the case was political suicide for those prosecutors naive enough to go against Benz.

But Cupp never questioned going forward. He was scared at times—many times—but his resolve to go forward never wavered.

On Tuesday, May 4, Detective Calloway returned to the Concept Homes Development to gather additional information about the Schwarz family.

There he interviewed Ida Falk, who told him that she and her family had lived on Triphammer Road for about 2½ years. Her thirteen-year-old daughter, Jamie, had talked to Detective Restivo on Sunday. Ida Falk had seen A.J. early every Thursday morning collecting aluminum cans from the neighborhood recycling bins. She believed Jessica Schwarz had been court ordered to perform community service and that one part of that community service was collecting aluminum cans. A.J. was made to gather them to assist his stepmother, she thought.

She heard Jessica swearing at A.J. on a daily basis. Even though she couldn't recall the exact words that were used, she said they were "dirty and vulgar." Also, Jessica was "always" referring to A.J. as stupid.

About a year earlier, she had seen A.J. in the front yard—for an hour or two—with his mouth taped shut. She, too, had seen him edging the lawn with regular household scissors.

Mrs. Falk told the detective that two or three months earlier her husband, Jarrell, had seen A.J. walking to school in the rain. Mr. Falk had slowed down to pick him up, but when he glanced in his rearview mirror, he saw that Jessica was right behind him. Assuming that she would pick the boy up, he continued on down the road. However, Jessica did not pick him up; she just passed him by.

After talking with Mrs. Falk, Detective Calloway spoke with her son, Troy, a fifth-grade student at Indian Pines Elementary School. Troy told the detective that, not long after they moved to Triphammer Road, he started going over to A.J.'s house to see if he could play—but most of the time, he was grounded and wasn't allowed. On one occasion, he saw A.J. with "brownish" tape over his mouth. Jessica had explained to Troy that A.J. was "being bad."

More recently—a month or so earlier—he had seen A.J. running down Triphammer Road naked.

At the house next door to the Schwarz home, Ron Pincus Jr. repeated the story to Detective Calloway that he had told Detective Restivo on Sunday: When he arrived home from work—about 1:30 in the morning—he had seen A.J. walking his dog. A.J. had asked him what he doing home so late. Pincus was tired and simply replied, "I have to get to bed." The boy told him good night and Pincus continued up the walk. He glanced over at the Schwarz house and noticed that the blinds were up in the living room and the lights and television were on.

About two weeks before that, he had seen A.J. edging his yard with scissors. Pincus said he felt sorry for him, so he went over and edged the Schwarz yard with his own edger. While he was there, he heard Jessica tell A.J. that he had a new nickname—"Jeffrey Dahmer." For the last two weeks of the young boy's life, that was what his stepmother called him.

He had seen A.J. swim on several occasions, but he was not allowed while the girls were swimming. A.J. was only allowed to go into the pool to clean it—before the girls got in—so they could have a clean pool to swim in.

Jessica had told Pincus a few weeks earlier that she hated A.J.—that she had always hated him. And that she could never bring herself to love him.

After the detective left, Pincus thought about how he had come home from work that previous Saturday night, bone-tired and looking forward to bed, and had been startled when he heard a rustling in the bushes next door. When he saw A.J. holding a leash, he realized that the noise he heard was the dog nosing around in the shrubbery.

A.J. seemed to want to talk, but Pincus was just too tired for chitchat.

Calloway then went to interview another neighbor whom Detective Restivo had talked to on Sunday—Eileen Callahan. She had only lived on Triphammer Road for about a year, but she had seen and heard a lot. She was a stay-at-home mom with three children and lived across the street and one house up from the Schwarzes.

Callahan's pregnancy with her third child had been a difficult one and she had spent much time resting on her living-room couch. From that location in her home, she couldn't help but notice the strange and bizarre behavior of her loud and obnoxious neighbor. She also witnessed the special wrath that Jessica seemed to have for her stepson.

Unfortunately for Eileen—and what she wouldn't find out for quite some time—was that her first name, though spelled differently, was the same as A.J.'s biological mother—Ilene. That fateful coincidence eventually caused her untold anguish, fear, and unwanted attention.

Not long after she and her family moved to Triphammer Road, Callahan had seen A.J.—on his hands and knees in the rain—edging the grass with a pair of scissors.

In October 1992, she had heard Jessica tell A.J. that she was "taking Halloween away from him," and asked him if he wanted her to take Christmas away too. And—in fact—Callahan had seen him cleaning out the garage on Christmas Day.

She had become so concerned about A.J. not being in school on Thursdays—due to the fact that he was collecting aluminum cans, and then later crushing them in his drive-way—that Callahan had called Child Protective Services to report it. She claimed that she was "put off" and told to call Indian Pines Elementary School—which she did. An employee at the school told her that they were aware of A.J.'s absenteeism.

About a month before his death, A.J. had told Eileen's husband, Rich, that he had to do chores from the time he woke up in the morning until the time he went to bed. And that his stepmother punished him by not allowing him to go to school.

In January 1993, when she saw A.J.'s black eyes and bruised nose, Eileen had seen enough. She called Florida's hot line, which had been set up for the public to report children who are known to be—or suspected to be—abused, neglected, or abandoned. As the public-service announcements promised, she called anonymously.

Well, not quite—she gave her first name, Eileen.

HRS protective investigator Barbara Black was assigned to the call and—as per local protocol—she called the sheriff's office to have them assign a detective from CAC to accompany her.

She and Chris Calloway went to the house on Triphammer Road and the detective spoke with A.J. The young boy adamantly maintained that he had fallen against the handlebars of his sister's bicycle as he was walking it into the garage to put it away.

Black detailed A.J.'s denial—and Jessica's ranting—in her report, including Jessica's complaint that she had had at least five abuse complaints against her and that she'd "had enough."

Jessica went on and on to Black about how the neighbors hated her and that Ilene was always calling in complaints against her and harassing her.

Barbara Black closed the investigation the same day she started it. Considering the information she apparently based her decision on, it is impossible to overstate how incredibly tragic her decision turned out to be. She placed a call to Joan Wyllner, A.J.'s protective supervision worker. It was Wyllner's responsibility to monitor A.J.'s placement in the Schwarz home. One must keep in mind, while reading the report, however, that Eileen Callahan left only her first name when placing the call to the hot line.

"Worker Joan Wyllner said she does not feel [Jessica] would hurt the child and fail to get medical care. She is very attentive to the child's medical needs. She had asked Broward [County] about closing the case last week. Joan feels natural mom (Ilene) somehow knows that this was asked. She always seems to throw a monkey wrench in when things go smooth.

"Joan saw the child January 4, 1993. No problems noted. (Joan did not wish to accompany this [protective investigator] and detective to the residence.)"

It appeared—even though the phone conversation with Joan Wyllner was put near the end of the narrative—that Black spoke to her prior to going to the scene.

As if that weren't tragic enough, what Eileen Callahan reported to Calloway left Scott Cupp truly speechless and incredibly sad. As he looked back, the overwhelming sense of hopelessness—of being trapped—that A.J. must have felt became clear to him.

Detective Calloway informed Eileen Callahan that he had been the one who had accompanied the woman from HRS to investigate the incident.

Eileen Callahan told the detective that, the day before the investigation, Jackie had come out of the house and went over to where A.J. was sitting on the driveway. She heard Jackie say, "What did Mommy tell you to say?" A.J. replied, "That I fell and hit my nose on the bicycle."

The day after the HRS/PBSO investigation was conducted at the Schwarz home, Mrs. Callahan received a phone call from the HRS investigator who had been with Calloway the day before. Unbeknownst to Eileen Callahan, her phone number had been recorded on the report of the complaint she made—which was now in the hands of Barbara Black.

Black told Mrs. Callahan to leave the Schwarzes alone and that she was not to call or make up any stories of abuse, and that if she did in the future—she could be prosecuted.

"She instructed me that she had spoken to me on a prior occasion, which I denied. She told me that if I continued to call, that they would slap a harassment charge on me, and that she would take my children instead. And that A.J. was lucky to be having a roof over his head. And gave me the supervisor's name and phone number—if I had a problem with the phone call."

At that time, Eileen Callahan was still unaware that her first name sounded the same as A.J.'s biological mother's—and she didn't know Barbara Black's name.

She was, of course, very upset by the phone call, so she called Joan Wyllner to make a complaint.

"I did tell her it was the woman that showed up at the [Schwarz] house because Barbara Black addressed herself as that. Ms. Wyllner said there was nothing she could do to find out who the person was that called me because there were so many people in that office. That there was 'no way' she could track it down. And then she went into great length explaining A.J.'s past.

"She was telling me that they had put him there so that he would be safe. The house that he grew up in or was living in—in Broward County—he was being abused there. Supposedly, he was sexually abused.

"She told me that Palm Beach County was looking into this as a favor to Broward County, that this was not Palm Beach County's problem. She told me if I wanted to file a complaint, that I could write a letter to H.G. Holley [state offices] complex. But she couldn't give me an address or a phone number, or her supervisor, or [whose] attention that I should mail the letter to."

Eileen Callahan told Joan Wyllner that A.J. was "going to end up dead" if HRS didn't do something about the situation.

There would be no more "harassing" phone calls to the

hot line complaining about A.J.'s treatment at the hands of his stepmother—save one last anonymous call, on May 2, in the afternoon, after his body was found.

At eight o'clock on Tuesday evening, May 4, Detectives Restivo and Waites, along with Sergeant Deischer, met with Mary Idrissi—A.J.'s third-grade teacher—at her home. She told them that A.J. was very wanting of attention—constantly wanting to be hugged and shown other signs of bonding. She further stated the he often talked about his home and appeared to be happy and, in fact, often referred to being happy living with his natural father and his two sisters [*sic*].

Idrissi described A.J. as being open and intelligent and able to cope with problems very well. She related a disturbing incident—which had taken place during the first week of school—involving the child and Jessica, in which Jessica spoke very demeaningly about him and recited his faults to her. Jessica continued to belittle him while he was standing right there beside her.

Idrissi sent weekly progress reports home with A.J. and often received belligerent replies from Jessica. He was not allowed to have school supplies or participate in school field trips, since he was not responsible enough to do so—according to his stepmother. She received these belligerent replies to the progress reports until—roughly—March 1993 when there was a meeting with her, Jessica and David Schwarz, and some representatives of HRS. Idrissi stated that during this meeting she was very positive and reinforced the fact that Andrew was happy being at home, which resulted in Jessica having a change in attitude toward her.

The teacher told the investigators that A.J. was absent from school more than was normal. He had been absent three or four days in January 1993, and when he returned to school, he had two black eyes and his nose was bruised. When she questioned him about what had occurred, A.J. told her that he had hit his nose on his bike and that he did not want his stepmother to be blamed.

Idrissi added that she often saw bruises on him, but they were in areas that would be common for a ten-year-old boy to have them.

CHAPTER 5

*Jimmy was Jimmy—retired NYPD—and not afraid
to voice his opinion, whether you wanted to hear it or
not. He would tell you like it was.*

—Detective Michael Waites

The morning after A.J.'s body was found, a woman named
Connie Mason called the sheriff's office and asked to talk to
a detective in reference to Jessica Schwarz. Jimmy Restivo
went to her home in Lake Worth to interview her.

Mason told Restivo that on April 19 she had attended a
group counseling session with Jessica, and had had a very
disturbing conversation with her about A.J.

Restivo: Would you tell me some of the things you remember her saying about A.J.?
Mason: She first caught my attention because she said
she had a little "Jeffrey Dahmer." After a few minutes,
she said it again and I questioned her on it and she
started telling me how he was abused by his original
mother—and that he was uncontrollable. She talked a
good twenty to thirty minutes about him.
Restivo: Just about A.J.?
Mason: Just about A.J.
Restivo: Did she ever say anything about hurting him
because he dunked one of the girls [under the water]?

Mason: She stated, I believe, that he held one of the girls under and she grabbed him by the throat and pulled him out of the pool, slammed him up against the fence, and said that she would "kill him and cut him up in pieces if he ever touched one of her girls again." Jessica said that she'd call the cops and turn herself in and go to prison for the rest of her life, but he would never hurt her children again.

Restivo: Did she tell you about something she had told a judge?

Mason: She stated she told the judge that if A.J. ever— I think this might've been in reference to molesting the girls—because I did ask about that. Was she afraid that he would do that to one of the girls and she, ah—

Restivo: You mean sexually molest?

Mason: Yeah. 'Cause he had been—she said that he had been. She said that she would kill him. She said, "I even told the judge I would kill him if he hurt one of my girls—and he still gave me custody of the kids."

Restivo: When she was saying these things, did you believe her? What was your reaction? Honestly?

Mason: I wanted to help her help the child—that's how I felt. That I could probably—by talking to her—help her love the child, as he needed more love. I felt like he needed more love, 'cause he was far from getting it, with her calling him a Jeffrey Dahmer. That's the wrong way.

Restivo: But she did talk about killing this little boy?

Mason: She said she'd kill him—several times. She said—not only the incident when she told him that she'd kill him—but she said to the whole meeting that if he hurt her girls, she would kill him. She said another thing about waking up in the morning. I wish I could word this right. She said everybody just had to leave her alone until like ten o'clock in the morning, as she was mean—extremely mean—in the mornings. And that A.J. just didn't comprehend that she was mean—to leave her alone. Sometimes he just didn't get it through his head.

Restivo: Did she ever indicate that she'd hurt him in the morning?

Mason: Not that I recall.

Restivo: Did she talk about her husband?

Mason: I know his name is Bear. I know she said he was big and she did talk—I just don't know what was said right now. It might come to me later. She did talk about him—I don't know. I believe he's on her side. You know, as far as taking control of A.J.

Restivo: Did she mention about how he would treat A.J.?

Mason: No. No. Not that I—

Restivo: Anything else come to mind, Connie?

Mason: The abuse, I say, would be from her.

Restivo: Excuse me?

Mason: I'm saying the abuse—I could tell it was being done by her. So, whatever she said about her husband, it didn't hit me like he was [abusing A.J.]. I thought she had a good husband because they had their home and a pool. I figured she had someone taking care of her family.

Restivo: Anything else come to mind?

Mason: I just think she held him under there.

Restivo: You think she held him under the water?

Mason: I do.

Restivo: Why do you get that feeling?

Mason: It just hit me in the gut when I seen it on TV.

Early in the afternoon on Wednesday, May 5, Detective Waites met with Ilene Logan (A.J.'s natural mother) and Patsy (A.J.'s half sister) at their home in Fort Lauderdale. Ilene told him that her ex-husband David Schwarz had been given temporary custody of both Patsy and A.J. because of an abusive situation that had occurred with another ex-husband. She said Patsy was the victim of the abuse and claimed that A.J.

had not been abused. David had been given temporary custody, with the court intending for both A.J. and Patsy to be returned to her.

She had since regained custody of Patsy and claimed that three weeks before her son's death, she had asked a judge for an emergency hearing to get A.J. back, but the request was denied.

Patsy told the detective that while she was living with David and Jessica, A.J. was fed only bread and water and sometimes was forced to eat bread off the floor. If he didn't clean the garage "good enough," he was not allowed to eat at all.

When he cleaned the kitty litter box, if he didn't do it right, "his face would be put into the litter box." He also had to clean dog feces from the backyard using his hands, but he was allowed to wear gloves.

Patsy told him about other incidents, including ones in which Jessica struck both her and A.J. She explained that she lived with Jessica and David from November 1990 until February 1992—when HRS removed her from their home. Arrangements were later made for Patsy to give a sworn statement in front of a court reporter—with Ilene present.

Later that day, Waites served a subpoena on the custodian of records for Indian Pines Elementary School for school records pertaining to Andrew J. Schwarz. The records showed that A.J. was just below normal in IQ testing. The principal of the school advised him that A.J. did not qualify for special learning disability classes, as had been requested by his stepmother.

Chris Calloway returned to Triphammer Road that afternoon to interview more neighbors. There he talked to an older woman, Shirley Leiter, who told him that every Thursday morning for the past year she had seen A.J. collecting aluminum cans from yellow recycling bins that the residents of the Concept Homes area put out in front of their homes for collection. The last time she saw A.J. was on April 29 when he stopped by her house to pick up additional cans that she had saved for him.

A.J. told her that he had been up since 4:45 that morning and that he was hungry. He couldn't go home and eat unless he had "a whole bunch of cans," and his stepmother would "put him in jail" if he didn't bring enough of them home.

Leiter had given him three doughnuts.

She had become very concerned after talking to him and, about 8:00 that morning, called the CPT. She was referred to a 1-800 number. She spoke to a man named Dave Davis, who told her to call Palm Beach County Truancy. Instead, she called the Indian Pines Elementary School and spoke to a lady whom she believed to be the principal. The woman told Leiter that the school would be taking care of the problem.

Three days later, A.J.'s body was found floating in the aboveground swimming pool.

Detective Calloway next talked to Ronald Pincus Sr., the father of the young man who had seen A.J. walking his dog in the wee hours of the night. Pincus Sr. told the detective that he had heard Jessica Schwarz verbally abuse A.J. on many occasions. The weekend before A.J.'s death—on Saturday—he heard A.J. saying, in a loud voice, "I have a big mouth. I get people in trouble. I'll never do it again." The boy was standing in front of his own house, but Pincus Sr. could hear him inside his home.

A.J. had been repeating the phrase for two hours when Pincus Sr. left at eleven o'clock in the morning. When he returned four hours later, A.J. was still standing there, repeating the same phrase, and continued until five o'clock in the evening.

He had also heard Jessica call the boy "Jeffrey Dahmer."

Pincus Sr.'s twelve-year-old stepdaughter, Jennifer Sullivan, told the detective that she had been in the Schwarz home at least ten times since January 1993. One of the times she was over there, she had heard Jessica tell A.J. that he was to be home by 2:10, and if he didn't make it home by then, she would "tie him up with duct tape, throw him in the road, and run him over."

On two different occasions, she had seen Jessica strike

A.J. About a month earlier, she had been over there playing in Lauren's room and heard Jessica say, "Come here, young man." Jennifer walked out into the living room and saw Jessica strike A.J. on the side of the face and he went into his room and cried. When she saw him later, his eye was red.

In January of that year, she was playing in the pool in the backyard of the Schwarz home. She looked into the kitchen area of the house after she heard A.J. cry out, "Don't do this! Please don't!" She saw Jessica strike A.J. in the eye three times with her hand. When she later talked to A.J. about it, he told her not to tell anybody or he would get in trouble.

During Scott Cupp's time in Live Oak—the seat of Florida's Third Judicial Circuit—he prosecuted a case against Luz and Guillermo Hernandez, charging them with criminal responsibility in the death of their four-year-old daughter, Sonia. Sonia had suffered from birth with severe brain disorders that left her unable to sit up, nearly deaf, blind, incontinent, vegetative, and prone to fevers and infections. She died of pneumonia in 1990. The problem was that her parents hadn't taken her to see a doctor for the two years prior to her death.

The prosecution alleged that the reason they didn't was because they had joined the End Timers, a religious cult led by Charles Meade. The End Timers espoused faith healing instead of doctors. The cult, Meade, and the manslaughter/child neglect case against the Hernandezes captured the attention of the *Miami Herald,* ABC's *20/20,* and the fledgling Court TV, which covered the trial live.

The trial brought Dr. Joseph Burton to town. The chief medical examiner for several counties in metropolitan Atlanta, Georgia, he specialized in pediatric pathology.

Largely because of him, the jury compromised and found the couple guilty of the medical neglect charge—but acquitted them on the manslaughter charge. The doctor convinced everyone that the child was well cared for by the parents and, in retrospect, Cupp felt that the jurors made the right decision. Little did he realize that one year later, their paths would cross again. But this time, if everything worked out the way he planned, Cupp would be asking him direct questions—instead of cross-examining him.

What Scott Cupp remembered most about Dr. Burton—from when he took the witness stand in Live Oak—was his presence and his demeanor. It was as much how he said things as it was what he said. He had an open, warm approachable manner, and Cupp couldn't help but like him.

His credentials were outstanding and he had a reputation for testifying for defense attorneys—as well as prosecutors. That told Cupp that he was brave. If he came to an opinion in a case, he wasn't afraid to say it—regardless of whom it helped or hurt.

After the Benz fiasco, Cupp felt as if all eyes were on him. Everyone involved in the investigation of A.J.'s death knew they needed a second opinion, but whose? They began making calls to various other medical examiners in Florida. Cupp didn't say anything, but his gut told him that everyone in Florida was going to back Dr. Benz.

And Cupp didn't just want a second opinion—he wanted a second autopsy.

How were they going to do it? Could they do it? He never had. At that point in Cupp's career, he had been involved in only a few homicides, and the Hernandez case was the first one in which he had been the lead prosecutor.

He began by telling Detective Waites, and Waites's superiors, about Burton—but Burton was in Atlanta. How could this be accomplished? What would state attorney Barry Krischer say? He had been in office just long enough to get the furniture in the right place—and Cupp was going to tell him he needed to go toe-to-toe with the chief medical examiner in a purely circumstantial-evidence homicide? Not only that, but the man he wanted to do the second autopsy was in Atlanta!

Cupp started by looking at the statutes, and what he found was Florida Stature 925.09, AUTHORITY OF STATE ATTORNEY TO ORDER AUTOPSIES: "The state attorney may have an autopsy performed, before or after interment, on a dead body found in the county when he decides it is necessary in determining whether or not death was the result of a crime."

He would later refer to this law as "the state attorney trumps the medical examiner" law. It didn't say anything about the autopsy being performed within the state, so maybe they could pull it off. Cupp decided to approach Krischer.

He knew he had a fighting chance. Krischer had a true commitment to improving child abuse prosecution in Palm Beach County, and had made it an issue in his campaign. When he took office, there were only three prosecutors doing child abuse for six criminal divisions. Krischer planned to give Cupp enough positions so that they would have one per division. Additionally, his background was solid.

Prior to becoming the state attorney, Barry Krischer had been the attorney for the Child Protection Team. It was obvious that when he spoke about legal issues involving child abuse, he knew what he was talking about. But how would he react to this? One could easily envision all sorts of very bad—and very public—endings. The media hadn't done much with A.J.'s death at that point, but they would. They were watching and waiting. Scott Cupp was hearing—which meant Krischer was hearing—that HRS "had really dropped the ball" this time.

Cupp had already been present at the hastily called meeting at the PBSO, attended by a rather large number of HRS personnel. He knew that was significant—for two reasons. First, it was at the sheriff's office—and not at HRS. Second, it was attended by a man from the inspector general's office in Tallahassee—an agency whose task was to conduct internal investigations of state agencies like HRS.

Many things were going on behind the scenes and probably none of them would be primarily designed to make the prosecution of A.J.'s killer any easier. They would have to move quickly.

The morning he planned to approach Krischer with the letter he wanted him to sign, Cupp arrived for work early. From here on out, he would be arriving for work early most mornings. He was surprised to find Krischer already at work in his office. No one else was there yet, so Cupp had his undivided attention.

Krischer asked, "What are you doing here so early?"

Cupp could tell from the look on Krischer's face that he knew it had to do with A.J.'s case. It was important to him that right from the beginning he didn't pull any punches. He wanted to convey very clearly that this case had enormous potential—if not handled correctly by everyone involved—to go very, very badly.

Cupp replied, "We need to talk."

"Okay."

Barry Krischer had a way of quickly reading a person's demeanor, and when necessary, he took on an almost fatherly tone and attitude. That would make them tell him everything—sometimes more than they had wanted.

This was one time Cupp held nothing back. He, quickly but thoroughly, told Krischer about the various meetings that had already taken place. Saying it to Krischer made Cupp realize just how extraordinary the case already was. Although it was only a few days old, it was already consuming many, many hours of a lot of people's time.

Scott Cupp could tell by Krisher's reaction that he was not surprised in the least about Benz's behavior. They spoke about HRS's role and the possibility of investigating them at some point.

Finally Cupp presented the letter he had prepared for Krischer's signature. He told him about the power he felt Krischer had—under the statute—to order a second autopsy. He told him about Joe Burton and how strongly he felt that a second autopsy—if Krischer would order it—had to be done by someone with no official ties, not only to Palm Beach, but to Florida as well.

Cupp told him there wasn't a doubt in his mind that Jessica had murdered A.J. And after viewing the tape of her at the sheriff's office, he knew—if given the chance—he could make a jury feel the same way. Not just convince them—but also make them feel the same way he was feeling.

The meeting didn't last as long as Cupp thought it would, and it didn't involve as many people as he thought it would. After twenty or thirty minutes, Krischer seemed to know all that he needed to, but he was intent on making sure that Cupp was okay with his own decision.

"Are you sure this is what you want to do?"

"Yes, sir."

Cupp's formality with Krischer told him that he was firm in his resolve to go forward—not just professionally, but personally as well. He was letting him know that he would do what needed to be done and see it through to the end.

Few state attorneys would want to inform the chief medical examiner that they were taking custody of a body and ordering a second full autopsy to be done. And, chances are, none of them would have signed the letter after barely reading it and making no changes—and without having a chief assistant state's attorney or deputy lend their counsel to the situation. By putting his personal and political trust in Scott Cupp, Krischer galvanized Cupp's resolve even more.

Five days after his tragic death—and four days after the first autopsy—A.J.'s body was packed in dry ice, placed in a container specially made for such things, and flown to Lawrenceville, Georgia, a suburb of Atlanta, to have a second full autopsy performed on him.

It was on Friday, May 7, that Detective Michael Waites had the somber duty of accompanying the body—transported by the Aviation Unit of the sheriff's office—at the request of the state attorney's office.

After Dr. Joseph Burton examined the body and performed the second autopsy, which took three to four hours, he advised Waites that the victim had been abused.

As Dr. Benz had done earlier in the week, Dr. Burton listed the cause of death as drowning, but he left the manner of death undetermined, pending microscopic examinations of standards recovered from various bruises on the victim. A complete copy of the autopsy report would eventually be provided to the sheriff's office, the Palm Beach County Medical Examiner's Office, and the Palm Beach County State Attorney's Office.

Scott Cupp would never forget A.J.'s second autopsy, which he had orchestrated successfully. As Joe Burton performed his work, Cupp was at home playing with his two daughters, four-year-old Kaity and two-year-old Elizabeth. He was trying his best to enjoy the evening. It was his thirty-seventh birthday.

CHAPTER 6

He never had the life of a child. He looked for af-
fection—and would cling to it when he found it. He
wanted to be a little boy, but never had the chance.

—Detective Michael Waites

The same day that A.J.'s body was flown to Georgia, Detective Calloway continued his investigation by doing a follow-up interview with thirteen-year-old Jamie Falk at her home. Jamie was a seventh-grade student at Christa McAuliffe Middle School. He asked if she had ever witnessed any abuse directed at A.J.

She told him that about a year earlier she had seen A.J. seated at the dinner table with a plate of food in front of him, but he had tape over his mouth. He could not eat the food but was made to sit there with his mouth taped.

On several occasions, she heard the stepmother screaming and hitting A.J., but she had only actually seen her strike him once.

Two months earlier, the teenager had taken it upon herself to call the HRS abuse hot line. She told the personnel at HRS that A.J. was "always getting hit," but since she had no proof, they told her they couldn't do anything.

Calloway then talked to another neighbor girl, twelve-year-old Serena Perryman, at her home. She told the detective that she had seen A.J. walking past her house on his way home from school three months earlier. Jessica Schwarz had come outside and yelled down the street to A.J. that if he did not get down to his house on the count of five, she would make him walk down the street naked.

Serena had also heard Jessica call A.J. a "fucking bitch" and many times she had seen bruises on A.J.

Next was nine-year-old Teresa Walton, a third-grade student at Indian Pines. The child told the investigator that she believed that Jessica Schwarz had made A.J. eat a cockroach. She was standing outside A.J.'s house when Jessica came to the front door—holding a cockroach in her hand—and called A.J. into the house.

Jessica told A.J. she was going to make him eat it because she had found the cockroach in the kitchen cabinets near the dishes and that he didn't do a good enough job cleaning the dishes.

Teresa walked into the kitchen and saw A.J. standing in a corner, "chewing on something."

The little girl also told the detective that A.J. was allowed only five minutes to eat his dinner, and if he didn't finish in that time, the food was given to the dog.

Teresa had also seen A.J. sitting at the dinner table with his mouth taped shut—with a peanut butter and jelly sandwich and Kool-Aid in front of him. His hands were behind the chair, but she didn't think they were bound. She believed that he was simply told to keep his hands behind the chair.

Over a 3½-year period, Teresa claimed that she had seen A.J. with tape over his mouth at least seven or eight times, and sometimes there was writing on the tape, such as "I'm an asshole" or "I'm an idiot." About two months earlier, she had seen him outside his house with silver tape—she thought it to be duct tape—over his mouth.

Later in the afternoon, Calloway met with a woman who had previously lived across the street from the Schwarzes. Gail Ragatz was a pest exterminator who had performed her services at the Schwarz house once a month.

She believed that A.J. had been abused—mentally and emotionally— by his stepmother.

In December 1992, Ragatz had gone over to visit, and while she was there, she saw Jessica put A.J.'s bowl of food next to the kitty litter box. Jessica told A.J., "If you want to act like a dog, you're going to eat like a dog." Ragatz remembered the incident vividly: the bowl of food contained macaroni and cheese and a hot dog with ketchup.

Yet another neighbor, Diane Mostov, related two strange incidents to Calloway. About one week prior to A.J.'s death, she was coming home from work at 5:30 in the morning and saw A.J. walking down the street carrying a garbage bag over his shoulder. It was still dark outside and she wondered what a child his age was doing out so early in the morning.

A few weeks earlier, she was taking her own child for a walk and passed the Schwarz house. It was early—between noon and one o'clock—in the afternoon on a school day and A.J. was sitting on the ground outside the garage door. He had no clothes on. He did not speak to her or ask for any help.

Mostov added that she was aware of the Schwarz family and "figured it was just one more of Jessica's unusual punishments."

On Saturday morning, Detective Waites returned to the Palm Beach County Medical Examiner's Office and A.J.'s body was released later that day to the funeral home that his natural mother, Ilene, had requested. He was buried the following Monday in Fort Lauderdale.

Detective Calloway returned to Triphammer Road to talk to Louis Steinhauer and his wife, Anne. The Steinhauers had lived directly across the street from the Schwarzes for about 1½ years. Mrs. Steinhauer said that about three times a week she would meet A.J. on the corner and drive him to school. She had asked A.J. if she could take him to school because she felt sorry for him, since he had to walk every day. A.J. accepted the rides from her—but only if she would pick him up on the corner, because he didn't want his parents to see him riding in a car.

During these rides, she learned that A.J. was grounded most of the time, and when she asked him what he was doing early every Thursday morning, he told her that he had to collect aluminum cans for his stepmother because she was on probation and made him collect the cans.

A.J. was up early every morning doing chores. He had to clean the garage about five days out of seven, but the Steinhauers had never seen the girls doing any chores.

Most disturbingly, Mrs. Steinhauer told the detective that on Saturday, April 24, she saw A.J. working in the garage, and Jessica had walked up behind him and placed her hands around his neck and picked him up off the ground. A.J.'s arms were limp at his side and his feet were off the ground. While holding him by the neck, Jessica started walking around the garage, saying, "See this! Look at this!" Mrs. Steinhauer believed she was showing A.J. certain areas in the garage that he may have missed cleaning.

Mrs. Steinhauer had heard—on a daily basis for 1½ years—A.J. being called "shit for brains," "stupid," and an "idiot."

Next the detective talked to Catherine Turner, the neighbor directly behind the Schwarz residence. She also had seen A.J. with a black eye and had asked him what happened. He told her that he "fell down."

Turner had baby-sat for Jessica in the past and said that they had changed the lock on A.J.'s room so that it was on the outside, instead of the inside.

Jessica had told Turner that she would make A.J. walk around the house naked as a form of punishment.

Turner told the detective that in the wee hours of the morning on May 2, she was awakened by a child's voice crying, "I won't do it again!" About five minutes later, she heard the same voice: "I won't do it again!"

She said that she did not recognize the voice, since she

had been sleeping, but the sound came from the back of her home.

Another neighbor, Bob Clayton, told Calloway that he had seen A.J. picking up aluminum cans around the neighborhood and had heard him being verbally abused by his stepmother.

Six months earlier—in reference to his ten-year-old daughter—Jessica had screamed at Bob Clayton, "Your little bitch is throwing things in my pool!" She cursed him and they had an argument about the accusation.

Clayton claimed that he had seen Lauren and Patsy swim naked in the pool many times—but the only times he saw A.J. swimming in the pool was when he was cleaning it.

When Detective Calloway interviewed Beth Walton on Monday, May 10, she said that she had met Jessica and her children in 1990 and had baby-sat for her on several occasions. One of those times, in October 1991, when Jessica arrived at her house with A.J., he was wearing a white T-shirt with the words "I'm a worthless piece of shit—don't talk to me" written on it. When Walton asked Jessica about it, she replied that she had written the words there because he violated one of her rules.

Jessica told her not to allow A.J. to talk to anyone or to watch TV while he was there.

Later in the day, Walton had an appointment at the NutriSystem Center, so she put another shirt over the one A.J. was already wearing. That way, he wouldn't have to lie if his stepmother asked him if he had left the shirt on all day.

On another occasion, when Walton was baby-sitting A.J., she gave him a peanut butter sandwich, and after he ate, he asked her if he could "wash" her bathroom—because she was nice to him.

On yet another occasion—in May or June 1992—A.J. was sitting at her kitchen table when Jessica appeared "obviously intoxicated." Jessica grabbed A.J., shook him, and smacked him in the head. Then she told him to tell the people—apparently HRS—that the only reason she took him out of school was because of doctors' appointments. At this time, Jessica was being investigated by HRS and the PBSO for physical abuse on A.J.—and drug abuse.

According to Walton, when Jessica grabbed A.J. and shook him, she told him that she was going to "knock the fucking crap out of him."

Jessica later told Beth Walton that A.J. was pulled out of school because he was supposed to wake her up on time— and he didn't. Also, he was supposed to empty a cat litter box and Jessica didn't think he had cleaned it well enough. Therefore, she was going to make him stay home from school.

Sometime in 1992, when A.J.'s natural mother was trying to get visitation rights, Walton claimed that Jessica had told A.J. that if he told the judge he wanted see his natural mother, she "would kill him."

On Tuesday, May 11, Detective Calloway interviewed Susan Simpson, a woman who had attended three group counseling sessions with Jessica Schwarz. Simpson told him that Jessica was "outrageous and obnoxious" during the meetings. Jessica talked about A.J. at every meeting and she called him Jeffrey Dahmer. Jessica also told her that she locked A.J. in his bedroom at night because she "was afraid he was going to be standing over her bed with a knife."

At one of the meetings, Jessica walked in and said, "Well, I fed the bastard."

Over the next several months, the investigation nearly came to a standstill until, finally, in the second week of August 1993, Scott Cupp received the autopsy report from Dr. Joseph Burton. An extremely complex case, Dr. Burton had spent numerous hours on its evaluation, as well as reviewing it with other experts on his staff.

It was his determination that if A.J.'s body had been found in any situation other than in water—and the postmortem and autopsy findings being as they were—that it was unlikely that the case would have been classified as anything other than a "homicide." He based his opinion, in part, on the numerous bruises, many of which were in locations that are not routinely found in accidental occurrences.

Dr. Burton stated in his report: "In arriving at a determination of cause and manner of death, the Medical Examiner must consider every aspect of the investigation. The determination of cause and manner of death is not dependant solely on the observations found at a postmortem examination and autopsy."

He explained that the autopsy was only a piece of the puzzle and must be put into context with the entire investigation—all the information known about the case.

"That is what I have done with this case and I have treated it as I would have, had it occurred in my own jurisdiction. This case has been reviewed in its entirety with four of my most experienced forensic investigators, having approximately sixty years of homicide and death investigation experience, collectively."

His entire staff—including other pathologists—was unanimous in its opinion.

They had found it fairly simple to rule out natural causes as the manner of death. A.J. had no significant underlying medical problems.

Nor was there anything to indicate a reason why he might have drowned accidentally—let alone any explanation as to why he might have been in the pool naked in the middle of the night or early in the morning. A.J. was a good swimmer and had no history of epilepsy or blacking out. The pool was only four feet deep, so even if he (at 4'4" tall) would have had cramps, he could have walked on his tiptoes and kept his nose above the water. Or he could have even bounced off the bottom to the pool edge—due to the small size of the pool.

The design and size of the pool also made it unlikely that he dived in, hit his head, and knocked himself unconscious. And the abrasions on his face, nose, and ears were not injuries caused by scraping or hitting the plastic-lined pool.

As to the possibility of suicide, Dr. Burton found it unreasonable to conclude that A.J. had taken his life intentionally by drowning. He had investigated many adolescent suicides during his career and could not recall a single one in which a child had committed suicide by drowning. He had also contacted other medical examiners in other jurisdictions around the country and could find no case in which a child of this age was felt to have committed suicide by drowning. Indeed, it is rare for adults to take their own lives in such a manner.

Was Andrew Schwarz's death a homicide?

Dr. Burton and his colleagues took many things into consideration.

"There is without question evidence of physical abuse to this child. The patterns of bruises on the scalp could—in no way—have been caused by some type of accident. They are multiple—involving all four quadrants of the scalp—and there are no lacerations or abrasions of the skin surface.

"The bruising on the upper inner left arm and behind the knees, as well as on the inner upper thighs are consistent with where someone may have forcibly held this child. Most of these appear to be of recent origin."

Burton determined that there was ample evidence from the investigators' interviews with neighbors and others that A.J. had been physically and emotionally abused—apparently, by his stepmother primarily.

"The investigative history and the postmortem examination and autopsies of Andrew Schwarz disclose irrefutable evidence that Andrew was physically abused."

In fact, Jessica Schwarz had been seen grasping A.J. beneath the head and holding him up off the ground by the neck—at some point previous to his death. Dr. Burton stated, "The bruises beneath his chin may certainly have been accounted for by such an act. This does not constitute proper treatment of a ten-year-old child."

He noted the information in the records that A.J. had been punished in the past by being made to run down the street naked:

"If this is true, it is certainly of interest that—when his body is discovered—he is naked. Ten-year-old boys are usually very self-conscious about their body. It is very unusual to find a child of this age who would be willing to swim in the nude—even in the middle of the night.

"In addition, the stepmother finding him missing from his room at 6:00 a.m., also is suspicious since she reportedly does not rise until 10:00 in the morning or later."

When David Schwarz found A.J. floating in the pool between 6:00 and 6:30 A.M., A.J. was already in a state of rigor mortis. Taking all factors into consideration—including the temperature of the water at eighty-two degrees, the size of the child, etc.—Dr. Burton concluded that the rigor mortis at least suggested that A.J. might have been dead for several hours prior to being discovered.

"When he went to bed, reports indicate that he was okay and no family member states anything about any visible injuries on his face.

"Yet on the face to the left of the mouth is a scrape-like abrasion. On the right side of the nose is a somewhat linear abrasion. Behind the ears are abrasions—one more intense than the other. Beneath the left arm is a recent bruise. On the inner aspect of the thighs there are recent bruises.

"The above pattern of injuries are consistent with someone having held Andrew's head with the hand placed behind the head and possibly another hand across the nose and mouth and submerging him until he aspirated enough water to become unconscious and die.

"This child's past psychiatric history is certainly questionable since most of the information given to treating physicians was supplied primarily by the stepmother. There is obvious bias in the stepmother's opinion of this child and her opinion is in direct conflict with some statements taken from school officials and from other people in the health care field.

"Although this child—at least by the parents' history—had exhibited in the past unruly behavior, possibly aggressive behavior, the circumstances of this case strongly suggest that this child's death is the result of physical child abuse with the terminal mechanism of death being submersion or drowning.

"The injuries to the scalp are sufficient in and of themselves to have caused the death of a child.

"In summary, at the very least Andrew's death should have resulted in an investigation and intervention on the grounds of physical and emotional child abuse. There is overwhelming evidence to support the above.

"The diagnosis of death by drowning does not exclude the manner of this occurrence as having been due to a 'homicide.'

"The evidence in this case overwhelmingly demands that the death of Andrew Schwarz should either be classified as 'homicide' or that the involved agencies should present all of the evidence to a grand jury or similar investigative body to conclude whether such a classification is warranted.

"There is nothing wrong with Dr. Benz having classified the death as 'undetermined.' In fact, I might also list the classification as such, although I feel more strongly now than when I was first involved in the case, that had it occurred within my jurisdiction that I would have classified the death as a 'homicide.'

"My report would reflect, as it does here, that the facts of the case not only suggest, but demand, that a grand jury or other body of non biased individuals review the case in its entirety and determine whether there is evidence for the legal system to proceed.

"If the determination is that there is not enough evidence, then at least it could be said that everything had been done to be sure that the questions surrounding his death were explored in their fullest in an attempt to speak for, to protect, and obtain justice, even though he has died."

Due to the findings of the autopsy, the case remained open pending further investigation.

"Hands/fists/feet" was listed as the suspected weapons that had been used on A.J. Schwarz.

Soon after he received the autopsy report from Dr. Burton, Scott Cupp asked a young colleague of his, assistant state attorney (ASA) Joseph Marx, to join with him in the investigation of A.J.'s death and—hopefully—the prosecution of Jessica Schwarz.

On the morning of August 11, Detective Waites asked David Schwarz to meet with him at the sheriff's office to discuss the finalized autopsy report.

Detectives Waites and Calloway interviewed Bear later that morning and explained the report—and Dr. Burton's qualifications to him. They also told him about the various bruises and injuries documented at the time of the autopsy.

When the detectives asked if he had any knowledge of problems between Jessica and A.J., David told them he did not. He added that when he had been employed as a truck driver, he had called home whenever he went on an overnight trip and there was never an indication of any problems.

David asked if he needed to contact an attorney and Waites explained to him that it was entirely his decision and that if he wanted to do that, the interview would be concluded until he had the opportunity to do so. David asked if he was being charged with any crime and the detective explained that, at that point, he was still being considered a witness in the investigation.

David decided to continue with the interview.

He felt that if problems existed between Jessica and A.J., his two other children would have told him about it. He claimed that Lauren or Jackie had never told him about any such problems. Lauren and Jackie were still in the custody of Jessica's parents.

Waites again described the bruising that was observed on A.J.'s body, and David had no explanation for—and claimed that he had no knowledge of—them.

When the detectives told him about the incident that Jessica had described to them in which A.J. was supposedly in the garage, striking himself in the head with a cane, David further claimed that he was not familiar with the incident and Jessica had never told him about it.

When asked what type of rewards A.J. received for good behavior, David said that he would get toys for "extra good behavior" and an "extra helping of food at dinner for daily good behavior."

When Waites asked him about the information that they had received in reference to A.J. collecting cans in the morning before going to school, David said that he did it to assist Jessica with her community service and claimed that the other two children also helped with collecting the cans. He said that he would wake A.J.—between five and six o'clock in the morning—before he went to work so that the boy could collect the cans before going to school.

To the best of his knowledge, David said the worst punishment A.J. had ever received was going to bed without dinner for one or two nights in a row. And that—at no time—had he ever seen A.J. being physically abused. Anytime he heard what he considered to be verbal abuse, or very loud yelling, at A.J., he would put a stop to it and did not allow it to continue.

Waites asked whether or not, if A.J. was being abused or physically punished, he would offer any resistance. David said that A.J. would not, and that he became very passive when anyone raised his or her voice at him.

He repeated the same story he had told them before about the morning he found A.J.'s body in the pool. Incredibly, he claimed that there had been no conversation between Jessica and him concerning A.J.'s death since May 2, the day A.J. died.

Soon after that, Michael Waites and Jimmy Restivo decided to "take another run" at David Schwarz. They really thought—especially Restivo—that armed with Burton's report, that Bear would turn on Jessica and give them something direct that had happened between Jessica and A.J. that night, early morning, or close in time to the murder.

When he didn't, they were left in the same position—there was no direct evidence that led to A.J.'s murder.

On August 31, Detectives Waites and Calloway went to the Schwarz home on Triphammer Road and attempted to interview Jessica Schwarz. When they arrived, Jessica spoke to them from inside the house and refused to unlock the door and talk face-to-face with them. She asked if she was under arrest and they told her no.

She told them that she needed to put some clothes on and then she would speak with them. A few minutes later, she came to the door and—speaking from inside the house through the locked door—told them to "fuck off."

Waites informed her to have her attorney, Sam Marshall, contact either him or Detective Calloway so they could set up an appointment to conduct an interview with her regarding the autopsy report.

At 12:30 that afternoon, Sam Marshall, who was representing Jessica in the dependency hearing involving Lauren and Jackie, contacted Waites, and the detective explained to him that they had received the final autopsy report, listing the manner of death as homicide. Not surprisingly, Marshall stated that he was not inclined to allow his client to be interviewed.

Later in the afternoon, Detectives Waites and Calloway met with Scott Cupp to review the investigation. As a result of the meeting, the case was tentatively set to be presented to the grand jury on October 5, 1993—unless there was a conflict with Dr. Burton's schedule. The possible charges that would be presented to the grand jury were first-degree murder, aggravated child abuse, emotional and mental abuse, as well as the possibility of an unrelated charge involving A.J.'s half sister Patsy.

CHAPTER 7

*I just can't help but feel that Andrew is programmed.
Things just don't ring true. His affect is flat.*

—Dr. Richard Zimmern

In September, Scott Cupp read—for the first time—the progress notes that Dr. Richard Zimmern had written over the period of time that he was A.J.'s guardian. It was, indeed, a poignant glimpse into the tragic life of Andrew J. Schwarz and the relationship he shared with the person who cared about him, perhaps more than anyone else—his volunteer guardian ad litem.

When Dr. Zimmern spoke to Jessica Schwarz on July 23, 1992, she told him that when she first met David, he was "on the rebound" from Ilene and that he had A.J. and Patsy every weekend.

It was obvious that Jessica had little regard for A.J.'s biological mother, Ilene, calling her "a slob and a slut. She is a game player and a manipulator." According to Jessica, Ilene appeared to be high on "speed or cocaine."

(This of course, was Jessica's opinion and the facts were not verified.)

Jessica told Dr. Zimmern that A.J. was a hyperexcitable child with a poor attention span, but that he got decent, passable grades.

His notes reflected some of her additional comments:

"He is impulsive with poor judgment and cannot be trusted alone."

Jessica claimed that A.J. tried to drown Jackie when she was two years old. She told the guardian that A.J. had had a near drowning experience when he was about two or three years old and was unconscious for several minutes, but he was not hospitalized.

After accusing Jessica of verbal and physical abuse, Patsy was removed from the Schwarz home in May 1992 and placed in foster care. The fact that Patsy had threatened suicide was instrumental in her being removed from the Schwarz home, but Jessica felt that Ilene had orchestrated the whole scenario for revenge.

Dr. Zimmern's notes from August 27, 1992, indicated that Jessica had finally set up an initial appointment for A.J. at South County Mental Health for September 10—even though he was supposed to have started counseling in March, immediately after his release from the Psychiatric Institute of Vero Beach.

Nor was he on the imipramine that had been prescribed for him. After A.J.'s discharge, Dr. Thomas Uttley, the doctor in charge of his case, had given Jessica one additional prescription for imipramine, but, according to Jessica, A.J. started to vomit the medicine.

At some point—again, according to her—she took him to a local family doctor who refused to renew the medication. The antidepressant is prescribed to relieve symptoms such as feelings of sadness, worthlessness, or guilt, loss of interest in daily activities, changes in appetite, tiredness, sleeping too much, insomnia, and thoughts of death or suicide.

A.J. was not on Medicaid at the time because HRS had suddenly dropped him from the program. Jessica claimed she was told that he was too old, yet the two girls and David continued to receive their cards. When A.J. finally received a card for August, Jessica called South County Mental Health to make the counseling appointment.

Jessica stated that she did not believe in counseling and

claimed that A.J. was never helped by imipramine. Ironically, she felt that what he needed was a strong, well-structured home where he would feel safe and wanted.

On September 18, 1992, there was a hearing before Judge Carney in the Broward County Courthouse. Through her attorney, A.J.'s biological mother, Ilene, asked that he be placed in a foster home, but the request was denied. The judge, however, was disturbed by the fact that A.J. did not start counseling until September 10—six months after his discharge from Vero Beach—and was also concerned about the variance in A.J.'s behavior in school and at home.

Dr. Zimmern's notes indicated that on October 7 he had had a long visit with David and Jessica in an attempt to become better acquainted with the family.

"Andrew was pleased to see me and readily talked about school. He quickly told me he didn't want to see his [biological] mother or sister—or even talk to them. He seems afraid that they will somehow re-enter his life. Andrew is a quiet passive child who appears to be easily dominated. I believe that he has many fears; he certainly is outwardly tense."

And, on October 29: "I just can't help but feel that Andrew is programmed. Things just don't ring true. His affect is flat."

There was another court hearing on October 30: "Andrew does not have to speak to or visit [with] Ilene Logan or Patsy Spence until he has Kathy Merritt's (his counselor) okay. Patsy is getting together with her mother and they will be united in the near future."

A few weeks later, Dr. Zimmern noted a telephone conversation he had with Jessica: "Andrew is getting into trouble in school and is not reporting his demerits to Jessica. He is hiding the teacher's notes. His schoolwork is going downhill. Jessica is angry with his teacher and the school in general.

"I have suggested he be placed on imipramine."

On November 24, he again visited the Schwarz home and discussed A.J.'s hyperactivity and talkativeness with Jessica. He urged her to take him to see his doctor and get a prescription for imipramine. They also talked about Jessica's handling of A.J.: "She is bugged by his 'lying.' She will not budge on softening her stand. I will approach his teacher and try to work from that end."

He visited Indian Pines Elementary School in December to talk to Mrs. Idrissi. Andrew was a good child in school, anxious to please, eager to help. Idrissi, aware that he was starving for affection and approval, gave him lots of both.

Dr. Zimmern suggested that there be no more notes home—that Mrs. Idrissi work out her own system of discipline within the class.

"Jessica Schwarz's character and attitude are now well known among the teachers at Indian Pines. Andrew will miss the December 10 [field] trip, which was lost because of lying and failure to bring home notes from the teacher. He knew, of course, that he would be punished and naturally hid the notes. Jessica is very resistant to changing her ways. Tough love!"

According to his notes on January 19, 1993: "Jessica and Andrew are a totally mismatched pair. Considering Andrew's current emotional developmental state, she is psychologically unable to give him the support he needs. Jessica must have significant problems herself. Her brazen, combative attitude is now well known in the neighborhood and in school. Everybody on Triphammer Road must hate her guts!

"Jessica has no concept of flexibility in her approach to Andrew. She has no concept of his emotional needs, and trying to meet those needs. Luckily, Mrs. Idrissi has the interest and capacity to mother him and give him the touching and hugging he needs. Home must be a dismal place for Andrew, including an absent father who gives him no support in any fashion.

"I think Andrew will be in reasonable shape as long as he has Mrs. Idrissi as a mother figure in school. I will try to call a conference on Andrew in June to decide whether or not he should remain with Jessica and David. They probably won't change and he will have to go to a foster home. I guess

Jessica just doesn't like him. She tolerates him, and his father just doesn't care. No one cares but Mrs. Idrissi and me."

On January 26, Richard Zimmern received a phone call from Ms. Janet Heinrich, the guidance counselor at Indian Pines Elementary School. She told him that a neighbor had reported that Andrew had a broken nose and two black eyes. Heinrich reported it to the abuse hot line and the call was referred to Barbara Black, the HRS investigator. Andrew was not at school that day or the day before.

"Ms. Black and a police officer went to the Schwarz home. They believe that Andrew's injuries were an accident, which occurred when he was on his bicycle. He has a broken nose?"

That afternoon, Dr. Zimmern visited Andrew: "He does indeed have a broken nose and two black eyes. He says that on Sunday the 24th at about two to three in the afternoon, he was walking his sister's bike into the garage when he tripped and fell against the handlebars." Nothing medically had been done for A.J. at that point, but he was scheduled to see his psychologist and family doctor the following day, on January 27.

"Andrew seemed depressed and subdued this afternoon. I told him I did not think he hurt himself falling against the bike handles. He persistently repeated the fall against the bike handle story. I just don't see how such a fall could generate enough force to break his nose."

That same day, Dr. Zimmern talked to Mrs. Idrissi on the telephone: "She cares for him a great deal. He has been absent nineteen out of the last forty-nine days."

On January 28, he noted that Andrew went to see his family doctor the day before, and, according to Ms. Black, his nose was not broken.

He talked to Mrs. Idrissi again on February 18: "Am concerned about Andrew's absenteeism in school; he has not been sick. Why would Jessica keep him home? She could be using school as a punishment since she knows Mrs. Idrissi cares for him. Andrew spends a lot of time in school getting hugs and touching from Mrs. Idrissi; he needs it badly. He is doing C work, which is remarkable considering his background. He is depressed and sad. No love or affection at home—just endless punishment."

On February 23, there was a staff meeting at the Center for Children in Crisis concerning A.J.: "The staff psychologist feels that Andrew is a very sick kid—almost at the end of his rope. Jessica Schwarz, a combative, rude, simplistic woman with no real love for Andrew, is the worst possible stepmother for him. Serious consideration is being given to removing him from the Schwarz home and placing him in a foster home. This home would have to be carefully selected; a warm loving person like Mrs. Idrissi would be fine. Barbara Black of HRS will set up a meeting in the near future."

In the column to the right of his notes, Dr. Zimmern jotted, "Need review in mid-May."

He talked to Jessica on February 24: "She is having health problems—either kidney or liver. Her auto license plates were stolen so she has no transportation. She is going to the doctor's tomorrow and plans to take Andrew with her because of a rash.

"She says Andrew is having problems in school again—behavior problems.

"Mrs. Idrissi tells me he just has his usual needs for attention and affection—plus his hyperactivity."

On March 2, he discovered that between September 14, 1992, and February 22, 1993—out of a total of fourteen appointments—there had been three cancellations and three no-shows. A.J. had not been to counseling since February 2.

The following week, Dr. Zimmern had a discussion with David and Jessica regarding their handling of A.J.: "They believe Andrew is irrevocably flawed because of his early years with his biological mother. They feel that little can be done to change this. Jessica's father has stated to her, 'His eyes are dead—he has no soul.'

"I urged them to believe that Andrew is an emotionally disturbed child who can be helped—even cured—through therapy and love and security.

"Andrew does well in school and this part of his life should be fostered and aided. Do not use school or any aspect of it as part of his home disciplinary regime. As soon as you are able he should be returned to his therapist.

"Andrew needs to know that you care, and that you believe in him. Try not to always outsize him. Find things that he can be praised for—he needs to feel good about himself.

"When Andrew's eyes go dead he is withdrawing from the world because he finds it all just too painful. His self-esteem is now so low—try to build it up any way you can.

"Andrew is a difficult person to live with because his past life was so bad. His present habits are ones he developed to cope with life as it was. When his life improves he will shed those habits because they will no longer be necessary."

On March 24, Dr. Zimmern made the following notation: "Andrew was in a fight yesterday. A local boy named Tristan mouthed Jessica—Andrew fought for his [step] mother's good name. For this he was punished—kept out of school and grounded. He is now grounded until Christmas of 1993. This means confined to the house and chores after school.

"Andrew is afraid he will be sent away to a foster home which he does not want. I believe he willfully disobeys and forgets his chores, homework, and jobs. It must be his way of fighting back, his way of being noticed, his way of asserting himself, his way of bolstering his self-esteem.

"Every Thursday, he collects cans from five to seven in the morning. I gather that on those days, he does not go to school.

"In many ways, Andrew's home is his prison.

"Jessica sees Andrew as a four-year-old emotionally who she cannot control. Andrew frustrates her—makes her angry. Jessica's method of handling this anger is a head on 'in-your-face', abrasive, verbal counter attack with threats, which totally undermine Andrew's security. He panics inside, another failure, which further undermines his fragile self-esteem. He fights back by disobedience and forgetfulness—the usual ploy of helpless creatures.

"Jessica states that Andrew has had a bad month—hitting girls—fighting with boys—not abiding by the rules—not listening to anyone."

On March 26, Dr. Zimmern attended a meeting at the HRS office; also present were Barbara Black, Dottie Daniels, who was Black's supervisor, the Schwarzes, and Mrs. Idrissi.

"Jessica came on strong at first with her profane, combative, 'in-your-face' attitude. This is wholly defensive and covers her insecurity and low self-esteem in the presence of people who could do her harm. She calmed down once she realized that this meeting was not a trial, and she had not been prejudged guilty of abuse and/or neglect.

"Mrs. Idrissi spoke well, indicating that Andrew was bright and capable. He does need a lot of support, including hugs and touching. He seems starved for affection. Mrs. Idrissi and Jessica exchanged verbal blows, finally coming to understand each other—without liking each other.

"The HRS supervisor made it plain to Jessica that they knew that unknown neighbors were calling in the abuse to harass her. She also made it plain that they have to follow the rules and investigate each call. She made it clear that HRS is not her enemy, but just an agency whose purpose here is to help Andrew. She suggested changes in Jessica's approach: less negativity, more kindness, more rewards on a day to day basis, trying to find positive things in Andrew's life to support.

"I stated that we all know that Andrew has had a horrible past which we are all trying to help him overcome. He needs support, he needs his counseling, and he needs steady school attendance. School is one place where he succeeds, where he has fun, where he finds someone to love him. He trusts [Mrs. Idrissi] and confides in her. Considering his past, Andrew is doing very well?

"Jessica has to be strict but needs to show warmth and acceptance. She needs to respect Andrew as a person, not think of him as an emotionally disturbed kid operating on a four-year-old level.

"No discussion of removing Andrew to a foster home.

"I believe real progress was made—all the parties said their piece. Jessica now knows we are not monsters out to get her, but people who want to help her keep Andrew in her home and provide for him in a useful and practical way.

"His new social worker is Sandra Warren."

On March 31, he noted: "Jessica had a fight with Ms. Russo of South County Mental Health. David was responsible for getting Andrew to the clinic. When he missed, he did not call. Ms. Russo is rightfully angry with Jessica and David. Jessica hung up on Ms. Russo, but called Sandra Warren at HRS to explain. She will attempt to mend the relationship and get Andrew started back in counseling.

"Jessica is also angry at all the little daily gifts Andrew receives from Mrs. Idrissi. She thinks he's being spoiled."

Dr. Zimmern made a quick visit to see Andrew on April 10 to give him and his sisters Easter baskets. "Everyone seems quite happy and together. Can a real family be forming at last? Andrew needs David's support and love—in a visible way."

He also visited A.J. on his birthday, April 24. "He had his usual long face and was cleaning up outside. I gave him his Battle Trolls, as he requested; he brightened up and began to show them to his sisters. Later we finished his outside chores together.

"Jessica wants to talk to me about Lauren—she has been acting up, and saying that Andrew gets all of the attention. We agreed to get together the first week in May."

And then the heartbreaking entry on May 3: "Andrew is dead. He was found in a pool yesterday. Heard the news on the eleven o'clock newscast. Schwarzes deny complicity. Jackie and Lauren removed by HRS. No details available."

And later in the day, he noted: "I spent the morning at the guardian ad litem office. I feel so badly. I should have pressed the panic button earlier, instead of waiting for the school year to end. I knew Jessica was a hard taskmaster, but I never thought of her as a sadist.

"Jessica called the office to talk to me. She said she

awoke between five and six in the morning to go to the bathroom. Going to the kitchen she noted Andrew's light on and his room empty. She checked the house and then woke up David. David found Andrew's body in the pool—already stiff. Saturday night the family had a happy time—singing and laughing.

"Jessica did not sound depressed or sad—just very angry. That seems to be her principal emotion—anger and hostility. Now her anger was aimed at HRS and the police, who took her daughters and placed them with her parents, up the coast a bit.

"When she called I thought we might cry together. She thundered—raging at the world as personified by the police and HRS. She had no soft spot in her heart for Andrew—no compassion—no feeling for his early suffering—or his current needs.

"God was unkind to Andrew. He gave him Ilene Logan and her lovers, followed by David and Jessica Schwarz. No one can hurt him anymore. In the end, we all failed him. I should have saved him; now I must live with my failure."

CHAPTER 8

Make no mistake—Richard cared deeply for A.J.

—Scott Cupp

Dr. Richard Zimmern's notes contributed much to the overall feeling of sadness, frustration, and anger that Scott Cupp was already feeling; but, most important, it strengthened his resolve to build a case against Jessica Schwarz.

At that time, Cupp had little respect for most in the child protection field. Rightly or wrongly, he perceived most as incompetent and untrustworthy, and he felt that most lacked sincerity. Richard Zimmern clearly was none of those things and Scott Cupp knew that A.J. was fortunate to have had him.

Ironically, Zimmern was the "volunteer" among all the "professionals," which perhaps spoke volumes about the system in place to protect abused children. Tragically—as even Dr. Zimmern himself acknowledged—in the end, he felt he also failed A.J.

Compounding Scott Cupp's determination was the psychosocial and psychological evaluation from the Psychiatric Institute of Vero Beach regarding A.J.'s hospitalization in February 1992. It should be noted that David and Jessica Schwarz were the sources for the information pertaining to A.J.'s behavior and history.

At the age of eight, A.J. spent six weeks in the psychiatric hospital for evaluation and treatment of underlying depression. The main concern was that he had been "irritable and unpredictable, as well as dangerous to himself and others."

Jessica and David saw him as "increasingly dangerous," claiming that he had "run into traffic recklessly, jumped off ladders, and attempted to drown his sister on various occasions."

David reported that A.J. did not talk clearly until about the age of five. He also told them that A.J. "drowned" at the age of three—he was underwater for three to five minutes.

A.J.'s natural mother abused alcohol and drugs and he was subjected to physical and emotional abuse from her during his childhood, and David claimed that Ilene had "disappeared with his children—out of state—for three years."

He also claimed that A.J. had "always been physically abusive towards pets, sisters, and smaller friends," and that he had recently "tried to drown" his younger sister.

By court order from Broward County, Ilene was not allowed to have contact with A.J., due to past abuse of A.J., and the boy claimed not to want any contact with her.

According to the report: "The patient (A.J.) has been abusive to the family members, and parents are having difficulty managing his behavior. More specific information has not been obtained due to stepmother's inability to engage in treatment, due to allegedly not being able to find transportation, as she cannot drive because she lost her license for six months. This is reported to the hospital two days after the patient's admission. The natural father cannot attend due to working as a truck driver, and being out of town for weeks at a time. We will need to further work with this resistance in order to engage the family in his treatment. This will be a very important component to this child's treatment.

"There appears to be little or no involvement at this time.

"It would appear there has been little consistency in this child's life."

During A.J.'s stay at the hospital, many psychological tests were administered, including the thematic apperception test (TAT)—a projective personality test that was designed at Harvard in the 1930s by Christiana D. Morgan and Henry A. Murray. One of the most widely used tests, it is one in which a person's patterns of thought, attitudes, observational capacity, and emotional responses are evaluated on the basis of responses to ambiguous test materials. The TAT consists of thirty-one pictures depicting a variety of social and interpersonal situations and the patient is asked to tell a story about each one.

A.J.'s TAT stories reflected his low self-esteem and poor body image, "partially rooted in his view of the world as an unpredictable place.

"There is anxiety regarding family gatherings, the mother figure and self perception, especially since he refused to make stories for these indicating, 'I can't, it is too hard. I can't even see their faces.' "

Also, he made a reference to missing one of his sisters, whom he believed to be in another state.

When A.J. was administered the Rorschach (inkblot) test, he saw alligators, fire, ghosts, lions, and dead dragons with blood on them. According to the psychological evaluation report, he was also preoccupied with angels.

The summary on the report read: "A.J. is a depressed and anxious youngster for whom hospitalization seems warranted at this time given his dangerous behaviors, and deterioration. He is experiencing a great deal of anger and sadness, which is believed to be at the root of much of his unpredictable behavior. Group therapy may help him begin to process these feelings, but individual therapy will need to be continued in order to boost his self-esteem.

"A.J. appears to be suffering from the loss regarding not only his mother, but also his sister. He will need to mourn and grieve in supportive therapy. Family therapy will be necessary to help A.J. bond more appropriately with current family members."

* * *

The case against Jessica Schwarz was presented to the Palm Beach County grand jury on October 4, 1993, and as a result—on October 8—a sealed indictment was delivered, charging her with one count of second-degree murder, four counts of aggravated child abuse (second-degree felony), two counts of felony child abuse (third-degree felony), and one count of witness tampering (third-degree felony).

The four counts of aggravated child abuse presented by the grand jury were that Jessica Schwarz had maliciously punished Andrew Schwarz by forcing him to eat food from a bowl placed next to a cat's litter box, by repeatedly forcing him to remain home from school, by forcing him to wear a shirt with the writing "I'm a worthless piece of shit; don't talk to me" (or words to that effect), and by forcing him to edge the family yard with regular house scissors—all causing him unnecessary or unjustifiable pain or suffering.

One of the counts of felony child abuse presented was that Jessica willfully (or by culpable negligence) permitted A.J. to suffer mental injury, by forcing him to sit naked outside his house.

The second count of felony child abuse presented was that Jessica willfully (or by culpable negligence) permitted Jackie to suffer mental injury by forcing her not to discuss the circumstances surrounding the life and death of A.J.

The count of tampering with a witness presented that Jessica did knowingly use intimidation or physical force, or knowingly did threaten or attempt to threaten, or did offer pecuniary benefit or gain to Jackie, with intent to influence her testimony.

At 1:00 that afternoon, Jessica Schwarz was arrested at her home on Triphammer Road. Jimmy Restivo, Chris Calloway, and Michael Waites went to the front door while uniformed patrol circled around to the back—to make sure she didn't try to make a run for it. Hoping they wouldn't have to break the door down, they banged on it until Jessica finally opened it, and they were able to serve the warrant.

Jessica had been talking to her attorney on the phone and

he was still on the line when the detectives entered. While the others read her rights to her and handcuffed her, Detective Waites picked up the telephone, which was on the floor, and informed Sam Marshall that Jessica was being taken to jail and that he could meet them there.

She was transported to the Palm Beach County Stockade and was held without bond.

On Friday, October 15, 1993, thirty-eight-year-old Jessica Schwarz pleaded "not guilty" to all the charges against her.

There was a two-hour hearing on Monday, October 25, 1993, to determine whether or not Jessica Schwarz should be released on bond. Her lead attorney, Rendell Brown, tried to convince the judge that his client was a responsible woman who—even when she knew she was going to be arrested— stayed to face the charges against her.

Scott Cupp painted a much more sinister picture—one in which Jessica Schwarz had assaulted her husband and even threatened some of the children in the neighborhood.

When Brown stated that A.J. had been placed in the care of Jessica and David because his biological mother had hit him in the head with a frying pan, Ilene Logan, who was seated in the gallery of the courtroom, cried out angrily, "You son of a bitch! No!"

Quite emotional, she struggled to stand up, but her father, who was seated next to her, held her down firmly and clamped his hand over her mouth in an effort to keep her quiet.

Apparently embarrassed and perhaps not wanting to be recognized later, David Schwarz wore dark sunglasses when he took the witness stand. When questioned, he quietly admitted that he did not attend his own son's funeral.

Cupp: You don't even know the day he died.
David: It was May 8.
Cupp (disgusted): It was May 2.

After viewing the videotape of Jessica ordering Jackie not to talk to the detectives, Judge Walter Colbath released

Jessica on $150,000 bond, with the stipulation that she was not allowed to leave her house—except to attend court proceedings. She was also prohibited from having any money or car keys.

And she was forbidden to have any contact with her daughters.

Jessica Schwarz's father, Edward Woods, paid the bond and she was allowed to leave the stockade late that afternoon.

One neighbor, after she learned of Jessica's release, was so frightened that she asked the police for additional patrols in the area.

On October 29, Detective Calloway met with twelve-year-old Ariel Walton, Teresa Walton's sister, at Christa McAuliffe Middle School. Ariel told the detective that she was Lauren Cross's best friend and that she used to visit Lauren "all the time."

She stated that when Jessica and her daughters would go to the grocery store or would leave the house for any reason, they would lock A.J. outside the house in the backyard area, on numerous occasions.

Ariel had heard Jessica frequently tell A.J. that she hated him. Jessica had also told her, "I'll never love that boy." And that she was going to "kill him someday and bury him under the pool."

She had seen Jessica strike A.J. across the face and head with her hands on numerous occasions. She, too, had seen A.J. perform the strange chore of edging the grass with scissors—and added that he usually cleaned the garage out "every day." A.J. was made to do "all the chores," but the girls did "next to nothing."

On one occasion, A.J. accidentally dropped some toothbrushes in the toilet, so Jessica told him that he wasn't allowed to brush his teeth anymore.

Jessica cursed at A.J. "all the time" and Ariel had overheard Jessica call him a "fucking retarded kid" and tell him that he was "no good."

About a year earlier, Jessica made A.J. eat a cockroach. She told Ariel that she was going to make A.J. eat every one of them that she saw in the house. Apparently, it was A.J.'s "job" to make sure there were no cockroaches in the house.

A little while later, Ariel saw A.J. using the garden hose to wash his mouth out, and he told her "the cockroach tasted nasty."

CHAPTER 9

Calloway put his heart into this case, just like he did every case he ever worked. I have worked with a lot of detectives and investigators over the years, and he is one that I highly respect.

—Detective Michael Waites

Scott Cupp went before the grand jury in November to question the HRS workers who had been responsible for protecting Andrew Schwarz—the same grand jurors who had indicted Jessica Schwarz the previous month.

Early in 1992, when Patsy claimed that Jessica had given her a bloody nose and was then returned to Broward County, A.J. remained in the Schwarz home, under the supervision of HRS.

Then in January 1993, Eileen Callahan made the "anonymous" phone call to HRS informing them that she believed Jessica Schwarz had broken A.J.'s nose. After the investigation by HRS and the sheriff's office, the charge was considered to be unfounded.

A few days later, A.J.'s therapist, after questioning him about his story that he hurt himself when he fell off a bicycle, expressed the opinion that she was not satisfied with his explanation.

The following week, Jessica took A.J. to see a counselor at the Center for Children in Crisis and the second counselor found that there was "rather severe and continuing emotional abuse" and recommended that there should be a more thorough investigation by HRS.

Incredibly, it was over a month later before the HRS workers even met with the counselors and school personnel to discuss A.J.'s case. The end result of the meeting was that everyone—including Jessica—agreed to work more closely together.

Barely a month later, A.J. was dead.

Andrew Schwarz had been in protective custody for thirty-six months—twenty-seven months longer than policy recommended.

The grand jury heard testimony from fifteen witnesses and reviewed numerous records and documents produced by HRS, the Child Protection Team, the guardian ad litem program, and the Palm Beach County Sheriff's Office.

Initially, all of the HRS workers were cleared of any criminal wrongdoing.

It seemed that no one in the system that had failed A.J. so miserably—and repeatedly—would have to take the slightest responsibility for his death or the abuse that he had suffered.

However, when the grand jury returned in December, they decided to revisit the case and then returned an indictment against Barbara Black. She was arrested and charged with extortion by threat—a second-degree felony punishable by up to fifteen years in prison. She had threatened Eileen Callahan, saying that she would charge her with an abuse complaint if she continued to call in about A.J.

Also, as a result of its investigation concerning the conduct of HRS during the time A.J. was under HRS supervision, the grand jury issued the following scathing report:

"It has been determined by the grand jury, based on the evidence presented, that HRS is not performing adequately to meet the public's expectations to protect the general welfare of children.

"The investigation revealed that HRS's policies and procedures were not followed. There was a lack of diligent follow-up and communication between counties, groups within the department, and with the police investigators.

"Caseloads are placed with unreasonable time constraints. The Child Protection Team professionals' recommendations were not implemented.

"Management of records was inadequate. It is difficult to determine if records are falsified and complete when they are not adequately maintained or systematically reviewed by management. There were important files that were not completely filled out in that there were omissions of important information. Changes were made to files contrary to standard record keeping practices. White-out, overwriting, cutting pages, and taping pages over each other were observed. It is an accepted practice to use a single line to strike out a sentence so that what was originally stated could be read; it would then be initialed and dated so it could be determined who made the change and when.

"Insufficient personnel was evident. Only one Quality Assurance person assigned to South Florida, regardless of how efficient and qualified, is not enough to ensure that the state policies are being implemented properly. Throughout the investigation, HRS witnesses testified that there are insufficient resources available to do detailed investigation with adequate follow-up visits, to ensure investigation with adequate follow-up visits, to ensure the welfare of the children they are to protect. Further testimony revealed there is a large workload coupled with mandated time constraints that demand quick decisions. Tracking and follow up of recommendations from the various staffing meetings to make sure each group carries out the recommendations appear to need more time than is permitted.

"Communication appears to be inadequate, as demonstrated by the current methodology and ineffectiveness of turning over cases from county to county and coordination with the police, guardian ad litem, and the Child Protection Team. Examples presented to the grand jury were: the lack of continuity with case workers changing jobs, the police not being fully informed of the circumstances surrounding an investigation they were called in to assist, follow up on a staffing meeting with the Child Protection Team where recommendations were agreed to but were not followed through, and the case closed prematurely.

"Andrew J. Schwarz's files had enough information in them to strongly suggest removing him from the home. There appeared to be an overwhelming drive by HRS to keep Andrew J. Schwarz with his natural father even when the Child Protection Team, staff meetings, and other documented information showed this was not in his best interest.

"Based upon testimony presented to the grand jury, it appears that responsibilities are either unknown or inadequately implemented. Various departments within HRS are performing different tasks concerning the same individual. When this occurs the various departments pass requests back and forth with little or no follow up. Independent verification and day-to-day supervision to assure personnel are taking on their assigned accountability is sorely lacking. Cases have been closed before all departments have completed all assigned tasks."

After reviewing the case, the grand jury made the following recommendations to HRS and, as appropriate, to the legislature:

"The supervisors should be more responsible for adherence to policies to ensure the workers make all appropriate collateral contacts. More emphasis must be placed on the quality of work, not the speed with which the work is accomplished or the quantity of cases closed. Supervisors and Quality Assurance personnel should monitor cases to determine if collateral contacts are actually being made. This monitoring should be documented when performed.

"HRS needs to ensure that their representatives perform their duties in a professional, encouraging, and non-threatening manner resulting in community cooperation as it relates to the safety and welfare of children. Based upon testimony presented to the grand jury, there is a genuine fear of the Department of Health and Rehabilitative Services' power to remove children from anyone involved (e.g. reporters of an incident) at the discretion of HRS personnel.

"A central filing system is needed that involves having one central file on each child which would include reports of abuse and neglect (including unfounded cases), foster care, counseling, medical reports, etc. These records must be made available to the various departments within HRS, the Court, law enforcement agencies, Guardian Ad Litem, and the State Attorney's office.

"The grand jury recommends that access to files on unfounded complaints be limited to the State's Attorney, law enforcement, the Court, and HRS. The name of the perpetrator and the file in which the complaint was [deemed] unfounded should continue to be withheld from any public request as an exception to Florida Statute 119. This recommendation is based on the concern that although one complaint may be held to be unfounded, additional complaints may reveal a pattern of abuse. This could aid in identifying and prosecuting the perpetrator.

"The grand jury feels it is questionable to have HRS investigating criminal activities even with the help of the police. HRS investigators are not trained in criminal investigations and should not be required to perform in this capacity. There are police criminal units trained in the investigation of criminal acts against children and would perform adequately if they were given complete history records of each case, ongoing and previous.

"When various departments pass requests back and forth to each other there should be a structured follow up. The various action items resulting from staffing meetings should be tracked to closure. This includes action items passed on to other departments and counties in south Florida. Independent verification and day-to-day supervision should ensure personnel are taking on their assigned accountabilities. Cases should not be prematurely closed before all departments have completed their assigned tasks.

"Additional trained personnel are needed in the areas of Child Protective Services, Child Protective Investigations, and Quality Assurance. In order to meet this criteria there needs to be sufficient resources.

"There needs to be more attention to detail when reviewing the case workers' and investigators' notes for trends, and that appropriate actions are initiated.

"In summation:

"It is the grand jury's desire that this report not be ignored but be carefully considered to determine the necessary changes the Department of Health and Rehabilitative Services must make to protect the children in its care and to prevent them from being abused again once they enter HRS's system."

Barbara Black was released on bond and continued in her role as an HRS child protection investigator.

On Thursday, December 23, there was a hearing to determine whether or not Jessica would be allowed to spend Christmas with her two young daughters.

Lauren and Jackie were present in the courtroom, seated between their father and their maternal grandmother. Except in the courtroom, Jessica had not seen them since her arrest.

Rendell Brown tried to convince Judge Colbath to allow the girls to have weekend visits with their mother, claiming that they had become depressed while living with their grandparents.

When Dr. George Rahaim testified, the psychologist told the judge that he had seen Jessica wave to the girls when she came into the courtroom and then make a "crude gesture" moments later to ASA Joe Marx, co-counsel for the prosecution. Although he couldn't say for certain that the girls had seen what their mother had done, he said that it was an example of her "silent manipulation. It's very subtle. These are girls riding to school in the rain while their brother had to walk. I liken it to a trustee in a concentration camp, where you have to live with unspeakable things happening to other people."

The psychologist also claimed that Jessica had engaged her daughters in a "conspiracy of abuse."

Judge Colbath ruled that the defendant could write letters to Lauren and Jackie and would be allowed to send them presents, but she could not visit with them, stating that he was "very concerned about the subtle abuse."

On December 28, Detective Calloway interviewed Laura Perryman (Serena Perryman's mother), who also lived on Triphammer Road, across the street and several houses down from the Schwarzes. Laura was known in the neighborhood to have a special talent for growing plants and that was how she came to know Jessica Schwarz.

Sometimes Jessica would send one of her children over to ask Laura Perryman a question regarding plants, and Perryman said that many times she walked over to Jessica's house to discuss plants with her. During those visits, she realized something was wrong in the household as related to A.J. She believed that he suffered from attention deficit disorder (ADD), as she herself had children who suffered the same disorder.

On one particular occasion—approximately one year before A.J.'s death—Jessica told Perryman that "A.J. tried to drown Jackie in the pool." Laura tried to explain to her that she believed A.J. had ADD and that children with that disorder are very impulsive and lack the ability to think before acting—and that she did not feel that A.J. would do anything to Jackie intentionally.

Jessica's reply was totally emotionless and cold: "If anything bad happens again, I'm going to kill A.J." When Laura Perryman tried to tell her that she did not actually mean that, Jessica Schwarz convinced her that that was exactly what she meant.

CHAPTER 10

You bring me a confession, I'll call it a homicide.

—Dr. James Benz, to Detective Jimmy Restivo

Rendell Brown filed a motion with the court to sever the abuse charges from the murder charge, and on Thursday, March 17, 1994, there was a hearing to address the issue. He successfully argued that there was no evidence linking Jessica to A.J.'s drowning, and the allegations that she had abused him previous to that could not be used to show that she caused his death.

Until Judge Colbath granted their motion to sever, Cupp had been operating under the naive assumption that there would be one trial. When he realized they would have to try an abuse case without a victim—with no mention that the defendant was being charged with his murder—he was momentarily devastated.

In essence, it meant that the jury would be allowed to know that A.J. was deceased and that he, obviously, was unable to testify. But they would be told that the facts and circumstances of his death had absolutely no relevance to and nothing to do with the issues involved in the trial.

The state would have to caution all of their witnesses to avoid mentioning his death—not to refer to his passing in any way that would draw any attention to his death. In theory, for all the jurors would know, A.J. had been hit by a car or died of cancer prior to the case going to trial.

The conditions of Jessica's bond required that she stay inside her house on Triphammer Road and that she refrain from communicating with any potential witnesses, in any way; but she had defiantly continued to be the terror of the neighborhood.

On April 13, 1994, at yet another hearing in Judge Walter Colbath's courtroom, Anne Steinhauer and Ida Falk testified that Mrs. Schwarz had stood outside her front door on the previous Sunday and shouted sarcastic, obscene remarks at them.

Mrs. Steinhauer told the judge that Jessica had shouted at her from across the street, "There's fucking Mother of the Year! There's fucking Mother of the Year!"

Both women testified that their daughters were so afraid of Jessica that they were having trouble sleeping. Ida Falk said that her daughter, Jamie, on one occasion had even hidden in the bathroom with a wooden bat.

"She's afraid Jessica is going to come over and hurt us."

The women were extremely relieved when the judge ruled that Jessica Schwarz had violated her bond and granted Cupp's request that she be returned to jail.

Everyone involved in the case—especially her neighbors—let out a collective sigh of relief. The overall stress level went down tremendously. Some of the kids in the neighborhood had literally been hiding in their rooms while she was on pretrial house arrest. It also went a long way in letting them know the authorities were working hard to protect them. All along, Scott Cupp worried that when it came time for trial, they would wilt and backslide when pressed on the stand.

Many times, lay witnesses' testimony at trial doesn't approach what it was when they initially gave their stories to the investigators. In this case, it was all the prosecution had.

Cupp was afraid if one witness started to back off, it would spread like a disease. If Jessica stayed out, he was afraid she would become a constant visual reminder to each of the witnesses that if she was acquitted, she'd be right back among them with no one to protect them if they had testified against her.

The following month, Jessica's attorneys, Sam Marshall and Rendell Brown, took a deposition from Dr. James Benz, the medical examiner for Palm Beach County. He, of course, would not be testifying in the abuse trial, but at the murder trial—for the defense.

He was brash, loud, and sarcastic, and he was "famous" for trying to shock people—especially jurors. It wasn't unusual for him to find a way to get the word "maggots" into his testimony—even when it didn't apply. Add to that the fact that he had a reputation for hating lawyers and it made for a rather bizarre deposition.

The tall, rotund man had been the medical examiner for Palm Beach County since March 1983, and he estimated that he had performed "approximately four hundred autopsies a year for the last ten years."

Peering at Sam Marshall through thick glasses, he stated, "I went to premedical school at Indiana University. I attended medical school at the Indiana School of Medicine. I had a one-year clinical internship at Lima Memorial Hospital in Lima, Ohio. All my other training has been at the Indiana School of Medicine. That consisted of four-years residency training in the area of pathology and in forensic pathology. I'm certified by the American Board of Pathology in anatomic pathology, clinical pathology, and forensic pathology."

Marshall: During the time that you've been the medical examiner, has there ever been a time where the state attorney has asked for a second opinion regarding autopsies performed by you? Other than this case?
Benz: Not that I can remember off the top of my head.

There was one other case that they didn't like my opinion. They had another pathologist review it, but I don't think he did a second autopsy.

Marshall: So you would say he just reviewed your opinion, but to your knowledge you can't recall other situations where another doctor did an actual postmortem—a second autopsy?

Benz: Not that I can remember.

Marshall: And were you aware of a second autopsy [that was] going to be done prior to it being done? Were you aware of that?

Benz: Yes. As I recollect, the state attorney came into the office and talked to me about it. There was a discussion as to the manner of death, primarily. And I had voiced my opinion on the death circumstances that the manner of death was undetermined. The police agency involved and the state attorney, as I recollect, felt this was a homicide. And so they wanted to find somebody else that would examine the child and see if they could come to a different conclusion.

Marshall: Do you know who preformed the second autopsy on Andrew Schwarz's body?

Benz: Yes. A pathologist by the name of Dr. Burton, I believe, in Atlanta.

Dr. Benz explained how, after conducting his autopsy on A.J.'s body on May 3, 1993, he came to the conclusion that the manner of death was undetermined.

"First of all, the child had evidence of having sustained child abuse somewhere in the past. Meaning he had bruises and things about his head and back and buttocks and so forth. He had a number of bruises that couldn't be readily explained by anything other than child abuse.

"Secondly, there was a history of child abuse—an alleged history of a history of alleged child abuse—by, I think, it was both parents—the father and the stepmother.

"And thirdly, the cause of death in my opinion was drowning.

"Understand that in my opinion the majority of the injuries that were present on his body were older injuries—a day or older than a day—other than some minor things."

He stated that he couldn't detect any significant trauma that was recent or that couldn't be explained by resuscitation efforts.

"And yet there wasn't any reasonable story or explanation in my opinion as to why this child was in the swimming pool and what exactly happened to him. There were certainly a lot—not a lot—but there were some suspicious circumstances.

"So you've got several things you can do. One is just pend the case, but eventually you're going to have to sign a death certificate.

"It was my opinion the child drowned and I couldn't come to any acceptable conclusion in my mind as to whether this was an accident or a homicide or even a suicide, although I thought that was a very remote possibility."

He explained that in order to complete a death certificate—"for the purpose of estates could be closed and things of that nature"—he completed the death certificate with the manner of death listed as "undetermined."

It was Dr. Benz's opinion—within a reasonable degree of medical certainty—that none of the bruises or injuries that he observed on the body of Andrew Schwarz were sufficient in and of themselves to cause his death.

"I didn't feel I had enough information to explain what exactly had happened to this child."

Marshall: And did you feel justified, based on having done the autopsy of Andrew Schwarz's body, to call his death a homicide?

Benz: No. If I would have, I would have so certified.

Marshall: Did you find any indication that Andrew Schwarz was gagged or tied up when he drowned?

Benz: No, I didn't find anything that suggested that.

Marshall: Did you find anything suggesting that Andrew Schwarz was physically held in the pool?

Benz: Not to my satisfaction—no.

Marshall: What would you have looked for?

Benz: You're talking about a ten-year-old boy. If somebody is going to take a ten-year-old boy and hold him submerged in the pool, you're going to have a struggle. You're going to have a fight on your hand[s]. You expect to see more damage. Then you track the more obvious things. He's in the backyard, there are neighbors, and this is one-thirty at night. You would expect to hear a struggle and I'm told nobody heard anything unusual.

Marshall: The information [that you received] is basically what was attached to your autopsy report, as it related to the investigation of facts that were supplied to you by the sheriff's office? That's the only information that was ever supplied to you?

Benz: I read the newspaper. I got newspaper clippings. There were suspicions about the case and so forth.

Marshall: Were there any taped statements of any witnesses provided to you—any police reports provided to you with statements of witnesses included?

Benz: All I got here is a report from South County Mental Health Center.

Marshall: What do you see your duty as being—[as] a medical examiner?

Benz: To investigate the death and, in those cases where an autopsy is required, do an autopsy, record, and document the findings, issue a death certificate.

Marshall: And as it relates to Andrew Schwarz—it's your opinion that this was not a homicide in the case of Andrew Schwarz?

Benz: No—I said it's undetermined. I didn't know whether it was or not.

Marshall: Your position is still that it's undetermined?

Benz: Right.

Marshall: So are you saying—just based on the medical

evidence—within the reasonable degree of medical probability, you didn't feel justified in calling this a homicide?

Benz: Not from the information that I have—no.

Marshall: And do you know whether or not there was any other information contained in Dr. Burton's report that's different from your report—in terms of actual medical findings?

Benz: Well, initially he received a lot more information than I had.

Marshall: Were you asked to look over any of this additional information by the state attorney to make a determination as to whether or not your position would change?

Benz: It's my position [that] the purpose of the medical examiner's office is to—by the laws of this state—determine the cause of death. Whether or not there's a crime involved or not is under the purview of the law enforcement agency—not this office. This office is not in the [business] of "playing Quincy" and go out and do our own individual investigation to see if a crime has been committed. That's in the purview of the law enforcement. So we try to stay out of that purposefully, so we don't conflict with the law enforcement agency that's conducting the investigation.

Now, in his report, Dr. Burton tended to advise the opinion that it was the duty of the medical examiner to see that justice was done—or some statement like that—which sounds great in the press and in the media. But I see nothing in the Florida statute concerning the medical examiner's office that relate to that issue.

Marshall: You don't see that as your duty—to see to it that justice is done?

Benz: No. I think it's more the duty of this office to do a careful and complete examination, tend to documentations, and to come to the best conclusions you can. But you work in conjunction with law enforcement agencies or various other agencies to gain information that will help you come to a logical conclusion, which you hope is the correct conclusion.

On cross-examination, Cupp asked the medical examiner if he had any problem with the concept—or the idea—that a second autopsy is done in a case.

Benz: Oh, there are a lot of cases that we'll do second autopsies.

Cupp: Do you mean by a separate pathologist?

Benz: Yes.

Cupp: This is something that's accepted in the medical examiner's field?

Benz: Yes.

Cupp: Happens quite a bit?

Benz: When I write a report [or when] you dictate a report, you know it's going to be reviewed and questioned. And in the same way in this state, the prosecutor has the ability if he wants somebody to do a particular autopsy—he can supersede the medical examiner to have it done someplace else. It was discussed with me.

Cupp: You had no problem with it up front?

Benz (arrogantly): No problem with it having been done obviously. I don't know how to put it, Mr. Cupp, other than: If you prepared a case for trial and you were all set to go and I said, "Well, I want somebody else to do it because I think somebody else can do a better job, so I'll have somebody else do this." I don't know how you'd feel about that.

Cupp: Did you feel that was said to you here?

Benz: Yes.

Cupp: Who said that?

Benz: Oh, the police.

Cupp: The sheriff's office?

Benz: Yes, oh, sure.

Cupp: Who said that?

Benz: I think there was a conversation. I don't know whether you were in the room or not, but yeah.

Cupp: You're not saying that the state attorney's office—

Benz—his voice rising—interrupted and claimed angrily that the "police" had looked at him and said, "Come on, God-damn it, you know this woman killed the kid. Goddamn it, you know that. What the hell's wrong with you? You know that!"

Cupp—struggling to maintain his composure as sprays of little "spitballs" flew from Benz's mouth and actually landed on him—feigned sincerity and asked mockingly, "Who said that?"

Benz admitted that he didn't know exactly who had said it—only that it was "one of the cops" who had said it "in a similar manner."

Cupp inquired, "I was present for that?"

Cupp said it as though he wasn't sure himself if he was at the meeting or not, and his tone implied, "Hmmm, I must have missed that."

As the doctor launched into a lengthy answer to the simple question, Scott Cupp stayed calm and tried not to react, in the hope that Benz would bury himself deeper.

"I don't know who was there. There was several police, a couple of my examiner assistants. My investigators are here—they remember. And my point is, it's not the purpose of this office to arrive at conclusions for the purposes of convicting someone of a crime. That's not the purpose of this office.

"I find that rather abrasive for a police officer to make that type of a statement in the first place. My reply to him was, yes, there was no doubt there was a lot of information alleging that these people had been abusive to that child.

"There were indeed a lot of physical findings on the body that tended to support that this child had been abused. But I found nothing that would allow me to think that this child had been murdered, and therefore I still to date have a number of unanswered questions.

"Here's a ten-year-old child. Why is he outside walking his dog at one-thirty—unsupervised? Does he do that often? Why is he in the pool? How'd he get in the pool? The father said he had to get the ladder to put it up against the pool and so forth.

"So there's a lot of unanswered questions. The whole thing just sounds hokey—or whatever word you want to use to try and describe it. There are too many unanswered questions. [There] just is not a clear-cut explanation as to how and why this ten-year-old boy came to his death by drowning in a pool. And there you have it.

"His findings are consistent with drowning, coupled with the information that he is found at the bottom of a swimming pool, your conclusion is that he drowned.

"Now, there are many things that could have happened to this child that might be different than what is laid out in front of me at this time. But as I say, that requires police investigation, not medical examiner investigation. Was there a crime committed? Who did it? And so forth.

"And then [there is] my opinion that this is not in the purview of this office and that indeed if this office provided that course, then we're treading into an area where it's a law enforcement agency and you're going to cross wires and there's going to be a lot of difficulties. It's going to create more difficulties than it's going to solve problems.

"Obviously we have to work with police and they get information, which they provide us. We get information, which we provide them. But most of the time—approximately ninety-five to ninety-eight percent of the time—the facts that are derived tend to support a conclusion [that] is acceptable to both people.

"In this case, obviously my conclusion [is] that I don't know how this child came to drown somewhere between one-thirty and six-thirty in the morning.

"You have a lot of unanswered questions for me and somebody may have the answers to all these questions. I assume they have sufficient answers to the question[s] because they're taking somebody up on a murder charge, and I presume for that they have a lot of facts to provide answers to the questions.

"But again that isn't in my purview, that's the state attorney's office purview. So I don't ask what they are—that's fine. The information that's been provided to me—these are my conclusions on them—and I have no reason to change them now."

Cupp: And I'm not asking you to. Could I get back to my original question? I just want to make sure that I'm clear. At the beginning of your last answer, you stated that you felt like you were—that the law enforcement officer was telling you he didn't like your results, so we're going to get a second autopsy?

Benz: Well, you're either saying that or they're saying we're going to find somebody who will be willing to state this is a homicide—and apparently you did.

Cupp: As you sit here today, do you feel that the state attorney's office was responsible for that or law enforcement?

Benz: Well, it's hard to say because you both came together to discuss it.

Cupp: Getting back to the contact you referred to with one of the law enforcement folks, but you don't recall which one it was. Did you feel threatened by that?

Benz: Not threatened—a little surprised.

Cupp: Did you take it that he was trying to influence you to—

Benz: Oh, yeah. I took it that he was trying to influence me.

Cupp: Did you report that to any of his supervisors?

Benz: No, he's rendering his opinion—fine.

Cupp: There's a difference. That was pretty strong. Wouldn't you agree there's a difference between rendering an opinion and threatening someone?

Benz: I didn't take it as a threat to me. He wasn't threatening me. I think what he was stating was a strong opinion as to how he felt about it and he may have had more information that I did. He may have interviewed these people and had formulated some feelings.

He obviously had forgotten that Scott Cupp had been present at the entire meeting, so Cupp knew Benz was lying about the yelling and intimidation—which made him even angrier at the medical examiner's behavior. Cupp had endured being roared at—and spit at—about an event that had never occurred. He wanted to stand up and yell back and push him out of his face. It made him go from fearing Benz's appearance at the murder trial to patiently planning for it—and eagerly anticipating it. Cupp wanted not just to neutralize him, but to show him to be a liar.

Cupp: Do you feel like you've been withheld information on this case by law enforcement or any other source?
Benz: Not necessarily, no.
Cupp: The reason I ask is your answer to one of Mr. Marshall's questions. You refer to Dr. Burton's report—that it appeared he had additional information that you didn't have. I might have misheard that. Did you feel he had additional information that you did not have?
Benz: Oh, yeah.
Cupp: Can you cite any of that?
Benz: He seemed to have the details as to what happened that night or some story in more detail than what I had—that I recollect.
Cupp: So you felt like you were given—I don't want to say inadequate, but . . . incomplete information?
Benz: No, I think they gave me what information they knew at the time. But this situation with Burton, this went on for—his report's in August. I mean, you're talking about he had phone calls, he had other stuff people were providing him with, other information all the way up

through August before he finally got around to getting a report to you.

Cupp: Yeah, I guess that's what I'm trying to get at. What additional information, regardless of what time he got it, do you feel that he received that you—for whatever reason—weren't provided?

Benz: I don't have any other comment on that.

On redirect, when Marshall asked the medical examiner if he could give a physical description of the police officer whom he had referred to—the one who had tried to influence his opinion. Benz replied, "No, I don't think so."

As Cupp walked to his car after the deposition, he thought, *Remember this—don't ever forget.* He was no longer even a little intimidated by Benz and his "expertise." He knew now that—for whatever reason—the medical examiner was willing to do whatever he could to beat him and defeat the case.

On Friday, May 27, 1994, tragedy and heartbreak shattered ASA Joe Marx's family as only violent and sudden death can. Joe's wife, Karen Starr Marx, also an attorney, was shot to death while filling in for a colleague at a pretrial deposition in a courtroom in Fort Lauderdale.

Their law firm represented the American Association of Retired Persons (AARP) in a lawsuit filed by sixty-eight-year-old Julio Mora against AARP and Clarence Rudolph, the director of the Broward County AARP.

Mora, a former employee of the AARP and representing himself, was sure that he had been illegally fired from his job. When the deposition was almost finished, he pulled a 9mm semiautomatic pistol from his briefcase, shot and killed fifty-six-year-old Clarence Rudolph, his former boss. He then turned the gun on Rudolph's attorney, forty-six-year-old Maurice Hall, and thirty-year-old Karen Starr Marx.

Hall was wounded in the abdomen and shoulder and survived the attack.

Karen Starr Marx died of her injuries a short while later. She was four months pregnant with the couple's first child.

Joe Marx was preparing to walk out the door of his office, on his way to a baseball game with his best friend, when he received the phone call that devastated his life.

After her death, Joe wasn't sure he would be able to continue with his participation in Jessica Schwarz's prosecution. When his friends gave him some excellent advice—not to quit his job or sell his house or make any other major decisions right away—he took some time off.

"It was the suddenness. You wake up one day—and you're preparing to get your extra room ready for a new baby—and the next thing you know, you're alone. I just felt like my whole world was collapsing—it really rocked my foundation. My family was great. The funeral was huge. I had a lot of friends and a lot of people behind me, but it was really difficult to think about doing anything important at that time—any important work."

After about two months—as the trial date loomed on the horizon—Joe "pulled himself together" and returned to work. He had invested so much time over the previous year leading up to the trial—arguing many of the motions, taking most of the depositions, and developing relationships with the witnesses—that he felt a very real commitment.

When all was said and done, he knew in his heart that his beloved wife, who often worked on behalf of children as a volunteer for the guardian ad litem's office, would want him to complete the task that he had started—to help with, and carry through with, the prosecution of Jessica Schwarz.

CHAPTER 11

I owe it to every kid who has ever been afraid to close his eyes at night or who has ever had to crawl beneath the tightening grip of weak men and women who would cause them harm. I owe it to every parent who would rather die for their kids than inflict the physical and mental scars of wicked words and degrading gestures—of closed fists and closed minds. I owe it to the public at large because they are demanding accountability for A.J.'s death. I owe it to my family and friends. And I owe it to A.J. May this trial earn him a grain of peace.

—Scott Cupp

The case against Jessica Schwarz was a testament to teamwork, persistence, and dedication. The man-hours alone were daunting—thousands of them, to be sure. The number of people unleashed by the state attorney's office and sheriff's office on a case as critical to the judicial process as this one—the witnesses that were questioned and the miles that were walked—was impressive. Scott Cupp was proud to be a part of it.

Yet—in the end—the strategy and the tactical plan upon which the case was founded was the responsibility of just one man—and Scott Cupp was that man. There had to be a

decision maker—the very nature of the business dictated it.
Make or break—that was where they were headed.

Cupp liked the pressure and thrived on the intensity. He
took pride in seeing beyond the mountains of paperwork to
the heart of the matter. He enjoyed dissecting the various—
and often conflicting—viewpoints of the team, and piecing
together the fabric of what he saw as most relevant. He ab-
sorbed energy and enthusiasm from the mounting scrutiny
of the press and the ever-present political machine.

The case against Jessica Schwarz was not based on physical abuse. He would not seize upon every abrasion or laceration—nor every unsightly bruise.

He would focus on the mental abuse that led to the physical abuse. He would let the jury see the kind of woman who
would force a nine-year-old boy to wear a T-shirt with the
words "I'm a worthless piece of shit, don't talk to me" written across the front of it. He would paint a picture of a
woman who would berate her stepson in public, screaming
at the top of her lungs and calling him hateful, despicable
names. And—with each word—she ate away at a mind so
perilously fragile that the boy would spend hours just staring
into space.

The only question was how the civilian witnesses would
do on the stand—especially the kids. There's never any guar-
antee of how a witness will come across to the jurors. This is
especially true of children. One of the worst feelings for a
prosecutor was sitting in the courtroom watching a child
slowly—during cross-examination—recant everything they
just said on direct.

But Scott Cupp was ready. He loved big trials, and this
would be a big one. The eyes of South Florida would be focused on the proceedings, knowing that the outcome would
cause judicial and legal ripples in every city and town where
child abuse occurred.

He knew he owed his best to the men and women who
had "busted their tails" for nearly sixteen months—bringing
it all together.

Jessica Schwarz's trial on the abuse charges was scheduled to start on Monday, August 22, 1994. Rendell Brown had filed a motion for a change of venue and, that morning, argued that Jessica could not get a fair trial because of the pretrial publicity.

Palm Beach County circuit judge Walter Colbath temporarily denied the motion until it could be shown whether or not an unbiased jury could be seated.

As it turned out, at the end of the day on Tuesday, a panel of six impartial jurors—three women and three men—had been selected to decide her fate.

It was dawn on Wednesday, August 24, 1994, when Cupp left home. According to pretrial ritual that had evolved over the years, the office was deserted when he arrived. He made coffee, put in a tape and turned up the volume, and concentrated on his opening statement. He never relied on notes but had scribbled some random thoughts on a half sheet of paper that wouldn't even make it out of his briefcase. The general thrust of the statement had been written in his head for days.

When his colleagues at CAC started to arrive, he closed his door. With the exception of Joe Marx, there was an unwritten "Do Not Disturb" sign on the door. It wasn't anything personal—he just couldn't afford to engage in idle chatter.

There's an edge that comes with the art of prosecution—and he knew he couldn't afford to go anywhere near a courtroom minus that edge. But the truth was—nothing could have stolen Cupp's edge that day. Not with this case.

Marx and Cupp arrived at the courthouse early. It was an old building—all wood and marble with high ceilings. The reporters were waiting, but most of them were savvy enough not to ask questions the prosecutors would have to sidestep or straight-out ignore. Cupp heard a "good luck" or two and nodded in reply.

They made their way to courtroom 445. The room was packed—spectators, reporters, family members, friends, and enemies. This was a big-time media trial and heightened security had been implemented—two extra guards, which meant two more guns, and two extra sets of eyes. Cupp hoped, as he touched base with the bailiff, the clerk, and the court reporter, that they wouldn't be needed.

Marx took a seat behind the table closest to the jury box and opposite the table reserved for the defense, and when Cupp finished making his rounds, he joined him.

Cupp ignored the gallery and the swell of whispers as Jessica Schwarz was escorted to her place at the defense table. Her lawyers had her wearing a bright-colored, flower-printed dress that looked out of place and contrived. Cupp couldn't decide whether they were going for the *Little House on the Prairie* look or Andy Griffith's Aunt Bea, but he hoped the jury would see through the deception. It was too bad that they wouldn't get to see her wearing her "Cops Are Pigs" T-shirt.

There was no question that Rendell Brown would be a worthy adversary; Scott Cupp had learned that well—first-hand. When Cupp was a new felony prosecutor, he and Brown had been opponents in a heroin possession and sale case, and he had actually been relieved when the judge put him out of his misery by dismissing the case.

Brown's long, scraggly gray-and-white beard—plus the fact that a couple of his front teeth were missing—made him look ten years older than his fifty years.

His overall appearance was one of a wise old owl, and he had a way of speaking that was unique. For example, he always pronounced the word "says" with a long *a,* instead of "sez." Anyone else doing that would—no doubt—sound stupid, but with Rendell it sounded learned.

He was also skilled in making up words. Early in the trial, he accused Judge Colbath of "vamping" him in front of the jury. Colbath's response was an incredulous and somewhat annoyed "What?" Never one to be nonplussed, Rendell repeated it like they were all idiots. They guessed he meant "disrespected," but a later check in the dictionary found no meaning for "vamp" that would have come close to fitting the occasion. With Rendell, they never knew what they were going to get.

Scott Cupp didn't know Sam Marshall very well, but his handling of the witness depositions hadn't impressed him; but he was Rendell's partner, and that spoke volumes.

A moment later, the bailiff stood and issued the customary "All rise!" The judge who entered the courtroom was the Honorable Walter Colbath. At fifty-eight, he was a physically imposing ex-marine who—by all accounts—had seen his share of combat in Korea.

There was a shift in the atmosphere of the courtroom with the appearance of the judge, and then the jury.

Cupp knew everything about the jurors—where they worked, what they did for fun, their families, their backgrounds, their likes and dislikes, their prejudices, and their proclivities. He studied their expressions, their dress, and their postures.

He believed if there was one thing a jury deserved, it's respect. Lose them on that account and he risked losing his case on that singular failing alone.

The jury was sworn in. Cupp's eyes moved across their faces: solemn, sincere, and uncertain. Who wouldn't be? His worry was not that the prosecution wouldn't be able to prove the charges against Jessica Schwarz—the evidence was overwhelming. Eyewitness testimony would validate all seven counts in such graphic terms that there would be no doubt. His fear was that the jury would not grasp the devastating effect the degrading, debilitating abuse had perpetrated—over a period of three years—upon the psyche of a child.

But Cupp would not allow himself to think that society had become that hardened. He had to believe that breaking the spirit of a ten-year-old boy—that twisting his mind—that battering his body—was deserving of quick and sure justice and the punishment that went with it.

Cupp could feel the blood pumping as the clerk announced the case: the *State of Florida* vs. *Jessica Schwarz*. The charges were read: Two counts of felony child abuse and five counts of aggravated child abuse. Jessica's trial on the charges of second degree murder and witness tampering hadn't yet been scheduled, but Cupp knew full well that the outcome of that trial would hinge in great measure on the outcome of this one.

Not surprisingly, Because of the unusual circumstances of the case, Judge Walter Colbath read the following instruction to the jury:

"The constitution of the state of Florida requires the state to prove its accusations against the defendant beyond a reasonable doubt. In doing so, it is not necessary for the state to present any testimony of the alleged victim, Andrew Schwarz.

"In this case, the alleged victim has become deceased and therefore, of course, is not available to offer testimony.

"The state and the defense attorneys have stipulated that the alleged victim, Andrew Schwarz, did not give his consent to the defendant to commit any criminal offenses against him and, therefore, you must not view failure to present testimony of the alleged victim as any consent on his part.

"You should further know that none of the circumstances or events which ultimately led to his death have anything to do [with] and are totally immaterial and irrelevant to the issues in this case.

"Do you-all understand that?"

The jurors indicated that they did, in fact, understand.

In his opening remarks, Judge Colbath made it clear that this was his courtroom, where his rules applied, and he wasn't about to tolerate any demonstrations or outbursts of any kind, and anyone who wanted to tempt those rules would be unceremoniously shown to the door.

When the judge had created the mood he was looking for, he gave Scott Cupp the floor.

As he stepped to the lectern, Cupp knew he would keep his opening remarks short and precise—twenty minutes. He was not going to waste the jury's time telling them what Jessica did. He would show them what she did with the evidence presented over the course of the trial.

He began with the customary "May it please the court. Mr. Brown. Mr. Marshall." Then he faced the jury and said, "Good morning, ladies and gentlemen."

The show of courtesy was a matter of protocol and good manners.

As he spoke, he looked each and every juror in the eye; and the genuine sincerity that he felt—after living this case for over a year—was reflected there.

His plan was to introduce an authority figure that the jurors, given their collective backgrounds, could identity with: someone of impeccable character, and—not coincidentally—the prosecution's first witness.

He promised them that they would hear A.J.'s third-grade teacher, Mary Idrissi, testify about her first meeting with Jessica Schwarz, at an open house for her students and their parents.

"Mrs. Idrissi will tell you that that meeting left an indelible impression on her.

"She will tell you that Mrs. Schwarz insisted that Andrew not be given any schoolbooks. You'll learn that Mrs. Schwarz would not sign the book verification sheet given to all parents that night. Why? Because Andrew had lost his books once before, and Mrs. Schwarz had refused to pay for them, and she wasn't about to sign this year. She told Mrs. Idrissi that if she were a good teacher, she would be wise to Andrew. That he was a liar. That he was dishonest. That she didn't trust him and he was sneaky.

"She said that he was not getting any school supplies because he didn't know how to take care of them. That he would never know how to take care of them. She reiterated to Mrs. Idrissi that Andrew was a very bad boy."

Cupp's eyes moved from one juror to the next.

"At that time, ladies and gentlemen of the jury, Andrew was all of nine years old."

He paused, letting that sink in.

"And where was Andrew while the defendant was calling him a liar? Calling him dishonest? Calling him a very bad boy?

"Well, you see, Andrew was standing right next to her—hearing every word—his eyes averted, saying nothing.

"This was his introduction to his new teacher."

Cupp spoke evenly. The calm had a purpose. He wanted to let the story create the emotion—to let the words reinforce the indictment.

"Andrew J. Schwarz was born to Ilene and David Schwarz in April of 1983. After his parents separated, Andrew stayed with his mother and his half sister Patsy.

"There were domestic problems. When the problems escalated, fate took a hand and Patsy and Andrew were removed from the house and placed with Andrew's biological father, David, and the defendant, Jessica Schwarz."

Cupp allowed the jurors a moment to glance in Jessica's direction—to get a look at the smugness on her face—to view the contempt that lay just below the surface.

"The defendant and David Schwarz had a younger daughter named Jackie. Mrs. Schwarz had a daughter from a previous marriage named Lauren Cross. Lauren was older than Andrew by two years—and the same age as Patsy.

"Andrew and Patsy arrived at the defendant's home in October of 1990."

Cupp informed the jury that the case that would be presented to them dealt with the time period between October 1990 and May 1993. He took a deep breath and then introduced them to A.J.

"So, who was this child that the defendant called a liar and a sneak? Well, as the school year progressed, Mrs. Idrissi will tell you that she noticed several things and she noticed them rather quickly. Right from the beginning, she noticed that Andrew was starved for attention. That he was constantly seeking her out for hugs and reassurance. In fact, she will tell you that the rest of the class eventually became so used to the steady progression of Andrew parading to and from his desk that they took it for granted. His attention span, she'll tell you, may have been short, but he was one of the most affectionate kids in her class.

"The other thing that became clear to Mrs. Idrissi—as the year progressed—was that Andrew was missing an inordinate amount of school. How many days? Forty-two out of one hundred."

Cupp allowed these numbers to sink in. Even he had trouble comprehending the astonishing number of days that A.J. was absent from school.

"You will come to find out that Mrs. Schwarz felt that Mrs. Idrissi was spoiling Andrew with all of this attention—with all of this support—with all of these hugs—with all of this encouragement. That what he needed—according to the defendant—was more punishment. That he needed more things taken away.

"In fact, the evidence will show that Mrs. Schwarz was withholding Andrew from school as a means of punishment. School was fast becoming Andrew's one safe place and she began to take that away from him."

Cupp opened his hand in the direction of the defendant and silently invited the jury to view the woman who would do such a thing.

"Things degenerated to the point that—during a face-to-face meeting between Mrs. Idrissi and the defendant—the defendant referred to Mrs. Idrissi as a maggot and a trouble-maker and a cause for much of the problems with Andrew."

Cupp turned and looked at Jessica and the jurors followed suit.

"What Mrs. Idrissi didn't know was that she was seeing only the tip of the iceberg. She didn't know of the litany of malicious and sadistic punishments that A.J.—as his friends would call him—was forced to endure at the mouth and hands of Jessica Schwarz."

The prosecutor turned his attention back to the jurors as he told them that several neighbors would take the witness stand and testify to the atrocities they had seen and heard at the Schwarz household.

As he recited some of the profanities they had heard, Cupp circled the courtroom for a moment. He didn't want the obscene words to cause the jurors embarrassment. The reaction he wanted was disgust. And outrage.

"James Ebenhack, a Palm Beach County fire rescue worker, lived in such close proximity to the defendant that he will come in here and tell you that he distinctly remembers hearing the defendant scream at A.J., 'I hate your fucking guts! You're a useless piece of shit!'"

There was a hum in the air as Cupp continued, "Patsy Spence—Andrew's half sister—lived in the defendant's home with A.J. from October of 1990 until February of 1992. In the beginning, Patsy will tell you, she shared a room with the defendant's older daughter, Lauren. She will tell you that things went along pretty well for a while, but eventually she was ordered out of Lauren's room and into A.J.'s room. She was forced to share a room with her younger brother.

"You will hear descriptions of the absolute barrenness of that room. But perhaps most chilling, you will hear a view from inside the asylum that only Patsy had—that only Patsy witnessed.

"This is what she saw the defendant do to A.J. . . ."

Cupp paused and took in the jury—one member after another.

". . . Because, you see, by now this little boy—Patsy's brother—had developed a bed-wetting problem. Imagine that."

Scott Cupp did not even attempt to keep the sarcasm out of his voice as he continued.

"And, of course, the natural reaction one would have to this—the way one would think to cure this—would be to take the child's face and nose and rub it into those urine-soaked sheets. That is what Patsy observed. The defendant rubbing A.J.'s face in sheets soaked with urine. . . ."

Cupp could feel the heat rolling up the back of his neck, and he took a moment to fill his lungs. He realized—listening to the room—that he wasn't the only one. He turned his eyes toward the front of the courtroom, and there was Colbath—with a look as hard as granite on his face—surely recognizing that this trial would cause ripples that would stretch far beyond the Fifteenth Judicial Circuit of Palm Beach County.

Cupp turned his attention back to the jury.

"The prosecution will also call Dr. George Rahaim, a local psychologist for the state's Child Protection Team. Dr. Rahaim will be allowed to render opinions as to the psychological effects of child abuse. He will also explain to you—in terms that we can all understand—the type of mental injury that these events caused Andrew."

Cupp looked at the jurors and knew that he had timed it just about right.

He concluded, "After all the evidence in this case has been presented to you, I'll have a chance—as well as Mr. Marx—to address you. At that time, we will talk to you about returning a proper and just verdict in this case, a verdict we believe you will find—beyond all reasonable doubt—to be guilty as charged.

"At this time, I thank you for your courtesy and your attention and your patience with all of us and ask you to pay the same courtesy to Mr. Brown."

Scott Cupp held their eyes for a moment; then he retreated to the prosecution table. It was a good start. He could feel it.

Judge Colbath then called upon Rendell Brown to make his opening statement.

"As His Honor most aptly explained to you, this is Mr. Cupp's and my version of what we expect the evidence will show in this case, and while we're trying to give you a road map, this—what we say to you—is not to be accepted as fact. The facts will come from the witness stand.

"Of course, if what our notions of what the evidence would divulge were the same, you'd not be here. We would not be here.

"But this is what we expect and know the evidence will show in this case:

"Jessica Schwarz was born and reared in Long Island,

New York, with a sister. Her father was an executive with a shipping company. Jessica was educated in New York.

"Sometime in her childhood, she was struck by the bug of driving a truck and made it clear to her father that that was her station in life. She wanted to be a truck driver.

"She bought a rig—in the language—and began to drive the rig to earn a living [right] out of high school. She married a trucker. They had a daughter, a daughter from whom you will hear. The marriage didn't work out.

"In the meantime, a person unknown to Jessica, David Schwarz, was married to a lady named Ilene and living in the Fort Lauderdale area. They, too, had a child—a second child for Ilene Schwarz, as she had a daughter, Patsy Spence, about whom you've heard and I'll tell you a little more about that.

"Patsy became the stepdaughter of David Schwarz in the marriage with Ilene. Together they had a child—Andrew Schwarz.

"As with Jessica Schwarz's [first] marriage, Ilene and David Schwarz's marriage did not work. They, too, were divorced. Ilene retained custody of Patsy, David Schwarz's stepdaughter, and Andrew Schwarz, their common son.

"David Schwarz later married Jessica.

"At a point, it became known to HRS and the authorities that some terrible things were going on in Ilene's household. Andrew Schwarz and Patsy Spence were taken from Ilene and given into the custody of a maternal aunt, a sister of Ilene.

"The maternal aunt kept these children for a short time, [then] called HRS and said, 'Hey, you've got to come get these kids out of my home.'

"David was contacted and asked if he would take custody of the children and, of course, he spoke with his wife and asked her how she felt about that. And Jessica Schwarz—there are two things she loves dearly, children and animals. And so her response was 'Sure, we'll keep both of them.'

"Now, Patsy Spence, mind you, is not the child of either David or Jessica.

"No one from HRS told Mrs. Schwarz—or David, for that matter—the depth of the problems of these children and particularly Andrew Schwarz. All they knew was that both kids were in counseling and Jessica had to take these children to counseling on a weekly basis.

"She did this, but no one told her what was really going on with Andrew, what had really happened to Andrew, and the depth of his problem."

Brown explained to the jurors that Jessica's mother had been keeping her granddaughter Lauren; but after the Schwarzes were settled in their home, Lauren came to live with her mother and stepfather. He also mistakenly told them that Jessica was pregnant with Jackie when A.J. and Patsy came to live with them. In actuality, Jackie was two years old at the time.

"Jackie was to live there. Andrew was to live there. And, of course, Patsy Spence was to live there—because Jessica's idea was that you shouldn't separate these children.

"They brought all of these children into the home. She and David went out, purchased a pool for the children, put it in the backyard so that Jackie and Lauren and Andrew and Patsy could enjoy the swimming pool and yet be in the yard where she could observe them.

"The neighborhood children—the ones that will come in here and tell you all of these horrible things—practically camped out at Jessica Schwarz's home.

"Now, you will—from time to time—learn that there were problems where the kids got upset with Jessica, because Jessica—and we make no bones about that—Jessica is a mother of tough love and tender mercies. She's a disciplinarian. 'When you're in my home, in my yard, you do it my way. You act as a child should act or you've got to go.'

"And that created some little problems—and you'll hear about the problems and the results of the problems from the children—as well as from their parents—as they come in here with their concocted stories, under oath, having to tell the truth and the whole truth, as Mr. Cupp said.

"And we talked to you on voir dire about a trucker's language. Jessica doesn't talk like a Sunday-school teacher—she doesn't. That's Jessica. When it is on her mind, she says it. It's over—we're on with it. Maybe it's not the way you would react or I would react—but it's Jessica.

"You're going to have another witness come in and say he heard Jessica Schwarz say, 'I hate his (A.J.'s) fucking guts.' So she's going to keep him at home to punish him? You'll have to decide whether that fits.

"Some of Jessica's neighbors—their response was to send HRS to Jessica's house. But, thank God, they did, because HRS has to keep records. And when HRS went to the home, they had to write the date, what they observed, and they also did it without—for the most part—without alerting her. In other words, just all of a sudden, they are at the door. And what did they find? Unfounded.

"And they didn't go by themselves. They went with a trained police officer. And they didn't talk to the kids in front of Jessica. They took them off [by] themselves—took walks with the children. No evidence. No evidence of any abuse. This is unfounded—unfounded. It wasn't happening. It did not happen. It did not happen."

Rendell Brown concluded, "Ladies and gentlemen, I think you have a broad overview of what the facts are going to be. Let me stop boring you and let you hear for yourself. I think once you've heard the facts, you'll do the right thing. And the only right thing will be to return a verdict of not guilty in this case.

"Thank you very much."

CHAPTER 12

Jessica is a mother of tough love and tender mercies.

—Rendell Brown

A.J. Schwarz's third-grade teacher, Mary Idrissi, was the first witness for the prosecution. The dark-haired, bespectacled woman was the mother of two teenage children and had been a teacher for over twenty years.

Looking very much the schoolmarm in her flower-printed dress, she reminded Scott Cupp of several of his own teachers from a generation earlier.

Sitting very straight in the witness chair, Mrs. Idrissi explained to the jurors that she first met Andrew at open house at the beginning of the 1992 school year. His stepmother, Jessica Schwarz, accompanied him.

"She came over to me with Andrew. The beginning remarks were that he was a lot of trouble—that if I was a good teacher—a wise teacher—I would recognize that he is a liar. That he's sneaky and don't let him buffalo me; be wise to his tactics and his head games; that he's not to be signed out any textbooks because he loses them and she will not be responsible for them. She continued to tell me what a problem he was, and the whole time this was going on, Andrew was standing right beside us.

"Andrew said nothing. His little eyes never left the floor. He was humiliated."

Cupp: Did she mention anything about school supplies?

Idrissi: Yes, she said that she would not be giving him any—that he loses them or destroys them—and that he would not have anything for school.

Cupp: What did he do for supplies?

Idrissi: I gave him his supplies.

Cupp: You spent money out of your own pocket?

Idrissi: Not really out of my own pocket, Mr. Cupp. A teacher is given a certain amount of money for supplies every year: crayons, pencils, notebook paper, pencil boxes. Basically, it's things that all teachers have and when Andrew came to my classroom on Monday, I took care of everything he needed.

Cupp: Did you think about it over the weekend?

Idrissi: Yes, extensively. I was very bothered by it—to have an encounter like that the first time I meet a parent. But more than anything, to do that in front of this little child that was so humiliated by it. It was unbelievable that the parent would do that in front of a child.

Cupp: And what happened on Monday—if anything—between you and Andrew?

Idrissi: Well, I was very eager to see Andrew on Monday because I wanted to assure him that I was very happy to have him in my room—that it was going to be a good year and a positive year. And if there was anything he needed, as far as supplies, textbooks, whatever—that I would take care of that. I told him, "You look like a good little boy to me—you don't look like you're any problem. I know we will be good friends."

Mary Idrissi told the jurors that as the year progressed she found Andrew to be very warm and friendly with a sense of humor—but that he was starved for attention and affection.

"Andrew would come to my desk an awful lot. In fact, so

much so that the other children in my classroom just kind of accepted that anytime at all—all through the day—Andrew would be coming to my desk. And the reason I allowed that was that Andrew could not stay on task. He would start a little bit of work and he'd be looking around and just fiddling—not bothering anyone—but just fiddling, not getting the work done.

"So when a teacher sees this off-task behavior going on, she shortens her lesson and checks them constantly. So if we were running spelling words six times each, I would have Andrew write them three times and let him come to my desk and let me see what he'd done well. This was the manner in my classroom. Andrew came to my desk; he would show me his words. I would give him many, many loves, hugs, and squeezes, and he responded to that and he completed his work. He was a very bright boy."

She stated there were about three parties in her classroom between August and December, but that—at the open house—Mrs. Schwarz had instructed her that Andrew was not to go on any field trips or attend any parties.

"He attended none. He attended no field trips or parties. He was absent on those days."

Cupp: Do you know his date of birth?
Idrissi: Yes, it is April 24, 1983.
Cupp: And, if I remember correctly, [in 1993] that was a Saturday. . . . Would that child's special day—so to speak—be the day before?
Idrissi: Yes, it was an honoring day.
Cupp: Was Andrew in school that day?
Idrissi: No, he was not.
Cupp: Let me ask you about the time period of school prior to the Christmas holidays. Did your class participate in any special school activity? What was that called?
Idrissi (crying): That was called "Holiday Shop."

Cupp: Mrs. Idrissi, are you okay?
Idrissi: I'm fine, thank you. I'm all right.

The jurors were asked to step into the jury room for a few minutes.

Mr. Brown (to Judge Colbath): The problem the witness is having—and we are having the problem with the spectators as well. . . . I just ask that you have the spectators—if they are overcome by crying—that they would leave the courtroom, please.

Judge Colbath (addressing the courtroom): I think you all heard what Mr. Brown just said. But, basically, if any of this testimony or any of the other testimony in this case affects you emotionally—to the point where you're visibly or emotionally distressed—please stand up and very quietly leave the courtroom.

After the jury was brought back into the courtroom, Cupp continued his questioning of Idrissi.

"I believe we were beginning to discuss the Holiday Shop?" Cupp resumed.

She explained that the Holiday Shop was an event that took place at her school, in the library, for a two-week period every December. The PTA sponsored it and it was an opportunity for the children to purchase Christmas gifts, Hanukkah gifts, and birthday gifts, at very inexpensive prices.

The teachers would escort their classes to the Holiday Shop and the children would go around with their lists and pick out their gifts and then bring them back to the classrooms. The teachers and the students would then gift wrap the presents before they were taken home.

"And it's a very, very exciting time for the children."

Cupp: Did all of your students participate in Holiday Shop?

Idrissi: Yes, they did—all of them, except Andrew. Andrew was not allowed to go. His stepmother would not allow him to go. He could not go—he did not have any money to go.

Cupp: But at some point, Andrew did participate; is that correct?

Idrissi: Yes, he did. The children don't go just once down to the Holiday Shop; they can go several times. If they keep bringing money in, they are permitted to go. Well, the two weeks was coming toward an end. Andrew had not been—as yet—and so I gave him two dollars to go down. And I told him that he could go and purchase anything he wanted for himself—didn't have to be a gift for home. Just with two dollars, you can buy a lot of nice little things. And what he bought was all for me. It was nothing for himself and I always treasured that—this was characteristic of Andrew.

(What the jury didn't get to hear was that A.J. had confided to his teacher that Jessica had told him, "If you buy anything for me, I would burn it.")

Mrs. Idrissi testified that Andrew walked to school and that he was frequently late.

Idrissi: We do report cards every nine weeks and about midway in that nine-week period, teachers send a progress report. But a lot of teachers send a weekly progress report. I send one every Friday and I, more or less, tell the parent how the child did that week.

Cupp: And did you, on occasion, receive these progress reports back from Andrew with writing on them from the defendant?

Idrissi: Yes, I would.

Cupp: What would be the tone of those responses?

Idrissi: They were usually rude—sarcastic.

Cupp: Could you give us an example?

Idrissi: My report was signaling that Andrew did not have a snack and asked her to please send something in.

Cupp: What was her response, if any?

Idrissi (referring to a page in a folder): Okay, this is from Mrs. Schwarz: "A.J. gets a daily snack, but he eats it on the way to school. Somehow you are so smart and I am wrong. You fix the snack and the problem; in other words, known as eating a snack on the way to school. Your problem—not mine. Oh, well." That was a frequent comment made to me: "Oh, well, your problem—not mine."

Scott Cupp was certain that the reason A.J. ate his snack on the way to school—if he even had one—was because he hadn't had any breakfast.

Cupp: Is it fair to say that the tone of the responses that you received were consistently negative?

Idrissi: Yes, sir, they were.

Cupp: Was there ever any positive or upbeat response that you received from the defendant on one of these progress reports or notes?

Idrissi: Yes, there was. This would have been after the HRS meeting. The meeting was March the 26th. I'd say it would probably be the first week after that. If it's all right, I'd just like to read. It says, "Mrs. I., I love you taking things away. It really brings the point home that no one is kidding as far as him being late. He had twenty-five minutes to get to school, so him being late—it took him fifty minutes to get to school? No way. And he's grounded for the weekend and if he is late again, well, let's just say he's going to cry a lot. He had 3½, 4 hours last night and still didn't finish his homework. Like being late, he just doesn't care and does what he wants. I look forward to him doing his handwriting over. I've tried. He hasn't done one thing about it. Boy, this is really working out and I'm sorry I didn't get along with you sooner. Sorry. Thanks. Oh, yes, we've gotten to the point with A.J., since he keeps doing the same things wrong over and over—we're talking years—he gets no breaks, no rewards when he knows better. He loves to play games with people's heads. He's never gotten one over on me; dared his dad once or twice—me, never—and I won't let that change. Beware of lies. Today he left the house at seven-thirty. Unless he's bleeding, no reason on earth he should be late—none."

Cupp: And that's the only response that you could possibly characterize as being positive or upbeat?

Idrissi: I began to, through the request of HRS, go through a series of behavior modifications of a reward system for Andrew. When I sent something home that was negative, the response was "I love you, now you're (in essence) responding to this and because you're now seeing that he lies. I wish I would have cooperated with you from the beginning." Now that a negative comment came home, the first response was, "Mrs. Idrissi, now we really see eye to eye."

Cupp: Did you ever receive—either in writing, over the phone, or face-to-face—any contact with Mrs. Schwarz that indicated, in any way, that she was happy or pleased with anything that Andrew had done?

Idrissi: None.

Cupp: Did she ever praise him?

Idrissi: Not that I ever heard. I never saw a physical touch. I never saw a squeeze or a hug, no.

Cupp: Did she ever support him in any way that you could tell?

Idrissi: She did say in a note back to me that "I'm very glad that Andrew is doing well in school, but he's not at home. He's not doing his chores at home. Therefore, Mrs. Idrissi, you can reward him, but I'm not."

Cupp: When was it that you had a face-to-face meeting with the defendant and there were others present?

Idrissi: My first meeting with other people was at the HRS meeting on March 26.

Cupp: Did Mrs. Schwarz say anything to you—or about you—upon entering the room?

Idrissi: Yes, she did. I walked in and she and Mr. Schwarz were in the room. There was no one in there but the three of us, and when I walked in, I heard her say to her husband, loud enough that I could hear it, "Here's the maggot. This is the woman that causes all the trouble." And her husband laughed at what she said.

Scott Cupp took the witness—month by month—through A.J.'s attendance record. He established that he was absent every Thursday, many Mondays, and all party days: he had missed 42 out of a possible 100. Idrissi stated that there were very few—if any—notes from home explaining his absences.

She also testified that she had never had a problem with A.J. vomiting in class.

Cupp (holding up a photograph): Was this Andrew?

Idrissi: Yes, it is.

Cupp: Was that his school picture?

Idrissi: Yes, it is.

Cupp: How old was he when he was in your class?

Idrissi: He was nine.

Cupp: This person that we've been speaking about throughout the course of your testimony, Jessica Schwarz, do you see her in the courtroom here today?

Idrissi: Yes, I do.

Cupp: Could you please point to her?

Rendell Brown spoke up quickly and stated, "We'll stipulate that the only female at the defense table is Jessica Schwarz." Brown then rose from his chair to cross-examine the witness.

Brown: Now, ma'am, you testified that you never had any problems with Andrew vomiting—I think was the term Mr. Cupp used—or regurgitating at school. Is that correct?

Idrissi: Yes.

Brown: And isn't it also true, ma'am, that you never administered the drug imipramine to Andrew Schwarz?

Idrissi: I'm not allowed to administer any drug, sir.

Brown: Do you know what imipramine is?

Idrissi: No, I do not.

When Mr. Brown prodded the schoolteacher to "admit to the court and the jury" that there were behavioral problems with Andrew in school, she firmly replied, "Not in my classroom."

The defense attorney then challenged her with an exhibit from her files.

Brown: Did you write at the bottom of that page, "Andrew needs to learn responsibility"? Did you write that?

Idrissi: Yes, I did.

Brown: Okay. Showing you a weekly behavioral report, I'll ask you if you wrote in red ink at the bottom of that? Would you read that—if you wrote it?

Idrissi: Yes, I did. It says, "Excessive talking and playing." I mentioned previously that Andrew was not on task. Not on task is not bad behavior. Andrew was not on task because I felt he was preoccupied with home life.

Brown: You really didn't have to think about the problem because you knew for a fact that Andrew had been in Vero Beach Hospital for six weeks based—just because he had problems. . . . Didn't you know that?

Idrissi: Somewhat.

Brown: Either you knew or you didn't?

Idrissi: I knew about it, but I didn't know the extent of it—but it certainly wasn't bad behavior.

Brown: But you'll agree, Mrs. Idrissi, that you received

a full report from the hospital reference Andrew's stay at the hospital, his problems, and ways to correct them; you'll agree with that, wouldn't you?

Idrissi: I did not receive that.

Brown (handing her a copy of the report): Now, Mrs. Idrissi, if you had seen that, if you had read that, it certainly would have given you some guidance as to how to deal with Andrew Schwarz; isn't that true?

Idrissi: Probably, but I've never seen that.

Brown: And there were step-by-step pronouncements as to what that child needed; do you agree with that?

Idrissi: Just reading it for the first time, I see something going on there. Again, I have not seen that. I have a degree in specific learning disabilities. Children in my school that are not qualified for a program—for whatever reason they didn't meet the criteria—oftentimes the administration puts these children in my classroom because they know I have a degree. I saw no signs of a child with learning disabilities—or [from] what I'm reading on that paper.

Brown: How long did you study to obtain your specialist degree in learning disability?

Idrissi: A year and a half.

Brown: And nothing in your studies prepared you for dealing with a child who had an imbalance of imipramine, did it?

Idrissi: No, it did not.

Brown: And you know from Mrs. Schwarz—among others—that when Andrew left the hospital, he was placed on a heavy dosage of imipramine, don't you?

Idrissi: I do not know that, sir, no. I did not know that he was on it.

Brown: The truth is, Mrs. Idrissi—as relates to you and Mrs. Schwarz—from the very first day, you had a personality conflict, didn't you?

Idrissi: She did not make a very good impression on me.

Brown: You didn't like her, did you?

Idrissi: I won't say I didn't like her. I did not like the way she demeaned and belittled this child standing in front of her. If you were going to talk about your child, whether you're a teacher or a parent—for heaven's sakes, would you do it when the child is in front of you?

Brown (ignoring Idrissi's comments): Isn't it a fact that on more than one occasion—when you sent Andrew's report card home—he signed it himself and brought it back to you? Isn't that true?

Idrissi: Only once he did that, sir, only once.

Brown: When a person does that, what do you call that?

Idrissi: Sir, you're not going to make me make this boy out to be a liar—a bad boy. Not at all.

Brown: I'm only asking you to tell the truth and answer my questions truthfully. I'm not trying to make you make anybody anything. My question is: what do you call it when someone signs their mother's name to their report card and brings it back to school?

Idrissi: I would call it he's afraid to show it to his mom.

Brown: Oh, I see. And there is no question that Andrew did that?

Idrissi: Yes, he did that, once.

Brown: You described Andrew as being warm and friendly?

Idrissi: Yes.

Brown: Isn't it a fact that Andrew had few—if any— friends in that entire school; isn't that true?

Idrissi: Totally false—totally false. He was loved by everyone. He was very well liked—very, very well liked. He had a sense of humor; he played all the games outside that my children played. He was never off by himself. He was very well liked, sir.

Brown: And I think you said earlier, there's no way I'm going to make you say anything negative about Andrew; that's basically what we're dealing with, isn't it?

Scott Cupp objected, "That's a misstatement of the answer and it's an unfair question."

Judge Colbath replied, "Well, I think it's a little argumentative. I'll sustain the objection."

With that, the cross-examination was completed, and Scott Cupp started the redirect examination:

Cupp: Did you get the impression—from your dealings with Andrew—that he was afraid of something or someone at his home?

Idrissi: Yes, I did.

Cupp: And is it fair to say the problems that Andrew had, they didn't create any kind of barrier with you and he and his learning?

Idrissi: No.

Cupp: You were able to have him learn?

Idrissi: Yes, he did learn.

Cupp: But he had a short attention span?

Idrissi: Yes, he did. He did short assignments. When he did that little assignment, he brought it to my desk, [and] I checked it over. I praised him; I complimented him; I hugged him; I gave him stickers.

Cupp: You touched him a lot?

Idrissi: Oh, yes, a lot.

Cupp: Did you kiss him on the cheek and on the forehead?

Idrissi: Many times.

Cupp: Did he ever return in kind?

Idrissi: Oh, yes. He was very affectionate, very warm.

Cupp: Could you describe Andrew's outward appearance when he would arrive at school?

Idrissi: He was very thin. I saw many bruises on him—a lot of bruising on elbows and knees and across the forehead. I found him to be extremely thin. He was wearing a lot of clothes that were too big for him, oversize clothes.

Cupp: What about his emotional state or his outward demeanor?

Idrissi: Well, other than the daydreaming, being off task, he was happy to be in school. He loved to be in school. He loved to be with the children. The minute he would come in the room, he would come right to my desk. He was very, very happy being in school.

Cupp: It's fair to say you liked Andrew?

Idrissi: Very much.

In his recross-examination of the witness, Rendell Brown tried to get Mary Idrissi to admit that the bruises that she had seen on Andrew's knees and elbows were typical of the bruises one might see on "most little third-grade boys" from playing.

Idrissi: Not two black eyes and a broken nose. No.

Mr. Brown (to Judge Colbath): Your Honor, may we excuse the jury?

After the jurors left the courtroom, Judge Colbath addressed the witness, "Mrs. Idrissi, I know this is difficult, but you're not here as an advocate. You're here to just answer questions. And just answer the questions that are asked of you without volunteering anything.

"I'm going to ask the prosecutors to please talk with their other witnesses. I know this is a very emotional subject for everyone and to please get them to not fall prey to becoming an advocate and just simply answer the questions."

Brown: I'm going to move for mistrial, Judge. This witness has sat here . . . it's obvious from the beginning, the game she's playing.

Colbath: I'm going to ask you not to make judgmental statements, "The game she's playing." That's judgmental. I get your point anyway.

Brown: I specifically asked about knees and elbows. Specifically, there's no way you can argue I invited that comment. Judge, for her to throw that out there—there's no way I'm going to be able to eradicate the prejudice that goes to my client in this case—based on those comments. I'm going to move for mistrial based upon those statements.

Colbath: I'm going to deny it, but I'm going to admonish the jury to disregard it. (Then Colbath spoke to the witness.) Mrs. Idrissi, we've had a very difficult time picking a jury. If your answers cause me to declare a mistrial, I'm going to be very upset.

The jury was brought back in and Brown continued his questioning of the witness.

Brown: Did you know, ma'am, that Andrew Schwarz had been in counseling since he was three or four years old?

Idrissi: Yes, I did.

Brown: And that Andrew Schwarz was approximately four years old before he was ever able to talk?

Idrissi: I did not know that, no.

That afternoon—after Mrs. Idrissi's testimony and the lunch break—Judge Colbath made a statement to the jury regarding Andrew's "broken nose."

He explained the following: "The state and the defense have reduced their earlier stipulation to writing and it definitely goes a little bit beyond what I've already instructed and I think it's very appropriate that I read it to you precisely as they have agreed to it because it's a little more far-reaching and sweeping than what I instructed you to and it is as follows: 'There's no medical evidence known to the state or to the defense that Andrew Schwarz ever had a broken nose.'"

CHAPTER 13

She would get screaming to the point that, frankly, you couldn't even understand what she was yelling at him.

—Gail Ragatz, neighbor

Joseph Marx called eleven-year-old Teresa Walton—clad in a bright, flowered dress with a very large lace collar—to the stand as the next witness for the prosecution. A friend of Lauren's, she estimated that she had been in the Schwarz home more than twenty times in the three years prior to A.J.'s death. She was only nine years old when A.J.'s body was found floating facedown in the family swimming pool.

She testified that she only had a chance to play with A.J. once or twice "because he was always cleaning" the kitchen, the living room, the girls' bedroom, bathroom; he was always mopping the floor and "things like that." She had also seen him cleaning the garage and witnessed him working in the yard, cutting the weeds with "haircutting scissors."

Teresa heard Jessica yell at A.J. "practically every time I went over"—many times cursing at him.

Marx (reassuring the little girl): Today is your day—you can say these things. Tell the jury what you heard the defendant say to A.J.

Teresa: Her calling him a "fucking asshole" and junk like that.

Marx: What did A.J. do when she called him a "fucking asshole"?

Teresa: Started crying.

Marx: Would she say that in front of people?

Teresa: Yes.

The little girl had been in the Schwarz residence at dinnertime and she stated that A.J. had special rules that he had to obey regarding how he ate his meal. Jessica would set the timer on the stove and he would have five or ten minutes to eat his dinner, and if he didn't finish eating in the given time, he had to put the rest of his food in the dog's bowl.

Marx established that Lauren and Jackie did not have to eat their meals in an allotted time.

Marx: Did there ever come a point in time that you saw an incident involving a cockroach?

Teresa: Yes. We were out washing Bear's truck and Jessica came out and said she found a cockroach on one of the plates and A.J. had to eat it.

Marx: Did you go inside? Did you see that?

Teresa: Yes. He was chewing when I walked in and then there was another half that he had in his hand.

Marx: Was he laughing? Did he think this was funny?

Teresa: No.

Marx: What was he doing?

Teresa: Crying.

Marx: Did you tell anybody about this?

Teresa: My mom.

She told the jurors that sometimes Jessica would punish A.J. by making him write, "I'm a liar. I should have never been born." She had seen him crying while he was forced to write the miserable words about himself and when he finished, Jessica hung the papers on the wall in his room.

She had also seen A.J. crying when Jessica had put "clear" masking tape on his mouth with the words "big mouth" written on the tape.

Teresa stated that "practically every time" she went over to their house, she saw Jessica strike A.J. across the face with an open hand.

> Marx: What did A.J. do after that happened?
> Teresa: He cried.
> Marx: Did you ever see Jessica Schwarz hug A.J.?
> Teresa: No.
> Marx: Did you ever see Jessica Schwarz kiss A.J.?
> Teresa: No.
> Marx: Did you ever hear Jessica Schwarz say one kind thing to A.J.?
> Teresa: No.

When she was asked to identify the defendant, Teresa was visibly shaking.

Rendell Brown started his cross-examination of the little girl by confirming that she had told her mother about the cockroach incident, and that her mother was Beth Walton.

> Brown: And she and Jessica just don't get along, do they?
> Teresa: No.
> Brown: They don't like each other, do they?
> Teresa (crying): Well, my mom liked her until what I told her about what happened in her (Jessica's) house.

Sobbing, she covered her face with her hands.

After a break to allow Teresa to regain her composure, Imogene Kelleher, the guardian ad litem who had been assigned to help the child witnesses during the trial, was allowed to sit by the young girl in the witness-box to reassure her. The judge instructed Teresa that she could not look to the woman for answers, and the defense attorney resumed his cross-examination.

Brown: You told Mr. Marx a minute ago that you actually saw Andrew eating a cockroach?
Teresa: Yes.
Brown: Now, was this a little cockroach or a big cockroach?
Teresa: I don't know. I didn't see the size.
Brown: But you definitely testified that you saw him put the cockroach in his mouth?
Teresa: Yes.
Brown: Now, do you remember ever telling this story any differently, Teresa?
Teresa: No.

She remembered talking to Detective Calloway, but insisted that she did not remember telling him anything different from what she was telling the jurors.

Brown: Did you tell him in that statement that you did not see the cockroach, but you saw him chewing it? Do you remember telling Detective Calloway that?
Teresa: No.
Brown: Now, you testified earlier that Bear was there?
Teresa: Yes.
Brown: And you're telling this court and this jury that you were in Jessica Schwarz's home and saw David Schwarz—Andrew's father—allow her to make him eat a cockroach?
Teresa: Yes.

A few minutes later, there was a conference at the bench when Marx objected to the fact that Jessica Schwarz was sitting at the defense table shaking her head and making facial expressions, "especially when there's a little girl up here."

After Judge Colbath asked Sam Marshall to "please admonish her," he addressed Rendell Brown. "I have a suggestion, if you don't object to it. If you just move yourself a little to the left, I think it would be—"

"You mean in front of the defendant?" Brown completed.

"You would put yourself between the two of them," the judge reasoned.

"That would be conspicuous, but I can do that."

Complying with the unusual—but understandable—request, Brown positioned himself between the witness and the defendant and continued his cross-examination.

> Brown: You also testified, I think, Teresa, that Mr. Schwarz was home and Mrs. Schwarz taped Andrew's mouth shut?
>
> Teresa: Yes.
>
> Brown: Where did the tape come from?
>
> Teresa: The drawer.
>
> Brown: Who got it out of the drawer?
>
> Teresa: Bear.
>
> Brown: Mr. Schwarz? Andrew's father? Got the tape out of the drawer?
>
> Teresa: Yes.
>
> Brown: And sat there while Mrs. Schwarz taped Andrew Schwarz's mouth?
>
> Teresa: Yes.
>
> Brown: And you sat there and watched this?
>
> Teresa: Yes.
>
> Brown: Teresa, let me ask you this: do you remember A.J. having a lot of fights with kids coming home from school?
>
> Teresa: Yes.

On the second day of the trial, the prosecution called Gail Ragatz as their next witness. During the time in question, she lived directly across the street from David and Jessica Schwarz. She worked for a pest control service and testified that that was how she became acquainted with the defendant. After Ragatz passed out flyers in the neighborhood, the Schwarzes started using the pest control service.

She met A.J. when he was about nine years old and saw the Schwarzes at least once a month—because of the pest control service—and occasionally throughout the month, as she had become friends with both David and Jessica and visited with them socially.

On one occasion, when she was at their home while they were having dinner, Jessica had fixed macaroni and cheese and hot dogs. Jessica put the plates on the table for the children, then turned around and said to A.J., "If you're going to act like an animal, you're going to eat like an animal."

Ragatz: The boy never did anything. She picked up his plate, took it over by the kitty litter pan—which was in his bedroom—and set it on the floor and grabbed him [by] the shirt, took him over, and made him sit on the floor. And as he was crying hysterically, she told him he was going to eat it, so he proceeded to eat. I left. I was mad.
Marx: Did you see Andrew Schwarz do anything improper before he was made to eat off the floor?
Ragatz: He didn't do anything.
(The jury would never hear that after A.J.'s death, Jessica Schwarz had called Gail Ragatz and told her, "Don't you ever tell anybody about that incident.")
Marx: Was that behavior anything unusual—for Jessica?
Ragatz: She was always verbally abusive with him. He was a "crackhead." He was a "bastard." He was a "bastard's baby." He was a "fuck face." She would get screaming to the point that, frankly, you couldn't even understand what she was yelling at him.
Marx: How did Andrew react when she did this?
Ragatz: Usually just close his eyes and go on.

Marx: Did it ever appear to you that he was afraid of her?

Ragatz: Absolutely.

Marx: Did she ever speak to you about how she felt about having Andrew there?

Ragatz: Yes, she did. She wanted him out of the house. She didn't like him.

(According to Ragatz, she had probably—over a period of time—seen Jessica and A.J. together approximately 150 times.)

Marx: Did you ever see Jessica Schwarz hug Andrew Schwarz?

Ragatz: Oh, no. No.

Marx: Did you ever see Jessica Schwarz kiss Andrew Schwarz?

Ragatz: No.

Marx: Did you ever hear her say one kind word to that boy?

Ragatz: No.

Marx (handing the witness a picture): One last thing. Do you recognize that?

Ragatz (crying): Yes. That's A.J.

Brown then cross-examined the distraught witness.

Brown: Mrs. Ragatz, isn't it a fact that you and Jessica were not friends; isn't that true?

Ragatz: We started out friends—yes.

Brown: Isn't it a fact, ma'am, that you and Jessica didn't get along at all; that you, in fact, did not like Jessica? Isn't that true, ma'am?

Ragatz: At the end—no, I did not.

Brown: Now, the day that you've testified about, the incident with the food . . . You and Jessica aren't getting along—you don't like her—at this point, right?

Ragatz: No, we were getting along, at that point.

Brown: How long did you stay there?

Ragatz: Two or three minutes and I got mad and I left.

He was sitting at the table, just as the other two children were, and didn't do anything.

Brown: If you were only there for two or three minutes, you [would] have no idea what transpired prior to those two or three minutes, would you—if anything transpired—would you?

Ragatz: No, I wouldn't.

Brown: And the truth of the matter is that Jessica has a tone of voice when she talks to everybody; isn't that true? I mean she's just a rough talking lady, isn't she?

Ragatz: She has an attitude, yes.

Brown: That's Jessica, isn't it? She talks to you that way, doesn't she?

Ragatz: Yes.

Brown: She talks to everybody that way, doesn't she? That's just the way she talks, isn't it?

Ragatz: I never heard her talk that way to her own children.

The next witness for the prosecution was fifteen-year-old Jamie Falk. She wasn't quite fourteen at the time of A.J.'s death, when she had approached Detective Restivo and asked to speak to him. Before Jessica Schwarz's bond had been revoked for shouting obscenities at her neighbors, Jamie had had trouble sleeping at night because of her fear of the defendant.

Aware that the teenager was nervous, Joseph Marx started by gently asking her to "sit up straight, get close to the microphone, and talk loud enough so the people in the back row can hear you, okay?"

Jamie had been friends with Patsy and Lauren and would go to their house "to talk and watch TV and watch movies and stuff." She said that "once in a while" A.J. would come into the room where they were.

"Usually he was, like, sweeping or something in the kitchen. He just always used to mop and clean the garage and pick up after the cats and dogs and stuff."

"Did you ever see Lauren and Jackie do these kinds of chores?" Marx asked.

"No."

The young witness testified that A.J. walked to school, while Lauren was allowed to ride her bike.

Marx: Did there ever come a day when it was raining out and you were late for class?

Jamie: Yeah. I missed the bus and my dad was taking me to school. It was raining and we drove by and A.J. was walking to school. We were driving up the road and we saw him, so my dad was going to stop and pick him up and drop him off at school, but we saw Jessica behind us, so we just—

Marx: Did your father keep driving?

Jamie: Yes, because he thought that she would pick him up, so we kept on driving.

But Jessica did not pick him up and A.J. continued walking to school in the rain.

Jamie also had seen A.J. sitting at the kitchen table with food in front of him, with tape on his mouth.

"He just looked embarrassed and scared and stuff. He was just sitting there. I felt bad. There was nothing I could do. I just—you know, I didn't—I felt weird. I just walked away."

Marx: Did you ever have an opportunity to hear Jessica talk to Andrew?

Jamie: Yeah.

Marx: Did she ever call him derogatory names—bad names?

Jamie: Yeah. She just used to call him stupid and worthless and stuff.

Marx: Did you ever see Jessica hug Andrew Schwarz?

Jamie: No.

Andrew Joseph Schwarz, also known as A.J.
(Courtesy of Palm Beach County Sheriff's Office)

Aerial view of the Schwarz home with the pool in back.
(Courtesy of Palm Beach County Sheriff's Office crime scene photo)

The front exterior of the house.
(Courtesy of Palm Beach County Sheriff's Office crime scene photo)

Passageway leads to the fenced-in backyard with the pool around the corner.
(Courtesy of Palm Beach County Sheriff's Office crime scene photo)

The pool with the recovered body of A.J. in the foreground.
(Courtesy of Palm Beach County Sheriff's Office crime scene photo)

The Schwarz living room.
(Courtesy of Palm Beach County Sheriff's Office crime scene photo)

The family's kitchen.
(Courtesy of Palm Beach County Sheriff's Office crime scene photo)

Jessica Schwarz's daughters' well-kept bedroom.
(Courtesy of Palm Beach County Sheriff's Office crime scene photo)

In contrast, the nearly closet-sized room where A.J. slept. *(Courtesy of Palm Beach County Sheriff's Office crime scene photo)*

The makeshift desk where some of A.J.'s handwritten punishment
assignments remained.
(Courtesy of Palm Beach County Sheriff's Office crime scene photo)

The clothes A.J. was wearing the night he died were found on the floor of his room.

(Courtesy of Palm Beach County Sheriff's Office crime scene photo)

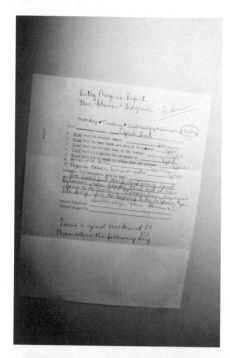

A favorable behavior report from A.J.'s teacher, Mrs. Idrissi. *(Courtesy of Palm Beach County Sheriff's Office crime scene photo)*

The second autopsy on A.J.'s body revealed bruising patterns consistent with abuse.
(Courtesy of Palm Beach County Sheriff's Office crime scene photo)

Joseph Marx, assistant state attorney at the time of the investigation and prosecution of Jessica Schwarz, is now a judge in Palm Beach County. *(Courtesy of Judge Joseph Marx)*

Judge Walter Colbath, who presided at Jessica Schwarz's trial. *(Courtesy of Judge Walter Colbath)*

Jessica Schwarz on the stand, being questioned by
her attorney Rendell Brown.
(Photo by Lannis Waters, The Palm Beach Post)

Scott H. Cupp in court. *(Courtesy of Scott H. Cupp)*

At A.J.'s school, a memorial plaque. (Note that his middle name is incorrect.) (Courtesy of Scott H. Cupp)

OUR LOVING FRIEND
AND A GOOD STUDENT
"A.J."
ANDREW JAMES
SCHWARZ
APR. 24, 1983 - MAY 2, 1993

Marx: Did you ever see Jessica kiss Andrew Schwarz?
Jamie: No.
Marx: During the entire time that you knew Jessica and Andrew Schwarz, did you ever hear her say one kind word to him?
Jamie: No.

Blond-haired, blue-eyed Troy Falk, Jamie's twelve-year-old brother, was surprisingly calm as he testified next—about an incident that had taken place one day after school.

"I had gotten home from school and I was showing my friend something . . . and I seen A.J. running down the street naked. He was across the street. He was, like, jogging, and kept on looking behind him."

"What was he doing with his hands?" Marx asked.

"He was, like, covering his privates. It was like he had his hands in front of his privates."

Marx asked the young boy to stand up and demonstrate for the jurors how A.J. had covered himself with his hands as he was running down the street naked.

"Did he look embarrassed?"

"Yes," Troy replied.

The witness said that Jessica was standing in the doorway while A.J. ran to the corner, and then "in a mean voice," she told him to "come back."

Marx: Did it look like—in your opinion—Andrew wanted to be running down the street naked?
Troy: No.
(Troy then testified that he, too, had seen A.J. with tape on his mouth.)
Troy: I went to the door to see if he could play. And when they answered, I seen tape on his mouth.
Marx: How close did you get to him?

Troy: Couple of feet away—about three feet away. [It was] like packaging tape—brown tape. They wrote "mouth" on it. He was just standing there.

Marx: Did he look like he was happy?

Troy: No.

And it continued—a long procession of neighbors and their children to the witness stand. After testifying to the verbal, psychological, and demeaning abuses they had seen and heard A.J. suffer at the hands of his stepmother, each one was asked the same series of questions:

"Did you ever see Jessica hug Andrew Schwarz?"

"Did you ever see Jessica kiss Andrew Schwarz?"

"During the entire time that you knew Jessica and Andrew Schwarz, did you ever hear her say one kind word to him?"

And time after heartbreaking time, the answer was always the same. Not one kiss. Not one hug. Not one kind word—ever.

CHAPTER 14

*My children's chores took maybe ten or fifteen min-
utes out of the day. A.J.'s took all day. I used to hear
her yell at him. I never really heard her talk to him.*

—Ida Falk, neighbor

After the lunch break, as rain poured down outside the
courthouse, Ida Falk knew that she would be the next witness for the prosecution. She was the mother of the two previous witnesses, Jamie and Troy.

She sighed as Joe Marx called her to the witness stand,
knowing she would have to repeat the hateful things she had
heard Jessica say to A.J.

Ida Falk had met the Schwarzes and become friendly with
them because her children played with their children; but the
friendship had ended when she saw some of the things that
were happening at her neighbors' home.

At first, she saw A.J. doing a few chores, like picking
things up in the yard or taking a bag of garbage out to the
curb, but then the chores escalated.

"Probably about a year after we lived there. He was always in the yard doing yard work. Any time I seen him outside he was working; he was doing yard work or cleaning the
garage or washing the cat litter box. My children's chores
took maybe ten or fifteen minutes out of the day. A.J.'s took

all day. I used to hear her yell at him. I never really heard her talk to him. She would cuss at him, tell him . . . she would tell him he was a stupid little f'er."

Marx: Tell us what you mean by f'er?
Falk (obviously embarrassed): Fucker.
Marx: What else would you hear her say?
Falk: That he was an asshole. She used to tell him all the time he was stupid or dumb.
Marx: What would he do when she would yell he was a stupid little fucker?
Falk: He would put his head down and keep doing whatever he was doing. She would tell him he was moving too slow; he was not doing things right—he was stupid.
Marx: Did you ever hear her talk to Lauren or Jackie the same way she talked to Andrew?
Falk: No.

She testified that while outside one day, she had seen A.J. working in his yard with tape over his mouth. He looked embarrassed and wouldn't make eye contact with her. On two different occasions, she had also seen him edging the lawn with "regular sewing scissors."

Falk: I saw him quite a few times—when he should have been in school—working in the yard. All day.
Marx: Did you ever see her—in the three years that you lived on Triphammer Road—come out of the house and give him a hug?
Falk: No.
Marx: Did you ever see her come out of the house and give him a kiss?
Falk: No.
Marx: During that time when he was doing all those chores, did you ever hear her say, "You did a good job"?

Falk: No.
Marx: Did you ever hear her say one nice thing to him?
Falk: No.
Marx: Did you ever see him vomiting on those days he
was home from school working in the yard?
Falk: No.
Marx: Was there anything about him that appeared
that he was ill?
Falk: No.

On cross-examination by Brown, Ida Falk admitted that she had had, over the period of time leading up to the trial, conversations with her children, Jamie and Troy, about the things she was telling the jurors. And that she had talked with some of her neighbors as well.

"In fact, that's been the hotbed of conversation in that neighborhood for over a year, hasn't it?" Brown asked.

"The hotbed of conversation? We try to not even think about it," Falk replied.

Her voice broke as she reluctantly admitted that even though she had seen A.J. out in the yard with tape across his mouth, and working in the yard when he should have been in school, she had never called anyone to report the situation.

"Are you all right? Do you need a break?" Brown queried.

Falk answered that she was okay.

Rendell Brown finished with his own series of questions. He asked her if she had ever seen Jessica Schwarz come outside her home and kiss Lauren. Or Jackie. Or David.

Mrs. Falk replied to each one that she had not.

Brown: She's just not a huggie-kissie kind of person,
is she? Is she, ma'am?
Falk: I don't know.

On redirect Marx asked Mrs. Falk what her impression was of A.J.

Falk: He was a nice little boy when he was at my house. He was always very polite. Every time when I would see him outside, he always waved and asked how I was, called me by name, always very polite.

Marx: When he was at your house, did you ever have a behavioral problem with Andrew Schwarz?

Falk: Never.

Marx: Mrs. Falk, when you saw what was happening at the Schwarz residence, did you call any authorities or did you tell anybody what was happening?

Falk: No.

Marx: Why not?

Falk: Because I was afraid.

Marx: Of whom?

Falk: Jessica.

It was the state's position that Ida Falk felt intimated by Jessica Schwarz because she had seen the defendant being arrested for "punching" her husband. Even though she hadn't actually seen the assault, she had seen Jessica being handcuffed and put in a police car, but the jurors would not be allowed to hear about the incident.

Brown (on recross): Why, Mrs. Falk, were you afraid of Jessica?

Falk: Because she was always screaming and yelling and I was just afraid of what she might do.

Brown: Now, Mrs. Falk, you know—do you not?—that several different departments have hot lines which are confidential for just that purpose, don't you? I mean, you know that, don't you?

Falk: I know there are several different hot lines. I didn't know they were confidential.

Scott Cupp called the next witness for the prosecution. Beth Walton, dressed in a short-sleeved, pleated white blouse and a dark skirt, tried to stay calm as she took the witness stand. The mother of four children, she had been in the nursing field for twenty years.

While she had been waiting to come into the courtroom, she had thought back to one of the days she had baby-sat for A.J. She liked A.J. and she was smiling when she opened the door, but when she saw the T-shirt he was wearing and the words written across the front, the color drained from her face and she gasped. Then she saw the look on his face: humiliation, defeat, despair.

"He's not to take it off," Jessica had told her in no uncertain terms. "He's violated the rules and now he has to pay the price. No television and no talking—not to anyone."

When the door slammed and Jessica disappeared down the walk, Beth Walton had looked down at the shirt again. The words read: "I'm a worthless piece of shit. Don't talk to me."

Now she would have the chance to tell a jury of Jessica Schwarz's peers.

Her long blond hair falling lightly over her shoulders, Mrs. Walton listened carefully to the young prosecutor's questions. She explained to the jurors that she and Jessica had been friends for a time, but then "the relationship between us got really bizarre." She had seen Jessica strike A.J. on two separate occasions.

"He had misbehaved. I was in her kitchen and she grabbed him. She just kind of shook him and kind of smacked him in the back of the head. He was cleaning out the track in the sliding glass door at the time. A second occasion, in my kitchen, she came—I was watching Andrew at the time—and she grabbed him."

She couldn't remember exactly how long A.J. had been at her house before Jessica came in, but she stated that it was "an hour or two."

Mrs. Walton recalled how "Jessica came in through the sliding glass door at the back of my house and grabbed

Andrew in the kitchen—by the shoulders—and shook him and was yelling at him that the sheriff's department was at the house. And that the only reason that he was being kept home from school was because he had doctors' appointments and he had better stick to that story and that if he was to deviate from that, there would be problems. She was extremely upset. She was kind of in a frenzy."

Mrs. Walton frowned as she demonstrated with her hands. "She was taking him and shaking him like this. His head was whacking back and forth. She shook him like a rag doll all over my kitchen. She was screaming at him.

"Andrew was standing there with his mouth hanging open. He wasn't saying anything."

Cupp: Leaving that time period for a moment, were there any other times or occasions where you would speak with the defendant and she would tell you about punishments that she would give Andrew?

Walton: There was one occasion when she told me that she went and took him out of school because she hadn't been woke up that morning and he hadn't emptied the kitty litter box and she went and took him out of school and brought him home.

Cupp: To punish him?

Walton: She was going to keep him home for the rest of the week and he was going to do chores for the rest of the week to punish him for not doing what she told him to do.

Cupp: Did there ever come a time when A.J. was in your home and he was wearing a T-shirt with some writing on it?

Walton: Yes, there was. On one morning I told Jessica I would watch A.J. for her. He showed up at my house with a T-shirt that said, "I'm nothing but a worthless piece of shit—do not talk to me." I then called Jessica. I said, "I have things I have to do and have to take A.J.

with me and I can't take him out in public in something like that." She insisted that he had to wear it all day long and he would be questioned as to whether he wore it or not.

Cupp: What did you do?

Walton: I put a button-up shirt over it and I told Andrew, I said, "Look, if Jessica asks if you wore the shirt, tell her yes and that way you can't be punished for lying or for taking your shirt off."

Cupp: Did you ever observe Mrs. Schwarz hug Andrew?

Walton: No. Not that I can recall, at this moment in time.

Cupp: Kiss him?

Walton: No.

Cupp: Be affectionate with him in any way?

Walton: No.

Cupp: Praise him?

Walton: No.

Cupp: Encourage him?

Walton: No.

Cupp: Do you ever recall an occasion where Mrs. Schwarz said anything positive or said anything that put Andrew in a good light?

Walton: It was around his birthday that she said she thought maybe she did love him. She wasn't really sure.

On that sad note, Scott Cupp ended his direct questioning of the witness.

Rendell Brown started his cross-examination.

Brown: As a nurse, obviously you're aware of the HRS hot line and those sorts of things?

Walton: Yes.

Brown: And did you report this incident when it happened?

Walton: What incident is that?

Brown: That you told this jury and court about with the T-shirt?

Walton: No, I spoke to Jessica about it.

Brown: Did you talk with any of the appropriate authorities about it?

Walton: No, I did not. I spoke to Jessica about it.

Brown: You didn't happen to have a camera on hand to take a picture?

Walton: No.

Brown: Now, you testified that on the one hand Mrs. Schwarz is saying to you that she can't stand him; she wants to get rid of him, meaning Andrew?

Walton: Yes.

Brown: And then she tells you—on the other—she's going to keep him home for a week to punish him?

Walton: Yes.

Brown: Do you see a contradiction in that?

Walton: Not really.

Beth Walton's nineteen-year-old daughter, Elissa, took the witness stand—very briefly—to confirm the story about A.J. wearing the T-shirt with the derogatory writing on it.

The last witness of the day was Catherine Turner, the neighbor who lived directly behind the Schwarzes. She had lived there for approximately five years and was the mother of a nineteen-year-old daughter and a twenty-three-year-old son.

Mrs. Turner had been in Jessica's home on several occasions, baby-sitting for her children, and she had never had any problems with A.J.

The jurors, however, would never get to hear that she had since become terrified of Jessica Schwarz—or that Jessica had threatened to kill her dog.

She told the jury about a time when she was baby-sitting

and A.J. was not allowed to be in the home like the rest of the children.

"He was told to stay in his room, by Jessica and her husband, David. It was in a room behind the garage. I assume it was his bedroom. All the locks [on the doors] were turned around so they were locked on the outside—all the children's bedrooms and the bathroom."

Cupp: So he could be locked in?
Turner: Right.
Cupp: Was he locked in when they left?
Turner: No.
Cupp: At some point, did he come out?
Turner: A couple of times he came out and I talked to him.
Cupp: How did he appear to you, at that time, and what was [his] demeanor, his mood?
Turner: He was a little sad.
Cupp: Did it seem that A.J. was punished more than the other children?
Turner: Yes. Just seemed that the girls were always running around outside and—most of the time—when I was baby-sitting, he had to stay in his room.
Cupp: So it wasn't just this one occasion?
Turner: Right.
Cupp: Were you ever told why?
Turner: Not really, no. She just said he was a bad boy and he had to stay in his room.
Cupp: But you never had any problems with him?
Turner: No, I never had any problems.

On another occasion, Jessica told her that she had made A.J. parade around the house with no clothes on.

"She said he had exposed himself in school and he had to learn his lesson and she made him walk around with no pants on. I didn't see it, but she told me about it."

Cupp: Did you ever have a conversation with Mrs. Schwarz where she told you anything about A.J. having a bed-wetting problem and what she was doing about it?

Turner: Yes. She wasn't really sure how to handle it, as far as I saw. I think one time she told me she felt like rubbing his nose into his bedsheets.

Cupp: Did she say she actually did it?

Turner: No.

Cupp: But she felt like it.

Turner: Right.

Cupp: When she spoke with you about these things, what kind of demeanor or tone of voice was she speaking to you in?

Turner: She was a little upset.

Cupp: Did you ever have occasion to see Mrs. Schwarz be affectionate with A.J.?

Turner: No.

Cupp: Did you ever see her hug him?

Turner: No.

Cupp: Did you ever see her kiss him?

Turner: No.

Cupp: Did you ever see her praise him?

Turner: No.

Turner had backed up somewhat from her deposition, where she had stated that she was afraid of Jessica—very afraid—and the reason was that Jessica had called her and told her if she didn't 'do something,' she was going to kill her Great Dane.

When Cupp asked Mrs. Turner if she recalled the deposition she had given on December 1, 1993, she said that she did. He asked her to read a portion of it to herself.

Cupp: Having read that, does that refresh your recollection as to what Mrs. Schwarz told you at that time?

Turner: Yes. She said that she felt like rubbing his nose

in the bedsheets like when a dog wets and you punish a dog.

Cupp: Well, didn't she, in fact, say that she did it?

Turner: I don't . . . She might have. It's been a while. It's a long time.

Cupp: Do you recall the following question and giving the following answer: Question: "Did she discuss with you the bed-wetting problem?" And your answer: "Yes, she said she was going to make him lie in it. I think one time she even tried—she tried to rub his nose in the sheets like a dog."

Turner: I might have said that.

Cupp: Do you recall being asked the following: Question: "Did she say she made him sleep on the floor because he wet the bed?" Answer: "No, she used to make him sleep in the bed with the sheets wet." Do you remember that question and that answer?

Turner: Yes, I do.

Rendell Brown then confronted the witness.

Brown: Now, ma'am, during the time you've known Mrs. Schwarz, the fact is that Mrs. Schwarz is just not a huggie-kissie person, period, is she?

Turner: No, I don't think she was to any of her children.

Brown: That was just Jessica?

Turner: Yes.

Brown: You didn't question whether or not she loved her children because of that, did you?

Turner: No.

Brown: Now, you saw the kids' rooms with the locks turned to the outside?

Turner: Yes.

Brown: Was it your interpretation of Mr. Cupp's question that that was to lock the children in?

Turner: I would think it would be to lock the children in myself.

Brown: That's just your assumption?

Turner: Well, that's what it seemed like to me, at the time.

Brown: But you never saw any of those kids locked in?

Turner: I never saw them locked in. I saw that the locks were turned around.

Brown: Now, Mrs. Turner, when you raised your hand and swore to tell the truth—the whole truth—you took that oath seriously, didn't you?

Turner: Yes, I did.

Brown: And in fact, that's why—when Mr. Cupp was asking you about Jessica having told you, or you remembered her telling you, that she rubbed his nose in the urine-soaked bed—the truth is, you don't really remember her telling you that?

Turner: I remember her telling me that, but I don't remember the precise words, per se.

Brown: Mr. Cupp asked you two or three times if Jessica told you that she had, in fact, done that?

Turner: Yes.

Brown: And your answer was?

Turner: Yes, she had told me that.

Brown: When you were giving your sworn statement, and this is back in December of '93, what you said was "And I think one time she even told me she tried to rub his nose in it—in the sheets."

Turner: Yes, I said that, yes.

Brown: But now you're telling the jury that you distinctly remember her saying that?

Turner: That's not what I'm saying. I said I thought. It's been a long time. I don't remember.

Brown: It's been a longer time than it was since 1993 when you made the statement?

Turner: Yes.

Brown: You don't really remember her telling you she did anything like that, do you?

Turner: Not that—she might have said it, you know.
She did say something to that effect, but I don't know
if she actually did it, if she really did rub his nose in it.
It was conversation. It was just back-and-forth conversation.

Brown: And during that conversation, she just might
have said that?

Turner: Yes. Well, she said she had thought about it or
was going to do it, but I never saw her do it. I never—
you know.

Brown: My question is, and I want to be clear in my
question so you can be clear in your response to this
jury: are you telling this court and this jury that you
have an independent recollection of Mrs. Schwarz ever
telling you that she, in fact, put that child's nose in any
urine-soaked bed?

Turner: She mentioned it, but—it's been so long, I don't
remember. I don't remember.

On redirect examination, Scott Cupp had only a few questions.

Cupp: When Mrs. Schwarz told you these things about
speaking about the bed-wetting, how did that make
you feel? Do you recall how you felt?

Turner: Well, I didn't think it was right.

Cupp: Was she laughing when she said it? Was she
saying it in jest or was she serious?

Turner: No, she wasn't laughing; she wasn't laughing.

Cupp: And did you do anything about what she told
you or any of the things that you observed? Did you
tell anybody; did you do anything?

Turner: No, I didn't.

At that point, Cupp told the judge that he needed to approach the bench. He told him that he intended his next
question to be, "Why not?" He explained that it was in the

record—she had stated it in her deposition—how "very afraid" she was of the defendant—and why.

Brown objected, saying it was "far beyond the scope of my cross."

Judge Colbath ruled in favor of the defense.

CHAPTER 15

*He said he couldn't go to school because he had to
collect aluminum cans for his [step]mother.*

—Candace Ahern

On Friday, fourteen-year-old Serena Perryman was the
prosecution's first witness of the day. She lived with her family four houses down from the Schwarzes on the opposite
side of Triphammer Road.

Home-schooled and extremely intelligent—literally a ge-
nius—she was very direct and slightly stilted in her speech
and delivery.

Serena testified that she had never been inside the Schwarz
house, but had played in the yard with Lauren and Patsy; and
in the three to four years that she had known the family, she
had never had the opportunity to play with A.J. because he
was "never allowed to play." He was made to do chores on a
daily basis, including watching Jackie, picking up "junk" in
the yard and driveway, and sweeping the sidewalk.

Until Patsy was removed from the Schwarz home and
placed in foster care, she was also required to do chores on a
daily basis, but not Lauren or Jackie.

Serena had seen many bruises on A.J.—too many to count—
and had witnessed the defendant strike A.J.

"I was standing on the sidewalk in front of their house.
Jessica opened the door, yelled obscenities at A.J., and

yanked him and struck him as they were entering the house. She said—I don't remember exactly, but she said 'fuck,' and something."

> Marx: Was that the only time you ever heard the defendant use the word "fuck" towards Andrew?
> Serena: No, lots and lots of times she used it.
> Marx: Would she use other derogatory names at Andrew?
> Serena: Yes.
> Marx: Would he be standing there when she'd be saying those things?
> Serena: Many times, yes. He generally wouldn't do anything. He wouldn't say anything, either. He just sort of looked down.

One day Serena had been outside "on the easement" in front of her house and saw A.J. walking home from school by himself. She looked down the street and saw Jessica at the front door of her house, "sticking her head out." Then she heard her yell "ferociously" at A.J., "If you're not home right this instant, I'm going to make you run down the street naked." A.J. started walking faster and looked frightened.

> Marx: Was there anything blocking your view or keeping you from hearing what the defendant said that day?
> Serena: There was nothing keeping me from hearing what the defendant said.
> Marx: Would A.J. always walk home and walk to school?
> Serena: Every time I saw him, yes.
> Marx: Did Andrew seem strange or abnormal to you?
> Serena: No, not at all. He was polite and respectful, sort of quiet.
> Marx: Serena, how would you describe Jessica Schwarz's attitude toward Andrew?
> Serena: Oh, it was very hateful—because the way she

looked and what she said to him, there was no warmth at all, just like cold.

Marx: Did you ever see this woman hug Andrew Schwarz?

Serena: No.

Marx: Did you ever see this woman kiss Andrew Schwarz?

Serena: No.

Marx: Did you ever see this woman say a kind word to Andrew Schwarz?

Serena: Never.

Brown, on cross-examination, tried—unsuccessfully—to convince the young witness that instead of A.J. "watching Jackie," what she actually saw was A.J. and Jackie playing together.

Brown: Now, do you know what kinds of things Andrew liked to do as far as playing is concerned?

Serena: No, because I never saw him play.

Brown: When you saw Andrew in the yard with toys, you chose to believe that he was picking up Jackie's toys; is that correct?

Serena: I didn't choose that—I saw that.

Brown: And, Serena, you say that you saw bruises all over his body?

Serena: All the parts that I could see that weren't covered with clothes. As long as I knew him, every time I came within a distance, I could see bruises on him.

Brown: Were these big bruises?

Serena: Some of them were, but others were medium-sized.

Brown: Would you agree if somebody were looking for those bruises, they should have seen them?

Serena: Certainly.

Brown: And I think you told Mr. Marx that the bruises we're talking about here were too many to count?

Serena: That's right.

Brown: Did you ever see Jessica hug or kiss Lauren?

Serena: I don't remember.

Brown: Have you ever seen Jessica hug or kiss anybody?

Serena: I don't remember.

Brown: How did you say you met Jessica Schwarz?

Serena: I met Jessica when they moved in. She was staggering down the sidewalk in front of her house and my mom asked her a question. I think she asked, "How are you doing?" And she said, "How should I be? I have four kids." And she continued staggering down [the sidewalk]. And later in the day, I saw her passed out under the neighbor's bush.

Her answer brought a degree of levity into the courtroom—for everyone, of course, except Rendell Brown. She just rattled off her answer before Judge Colbath—or anyone—could stop her. It was obvious by the way she said it that it was absolutely, 100 percent true. That was as close as anyone would have even thought about laughing out loud during the trial. For a very brief period of time, it reduced the tension.

Not surprisingly, Brown asked to approach the bench.

Brown: Your Honor, I'm going to ask the court to take the responsibility to direct these witnesses as to what is and not coming in, in this trial. Now, I mean you're going to tell me, "You asked her." The idea is to keep this stuff out. I asked how she met her and she goes into [a] diatribe, but the court has already said this is not coming in, in this trial.

Judge Colbath: I know we've touched on this subject and I understand your dilemma, Mr. Brown, but, as I said before, short of listening to the testimony out of the presence of the jury, I don't know how anyone could ever have anticipated this kind of an answer. It is a very truthful answer.

Brown: I don't know if it's truthful.

Judge Colbath: Let me say this: it's certainly a responsive answer, whether or not it's truthful, at least from the viewpoint of a fourteen-year-old girl. Can you switch gears?

Brown: I'm going to have to.

Judge Colbath: Let's move on.

Brown (to the witness): Serena, do you recall the last time you spoke with Patsy?

Serena: No, I don't.

Brown: Can you get us in the ballpark?

Serena: I don't remember.

Brown: Now, you never saw Andrew Schwarz naked, did you?

Serena: No.

Eleven-year-old Brittany Ahern was the next witness for the prosecution. Scott Cupp informed the judge that her mother would be the next witness, so she was not present in the courtroom. Imogene Kelleher, the guardian ad litem, sat next to her while she was on the witness stand.

Outside the presence of the jury, the judge addressed the little girl. "Brittany, some of the questions that either Mr. Cupp or Mr. Brown may ask you could possibly deal with when certain events took place, when did you do this or when did you see this or something like that. Try not to refer to A.J.'s death as a point in time to reference your answer. Do you understand what I'm saying?"

The girl answered, "No, I don't."

Judge Colbath patiently tried to make it clearer to the child. "Well, in other words, if Mr. Cupp or Mr. Brown say, 'Well, Brittany, when did this take place?' Instead of saying, 'Oh, it was right after A.J. died or it was just before A.J. died,' try to give a month and a year, if you can do that. Do you understand what I'm saying?"

Brittany answered, "Yes."

The jury was brought in and Cupp elicited the information from the girl that she and Lauren Cross, Jessica's daughter, had been classmates and friends. And that the first time she had been in the Schwarz home was to attend Lauren's party for her tenth birthday.

Having been a "latchkey kid," her mother made arrangements with Jessica for Brittany to go there every day after school until about 6:00 or 6:30 in the evening so she would have someone to play with, and her mother also dropped Brittany off in the mornings on her way to work so she could go to school with Lauren.

Brittany testified that she had seen Jessica hit A.J. "kind of hard" with her hands "a lot of times" on his face, his head, and his butt.

Cupp: Did you ever see Jessica punch A.J.? Do you know what I mean by punch?

Brittany: Yes.

Cupp: How do you punch somebody? Show me. Hold up your fist.

(The witness balled up her fist and showed it to the prosecutor.)

Cupp: Did you ever see Jessica punch A.J.?

Brittany: Yes.

Cupp: On what part of A.J.'s body would Jessica punch him?

Brittany (hesitantly): I—I don't remember.

Cupp: Were you ever over at Lauren and A.J.'s house at one time when A.J. got home from school late?

Brittany: Yes.

Cupp (gently): Could you tell us what happened? Take your time.

Brittany: One day, he came home from school and he was late—because he was supposed to be home by a certain time and he wasn't—and she yelled at him and made him take off his clothes and run down the street naked. I didn't see it, but then later on in the day, kids were saying, "Why was A.J. running around the street naked?"

Cupp: Did you hear Jessica tell A.J. to take his clothes off?

Brittany: We were in the kitchen and the kitchen was kind of connected to his room and she was telling him.

Cupp: What made him come back?

Brittany: She called him back.

Cupp: What did A.J. do after he got back?

Brittany: He was crying—in his bedroom.

Cupp: Did you ever hear Jessica curse at A.J.?

Brittany: Yes.

Cupp: Now, I think it would be okay with your mother—just for today, just this one time—that you say what you heard. Is that okay?

Brittany: Yes. She would call him "asshole" and "shit for brains."

Cupp: Did you hear it just one time or more than one time?

Brittany: More than one time.

Cupp: All the times that you went over there, did you ever see Jessica hug A.J.?

Brittany: No.

Cupp: Did you ever see her kiss him?

Brittany: No.

Cupp: Did you ever see her help him do anything or encourage him?

Brittany: No.

Cupp: Was she ever nice to him—at all?

Brittany: I don't think so.

On cross-examination, Brittany reiterated for Rendell Brown that she never personally saw A.J. running down the street naked—that she heard it from Troy Falk.

Brown: Now, during the times that you remember seeing Jessica hitting Andrew, you said she hit him hard?

Brittany: Yes.

Brown: Was it hard enough to cause bruising?

Brittany: Yes.

Brown: Did you see bruises yourself?
Brittany: Sometimes I would see bruises.

Scott Cupp's redirect questioning was brief and to the point:

Cupp: Brittany, when you were over there when A.J. came home late and Jessica told him to take his clothes off and run down the street—what did Jessica say to you and Lauren?
Brittany: She told us—she told me, "Now don't go telling your mom about this."
Cupp: You heard her tell A.J. to do this, right?
Brittany: Yes.
Cupp: But you didn't walk outside and watch him do it?
Brittany: No.
Cupp: You never talked to those kids about this, did you?
Brittany: No. I heard what Troy said on television.

Candace Ahern, Brittany's mother, took the witness stand next. She testified that on one of the afternoons when she went to pick Brittany up at Jessica's house, A.J. was outside and she noticed that his eyes and his nose were swollen and black and blue.

"It was so noticeable that his nose didn't look like a nose; it was almost disfigured-looking."

A.J. followed her into the house and, when they were inside, she asked A.J. what happened to his face—and Jessica laughed at him.

"She laughed hysterically, laughed at A.J. and his face, and called him 'shit for brains,' which I thought was abusive."

"What was A.J. doing?" Cupp asked.

"Crying. He started to cry," Ahern replied.

One morning, when it was raining, she was taking Brittany to school and went by to pick up Lauren. She saw A.J. and offered him a ride to school too.

"He said he couldn't go to school because he had to collect aluminum cans for his [step]mother."

On another occasion, Jessica called her and was complaining about A.J., telling her that he was "giving her a very hard time and he was very hard to handle." Mrs. Ahern told her that if he was that difficult maybe she should give him back to his mother.

"What was her response?" Cupp asked.

"That she did not want to pay child support."

Jessica Schwarz shook her head from time to time and scribbled on a notepad at the defense table as she listened to the accusations. Her defense attorney then began his cross-examination of the witness.

Brown: Now, Mr. Cupp asked you about a swollen nose and black eyes?

Ahern: Yes.

Brown: And you were going to tell this court what Andrew said to you about that and he stopped you. Did you ask him what happened? Did you ask how he got the swollen nose and black eyes?

Ahern: Yes, I did. He said he ran into something in the garage.

Brown: Okay. He told you he was riding the bicycle in the garage, didn't he?

Ahern: I think that's what he said.

Brown: His little sister's bicycle?

Ahern: It was a little bicycle.

Brown: Somehow he ran into the wall with the bicycle; isn't that what he told you?

Ahern: That's what he told me.

Brown: Andrew never told you that "my [step]mother makes me collect cans," did he?

Ahern: He said, "I'm collecting cans for my [step]mother."

Brown: Okay. He never told you that she made him collect cans?

Ahern repeated: He said, "I'm collecting cans for my [step]mother."

Brown: You never talked to HRS about any of this stuff that you told us?

Ahern: No, sir.

Brown: Did Mrs. Schwarz ever tell you about the effort she was making to get HRS to do something about the problems with Andrew?

Ahern: An effort? No.

The next witness was Anne Steinhauer, the neighbor who lived directly across the street from the Schwarzes. An attractive young mother, with very long hair and impeccable makeup, she knew A.J. because occasionally he came over to her house to see if her little girl could play with Jackie, and she also "took him to school once in a while."

Steinhauer: I always thought he was very thin, but he was always very polite. When I took him to school in the morning, he always said, "Thank you, I appreciate the rides." He was a nice boy.

Marx: When you picked him up to go to school, did you see him with lunch?

Steinhauer: One time I took him to school, he had a banana and an apple.

Marx: How many times did you take him to school?

Steinhauer: I took him pretty regularly. Whenever I would pass him, if he were on the road, I'd ask him if he wanted a ride.

Marx: More than twenty times?

Steinhauer: Oh, yes.

The young boy would get in the car, look from side to side, then "scrunch down" underneath the window so no one would see him. He told her he wasn't allowed to have rides to school.

Many, many times, she had seen A.J. doing chores.

"He cleaned the garage, seemed like every day. He would pull everything out of the garage, put it into the driveway, sweep out the inside of the garage, and then he'd haul everything back inside. He did this almost every single day. I can't understand how a garage can get that dirty.

"He used to mow the lawn with an electric lawn mower. He fed the cat; he'd clean the litter box.

"He was—all day he was outside doing chores from when he got up until it got dark at night. He was out there all day. When I got up, he was already out there when I got to the front of my house. I usually get up about seven A.M. and he was probably out there until the sun started to go down."

She had seen A.J. sweep the driveway and the sidewalk—with a paintbrush.

"It seemed like he was trying to be very particular; he was trying to get every piece of grass, and the whole time he was out here, he was screaming, 'I [am] bad, do bad things and I do bad things and I get people in trouble and I won't do it again.' He said it all day.

"Jessica would come to the window in the front and she'd say, 'I can't hear you.' And then David was in and out all day, saying, 'I can't hear you. Say it louder.' And then A.J. would say it and then she'd say, 'I can't hear you. Say it louder.' It was just all day long."

Marx: Did you ever see A.J. playing?
Steinhauer: Playing? No, I never saw him have any friends over or anything.
Marx: Did you ever see Lauren and Jackie doing chores?
Steinhauer: Doing chores? No, they were always playing in the driveway or on the sidewalk out front with their friends.
Marx: Did you ever hear the defendant call A.J. derogatory names?
Steinhauer: Yes. It was quite often; she'd say that he was worthless, he was no good, he would never make

anything of himself, he had shit for brains, and he was a worthless piece of shit that would never go anywhere or do anything with his life.

Marx: Did there ever come a point in time when you saw the defendant strike or accost Andrew Schwarz?

Steinhauer: I never saw her hit him, but one time—when he was out cutting the grass—she came up behind him and she put her hands around his neck. She had like a chokehold around his neck and she picked him up and his feet were like six inches to a foot off the ground and she was swinging him around showing him things in the garage. The only thing I could hear her saying was "Look at this and look at this." And then when she let him down, she dropped him. She didn't let him down—she just dropped him. (While she was testifying about what she had seen, Steinhauer placed her hands around her neck to demonstrate how Jessica was holding A.J.)

Marx: Did he fight back?

Steinhauer: No, he just let his hands swing from side to side. He didn't grab onto her arms to try and release the hold or anything.

Marx: Approximately how big was this little boy?

Steinhauer: He was probably fifty pounds—if that. He was very thin. He wasn't a very big boy at all.

Marx: What did you do after you saw these things take place?

Steinhauer: Well, in January, I called Child Protection Services, but when I felt that they didn't do anything, I didn't call anymore. I felt nothing was being done and I had done my part.

Marx: Did you ever see the defendant hug Andrew Schwarz?

Steinhauer: No.

Marx: Did you ever see the defendant kiss Andrew Schwarz?

Steinhauer: No.

Marx: Did you ever hear the defendant say a kind word to Andrew Schwarz?
Steinhauer: No.

On cross-examination, Rendell Brown asked Mrs. Steinhauer if she had ever seen A.J. with any bruises; the witness replied that she had seen him with two black eyes. Other than that, she had not.

Brown: And you saw him practically every day, didn't you?
Steinhauer: Not every day, but I saw him regularly, yes.
Brown: And you saw him up close because you had him in your van. You drive a van, right?
Steinhauer: Yes.
Brown: So you had a pretty good look at him?
Steinhauer: Well, I wasn't looking at him while I was driving. He'd get in—I wouldn't inspect his body when he got in my car to see if he had bruises.
Brown: Did you ever see David kiss Andrew?
Steinhauer: No.
Brown: Did you ever see David hug Andrew?
Steinhauer: No.

After the lunch break, Eileen Callahan was the next witness to take the stand. The young mother of three young children had, at one time, been a neighbor of the Schwarzes—and was the victim of Barbara Black's threats.

Even though A.J. had only been to her house twice to play with her children, her impression was that he was "a very nice little boy."

In May 1992, she had seen A.J. working in the yard in the rain—on his hands and knees—edging the sidewalk with a pair of household scissors.

Marx: Is this the only time you saw Andrew doing chores?
Callahan: No.

Marx: Did it escalate during the time you were living there at Triphammer Road?

Callahan: Yes. I saw Andrew cleaning the car, washing the car, cleaning out the garage on weekends, mowing the yard with an electric lawn mower, raking up pine needles—or leaves, if you will. I saw him cleaning out the cat litter box. One weekend I saw him cleaning the cab of a big tractor-trailer truck.

Marx: Would this go on all day?

Callahan: Yes.

On another occasion when she saw A.J. edging the lawn with scissors, her husband went over to help him with some of the yard work. When she saw A.J. the next day, his eyes were black and blue.

Marx established the fact that during the period of time in question, Mrs. Callahan was a stay-at-home mom who had been pregnant and "couch ridden."

Marx: Did there ever come a point in time that you made a phone call in regards to what you saw? Was that after you saw him with the black eyes?

Callahan: Yes. I called the state attorney's office, the hot line number to get some information, ask questions, and then I called Child Protective Services.

Marx: Do you know if somebody came out to the Schwarz residence in regards to that phone call?

Callahan: Yes.

And then the same series of poignant questions with the same series of heartbreaking answers, establishing that the witness had never seen Jessica Schwarz hug A.J., or kiss A.J., or even say one kind word to him.

The next witness was Margaret Pincus. She and her family had lived next door to the Schwarzes and she, too, had seen A.J. down on his knees, trimming the lawn "around the edges" with a pair of household scissors.

"When I walked out, it was maybe late morning and he was out there—seemed like it was all day long because it was getting dark when he went in the house. I heard noises coming out of the house and to the effect of 'Say it louder—I can't hear you!' It sounded like Jessica, but I couldn't swear to it."

Cupp: Did it sound like an adult female?
Pincus: Yes.
Cupp: And what was A.J. saying, if anything, that he had to yell louder?
Pincus: "My name is A.J. I lie on people to get them in trouble and I'll never do it again."
Cupp: Did you hear him saying this throughout the day?
Pincus: Repeatedly. All day long.

CHAPTER 16

There is much I could say about Richard and his devotion, work, and love for A.J. He needs no one to apologize for him—or to make excuses for him. Certainly no one has the right to question whether Richard could have or should have done more to help A.J. No one has that right. No one cared more during those last months. No one.

—Scott Cupp

Scott Cupp's next witness was the gentleman that he had grown, over the months since A.J.'s death, to care deeply about—and even feel protective of: Dr. Richard Zimmern, Andrew Schwarz's guardian ad litem. Although he was an average-looking man, with neatly combed salt-and-pepper hair, his kindness and his humanity were anything but ordinary. A.J.'s death had broken his heart.

Well-dressed—but casual—in his blue button-down collar shirt, gray dress pants, and sport coat, Dr. Zimmern entered the courtroom and walked slowly to the witness stand.

In his soft voice, the retired pediatrician from Connecticut explained to the jurors that a guardian ad litem is a volunteer who is appointed by judges in various courts to aid and assist any child who is going through the legal process. He had been a guardian for almost four years and had been A.J.'s from July 1992 until May 1993.

"At that time, in July of '92, A.J. was scheduled for a hearing before Judge Birken in Broward County."

Cupp: So this case, A.J.'s case, was not a Palm Beach County case, but it was a Broward County case? But A.J. was physically living in Palm Beach County; is that correct?
Zimmern: Correct.
Cupp: Would it be a fair statement that your role as a guardian in Palm Beach County was kind of a courtesy to the program in Broward so that that guardian wouldn't have to come all the way up to Lantana or Lake Worth?
Zimmern: Correct.

When he first got the case, Dr. Zimmern went to meet with Jessica and David Schwarz, which was the normal routine, so that he could gather enough background information so that he would be able to present a reasonable and coherent report to the judge. He had a heavy caseload at the time and was told by his supervisor that he would just be covering for Broward County and that it was routine—a court hearing that had to be covered.

He had no idea how complex the case was, how much background there was, or "all the ins and outs of what was going on."

"And, of course, you get paid the same thing for this case that you get paid for all of your cases—and that's what?" Cupp asked.

"We're all volunteers."

At some point, Dr. Zimmern became aware that A.J. had been hospitalized in 1992 for six weeks in the Psychiatric Institute of Vero Beach. As part of his role as a guardian, he requested copies of the discharge summary, the admitting history, and the physical evaluation.

Cupp: And there were several rather specific things that were to happen—according to the hospital?

Zimmern: Yes, there were.

Cupp: You being a pediatrician and physician, you would be familiar with drugs, certain types of prescription drugs that are dispensed and prescribed by physicians? Are you familiar with imipramine?

Zimmern: Imipramine is a drug that has been discovered to have certain calming effects in hyperexcitable children.

Cupp: Anxious children?

Zimmern: Anxious children, learning-disabled children. When it works, it has a very dramatic effect.

Cupp: And one of the recommendations from Vero Beach was that A.J. be placed on imipramine; is that correct?

Zimmern: Yes.

Cupp: When you picked up the case, did you become aware that Andrew was not on imipramine? How did you become aware of that?

Zimmern: In my discussions with Jessica Schwarz, I kept asking her about the drug and two things came out: Number one—he had vomited the drug.

Cupp: According to—

Zimmern: According to Mrs. Schwarz.

Cupp: During the time that you were his guardian, through his third-grade year, he wasn't on imipramine at all?

Zimmern: As far as I know, he was never placed on imipramine. (The guardian had visited Andrew approximately seventeen times, had taken copious notes, and dated them.)

Cupp: I believe you visited Andrew on January 26 of '93. Do you recall that? Did you observe anything unusual about his appearance?

Zimmern: Yes, I observed that he had two black eyes and a swollen nose.

Cupp: Were these . . . I mean, there are black eyes—and then there are black eyes. Was this just a little reddening under the eyes?

Zimmern: No, these were good black eyes.

Cupp: Did you notice anything about his demeanor or his affect?

Zimmern: Well, he was depressed. He seemed to me to be depressed, subdued, looking down. He frequently—when he was upset—would sort of look down, sort of hunch.

Cupp: Another one of the discharge recommendations from the Vero Beach hospitalization was that he, as well as family—including Mrs. Schwarz—needed desperately to get into counseling; is that right?

Zimmern: They recommended counseling.

Cupp: Individually and family?

Zimmern: Yes.

Cupp: How long of a delay was there from the time that he was discharged to when any counseling ever took place for Andrew?

Zimmern: He was discharged on March 20, [1992], and I believe his first appointment was September 10. A little less than six months. Andrew had fourteen appointments; three were canceled, three were no-shows.

Cupp: Did you ever have a conversation with Mrs. Schwarz in which she relayed how she felt about Andrew? Was there one conversation in particular that disturbed you? And what phrase or what terms did she relay to you to describe him?

Zimmern: The phrase that scared me was "His eyes are dead. He has no soul."

Dr. Zimmern then told the jury about his visit to see Andrew on April 24, 1993—his tenth birthday. When he pulled up in front of the house, the young boy was edging the lawn with a pair of household scissors. During the time he was there, there was no talk of a birthday party or of any other birthday gifts.

Cupp: And you brought him a birthday present?
Zimmern: Yes, he had wanted some Battle Trolls.
Cupp: How did he feel about that?
Zimmern: Well, he was kind of sad that day, but the trolls cheered him up.
Cupp: Did you ever see Jessica embrace or have any physical contact or affectionate connection with Andrew?
Zimmern: No.

On cross-examination by Rendell Brown, Dr. Zimmern admitted that the only time he had seen Andrew with any bruises was the one occasion when the child's face was injured.

Brown: And your visits were actually drop-in kinds of visits, weren't they?
Zimmern: My visits—all of them were appointments.
Brown: You had an appointment on the day of his birthday?
Zimmern: I would usually call to make an appointment. The only time that I didn't was his birthday, I guess, and Easter. But Mrs. Schwarz knew I was coming the day of his birthday because she was the one who told me to get Battle Trolls.
Brown: Was that in response to asking her what he would like for his birthday?
Zimmern: Correct.
Brown: And did she say to you, "No, he can't have anything for his birthday"? She didn't tell you that, did she? In fact, she said, in response to your question, "He would like some Battle Trolls"?
Zimmern: Correct.
Brown: And she allowed you to bring those Battle Trolls and give them to him, didn't she?
Zimmern: Yes.

Brown: Let me ask you, sir, if you'll look at that report and tell me if you recognize that report?

Zimmern: Yes, I do recognize it. This is my report to Judge Birken at the first hearing in September of '92.

Brown: As a guardian ad litem, reports of minors—which are otherwise confidential and not reviewable by the public—are reviewable by you; is that correct?

Zimmern: Yes.

Brown: You can get into the reports and read the reports? And, in fact, that becomes sometimes necessary for a guardian ad litem to do his job properly; isn't that true?

Zimmern: Yes.

Brown: And did there come a time when you began to get into the reports regarding Andrew Schwarz? His files, the proceedings that were going on in Broward and what those proceedings were about? You read all of that stuff?

Zimmern: I read the stuff that I was given.

Brown: Now, Jessica and David Schwarz lived in Palm Beach County at all times that you were aware of them; isn't that correct?

Zimmern: Yes.

Brown: And yet there was a court proceeding going on in Broward County; isn't that correct? And there was a reason for that, wasn't there?

Zimmern: Yes, I presume that it was because the case originated there.

Brown: And who lived in Broward County, where the case originated?

Zimmern: Ilene Logan, his natural mother, and—at that time—Patsy, his sister.

Brown: You've indicated that you have some knowledge about a drug called imipramine?

Zimmern: Yes.

Brown: It's intended to alter certain behaviors; wouldn't you agree?

Zimmern: It is a mood-ameliorating drug.

Brown: And the behaviors that it's intended to correct are those organic behaviors that usually have set in on a person by the formative years—which is four to five years of age; isn't that correct, Doctor?

Zimmern: Partially. Imipramine can be used for learning disabilities, for children who have hyperexcitability syndromes and it also can be used in certain situations as a plain old tranquilizer. If something is congenital and it is an inborn condition, then it will become apparent. However, it becomes apparent at different times in different situations. Learning disabilities generally don't become apparent until kindergarten or first grade when a child is put under the stress—the actual stress of learning.

Brown: The cause, however, is generally set in the formative years; wouldn't you agree with that?

Zimmern: It's hard to give that a precise yes or no, black and white, because—actually, I'm not an expert witness on this.

Brown: You were a little bit out of your area when you started with Mr. Cupp with those answers, weren't you?

Zimmern: I would disagree. Any practicing pediatrician, using imipramine all the time, learns to use it, to adjust dosages, knows the side effects.

Brown: You will agree that at some point you concluded, from your involvement with Andrew Schwarz, that not only should Andrew continue his counseling, but there should be intensive counseling offered to the family as well; isn't that correct?

Zimmern: The recommendation for the family counseling came from Dr. Uttley in his discharge recommendations. I really pushed mostly for Andrew's counseling.

Brown: And the truth of the matter is, Doctor, that not only did you push mostly for Andrew's counseling, but so did the entire Child Protection Team; isn't that correct?

Zimmern: Well, they were pushing for counseling, of course.

Brown: For Andrew, I mean?

Zimmern: For Andrew, yes.

Brown: And during your involvement with the Child Protection Team and with HRS, never once, never once did anybody push for counseling for the family—as the law requires, did they? Did they, Doctor? Did HRS ever make any recommendation or push for counseling for the rest of the family other than A.J., to your knowledge?

Zimmern: Not in my presence.

Brown: Now, there is no question that Dr. Uttley, who treated this child for six weeks, who determined what his problem was, and who put him on the medication to try to help him, made the recommendation that there be intensive counseling for the rest of this family as a part of this discharge summary, didn't he?

Zimmern: Correct.

Brown: Now, Doctor, the truth of the matter is that from the very beginning, when you first met Jessica Schwarz, she was telling you then that Andrew needs help, emotional help, wasn't she? Isn't that true?

Zimmern: No, it's not true. As a matter of fact, sir, quite the reverse. Mrs. Jessica Schwarz was quite clear that she didn't believe in counseling and she didn't believe in drug therapy.

CHAPTER 17

The overwhelming thing I remember about Richard was his kindness—his humanity. Easily loved. When he broke down on the stand—briefly—I wanted to leave the courtroom. It was horrible! It broke my heart. I wanted to scream. He loved A.J.

—Scott Cupp

Rendell Brown then requested that the doctor read his entire guardian ad litem report to the jurors, and Dr. Zimmern was eager to comply. "Certainly. Sorry, I'm meticulous." The transcript was as follows:

"History: Andrew Schwarz comes from a highly dysfunctional family setting. He was abused and neglected by his drug abuse natural mother and suffered verbal and physical abuse from her paramours.

"Andrew has been living with his father and stepmother, David and Jessica Schwarz, since he was adjudicated dependant in mid-1990. Mr. Schwarz was given custody of his son November 19, 1990.

"Andrew received outpatient counseling at the Youth Services Bureau in Palm Beach County in 1991. On February 6, 1992, he was admitted to the Psychiatric Institute of Vero Beach under the care of Thomas E. Uttley to remain there for six weeks. Reasons for admission were withdrawn behavior, depression, thought-processing problems, suicidal behavior and violence towards his younger sister.

"His discharge diagnoses were depressive disorder, post traumatic stress disorder with extreme anxiety, specific learning disability, parent/child problems, extreme and enduring psychosocial stress factors.

"Discharge recommendations were six months of antidepressant medication, imipramine, 125 milligrams per day and in divided doses, intense and extensive individual and family psychotherapy to work through issues of loss and abandonment.

"He had classes at [Indian River Memorial Hospital] and laboratory monitoring of his drug levels. Andrew was discharged on March 20.

"On May 1, 1992, Judge Birken decreed that the natural mother and sister of Andrew Schwarz were enjoined and restrained from contacting him, either directly or indirectly; also, that no adult was to disparage any other involved adult in his presence.

"On the same date, David Schwarz signed a protective services plan in which the following problems were identified: Medical needs, social stimulation and non compliance with HRS.

"Sources contacted: Andrew Schwarz, child; Jessica Schwarz, stepmother; David Schwarz, father; Ms. Heinrich, guidance counselor at the Indian Pines school; Linda Hunter, second grade teacher, Indian Pines school.

"Source unable to contact: Thomas Uttley, psychiatrist at the Psychiatric Institute of Vero Beach.

"Updated findings: Jessica Schwarz, Andrew's stepmother, reports as follows: In 1990 HRS placed Andrew and his sister, Patsy Spence, with the Schwarzes. Andrew has made great progress while in their care. When Mrs. Schwarz first met him six months ago, he was a frightened waif who would hide his face and was totally inarticulate, malnourished, dirty, and ate ravenously with his fingers.

"While in Palm Beach, Patsy received counseling at the

Center for Children in Crisis. Patsy, who will be thirteen years old next month, accused Mrs. Schwarz of verbal and physical abuse. She also threatened suicide, which apparently triggered the hearings that placed her in foster care.

"Mrs. Schwarz feels that the children's natural mother, Ilene Logan, whom she regards as a slob, a slut, a game player and a manipulator, orchestrated these actions for revenge.

"Mr. and Mrs. Schwarz attended court ordered parenting classes in 1990. She used the principles learned in those classes as a basis for handling Andrew, keeping her wall chart, recording of his bad deeds and rule infractions.

"Andrew kept breaking rules repeatedly and therefore never won praise for good behavior. He was always behind and consequently grounded far into the future.

"Mrs. Schwarz would arrange deals in which a large number of bad deeds would be exchanged for a few good ones, but this did not work very well.

"Mr. and Mrs. Schwarz attended two of the sessions held for parents at the Vero Beach hospital. It was hard for them to get there, considering their routine. They did attend the discharge meeting and received advice and instructions, according to Mrs. Schwarz.

"Andrew remained on imipramine for a short while but he was vomiting the pills. When the hospital prescription ran out, a local family doctor refused to renew the medication.

"Due to errors in administration, Andrew did not receive a medical card until August, 1992. Mrs. Schwarz then called South County Mental Health Unit and arranged for an appointment on September 10. Her husband and two other daughters did receive their cards. HRS reportedly told Mrs. Schwarz that Andrew was dropped because he was too old.

"Mrs. Schwarz feels that Andrew is an extremely excitable child with a poor attention span; that he's impulsive, has poor judgment and cannot be trusted alone. She's upset by Andrew's lying, sneaking about, and his refusal to talk. She feels he knows what he is doing and uses rule infractions as a way to get attention; that he's 'a bad boy with a grin on his face.'

"Mrs. Schwarz acknowledges that she's a tough, combative person, not a warm or touchy-feely person. She believes in tough love and thinks that psychological counseling is of little value. She also feels that Andrew was never helped by imipramine and that he needs a strong, structured home with firm rules and prompt punishment for all deviations. Here he would feel safe and wanted.

"David Schwarz is a long distance truck driver who's rarely home. He's had a difficult life but recalls Andrew's birth in 1983 affectionately. Even though Patsy was not his child, he loved her, and was happy to take her into his home, as well.

"Ilene Logan told Patsy that Mr. Schwarz was her father and that he did not want to accept Patsy and Andrew. Mr. Schwarz has been baffled by Andrew's increasing depression and withdrawal over the past fifteen months, accompanied by sleep disturbance, insomnia and bed-wetting. His son's impulsiveness, unpredictability has frightened him. Mr. Schwarz really doesn't know how to handle Andrew so he tries to keep order and keep his child safe.

"The guardian ad litem walked with Andrew about his neighborhood for about an hour. He was quiet, nonspontaneous, and did not engage in any conversation but would answer innocent questions. He did not permit prying into his thoughts by a stranger.

"Andrew did say that he does not want to see or speak to his natural mother and stepsister.

"Mrs. Schwarz told me that Patsy told Andrew she hated him and that she had physically abused him.

"Linda Hunter, Andrew's second grade teacher, said she loved Andrew and described him as a very bright child who was never a behavior problem, never acted strange or irrational, and never did anything in school to hurt himself or other children. She thought that Andrew was scared to death of something or someone. He was very loving toward her and she felt he needed love in return.

"Ms. Hunter said she often sent good behavior notes home and would receive strange letters filled with negative things about Andrew. He was forbidden by his stepmother to receive any snacks or goodies in school, attend any school parties, or go on any field trips. Mrs. Schwarz explained to Ms. Hunter that these prohibitions were necessary to balance the long list of bad things he had done at home and that he was deeply indebted—behavior wise.

"Ms. J. Heinrich, guidance counsel [or] at Indian Pines school, could tell the guardian ad litem very little about Andrew because she had been forbidden by Mrs. Schwarz from speaking to him or to his sister, Patsy, when Patsy was in school. She said that when Patsy was in school there, she acted like a little mother to Andrew and was very concerned about him. Andrew seems immature to Ms. Heinrich. She also said he's frightened, doesn't smile, although he always says everything is fine. She feels he's afraid to speak out.

"At the request of the Schwarzes, Andrew has been before the Child Study Team three times. On each occasion they concluded he was not a candidate for classes for the emotionally disturbed. They felt that Andrew was not a behavior problem, but did have trouble concentrating. They also found a conductive loss in the child's left ear and requested the parents follow through with their family doctor.

"In 1991, Andrew did receive counseling at school from Ed Carpenter of the Youth Services Bureau. In general, Ms. Heinrich feels that Mrs. Schwarz has been hostile to her, and the teachers in this school, in their efforts to help Andrew. She has written negative notes to the school and has not been at all friendly.

"Dr. Thomas Uttley, attending psychiatrist at the Psychiatric Institute of Vero Beach, did not return the guardian ad litem's calls.

"Summary: Andrew is a depressed, anxious child with severe and long standing parent problems. Last spring he became suicidal, withdrawn, and was unable to assess reality. He may have come close to a psychiatric breakdown. If Andrew cannot live in our world, he will withdraw into his own.

"Andrew seems to do well academically in school so far. Intellectual observations are not onerous in this early grace period. This may change as the material studied becomes more difficult and requires increased concentration and effort. Andrew's behavior in school has been fine, as well. He has not been a problem to his teacher, his peers, or himself.

"However, Andrew does not function well at home. He cannot follow the family rules, resists doing his assigned chores and is just generally uncooperative. Something is wrong here. Changes must be made. Why is Andrew so cooperative in school and so rotten at home?

"Andrew loves and needs Mr. and Mrs. Schwarz. When they did not visit during the visiting in Vero Beach he was overwhelmed and de-compensated completely. Perhaps Jessica Schwarz should alter her patterns to fit the patterns of his illness. Certainly the family, Andrew, Jessica, and David—if possible—would benefit greatly from individual counseling and imipramine for the six months suggested by Dr. Uttley in his discharge recommendations.

"Andrew suffers from poor self-esteem and a sense of rejection. He perceives himself as worthless, with a lack of identity. Andrew needs to be built up and given this identity. His self-esteem should be enhanced and he can no longer be rejected as a bad boy, unworthy of love or respect.

"The guardian ad litem strongly recommends that Andrew continue in individual counseling and Jessica Schwarz and Andrew participate in family therapy; David Schwarz, too, if possible."

Zimmern: And that's it.
Brown: You do not have the signature page?
Zimmern: Sorry. "Andrew must be treated again with imipramine, as suggested by Dr. Uttley, and HRS con-

tinue supervising this family, the court review this case in six months, the guardian ad litem continue to monitor the case."

Brown: Now, Doctor, it's exceedingly clear that this entire family needed help to deal with this situation; isn't that true?

Zimmern: I would say yes.

Brown: Now, you're not a part of the Child Protection Team, per se?

Zimmern: No.

Brown: So getting the family counseling and that sort of thing is not really your bag, is it? That's what the Child Protection Team does?

Zimmern: It's not my job to arrange for counseling.

Brown: But when a father comes to you and says, "I really don't know how to handle my child, so I just try to keep order and keep him safe," doesn't that sort of set off red flags that he's asking for help? That the family needs help?

Zimmern: The family needs help in handling Andrew and Andrew needs help in handling himself.

Brown: And you're not a trained psychologist?

Zimmern: No.

Brown: But you were able to see the need here?

Zimmern: I was able to see the need that Andrew had for help.

Brown: Okay. What about Mr. Schwarz and Mrs. Schwarz?

Zimmern: Yes, I would say that both Mr. and Mrs. Schwarz needed help.

Brown: Now, you also said that there were no problems with Andrew as far as behavior at Indian Pines is concerned, correct?

Zimmern: No, there were no problems according to the two teachers, Ms. Hunter and Mrs. Idrissi.

Brown: Did that have anything to do with any requests on your part to the school regarding his behavior, sir?

Zimmern: Yes.

Brown: Did you personally ask Mrs. Idrissi to set a different standard of rules and regulations for Andrew than the rest of the children? Did you?

Zimmern: I certainly did.

Brown: My question is: if his behavior is on par, there's no need to do that, is there?

Zimmern: I really can't answer that yes or no because there are . . . All right, yes, if his behavior is on par, there's no need to do that.

With that, Rendell Brown ended his cross-examination. Scott Cupp then began the redirect questioning.

Cupp: You've already testified that you couldn't get anything out of Andrew Schwarz? He wouldn't talk about what was going on inside the home?

Zimmern: Absolutely not.

Cupp: Ms. Heinrich, the guidance counselor? Usually a pretty good source of information for you—for kids in your cases? Now, reading briefly from your report, "Ms. J. Heinrich, guidance counselor at Indian Pines, could tell the guardian very little because she had been forbidden by Mrs. Schwarz from speaking to him or his sister, Patsy." So, she couldn't give you any information?

Zimmern: No.

Cupp: And the other source you had—other than the other two I'll get back to—was Linda Hunter? The second-grade teacher?

Zimmern: Yes.

Cupp: And Linda Hunter basically said, in a nutshell, "When I have the kid, he's fine, there's no behavior problems, he's a good kid, sweet kid. . . ." All the rest of the adjectives, correct?

Zimmern: Correct.

Cupp: So that leaves two people who—

Zimmern: David and Jessica.

Cupp: So at that point, all the information that you had, all the history was coming from the defendant? And her husband?

Zimmern: Yes.

Cupp: And they painted a pretty bleak picture of Andrew, didn't they?

Zimmern: Yes.

Cupp: Isn't that the same basically, with the intake at Vero Beach, the history source for A.J. for the hospital was the very same two people?

Zimmern: Yes.

Cupp: So all you really had to go on, at that point, was what she said?

Zimmern: Yes.

Cupp: Did you later come to find out that practically everything that she had told you about Andrew was false?

Zimmern: Yes.

Cupp: During the six weeks that Andrew was in Vero · Beach . . . it's a little ways from here? At least two hours?

Zimmern: Two hours.

Cupp: Andrew gets delivered up there and he's there for forty-two days and his loving stepmother and bio-logical father see him twice; is that right?

Zimmern: Well, that's the information I had.

Cupp: And it's in the records?

Zimmern: Yes.

Cupp: Isn't it also in the records that that was a major source of problems for him while he was there, that he would—the term, I think, is "decompensate," when they would not come to see him?

Zimmern: Yes.

Cupp: You can't have group therapy when you're by yourself? You can't have family therapy when you don't have a family?

(Dr. Zimmern sadly agreed.)

Cupp: When did A.J. arrive to live with the Schwarzes?

Zimmern: I think it was November of 1990.

Cupp: When you have this conversation that you've read to the jury about David Schwarz being baffled by Andrew's depression and withdrawal over the past fifteen months . . . Now, he told you that—sometime after Andrew arrived—these things happened; is that right?

Zimmern: Yes.

Cupp: After Andrew arrived in the Schwarz home—he was there for many months—and then for the past fifteen months, when David was talking to you, we've got problems of sleep disturbances, insomnia, bed-wetting, increasing depression, withdrawal?

Zimmern: Yes.

Cupp: So they started when he was in the Schwarz home, right?

Zimmern: These symptoms started in the Schwarz home.

Cupp: According to David?

Zimmern: According to David.

Cupp: And the point is that Mr. Schwarz specifically told you that these conditions started occurring some fifteen months prior to the time he talked to you?

Zimmern: There was an acute onset fifteen months prior to our conversation.

Cupp: That would have been during the time period that he was in the home and in the primary care of the defendant; is that correct?

Zimmern: Correct.

CHAPTER 18

The most important thing in this little boy's life was that he do his work and get it all done.

—Dr. George Rahaim

In an earlier hearing, Judge Colbath had ruled that—because of her fear of the defendant—it would not be necessary for Patsy Spence to come into the courtroom and take the witness stand; but, instead, she would be allowed to testify via closed-circuit TV, from his chambers.

A therapist who had counseled the young girl had testified at the hearing that Patsy had nightmares about Jessica and not being able to save A.J.

From the adjoining room, Scott Cupp established that Patsy Spence was almost fifteen years old, her natural mother was Ilene Logan, and that there had come a time when she and her half brother, A.J., had had to leave their mother's home. They lived with an aunt for a short period of time and then were placed with Jessica and David Schwarz, even though Patsy was not a blood relative of either one of them.

When they first went to live with the Schwarzes, the only other child in the home was David and Jessica's natural daughter, Jackie, who was two years old at the time.

At first, Patsy and A.J. were treated well.

At some point, Lauren, Jessica's natural daughter from a

previous marriage, came to live with them. She was a few years younger than Patsy and they shared a bedroom for a while. According to Patsy, the girls got along "all right" at first.

Cupp: Did there come a time when you could no longer stay in the same room with Lauren?
Patsy: Yes.
Cupp: Tell me what happened that caused that?
Patsy: When I let one of my friends come in to use the phone and Jessica came home and she caught him leaving the house, so she put me in my brother's room.
Cupp: Was that during the day or at nighttime?
Patsy: Around like five.
Cupp: About how old was the boy?
Patsy: About thirteen or fourteen.
Cupp: And about how old were you?
Patsy: About twelve or thirteen.
Cupp: Who else was home when the boy came in?
Patsy: Just me and Lauren.
Cupp: What happened when Jessica came home?
Patsy: She started hitting me.
Cupp: Was her hand open or closed?
Patsy: Open and closed.
Cupp: So she slapped you?
Patsy: And punched me.
Cupp: What part of your body did she punch?
Patsy: My face. My nose started bleeding.
Cupp: Did she say anything to you?
Patsy: She was calling me names, like "bitch," "cunt," "slut," "whore."
Cupp: After that, what was your punishment?
Patsy: To sleep in my brother's room for a year.
Cupp: Did you ever get to sleep in the room with Lauren again after that?
Patsy: No.

According to Patsy, there were many times—when A.J. didn't do his chores right—that Jessica punished him by making him eat bread and water while sitting on the floor in his room.

Patsy could not remember A.J. ever having a problem with wetting the bed when they were living with their natural mother, or at their aunt Dodi's house, or while they were in foster care. And he did not have a problem with it when they first came to live with Jessica and David.

But at some point after Patsy was staying in the same room with him, A.J. started wetting the bed.

Cupp: Would Jessica do anything?
Patsy: She would rub his nose into it.
Cupp: Did you see this happen?
Patsy: Yes.
Cupp: What would A.J. do when this would happen?
Patsy: Cry.
Cupp: Did you ever see Bear do that?
Patsy: No.
Cupp: Did Bear even know that it was happening?
Patsy: Yes.

Patsy was so afraid of Jessica that even after she was removed from the Schwarz home and placed in foster care—leaving A.J. behind—she didn't tell anyone about the abuses she had seen.

The state offered Dr. George Rahaim, the next witness, as an expert in the field of psychology in connection with child abuse. He was the team psychologist for the Child Protection Team.

As a result of his involvement in the case of Andrew Schwarz, he had reviewed a huge amount of material: records of the Child Protection Team, a complete set of records of A.J.'s six-week hospitalization, school records, and "an enormous pile of HRS records," records from the South County Mental Health Center, the Atlantic Counseling Center in

Delray Beach, the records of the guardian ad litem, and the medical records of Dr. Sheju Ukuedojor.

He reviewed the police reports documenting interviews with the Schwarz family and most—if not all—of their neighbors and many of the depositions. In addition, the psychologist interviewed Mary Idrissi, A.J.'s third-grade teacher, and viewed the videotape of Jessica, Lauren, and Jackie.

Upon A.J.'s admission to the Psychiatric Institute of Vero Beach, he was immediately placed on suicide precaution—someone looked in on him every fifteen minutes—day and night.

The psychologist testified that Dr. Uttley, the attending psychiatrist, prescribed imipramine (an antidepressant) and Ativan (a tranquilizer) for A.J. The child underwent psychological testing and evaluation and a physical. Dr. Uttley also ordered that he have individual counseling, group counseling, and family psychotherapy.

"He participated there in a great many therapeutic activities: counseling with staff, group therapy with other patients and staff, play activities. He went to school there. He was prescribed medication, took the medication."

Jessica and David had given a history that he suffered brain damage by virtue of being a cocaine baby, suffering fetal alcohol syndrome, having been struck in the head with a frying pan, and, ironically, a near-drowning experience very early in his life.

A.J. had a CAT scan, at least two electroencephalograms, blood tests, thyroid profile, and a battery of psychological tests.

Even though the psychological records indicated that some of his behavior was abnormal, Dr. Rahaim had found no evidence that Andrew Schwarz, who had been investigated quite thoroughly, had any organic problem or abnormality with the functioning of his brain—no brain damage.

"The medical records ruled it out quite conclusively."

Dr. Rahaim testified that when Andrew Schwarz's intelligence capacity had been tested in school in March 1990, his

IQ had been 101—average. He was tested again in October 1991 and his IQ was 91—low average. A.J. was tested a third time in February 1992—during his stay in the psychiatric hospital—and, astonishingly, his IQ was 86—very low average. In less than two years, there had been a 15-point drop in A.J.'s IQ.

"That's a serious drop in intelligence ability."

At one point, during A.J.'s hospitalization, he was given a list of twenty goals and asked to check off the ones that were important to him. He checked all twenty items. Then he numbered the three most important ones: Get my chores and schoolwork done. Do better in school. Understand my feelings better.

"The most important thing in this little boy's life was that he do his work and get it all done."

He was not quite nine years old at the time.

"He asked the staff if he could please not leave the hospital, that he wanted to stay there because he was allowed to do things there."

A.J. suffered from depression and also experienced many of the symptoms of post-traumatic stress disorder: nightmares, insomnia, very frequent agitation, and constant fear.

"He was a remarkably passive person, exhibited a passive withdrawn approach to almost everything. He also was very agitated and he exhibited behaviors that you think of when you think of somebody who can't stand to be in their own skin—they're constantly fearful and anxious. All during the hospitalization, they noted that over and over."

A.J. had become a bed wetter, but the problem disappeared while he was in the hospital.

"The bed-wetting appears to have started very early in 1991, a few months after Andrew arrived at the Schwarz home. It continued until the day that he was admitted into the psychiatric hospital. I think the bed-wetting was one of many, many symptoms of being abused and harmed."

A.J. found himself sobbing in front of other people in school and other places—"just broken-down sobbing." He exhibited regressed behavior—fingers in the mouth, baby talk—one of the hallmarks of an abused child.

"Andrew experienced just an overwhelming anxiety and agitation, what I think is best described as kind of a constant sense of dread and fear."

A.J. became close to psychotic in the hospital when there were no visits and when visits were promised, but they did not occur.

"My understanding [is], except for the time that he was actually brought to the hospital, that Jessica Schwarz visited him once and that David Schwarz visited him once, even though there were apparently many telephone calls and one letter literally begging for them to be involved with the child, letting them know that the child was decompensating, was deteriorating because of no access to the parents—that they expected that the child would do very, very badly because of no involvement of the parents in treatment."

Overwhelming insecurity and need to be made secure and safe. Constantly needed to be hugged and touched and made to feel safe. Grabbed the staff and tried to hug them. Always wanted to be hugged and comforted. Withdrawn. Preoccupied. Passive. No spontaneity except for needing security. No spontaneous information.

"He was described as having problems that he was keeping deep inside; that he was so withdrawn that he couldn't tell you much about his life. His thoughts were disorganized. He couldn't think straight, if you will. His affect was flat. You didn't see emotion, you know, laughter and things like that. He was just zombielike.

"He had no trust in anyone. He wouldn't complain. If you asked him what was wrong, he'd tell you 'he' was wrong. His identity was just very badly shattered. In my opinion, he felt like he was worthless—that all bad things were due to him."

He was unable to have relationships, to personally have friends, to share stories, or to trust anyone.

"And there was a deep overwhelming learned humiliation about the boy."

The continued use of derogatory words by the defendant ground down his spirit. He was so frequently and consistently degraded that "he knew that it was true."

"Children up to around the age of eleven or twelve are learning who they are and what they are, if you will. They are learning their identity. The effect of this constant cursing, being put down, belittled, degraded, was that he learned that he was garbage—not even that he felt like it or thought it—but that was him and that's overwhelmingly destructive."

Dr. Rahaim testified that the date of Dr. Richard Zimmern's report—September 9, 1992—was significant in isolating a time period. David Schwarz had told the guardian ad litem that he was baffled by A.J.'s increased depression and withdrawal over the previous fifteen months, accompanied by sleep disturbance, insomnia, and bed-wetting. His son's impulsive, unpredictable behavior frightened him.

"What he indicates is that the date of onset of all of these symptoms of abuse was a few months after A.J. came to live in the Schwarz home."

At the time of A.J.'s discharge from the psychiatric hospital, there was a very angry telephone conversation between the social worker and Jessica Schwarz. In this exchange, Jessica indicated that she was not going to come up there, and if they wanted to discharge him, they could discharge him. However, they'd have to bring him back home because she wasn't going to come and get him.

"It's hard to have family therapy without a family?" Cupp proffered.

Dr. Rahaim agreed.

"I certainly thought that the child needed to be removed from that home. It was my opinion that the child was a targeted child, he was being abused, and that the best thing we could do to protect him was to get him out of there.

"I felt that this child was at terrible risk. I thought he was at the end of his rope. I thought we had to get him out of there quick."

CHAPTER 19

He told me that he didn't want to talk to his natural mother because she and her men friends had been mean to him in the past. He said they had beaten him with belts and belt buckles. He said he wants to remain with his dad.

—Janie Sutherland

The prosecution rested its case and Rendell Brown called Janie Sutherland to the witness stand as the first witness for the defense. She was employed by the Juvenile Justice Department, but in 1991, she worked for HRS in Child Protective Services.

"I was given a caseload and it was my responsibility to monitor that particular case. My duties included home visits, court, and basically just supervising the child."

She was neither present at the dependency hearing on August 17, 1990, when Andrew Schwarz was adjudicated dependent and placed under protective supervision, nor at a review hearing on November 19, 1990, when A.J. and Patsy were placed in the custody of David and Jessica Schwarz. She was aware that the children had lived with a maternal aunt before being placed with the Schwarzes.

As a part of her duties, she became involved with the supervision of A.J. and Patsy during the time that both children were living with Jessica and David.

The purpose of home visits was to monitor the case and to make sure that there wasn't any abuse or neglect going on in the home, and to inspect the physical surroundings to make sure the home was adequately kept, safe, and clean. She was to make unscheduled and unannounced visits, with the expectation that if something was going on, there wouldn't be a chance to cover it up.

"Most of the time when you visit the home, you try to get the family—the mother and the father and the children—there when you conduct. A lot of times it's done one-on-one because you want to talk to them to find out if there are things going on in the home that you should know about."

Sutherland discussed the need for counseling and therapy with the defendant, and Jessica told her that she had signed up A.J. for special classes in school and expressed a desire to get both of them in counseling. She agreed that A.J. needed extensive counseling and therapy.

"From my recollection, they appeared to have adjusted well to the new placement."

On February 20, 1991, Sutherland visited the Schwarzes because she had received a report from a protective investigator that "something" had occurred in the home. Because there had been an allegation of abuse, she was specifically looking for scars, bruises, or a difference in their attitude and behavior.

"You're looking for physical evidence in the home—all sorts of things."

Brown: And when you saw them, how did they appear?
Sutherland: It appeared that nothing was wrong.
Brown: They appeared fine, just fine?
Sutherland: Just fine.

On March 13, 1991, she had made a regular home visit and her observations regarding the children were that "everything appeared to be intact—the kids appeared to be okay." They were in counseling and therapy.

When she visited on May 7, 1991, she observed that A.J. "seemed very hyper, but for the most part—other than that—everything was fine."

Sutherland testified that, according to her notes, when she visited on August 16, 1991, the children had just eaten lunch and were playing outside in the pool, including A.J.

"Incidentally, did Jessica say any nice things about A.J.?" Brown posed.

"She said that he had done better in school despite the fact that he still has problems retaining information. She said he did better," Sutherland replied.

During an office visit with A.J. and Patsy on August 30, 1991, A.J. again was very hyper and disruptive.

Her observation on October 15, 1991, was that they both "looked well and healthy and are doing much better in school."

After his six-week hospitalization, she visited A.J. on April 13, 1992, and he told her he was "doing good" and that his behavior and grades were good and had improved.

"He told me that he didn't want to talk to his natural mother because she and her men friends had been mean to him in the past. He said they had beaten him with belts and belt buckles. He said he wants to remain with his dad."

Brown: Now, from the beginning of your supervision with him, up to this point had he told you anything like that about Mrs. Schwarz—Jessica?
Sutherland: No.
Brown: And had you seen any evidence of anything like that from Jessica Schwarz?
Sutherland: No.

When Sutherland made an unannounced visit to the Schwarz home on May 8, 1992, only A.J. and his stepsister, Lauren, were at the house. A.J. explained that his stepmother had gone to the store and would be right back.

A.J. told her that when he went to court on May 1, the judge in Broward County spoke to him in his chambers and told him that his natural mother was ordered not to see him—she had no visitation rights.

"He said that also applied to Patsy."

A.J. told her that he was doing fine and that there were no problems and she testified that she did not observe any scars or bruises that day.

She told the jurors that during the period of time that she was making visits to the Schwarz home, no one in the neighborhood—adult or child—had ever come to her and told her anything about any problems with A.J. And even though she had visited with Patsy on numerous occasions, sometimes outside the presence of Jessica, Patsy had never told her about anything improper that Jessica was doing to A.J.

In fact, when Patsy left the Schwarz home, Sutherland was the one who drove her away from the house and had talked to her during the ride.

Brown: And she never once ever mentioned to you anything about Jessica Schwarz doing anything to that child, did she?
Sutherland: No.

On cross-examination, Janie Sutherland said she didn't recall who Patsy's teachers were during the time she was supervising her, but that she had spoken to one of them on one occasion. Just prior to Patsy being moved out of the Schwarz home, Sutherland had picked her up from school and had a conversation with the teacher about Patsy being upset.

Cupp: Prior to that, did you ever have a conversation with her teacher?
Sutherland: I don't think so.
Cupp: How about Andrew—who was Andrew's teachers during that time period?
Sutherland: I don't remember.
Cupp: Was there ever a time when you knew? At the

time that you were supervising Andrew, did you know who his teachers were?

Sutherland: I basically dealt with his therapist.

Cupp: So you never spoke with his teachers for any reason?

Sutherland: I may have. I can't recall at this time.

Cupp: Is there anything in your records that would refresh your recollection?

Sutherland: I don't think so.

Cupp: So, it's fair to say if it's not in your records, you never talked to them?

Sutherland: I may have. I don't recall.

Cupp: Wouldn't that be something that you would note in your records if you talked to a child's teacher to verify how they were doing, or if there were any problems you would note that—just like you would note when you go out to the home?

Sutherland: Yes. (She reluctantly admitted that some of her monthly "visits" were telephonic.)

Cupp: In fact, you could go an entire month without seeing the child if things were going along reasonably well. You could call up just to check in and see how everything was going; is that right?

Sutherland: I may.

Cupp: So, it's fair to say that the source of information for you in determining whether or not the child or children were doing okay, [it] would be the family, right? That's all you had to go on, was what Jessica said was going on?

Sutherland: No, home visits, and I talked frequently with their therapist or their counselor. (She admitted there was a period of time when A.J. was having a difficult time getting to counseling and he had missed quite a few sessions.)

Cupp: Isn't it fair to say that when A.J. would tell you about his wishes and wants, you really don't know

what the source of that information was—you don't know if that was him telling you his true wants, or somebody else telling him, "This is what you better say"?
Sutherland: No, I don't.

The next witness for the defense, Joan Wyllner, testified that she had been employed by HRS in several different positions for approximately 5½ years. In her capacity as a protective services officer, the management of A.J.'s case had been transferred to her, and as part of her duties, she visited the Schwarz home approximately once a month and kept records of her involvement.

When she arrived at the Schwarz home on August 20, 1992, she observed that the house was in a nice area and that there was a pool in the backyard and a security fence. In terms of cleanliness, it "appeared to be acceptable."

She visited again in September and October and saw no evidence that A.J. was being physically abused.

Brown: What are you looking for when you visit with a child?
Wyllner: Whether there's any indication of abuse, obvious neglect, whether the house is unsafe, if there's food in the refrigerator, if the child is receiving medical care, things along that line are things that we would look for.
Brown: And up to this date you haven't seen anything?
Wyllner: Nothing beyond our guidelines.

She continued her monthly visits and, on more than one occasion, she talked to A.J. about his feelings in regard to living with his father and stepmother.

"He wanted to stay with his father."

Even though the household, of course, included Jessica, he specifically said he wanted to be with his father—to stay with his father—and he did not want to have contact with his natural mother.

Brown: Did he ever mention anything to you about Patsy?
Wyllner: That he didn't want contact with either of them.
Brown: Now you've told us that Andrew indicated he wanted to be where he was. Did you get any indication that he was not wanted there?
Wyllner: I don't recall any specific statement like that, no, sir.

On cross-examination, Wyllner testified that the supervision of Andrew Schwarz was done as a courtesy to Broward County, where the case originated, and that her unit had him for a relatively brief period of time—approximately five or six months.

Cupp: It was not too long after you got into the case that you made it known, in a letter, you thought you had this situation figured out, right? You wrote a letter?
Wyllner: I wrote a letter requesting guidance from Broward.
Cupp: The point of your letter is you thought that protective supervision needed to fold up their tent and go home—these folks didn't need it?
Wyllner: I was reacting—that was the letter I wrote, yes, sir.
Cupp: And it accurately reflected your opinion—based upon your time with the case and dealing with the family—that you didn't think they needed protective supervision services any longer?
Wyllner: Given what I had in the file at the time, no, sir, I didn't.
Cupp: Because you-all have a pretty heavy caseload?
Wyllner: Yes, sir.
Cupp: If you can reduce it by one, you can spend more time with the others?
Wyllner: Yes, sir.
Cupp: By the way, had you reviewed anything about the Vero Beach hospitalization of A.J.?

Wyllner: I believe I had a copy of a report in the file.

Cupp: Did you review it?

Wyllner: I read it over.

Cupp: What did you learn from that; what do you remember learning?

Wyllner: I really don't recall any details about it other than he was on some kind of medication when he left Vero Beach.

Cupp: Did you also become aware that one of the big problems with his hospitalization was nobody was coming to see him?

Wyllner: No, sir, I don't recall.

Cupp: So you didn't read that?

Wyllner: I don't recall.

Cupp: Nobody made you aware of that?

Wyllner: I don't recall being told that.

Cupp: Did you learn that part of his problem was that his family was not coming up there participating in his therapy? Did you learn that before you wrote that letter?

Wyllner: I don't recall that.

Cupp: Do you think that would have been important to know?

Wyllner: I was going with what I understood at the time.

Cupp: Did you read his discharge summary?

Wyllner: I read over the file. I don't have any clear recollection of what specific things were included, no, sir.

Cupp: So, you don't know whether or not this little boy came out of Vero Beach as a pretty vulnerable kid? You don't know that? You didn't know it then and you don't know it now?

Wyllner: He was supposed to be in therapy, so I assume there were things to be done by the therapist, yes, sir.

Cupp: How were they doing in therapy during the six months that you had them? Were they going?

Wyllner: I believe they were. When I spoke with the

guardian, he said that they were going to counseling on a steady basis. I had been told, by Mrs. Schwarz, that she made arrangements for him to be seen in South County.

Wyllner didn't recall ever talking to A.J.'s guidance counselor, but said it was possible that she talked to his teacher, because she had spoken with "someone at school," but didn't recall who it was.

"Did you learn from Dr. Zimmern that he was prohibited—by Mrs. Schwarz—from speaking with A.J.'s guidance counselor? Did you learn that?" Cupp questioned.

Wyllner said no.

She then testified that in January 1993—when there was an allegation that the defendant had physically abused A.J.—she was transferring into another unit and was not seeing clients at that time.

Cupp: I'm not sure I understand. Were you the supervising worker or not?

Wyllner: I was still on the file as a supervision worker, yes, sir.

Cupp: What's the difference between a protective supervision and child protective investigator?

Wyllner: The investigator is the one that gets the abuse call and goes out and does the actual on-site investigation to determine whether the allegation is confirmed or not.

Cupp: And that wouldn't be your job—that would be somebody else?

Wyllner: That's somebody else's, yes.

Cupp: And you recall that this one in January—that worker was Barbara Black?

Wyllner: I believe so, yes, sir.

Cupp: And you know that because you talked to her before she went out there, didn't you?

Wyllner: I talked to her the day that she—yes.

Cupp: Before she went out?

Wyllner: Yes.

Cupp: And you told Barbara—before she went out—that this sounded like, or words to this effect: that there was probably nothing to it; that your understanding from dealing with the case was that Ilene—the biological mother—was always in the neighborhood stirring up [trouble] and calling in false reports. Didn't you give Barbara Black that type of information?

Wyllner: That was my understanding, yes, sir.

Cupp: You knew the biological mother to be Ilene?

Wyllner: I knew—yes, sir.

Cupp: Ma'am, do you recall when Barbara Black spoke to you, she told you that the person who called in the complaint was a person by the name of Ilene [*sic*], but she didn't know the last name? Do you recall that?

Wyllner: I—no, sir.

Cupp: You've had occasion to have seen this [abuse report], haven't you—the one that we are talking about regarding the January incident?

Wyllner: It was probably in the file. I haven't seen it since. The reporter information is not supposed to be on it when we get it. It's usually available to the investigator, but most of ours did not include it when we got the copy.

Cupp: If I hand you a copy of it that contained the information about the reporter, might that refresh your recollection as to who the reporter was?

Wyllner: Possibly.

Cupp (handing her the report): Just look at it in terms of the reporter information, if you will, ma'am?

Wyllner: It says, "Ilene."

Cupp: It says, "Ilene unknown"?

Wyllner: Yes, sir, spelled the way I understand the mother to spell her name.

Cupp: So you made an assumption, when Barbara Black called you, that the source of the report for these allegations of two black eyes and a suspected broken nose was the biological mother?

Wyllner: I don't recall what I thought, at the time.

Cupp: But that's what you told Barbara Black, isn't it?

Wyllner: That there had been earlier situations where the natural mother had tried to cause problems and was involved in court issues with the Schwarz family.

Cupp: And you didn't know that a neighbor—a new neighbor—moved in across the street by the name of Eileen Callahan?

Wyllner: No, sir, I didn't know the name of any neighbors.

Cupp: So you came to the assumption and you conveyed that to Barbara Black and she went out there that day with that assumption?

Wyllner: She went out there that day. What she thought, I don't know.

Cupp: But she spoke to you before she went out there?

Wyllner: Okay.

Cupp: You don't do this kind of work anymore, do you?

Wyllner: No, sir.

CHAPTER 20

He had a very low self-esteem. This is one of the things I was working on and A.J. wanted to be accepted so badly he would play the role of whatever you want him to do, to be accepted.

—Edwin Carpenter

The following day, August 30, 1994, the next witness for the defense was Edwin Carpenter, a Juvenile Family counselor with the Department of Public Safety, Division of Youth Affairs.

"We, as a service, are a family counseling service, voluntary, meaning that the client has to volunteer. They may enter or leave the service at any time. We go into the home or into the school or whatever is needed to work with the family with whatever problems we see. Basically, we're short term, three months, but sometimes we go beyond that. Volunteer means that even if they are referred, they have to agree to the counseling, or the service is not available."

He testified that no one who received this counseling was under a court order to be there, and that he had counseled Mr. and Mrs. Schwarz and A.J., having been in their home eleven times between May 21, 1991, and September 24, 1991. Also, he had seen A.J. at school on five different occasions, and he claimed that Jessica had not resisted his efforts to talk with the boy at school.

Carpenter stated that the conditions in the home were "very sufficient" and he had not observed any signs that A.J. was being abused.

Brown: Did the Schwarzes pay for these services?
Carpenter: No.
Brown: Were there occasions when you talked with Andrew alone?
Carpenter: Sometimes in the home we'd go to his room, other times in the living room, and then at the school I'd be dealing with him.

Carpenter explained that when he first started working with A.J., he made an agreement with him that he did not have to talk about anything that he didn't want to, but that if he did talk, he had to tell him the truth. The counselor explained to him that later he would have to tell the court what A.J. really wanted, so they would need to talk about things so he would know what to say.

A.J. told him that he wanted to live with his father; he did not want to go back to his natural mother because of "the way he was treated there." The counselor didn't think A.J. had told him about all the "bad things" that had happened while he was living with his natural mother because sometimes A.J. would say, "I don't want to talk about them."

Brown: Did he ever—in that conversation—tell you that while living with Jessica Schwarz, bad things were happening?
Carpenter: No.
Brown: What else did he tell you, other than not wanting to live with his mom who did bad things to him?
Carpenter: He said that he never felt loved. He felt his father loved him.
Brown: What about his stepmother?
Carpenter: He said she loved him in her own way. His

definition of love was taking care of him and he said, "She takes care of me."

Carpenter suggested to the family that it would help A.J. if they would show him physical affection—by hugging him and getting close to him.

"I never observed this, but they would sit close to him and put their arms around him."

When HRS asked the counselor to make recommendations, he suggested that the family have long-term counseling.

"Now, once you make the recommendation, do you know who carries it through or who's supposed to carry it through?" Brown queried.

Carpenter answered, "The family."

On cross-examination, Carpenter admitted that he did not know what went on in the Schwarz home when he was not there.

Cupp: Didn't it disturb you that one of the things that you observed was A.J.'s definition of love—in regards to his stepmother—was she takes care of him; did that disturb you a little bit?

Carpenter: Yes, it did. Because, knowing what he had told me about his previous family life, I thought he needed more than just taking care of—but taking care of was very important to him.

Cupp: He needed hugs and kisses?

Carpenter: He needed a lot of help with emotional—maintaining his emotional balance.

Cupp: Did you ever hear the expression "Throwing gasoline on a fire"?

Carpenter: Yes.

Cupp: Last thing [he needed] to be told by his stepmother is that she hated him?

Carpenter: That would be devastating to him.

Cupp: The last thing he needed to be told by his step-mother was that he was a useless piece of shit?

Carpenter: This would be devastating to him.

Cupp: The last thing he needed was to have his step-mother force him to eat a cockroach?

Carpenter: Yes.

Cupp: What would that do?

Carpenter: He had a very low self-esteem. This is one of the things I was working on and A.J. wanted to be accepted so badly he would play the role of whatever you want him to do, to be accepted.

Cupp: He wanted to be loved?

Carpenter: Yes.

Cupp: He wanted her to love him?

Carpenter: Yes.

Cupp: Did you see any evidence that she ever, in fact, loved him?

Carpenter: You'll have to define love because in A.J.'s terms—taking care of him—she loved him. I think she tried in what she defined as love.

Cupp: And again, the time period that you dealt with, I mean, you were wrapped up and done by September of 1991?

Carpenter: That's correct. (He had never seen A.J. in 1992 or 1993.)

Cupp: You don't know what the dates of these offenses are, do you?

Carpenter: I have no idea.

Cupp: Mrs. Schwarz didn't have to do anything as far as this counseling; all she had to do was be home?

Carpenter: That's correct.

Cupp: She didn't have to go anywhere, write anything down?

Carpenter: No.

Cupp: She didn't have to pay?

Carpenter: No.

Cupp: All she had to do was sit on the couch?

Carpenter: Correct.

Cupp: Isn't it true that they knew that what they told you—you were going to turn around and tell HRS?

Carpenter: Yes.

Cupp: So that everything that A.J. would tell you he knew would get back to Jessica, right?

Carpenter: Not necessarily. The rules of confidentiality would not allow me to tell the family what he told me in private. I would only tell in open court with a subpoena.

Cupp: Did you explain the rules of confidentiality to A.J.?

Carpenter: Yes.

Cupp: Do you think he understood you?

Carpenter: Yes.

Cupp: Do you think he believed you?

Carpenter: Yes, because at times he would say, "I don't want to talk about it," because he understood our contract with each other.

Cupp: Did he tell you that he didn't want to talk about things [in] reference to his stepmother and the home?

Carpenter: Sometimes he just wouldn't talk.

Cupp: Just wouldn't talk?

Carpenter: Yes.

Sandra Warren, who had been employed by HRS, Child Protection Services, for eighteen months, was the next witness for the defense. She explained that when visiting with children under her charge, she always checked to see if there were any visible marks on the child.

"We don't necessarily lift their clothing or anything like that every time we visit them, but we check to see if there's anything readily visible and then we just talk with them. It depends on what particular problem occurred that got us involved with the family as to what kinds of things we may be discussing."

Warren testified that she explains to the child—to the best of her ability—that what he says is going to be kept confidential and tries to ascertain that the child understands that.

When she first visited with A.J. on March 17, 1993, he was in his bedroom, lying on the bed, and she talked alone with him.

Brown: Did you talk with him about his natural mother and sister?

Warren: Yes. He told about his feelings about them. He told me that he did not like to talk about them, that he would feel sick when he would think about them.

Brown: Isn't it true that what he really said, "It makes me actually throw up"?

Warren: Well, in my notes when I made that reference, it's referring to when his mother is actually around.

She had participated in a meeting—a roundtable discussion—about the Schwarz family and A.J., and as a result of that meeting, a conclusion was made regarding Andrew Schwarz's placement with Jessica and David.

"It was felt that he should stay where he was at, with some changes in discipline and controlling his behavior and such. The child had indicated to those that were at this meeting that that's where he wanted to be."

According to the report from the March 26, 1993, meeting: "In the end it was decided that this is still the best placement for Andrew and that he's happy there and obviously loves them both very much."

Brown: Do you recall how many notes or how many notations in your file you made of bruises?

Warren: I don't recall how many.

Brown: Did you make any?

Warren: Yes. I know of one specific area that I made a

notation of a bruise. That would have been on March 17. He had bruises under his eyes and over the bridge of his nose.

Brown: Did you personally ask Andrew how that happened?

Warren: Yes. Something to do with some sort of a bike accident.

Brown: He had a bike accident and hurt himself; isn't that what he told you?

Warren: Yes, that's what he told me.

The "bike accident" happened on January 24 and, indeed, Dr. Richard Zimmern observed A.J. with two black eyes and a swollen nose on January 26. Sandra Warren saw the "bruises under his eyes and over the bridge of his nose" on March 17. Seven weeks later, the bruises were still visible.

Sadly—tragically—the cross-examination was notable because it showed—as it had with the previous defense witnesses, with the possible exception of Edwin Carpenter—how little the very people who were supposed to be protecting him knew about Andrew Schwarz.

Cupp: At the time that you entered A.J.'s life, do you know how many people—HRS, counselors, and doctors—he had seen by that time?

Warren: No.

Cupp: It was a bunch, wasn't it?

Warren: I have since learned that.

Cupp: Isn't one of the first things you do when you pick up a case is review—or try to review—what's occurred with the child prior to the time you get the case; you want to know the background, right?

Warren: That's correct.

Cupp: Who was the worker before you?

Warren: Joan Wyllner.

Cupp: Who was the worker before Joan Wyllner?

Warren: I don't recall.

Cupp: Do you know who Janie Sutherland is?

Warren: Yes.

Cupp: She's a supervision worker just like you?

Warren: She was, at that point.

Cupp: You didn't come across her name at some point?

Warren: I don't recall.

Cupp: Did you review the records?

Warren: I reviewed the records that were in the file.

Cupp: And who's Edwin Carpenter?

Warren: I don't recall.

Cupp: Do you know him as a counselor?

Warren: I've only recently met him, so at that time I did not know him.

Cupp: But you did not come across anything in the records, or did you know that A.J. had seen Edwin Carpenter?

Warren: Him specifically, no. Not that I recall anyway.

Cupp: Did you review the Vero Beach psychiatric records?

Warren: Yes.

Cupp: How was the counseling going with A.J., the family counseling, the individual counseling?

Warren: At the time I was involved with the case, it was not going at all—they were not going.

Cupp: Cause you any concerns?

Warren: Yes.

Cupp: Why?

Warren: Why what?

Cupp: Why did it cause you concerns?

Warren: Because according to what I had seen in the file, he needed to be in counseling—or being treated, I should say—at South County Mental Health.

Cupp: What about the family counseling?

Warren: I don't recall any—my feelings about it—at the time.

Cupp: Did you review the discharge recommendations by Dr. Uttley?

Warren: I don't recognize that name.

Cupp: Did you review the discharge summaries from the Vero Beach psychiatric hospitalization?

Warren: Yes.

Cupp: Do you recall what they were?

Warren: No.

Cupp: Do you know if any of the recommendations— were any of them being implemented by Mrs. Schwarz or by anybody?

Warren: I don't recall the recommendations, so I can't speak of them.

Cupp: Was he on imipramine, to your knowledge?

Warren: He had been. I don't believe he was at the time I was involved with the case.

Cupp: Why not?

Warren: Why wasn't he?

Cupp: Yes, ma'am.

Warren: There was a problem with Medicaid and communication between South County that was providing that for him and him being able to access it.

Cupp: So he just wasn't on imipramine?

Warren: To my knowledge, he wasn't.

Cupp: And he wasn't in family counseling?

Warren: To my knowledge, he wasn't.

Cupp: And he wasn't in individual counseling?

Warren: That I don't know.

Cupp: You were his protection supervision worker, weren't you?

Warren: Yes.

Cupp: That's your responsibility to know what's going on with the child?

Warren: Right.

Cupp: You don't know whether he was in individual counseling?

Warren: I had this case for a very short time. I spent
most of it trying to find the answers to those questions.
Cupp: Now, at this meeting when it was decided by the
powers-that-be that A.J. would stay where he was at,
Dottie Daniels was at that meeting, wasn't she?
Warren: Yes.

Cupp established that Dottie Daniels was a child protective
investigator supervisor. It was a child protective investigator's
responsibility to respond to and investigate calls that came into
the abuse hot line, which was not part of Sandra Warren's
duties because she was a protective supervision worker.

Cupp: But you have access to their reports, don't you?
Warren: Yes.
Cupp: And, in fact, one of the things that you have to
do when you get on the case, to properly supervise it,
is you have to be aware of any prior abuse complaints
and what happened?
Warren: That's correct.

Scott Cupp knew that one of the reasons it was decided at
the meeting that it was all right to leave A.J. in the Schwarz
home was that Dottie Daniels, Barbara Black's supervisor,
had stated—in no uncertain terms—that it was her opinion
that all the abuse complaints coming from the neighbors
were harassment. Also, she felt it was "going to cease," and
that it was directly as a result of the biological mother.

Cupp: Did you know Dottie Daniels to be Barbara
Black's supervisor, at that time?
Warren: Yes.
Cupp: Was Barbara Black at that meeting?
Warren: Yes.
Cupp: Was Barbara Black, child protective investiga-
tor, assigned to go out and investigate these allega-
tions that led to the black eyes and the bruised nose?

Warren: I don't know specifically what the allegation was at the time she went out.

Cupp: But you know her to be the investigator who went out on that particular call?

Warren: I don't know that.

Cupp: What counseling or what therapy or treatment was A.J. receiving for his bed-wetting problem?

Warren: I don't believe I've discussed that with anyone. I don't know.

Cupp: Nobody—Mrs. Schwarz never reported to you that she was having a problem with A.J. wetting the bed?

Warren: Not that I recall.

Cupp: That's something that you would note?

Warren: Yes, it would be.

Cupp: Why would you note that?

Warren: Because a child of that age—that might be an indicator of some other problems, something might be causing that.

Cupp: Like?

Warren: If it were something that happened on a regular basis.

Cupp: Like?

Warren: I don't—I'm not an expert in that field. I don't know.

Cupp: But you've received training in the area of child abuse, haven't you?

Warren: Yes.

Cupp: That's what you do. That's what you were doing at the time; you were dealing with abused and neglected children, correct?

Warren: Correct.

Cupp: Haven't you been taught that it's one of the hallmark indicators of abuse—if the bed-wetting is not tied to a physical problem?

Warren: Bed-wetting may be an indicator of a physical problem or possibly abuse problem.

Cupp: Assuming—assuming it's not tied to a physical problem, aren't you taught that's one of the hallmark indicators of stress on a child?

Warren: I can't recall if that was ever mentioned in any of my training.

Cupp: Okay. Is it fair to say from your involvement with Andrew that probably the most important thing in his life at that time was school?

Warren: I never discussed it in those terms with him. I really don't know.

Cupp: You didn't get that impression?

Warren: I don't know.

Cupp: But you did testify on direct that you were aware of the incident—the bicycle accident—and you spoke with Andrew about that?

Warren: What I knew of that accident was what Andrew told me.

Scott Cupp knew, in fact, that Barbara Black had made it known in writing that she had concerns about Andrew being able to tell the truth.

Cupp: You know that Barbara Black was indicted as a result of her activity?

Warren: I don't know what happened with Barbara Black.

Cupp: You don't know what happened with Barbara Black?

Warren: I did not follow that.

Cupp: No further questions.

Years later, when asked about Sandra Warren, Scott Cupp replied, "I couldn't pick her out of a lineup." But he remembered quite clearly what he was feeling as he cross-examined her: "Anger, disgust, utter frustration. If ever [in my opinion] one person in that inept agency personified their overall incompetence, it was her—only she was incompetence with an attitude."

CHAPTER 21

*We tried to instill in the kids common sense and com-
mon decency even if we did not have too much money.*

—Helen Woods

Lauren Cross, now almost twelve years old, was the next
witness for the defense. Her testimony was intriguing and
notable, but not surprising, in that she contradicted almost
everything that over a dozen prosecution witnesses—neighbors and their children—had sworn was the truth. And many
times, she spoke of A.J. in the present tense.

She did, indeed, attempt to paint the Schwarz family life
as quite "normal" and emphatically rejected each of the
abuse allegations against her mother. According to Lauren,
Jessica did the cooking for the family, but sometimes Bear
fixed biscuits and gravy for breakfast on Sunday. Her mom
always cooked enough food for all the children, no one was
denied any food, and A.J. was never put on a diet other than
their regular meals. His food was not different from Lauren,
Jackie, and Patsy's, and they ate as a family—in the kitchen.

Brown: Do you recall an incident when Gail Ragatz
came to your home and your mother made Andrew sit
on the floor near the cat litter box and eat his dinner?
Lauren: No, he never did that. He always ate at the table.

Brown: Did you ever see your mother handle a cock-roach?
Lauren: No, she doesn't like bugs.
Brown: Do you ever recall a time when A.J.'s mouth was taped shut by anyone in your house?
Lauren: No.

On and on, it went. All the children were allowed play-time—including A.J. Jessica—and sometimes Patsy or Lauren—helped A.J. with his homework.

Brown: Did Andrew have any toys?
Lauren: Yes, he had quite a bit of Ninja Turtles and re-mote control cars and trucks, and he had a big teddy bear thing or something like that and stuffed toys.
Brown: Were these the things that Andrew enjoyed playing with?
Lauren: Yes.

She said that A.J. had a bicycle but was not allowed to ride it to school.
"We tried it once but he almost got hit by a car and he's not too careful, so he walked."
Lauren admitted that sometimes she got in trouble with her mom. For punishment, Lauren would have to take a bas-ket of unmatched socks into her room and match them up, or a television show would be taken away for the night, or "just something simple like that." Jessica did not hit her—or A.J.

Brown: Now, when your mother talked to you when you got in trouble, how did she talk to you?
Lauren: Loud. She didn't talk, she yelled—well, not like bad or anything, but she wasn't calm either.
Brown: Did you ever hear her yell at anybody else?
Lauren: Yes. Everybody. Almost everybody yelled at each other once in a while in the house.

Brown: What about neighbors; did you ever see her yell at the neighbors?

Lauren: Yes.

Brown: Was she just a kind of person who yelled when she got upset?

Lauren: Yes.

Jessica got upset and yelled at A.J.—just as she did Lauren—when he didn't do his homework. Her mother was concerned about A.J.'s schoolwork and about him getting his work done.

"That's why she yells and tells him to do better."

Lauren said that when she had a chore to do—like cleaning her room—she had to stick with it until it was finished, but she was allowed to stop and eat dinner and then go back to her chores. And she claimed it was the same way with A.J.

Both David and A.J. cleaned the garage, and since A.J. liked to mow the lawn—and David had taught him how to use the weed whacker—the upkeep of the yard was A.J.'s responsibility. And, of course, she had never seen A.J. use household scissors to trim the yard.

They had a party for A.J.'s birthday in 1993 with cake and presents, and "we had his friends come over." He was allowed to invite anyone he wanted.

Lauren did not recall a time when it was raining and A.J. had to walk to school while she rode in her mother's car.

Brown: Did that ever happen?

Lauren: No, we all—she drove us. My mom drove us.

Brown: Would A.J. be in the car when it rained?

Lauren: Yes.

Brown: I want you to think about this question, and tell me if you ever recall coming home and Andrew running—or your mother ordering Andrew to run—down the street naked?

Lauren: That never happened.

Brown: Do you ever recall hearing your mother ordering A.J. to take off all of his clothes?
Lauren: No, she'd never do that; she never did.

And she had never seen her mother keep A.J. home from
school for punishment—or go to school to get him and bring
him home to do a chore. Lauren claimed that A.J. got sick more
than the rest of them because he was "thinner and skinnier."

Brown: Now, do you recall what kind of illnesses he had?
Lauren: Stomach virus. I think he had the flu once and
he had a stomach virus a lot. Sometimes he'd just go to
the bathroom and throw up.
Brown: Did he do that a lot?
Lauren: Yeah.

She had never seen A.J. wearing a T-shirt with any writing
on it—other than T-shirts that were bought with words im-
printed on them.

Brown: Lauren, I don't want to embarrass you, but I
want to ask you this question: did you ever hear your
mother say to Andrew, "I hate your fucking guts"?
Lauren: No.
Brown: Did you ever hear her say to him, "You're a
useless piece of shit"?
Lauren: No.

In reference to A.J. wetting the bed, Lauren said she did
not recall a time when her mother rubbed A.J.'s nose in the
wet sheets.

Brown: Did you ever see this happen?
Lauren: No.
Brown: Did Andrew ever tell you that it happened?
Lauren: No, because it never did.

According to the young girl, her mother tried to stop the bed-wetting problem by reading a home remedies book. When A.J. had to go to the bathroom, Jessica would tell him to wait for five minutes before he went—to strengthen his bladder.

Brown: How did you get your school supplies?
Lauren: My mother would take me out and buy them.
Brown: How did Andrew get his school supplies?
Lauren: Same way. We'd go together and we'd both have our list and we'd do his list and then go clothes shopping and then go home.
Brown: Now, Lauren, when did you first meet me?
Lauren: Today.
Brown: Have you discussed any of these matters—about which you have testified to—with your mother?
Lauren: No.
Brown: You understood the oath you took to tell the truth?
Lauren: Yes.
Brown: So help you God?
Lauren: Yes.
Brown: Have you told the whole truth?
Lauren: Yes.

Even though she was incarcerated, it seemed that Jessica Schwarz had the ability to control what her children told others about their home life—even under oath. The young girl was no doubt—if nothing else—the victim of her mother's intimidation. Not to mention the fact that Lauren had witnessed firsthand what her mother was capable of doing to a child.

The next witness for the defense was Jessica's mother, Helen Woods, who testified that she lived in Palm Bay with her husband and her two granddaughters, Lauren and Jackie. She and her husband had moved there two years earlier from Long Island, New York, where Jessica had grown up along with her older sister.

Mrs. Woods testified that she didn't think her method of discipline with her children was different from anybody else's.

"If the kids did anything wrong, privileges were taken away."

If they didn't finish their meal "properly" or eat as much as she thought they should, they did not get dessert or get to watch television. They had to go to their room, play there, and "that was it."

While Jessica was growing up, Mrs. Woods learned that her daughter wanted to become a truck driver.

"Did she realize that dream? Did she become a truck driver?" Brown asked.

Helen stated that yes, she did.

Like Lauren before her, Mrs. Woods described the Schwarz family and their lives as nothing out of the ordinary.

"A.J. was into Ninjas—the Ninja Turtles—and I myself bought him quite a few every birthday, Christmas; also [I got him] a wooden toolbox with little miniature tools that boys could use. He had a couple of board games, but I really couldn't tell you names of them because the kids always interchanged their toys anyway. He had trucks. He loved the little miniature cars and I had gotten him—for one of the birthdays or something—a carrying case for all of these little cars."

Jessica had also bought toys for A.J. and, "of course," she allowed him to play with them—and with other children. And A.J. had a bicycle. Both she and Jessica bought A.J. his school supplies, but "I think, by and large, it was Jessica who paid for most of the school supplies, but I did—even if it was just pencils—just to let him know that we cared."

Jessica cooked the meals and there was no scarcity of food.

"She cooked very balanced meals and lots of it. The biggest eater was Andrew."

Brown: Did you ever witness Jessica feeding Andrew bread and water for dinner?
Woods: No.
Brown: Did you ever see your daughter playing with cockroaches?
Woods: No, no, no way at all. First of all, we did not have cockroaches in our house. If I had spotted one, I'd have the exterminator there the next day. But I never saw her playing with any sort of bugs or cockroaches or whatever.

When Mrs. Woods stayed with the children for about a week while Jessica was in the hospital, A.J. walked to school while Lauren rode her bike, but if it rained, she drove them.

Brown: During the time that you were in the home, did Jessica ever tell you to keep Andrew at home as punishment? At home from school, I mean?
Woods: Definitely not, no.
Brown: Did you ever see Jessica hugging Andrew?
Woods: Yes, I have.
Brown: How often did you see her hug him?
Woods: Well, as I say, I wasn't a constant visitor down there and I can't say that it happened three times a day or anything like that, but I've seen her on occasions hug Andrew the way she hugged Lauren and Jackie. (She had heard Jessica yell at A.J. and the other children as well.)
Brown: Did you ever hear her use profanity with the children?
Woods: Certain words, yes.
Brown: You have never seen Jessica rub Andrew's nose in urine-soaked linen, have you?
Woods: Definitely no.

Brown: Do you recall, ma'am, Andrew, along with Jessica and the rest of the family, visiting your home Christmas of 1992?

Woods: Yes.

Brown: Did you have an opportunity to observe Andrew and the way he acted, talked, and things of that sort?

Woods: Yes.

Brown: Now, did your grandson walk like a zombie at that point?

Woods: No.

Brown: Did he act like a zombie?

Woods: No.

Brown: Was he lucid?

Woods: Yes.

Brown: Was he coherent?

Woods: Absolutely.

When questioned about her observance of A.J.'s table manners, she replied that "his table manners were fine," and that he did not "gulp down his food" as if he had been trained to eat in five minutes.

Brown: Did he eat lots of food?

Woods: He certainly did.

Scott Cupp started his cross-examination by asking Mrs. Woods about Jessica's upbringing.

Cupp: Your daughter did not grow up underprivileged, did she?

Woods: No, she did not.

Cupp: She didn't want for anything?

Woods: Oh, that's carrying it a bit far.

Cupp: Well, she was raised well?

Woods: Yes, she was raised well. We tried to instill in the kids common sense and common decency even if we did not have too much money.

Cupp: She grew up in Glen Cove, Long Island?

Woods: Yes.

Cupp: She lived in the same home her entire life? She wasn't moving around from place to place to place and she had one mother and she had one father?

Woods: Yes.

Cupp: She graduated all the way through the same school system?

Woods: Yes.

Cupp: She had two caring, loving parents? Who tried the very best they could to teach her right from wrong?

Woods: Yes.

Cupp: As far as you know, you did that?

Woods: Yes.

Cupp: Now, you've testified that on approximately five occasions you were in the Triphammer [Road] home. You went there approximately five times?

Woods: I believe so, yes.

Cupp: Over about a four-year span?

Woods: Probably.

Cupp: So, you only can tell us and tell this jury what went on when you were there, right?

Woods: Of course.

Cupp: You don't know what happened when you weren't there?

Woods: No.

CHAPTER 22

I may not be able to clearly define evil for you—not as a black-and-white statement lifted from the pages of a dictionary—but I can say without equivocation that I know it when I see it, and Jessica Schwarz will forever personify it in my eyes.

—Scott Cupp

"This was what I, Scott Cupp, knew about Jessica Schwarz. I knew that she had tapped a dark place inside of me that held every negative emotion I was capable of feeling. I'd experienced hate, loathing, anger, and vengeance, and I knew how detrimental that could be in extracting the truth. I knew that she had come to represent the very heart of evil in my eyes, which might have been a powerful motivator, but if it had blinded me to the facts and the nuances behind the facts—in the end—I would have hurt our case.

"The nefarious image of the woman was—above and beyond all else—directly related to the despicable abuses she had perpetrated, day in and day out, upon A.J., true—but it was more than that. It was the look on her face—part amusement, part vindictive, part raptorial—that conveyed the message that A.J. had gotten exactly what he deserved, and that she was just as happy as a clam to have been the one who saw to it. The psychological pieces that breed remorse did not exist in her.

"Jessica was a brute and a bully, but she wasn't stupid. Intimidation had become an art form for her. She had been successful at intimidating her powerfully built husband to such a degree that he had stood by and allowed her to throw his son around by the neck—and while she forced him to run down the street naked because he wasn't walking home from school fast enough to suit her.

"She had frightened her neighbors so effectively that most of them were afraid to call the police or social services—or anyone else—after hearing Jessica call her stepson names so denigrating you wouldn't address a dog that way. She had so intimidated this innocent ten-year-old—a kid whose biggest crime was a mischievous streak about the same size as any other ten-year-old boy's—that his IQ had dropped from 101 to 86 in less than two years.

"I knew that she—during that time—had destroyed a human being and had taken pleasure in it. I may not be able to clearly define evil for you—not as a black-and-white statement lifted from the pages of a dictionary—but I can say without equivocation that I know it when I see it, and Jessica Schwarz will forever personify it in my eyes.

"What I also knew was that the dark place inside of me was at war with the detachment, the calm, and the professionalism that had characterized my approach to every case I'd ever prosecuted. By the time Jessica took the stand that morning, the war had to be over—the dark place defeated, imprisoned, and silenced.

"I concentrated on my choice of tie, something conservative to go with the charcoal gray suit I'd laid out the night before, and let my mind replay the dream one more time. I knew it well by then, since it had robbed me of much needed sleep for the previous weeks.

I'm traveling by car with my family. It's a black night and the road is deserted. Torrential rain makes driving impossible. I'm as lost as I've ever been. We stop in front of a lonely Tudor mansion overgrown with vines and shrouded in darkness. I venture to the door. No one responds to my knock, so I push past the door and go inside. Not a soul; not a hint of light.

Sheets have been draped over the furniture and the drapes are drawn. I shiver. All at once, I glimpse a flickering light—like flames from a dying fire—coming from a nearby room. I follow it. The room is overwhelmed with chairs—hundreds of them—and the legs of the chairs form an impenetrable lattice.

Beyond the chairs, I see movement. A small, lithe shadow darting frantically in front of the fire. It's A.J. Trapped and inconsolable. When I realize the fire is dying out and the shadow is fading, I wake up. Every time. Even before I can call his name.

"'Okay,' I told myself, 'so you may not be able to call his name or reach out to him—but you can make sure his voice is heard.'"

Finally it was the moment Scott Cupp had been waiting for. Jessica Schwarz's direct testimony had been a marathon—lasting five hours—full of denials and, of course, an explanation for everything.

One of the more memorable moments was when Rendell Brown asked Jessica about the incident with Patsy—when the young girl had allowed the boys to come into the house to use the telephone. Jessica denied punching her with her fist, but she admitted slapping her once with an open hand.

"Well, part of her story was true—I had a rule when my husband and I weren't in the house—I said to all my kids, and this is just something I made up, I guess. I said, 'If somebody knocks at the door, I don't care if it's God handcuffed to a cop, if you didn't dial 911, or pray to God to come on down—don't open the door.'"

And her version of the Holiday Shop completely contradicted the testimony of Mary Idrissi.

"I gave him two dollars to go to the Christmas store. The things are very cheap, inexpensive; so, yes, that's considered a lot for that particular store. He bought a key chain for his father; it was gold—the color gold—with a black inset that said, 'Number one dad.' He bought me a Christmas angel candle and he bought Lauren a big red-and-white pencil that looks like a candy cane and then that's it. He ran out of money, so what he had done for Jackie was he made a homemade hanging ornament for the tree."

Jessica had testified on direct examination that A.J. had had a cat named Bud, but she claimed that "something" happened to it.

"I came in on the tail end of it, but I saw it happening. Bud was a little kitten—fit in the palm of your hand, just about—and Andrew was taking the cat and smashed its head into the wall, and after that, the cat just started hissing and scratching and biting at kids, so I gave it to a family with no children."

And then the final few minutes of her direct testimony with Rendell Brown—several times—referring to A.J. as Jessica's "son":

Brown: You indicated that many of the absences of Andrew Schwarz were unknown to you because nobody sent you reports?

Jessica: Right.

Brown: Did you ever keep him out of school to punish him?

Jessica: No, I did not.

Brown: Did you ever write, "I'm a worthless piece of shit, don't talk to me" on a T-shirt and make Andrew wear it?

Jessica: I never wrote on his shirt, and no, I never did write that. I never did write on anybody's clothes.

Brown: And you never—that scissors stuff never happened?

Jessica: No, no.

Brown: Did you ever make your son run down the street naked?

Jessica: No.

Brown: Did you ever rub your son's nose or face in any bedsheets—any urine-soaked bedsheets?

Jessica: No, I did not.

Brown: Did you ever say to your son, "I hate your fucking guts"?

Jessica: No.

Brown: Did you refer to him as a "useless piece of shit"?

Jessica: No, I did not.

Brown: Did you have any goals or aspirations as relates to your relationship with your son?

Jessica: Yes. I wanted him to be happy and stay at the house and just grow up there with us.

Brown: Did you ever come to a point where you just wanted Andrew out of the house?

Jessica: Yes.

Brown: Did you ever talk to anybody about that?

Jessica: Yes.

Brown: How was that resolved?

Jessica: They just left him in the house.

Brown: Did that upset you?

Jessica: It didn't make any sense to me, but it didn't upset me.

Brown: Where did you want him to be?

Jessica: I wanted him to stay with us in the house, but if that wasn't working, I wanted him—I felt he needed more than once-a-week treatment.

Brown: When you were talking to HRS about the treatment, did you specify to them what you wanted or what you thought he needed?

Jessica: At one point, yeah.

Brown: What was that?

Jessica: Hospitalization.

Scott Cupp reminded himself that if she had told the truth from the beginning, there would be no reason for a trial—and no chance for him to expose her for what she truly was.

It was one o'clock in the afternoon and the heat outside was oppressive and laden with humidity—typical West Palm Beach. Cupp was grateful for the air-conditioning circulating in the courthouse on North Dixie Highway—but a courtroom filled to the brim with people high on anticipation tended to negate the cool air.

He took his seat next to Joe Marx. Clearly, with the loss of his wife and unborn child, the last three months had taken a toll on Joe, but despite the turmoil, he had done his job well.

"Shall we do this thing?"

Joe nodded. "Take her down, chief."

Cupp scanned the defense table. Jessica was wearing the same flower-print dress; her puffy cheeks were blushed with makeup. She didn't look especially comfortable with either the dress or the makeup.

When Judge Colbath entered the courtroom, everyone rose in unison.

At 1:05 P.M., the jurors were escorted back into the courtroom, and as they took their seats, Cupp did his best to make eye contact, but they were more intent on Jessica's short trek back to the witness stand.

After the judge reminded her that she was still under oath, he nodded in the prosecutor's direction and Cupp positioned himself at the lectern.

"Tell us, Mrs. Schwarz, what was Andrew's favorite color?"

She hesitated and lifted her shoulders slightly in a dismissive shrug.

"Blue," she answered in a tone that suggested the lack of importance in the answer.

Scott looked her straight in the eye—the very last thing he wanted was for her to feel comfortable or confident. He wanted the jury to have a clear view of the woman behind the facade that her defense team had attempted to create with their direct examination.

Cupp: Your testimony to this jury is that at nighttime you would go in his bedroom and you would hug Andrew and kiss him good night?

Jessica: I never said I would go in. I said I would hug and kiss him good night.

Cupp: Every night prior to going to bed?

Jessica: Every night, yes.

Cupp: When you were growing up, is that the way your parents treated you?

Jessica: Hugging and kissing before [bed]?

Cupp: Yes.

Jessica: Yes.

Cupp: You weren't abused?

Jessica (a shade of red creeping into her cheeks): No.

Cupp: You weren't told that you were hated? (Every question was asked as if it had "like A.J. was" attached to it.)

Jessica: No, I wasn't.

Cupp: You weren't made to say things that demeaned yourself?

Jessica: No, I wasn't.

Cupp: You weren't made to say things that demeaned yourself in front of your friends? In front of your neighbors?

Jessica (her voice rising): No!

Cupp: You weren't given bizarre punishments? (He told himself to press—not push.)

Jessica: No.

Cupp: You were taught right from wrong?

Jessica: Yes, I was.

Cupp: Did your parents ever punch you?

Jessica: Yes.

(Cupp paused. A hush fell over the courtroom. It was certainly not the answer he had expected.)

Cupp (incredulous): They punched you?

Jessica (her cheeks flushing red): Punch? I thought you said "punished." I'm sorry. (She glanced at the jury, then back at Scott.)

Cupp: Did they? Punch?

Jessica: No!

Cupp: Did they swear at you?

Jessica: They swore.

(Now Cupp pushed.)

Cupp: To your face when you were nine years old? Did they swear at you and tell you, "I hate your fucking guts"?

Jessica: No! Neither did I.

Cupp: My question was: did your parents do that?

Jessica: No.

Cupp: Did your parents make you do yard work?

Jessica (shrugging): Yes.

Cupp: Did they make you go out with a little pair of household scissors and trim the lawn?

Jessica: No!

Cupp: Did they make you go around with a paintbrush and sweep every single blade of grass off the walk and back into the yard? Did they make you do that?

Jessica: No.

The slight rustling in the courtroom told Scott Cupp that everyone was thinking: *Then why did you make A.J. do that?*

Cupp: How much child support did you and your husband have to pay for Andrew before he came into your home?

Jessica: I didn't have to pay any.

Cupp: How much did your husband have to pay?

Jessica: I don't know.

Cupp: But he had to pay child support?

Jessica: I don't know.

Cupp: You don't know?

Jessica: I don't know what the whole situation was. I know that he owed money.

Cupp: And isn't it true that if Andrew went back to his original placement with his biological mother, that your husband would have to pay child support?

Jessica: No matter where Andrew lived, my husband would've had to pay, yes.

Cupp: When was A.J.'s birthday?

The sudden change in direction obviously surprised her. Jessica blinked and Scott could see her searching her mind for the date.

Jessica (finally): April 24, 1983.

Cupp: And he didn't go to school the day before his birthday, did he?

Jessica: To my knowledge, he did.

Cupp: In 1993?

A.J.'s birthday was on a Saturday that year, so his "special day" at school with his classmates would have been on Friday. Even though Mrs. Idrissi had testified quite the opposite, Jessica Schwarz insisted several times that "to my knowledge," A.J. had gone to school that day.

Cupp: Your testimony is that you sent A.J. to school that day?

Jessica: To the best of my knowledge, yes.

Cupp: How many other parties and school activities were there in his '92 to '93 school year—that you remember—I mean like special days, like Halloween, Christmas, field trips?

Jessica: Halloween, Christmas . . . I think there was the zoo, Thanksgiving, Easter. . . . There was also a carnival that the whole school was involved in.

Cupp: And isn't it true that, due to your instructions to Mrs. Idrissi at that open house, he was to participate in none of those?

Jessica: No, that's not true.

Cupp: That's just not true?

Jessica: That's just not true.

Mrs. Idrissi's earlier testimony had been so powerful and so emotional that the jury had very obviously been swept up in it, and Scott used that—intentionally pitting Jessica against her.

Cupp: Mrs. Idrissi is mistaken?

Jessica: Yes, she is.

Cupp: And she's mistaken because she doesn't like you?

Jessica: We didn't like each other.

Cupp: You couldn't get any cooperation from Mrs. Idrissi or—as you called her—"the maggot"?

Jessica (smugly): I never called her that. Didn't even recognize her that day.

Cupp: Well, Mrs. Idrissi was spoiling Andrew, wasn't she?

Jessica: Well, as she put it in her testimony, she changed the rules for him.

Cupp: So, Mrs. Idrissi—who has thirty children to educate—has the audacity to single your child out and spoil him, right? That's what she was doing?

Jessica: In essence, she was changing the rules for him.

Cupp: Isn't it true that she was trying to get A.J. to learn—trying to help him learn?

Jessica: No.

Cupp: Isn't it true that she was trying to compensate for what he wasn't getting at home?

Jessica: No.

Cupp: All the love and affection that Mrs. Idrissi was giving A.J. at school—he was getting that at home?

Jessica (without emotion): He was getting that at home.

Cupp: Uh-huh. This was a kid who just had this enormous thirst for attention and need to be loved, right?
Jessica: Right.
Cupp: So abnormal that even when he was in Vero Beach for six weeks—and you visited him twice—he's basically clutching at every nurse every time they come in, wants to be hugged, wants to be stroked, wants to be a kid?
Jessica: Yes, A.J. did that to everyone all the time.
Cupp: And to you?
Jessica: And to me.

Cupp moved away from the lectern. He took two steps toward the defendant and listened to the shuffling in the gallery behind him. His intention was to take the jurors and the spectators on a journey through the Schwarz household, where not a single picture of A.J. was ever hung on a wall or set on a desk or displayed on a dresser. Not one. Compared to dozens of pictures of the girls. Not a single one of his drawings from school on the refrigerator. There were no trinkets or souvenirs.

But Jessica had a different story.

Cupp: Oh, how many pictures of A.J. did you have hanging in your house in April of 1993?
Jessica: The hanging pictures?
Cupp: Okay, hanging, sitting up on a table, on your dresser, in the kitchen, on the refrigerator, anywhere in the house?
Jessica: Anywhere in the house?
Cupp: Yes, ma'am. If somebody walked in, how many would they be able to see?
Jessica: Two of them were in the hallway, one was in the living room, and the rest were in my photo album.
Cupp: So, your answer to my question is you had three?
Jessica: Yeah.

Scott then questioned her about A.J.'s bedroom—a room so barren that it had been described to him as "the dark side of the moon"—so drastically in contrast to the well-appointed rooms of Jessica's daughters that it made him embarrassed, angry, and resentful. The lack of pictures, the barren bedroom, the dearth of toys—all destined to help crush and break A.J.'s spirit.

"And you felt about A.J. as if he was your own son?" Cupp asked.

"As if he was my own," Jessica replied.

He asked her about A.J.'s nightly bed-wetting—a problem he had never exhibited before he arrived at Jessica's house. He quizzed her about the locks on A.J.'s bedroom door. He asked her why she prohibited the guidance counselor from speaking to A.J.

When she vehemently denied the accusations, he—struggling to minimize the sarcasm that he felt—said to the defendant, "This is a big conspiracy, isn't it?"

Jessica replied, "I don't know what this is."

Cupp questioned her about A.J.'s half sister Patsy and the incident that caused her to be taken out of the home for good. It, of course, began when Patsy allowed two boys inside the house without permission and it ended with a fist in her face.

Cupp: You've already testified that you've got a bad temper—or words to that effect?

Jessica: I don't remember saying that.

Cupp: Well, do you have a bad temper?

Jessica: I have a temper.

Cupp: And you're loud?

Jessica: Yeah.

Cupp: And you're crude?

Jessica: Yeah. I can be.

Cupp (calmly): So at the time this happened with Patsy, you were upset?

Jessica: Yes.

Cupp: You were angry.

Jessica: Yes.

Cupp: You lost your temper a little bit.

Jessica: Yes.

Cupp: And you balled up your hand into a fist and you punched her in the face.

Jessica: No, I did not.

Cupp: And her nose bled.

Jessica: No, it did not.

There was an edge of frustration and desperation in her voice, and the anger that Cupp wanted the jury to see crept to the surface as well.

Cupp (pushing): In fact, you knocked her down—you hit her so hard.

Jessica: No, I did not!

Cupp (glancing briefly at the jurors): Tell us. At the parenting classes you attended—were you taught to humiliate your child?

Jessica: No!

Cupp: Did they teach you that an appropriate method of punishment was to have your child wear a T-shirt with derogatory words on it?

Jessica: No.

Cupp: Did she go over bed-wetting—at all—at the parenting classes?

Jessica: I don't remember.

Cupp: You don't remember anybody ever telling you that a recognized method is to take the child's head and rub his nose into the urine-soaked sheets—like a dog?

Jessica (her face red with anger): I didn't even do that to my dogs. I didn't do it to my dogs or my children.

Cupp: You didn't do it to your dogs—you just did it to A.J.

Jessica: I didn't do it to Andrew!

Cupp: Isn't it true that the pets got treated better in your house than Andrew?

Jessica: No.

Cupp: Did they tell you to use nudity as a punishment? Has anyone ever told you that that's a recognized way to punish a child?

Jessica: Absolutely not.

Cupp: Or making him walk to school in the rain while you give another child a ride?

Jessica: I never did that, so I wouldn't know what it was used for.

CHAPTER 23

*We always remembered how Corporal Hopper
pointed out later to us that she noticed rather quickly
that morning that something didn't feel right to her inside the home. It was like A.J. hadn't "lived" there.*

—Scott Cupp

From there, Scott Cupp delved into A.J.'s six-week odyssey
at the psychiatric hospital in Vero Beach, so physically and
emotionally whipped that the doctors, fearing for his life, ordered around-the-clock supervision. After acknowledging
how extraordinarily traumatic that must have been for A.J.,
Jessica admitted that she and his father went to visit the fragile nine-year-old a total of two times—one of those being the
day they dropped him off.

When Cupp made it clear that the hospital staff at Vero
Beach literally begged Jessica and David—the boy's own father—to come visit him more often, the emotion in the courtroom was palpable. And when he threatened to use the
records to prove that they refused to come to the hospital to
pick A.J. up after his discharge, the tension running through
the room was like an electrical current.

Cupp revisited the perverse practice of keeping A.J. out
of school as a form of punishment. He'd already established
that out of the forty-two days that A.J. was absent during his
tumultuous third-grade year—Thursday was a given. Thursday

was recycling day on Triphammer Road, and a half-dozen neighbors had already testified to the number of times they witnessed A.J. out at 5:00 in the morning, picking up cans for Jessica.

He didn't expect Jessica to admit that A.J. was forced to get up at 4:30 in the morning to collect cans for her benefit—that wasn't the point. Cupp wanted the jury to hear her lie in the face of the witnesses they had already heard from. He wanted them to experience her arrogant attitude toward A.J.'s repeated absences. He wanted them to feel her smugness.

Cupp: Never made it to school on a Thursday, did he?
Jessica (flippantly): Looks like he didn't.
Cupp: There were a lot of cans out on those Thursdays, huh?
Jessica: Yep.
Cupp: And A.J. was out there collecting them, wasn't he?
Jessica: Not to my knowledge.
Cupp: But he didn't make it to school those days. You sent him, though, right?
Jessica: I sent him to school.

The defense team had attempted to paint Jessica Schwarz as a woman possessed by her affection for children and animals, but Scott Cupp attacked her claim that the Schwarz house was a hangout for all the neighborhood kids by showing just how few of their names she even knew—except for the ones who had testified earlier.

When Jessica denied trying to prevent HRS workers from talking to her children, Cupp asked, "Isn't it true that you threatened A.J. about talking to anybody from HRS about anything that went on in your house? Threatened him in front of your neighbor Beth Walton?"

"No, I didn't threaten him in front of anybody," she replied curtly, her body language revealing her arrogance. She couldn't conceal it—but Cupp sensed that she really didn't want to.

Cupp: When A.J. had the incident with his eyes and nose—you didn't see it happen?

Jessica: No, I didn't.

Cupp: Shortly after he came into his home, his nose literally started getting big in front of you? And that struck you as funny?

Jessica: Well, it just sort of looked funny and I did laugh. (Incredibly, she appeared to be fighting off a grin even as she spoke. Cupp plunged ahead.)

Cupp: And he didn't cry?

Jessica: No, he wasn't crying and there was no blood.

Cupp: And his nose was—your words—getting bigger in front of your face?

Jessica: Yes.

Cupp: In fact, whatever hit him, hit him so hard that the next morning you literally had to wash his eyes to get them open because he could not open them—isn't that what you told us earlier?

Jessica: I don't remember saying I was washing his eyes open—but they were black in the morning.

Cupp: And you couldn't get them open?

Jessica: I didn't say that.

Cupp: Do you remember giving a statement about that at another time?

Jessica: No, I don't remember it.

Cupp: If I showed you the statement, would it refresh your recollection?

Jessica: It might.

Scott Cupp, not wanting to break the momentum, made a quick decision to move on—for the moment.

Cupp (staring at her): And isn't it a fact that the reason why you finally took A.J. to the doctor was that the detective who came out to the house told you, "You better get that kid to the doctor"?

Jessica: No.

Cupp: No. (He repeated her denial to underline yet another lie, spoken under oath.) Detective Calloway didn't have all the information, though, did he?

Jessica: I don't know what you mean. He got all the information—from A.J., mainly.

Cupp: Did he talk to Jackie?

Jessica: Yes. He talked to Jackie—alone, as a matter of fact.

Cupp: After you told Jackie what to say, right?

Jessica: Absolutely not. You don't tell Jackie what to say. Jackie says whatever she wants.

Cupp: Isn't it true that A.J. and Jackie went across the street to Eileen Callahan's house? And when Ms. Callahan saw his eyes and nose and asked him what had happened, it was Jackie who said—

Rendell Brown objected, saying it was hearsay, and Cupp withdrew the question. The defense attorney's timing was good—good for the prosecution. It left the jury filling in Jackie's words.

Cupp then produced the statement that Jessica had given to Detective Michael Waites on May 2, 1993, in which she told him about the incident with A.J.'s black eyes. He handed the statement to her and asked her to read a portion of it to herself.

Cupp: And you told him his eyes were so black and blue that you had to wash his eyes out?

Jessica: I said they were really black and they were really swollen. I didn't remember having to wash his eyes open, but if I said it, I did it.

Cupp: And they really hurt?

Jessica: Yes.

Cupp: And he didn't cry?

Jessica: No, he didn't. He wasn't struck with anything. He hit—he fell into the bicycle. No one struck him in any way, shape, or form.

Cupp: You never struck him?
Jessica: No.

Candace Ahern had testified earlier that Jessica had laughed at the condition of A.J.'s nose and eyes and made fun of him in her presence, but when Cupp questioned Jessica about it, she denied it.

Cupp: You didn't laugh at him in front of her and call him "shit for brains"?
Jessica (nonchalantly): Not in front of Candace Ahern.
(Her answer couldn't have been more perfect for the prosecution.)
Cupp: How about not in front of Candace Ahern?
Jessica: Yes.
Cupp: And you called him "shit for brains"?
Jessica: And HRS called me about that and I told them.
Cupp: And that didn't happen in front of Candace Ahern? That happened a different time?
Jessica: I don't really remember.
Cupp: You testified—on direct—that he was hiding food in the garage and he never told you why. He didn't have an explanation?
Jessica: He wasn't admitting to anything. I asked him if he was the one hiding the food.
Cupp: And didn't you say that he denied that there was food there or said, "What food?" That's why you took him around to show him?
Jessica: Yes.
Cupp: And you—of crude character, allowed—did you say sometimes you're abrasive? Some people think you're abrasive?
Jessica: Oh, yes.
Cupp: And you were angry. Here's this kid opening up the food and he's laying it around—hiding it in the garage. You were angry, weren't you?
Jessica: I wasn't angry.

Cupp: Calm? You calmly just rested your hand on his neck and showed him here and showed him there? That's Jessica?

Jessica: I wasn't crazy. I was just walking—look here, look there.

Cupp: You'd never picked him up by his head and dropped him?

Jessica: No.

Cupp (with measured sarcasm): Not Jessica?

Jessica: That's right.

The buzzing in the gallery suggested strongly that the spectators—at least—didn't believe her, and Judge Colbath was forced to quiet them with a sharp crack of his gavel.

Cupp: Your testimony—so I'm clear—in reference to Richard Zimmern . . . when he drove up to your house on A.J.'s birthday, A.J. was not trimming the sidewalk with scissors?

Jessica: That's exactly right.

Cupp: He was not?

Jessica: No, he was sweeping with a broom—a full-sized broom.

Cupp (pointedly): Dr. Zimmern is mistaken?

Jessica: Absolutely.

Cupp: I guess he's just getting old and senile?

Not surprisingly, Rendell Brown strenuously objected and Scott Cupp quickly withdrew the question, knowing the point had already been made.

"Isn't it true," Cupp continued, "that—after you were all interviewed by the police in May—you told the girls, 'Don't tell them anything. I could go to jail'?"

Brown quickly came out of his chair, protesting, "Your Honor, I'm going to object—"

But before he could finish, everyone in the courtroom heard Jessica say, "I told Jackie that."

The defense attorney was stunned. Everyone was stunned.

Cupp (quickly continuing): And where was Lauren?
Jessica: She was there.
Cupp: She was standing right next to you?
Jessica: Yes.
Cupp: Your testimony is that you felt equally fond of all three children—Lauren, Jackie, and A.J.?
Jessica: Right.
Cupp: Do you think maybe A.J. was hiding food because he was not getting enough to eat?
Jessica: Absolutely not.
Cupp: You weren't giving him a limited amount of time to eat? Is that what you were using the timer for?
Jessica: I was using the timer for bed-wetting when he first moved into my home.
Cupp: When A.J. was placed on the imipramine—when he came home—how long was it before he started throwing it up?
Jessica: I really don't remember.
Cupp: And then you took him off it?
Jessica: If he threw it up, I took him off it until he felt better.
Cupp: But he never had a problem tolerating it for six weeks while he was in Vero Beach, did he?
Jessica: I guess not, if that's what they say.
Cupp: Isn't it true that you told Dr. Zimmern that you didn't think the imipramine was helping A.J. and you took him off of it?
Jessica: No. I told him about the throwing up.
Cupp: That was never a point of contention that Dr. Zimmern thought he should be on the imipramine? Was that something you disagreed with him about?
Jessica: No, I didn't disagree about him being on the

imipramine. I just took him off of it until he stopped throwing up and felt better.

Cupp: Did you also tell Dr. Zimmern that you didn't think the counseling was helping A.J.? That he didn't need counseling—he needed discipline?

Jessica: He asked me a point-blank question. He said, "Is Andrew getting any better with everything that's going on in the home, in school, and in counseling?" And I said, "It gets better and it gets worse, but the overall picture—I think he needs more help."

Cupp: You didn't tell Dr. Zimmern that you didn't believe in counseling?

Jessica: I told him I didn't believe in it for me, but I would participate.

Cupp: Oh, I see. During the 1992 to 1993 school year with Mrs. Idrissi, he was not on imipramine during that year, was he?

Jessica: Yes, he was.

Cupp: Your testimony is that he was on imipramine during his third-grade year with Mrs. Idrissi?

Jessica: Yes, I think so anyway.

Cupp: You're not sure now?

Jessica: Well, I'm about 100 percent sure, but on and off. Again, it was always on and off, so I really don't remember the exact date.

Cupp: Wasn't that the time period when you said that Dr. Ukuedojor wouldn't prescribe it?

Jessica: What I had originally said was that I was getting stuck with having to find someone to prescribe this.

Cupp: And Ukuedojor prescribed it?

Jessica (rambling): He did. Nobody was doing the blood levels is what it was. He had to have blood levels, blood taken and levels—however they do it—on a monthly or weekly basis. That much I don't really remember, but nobody wanted to take the responsibility for taking the blood; so in essence, they turned it around

and said if we don't take the blood we can't prescribe
the pill, so I had called Dr. Uttley and begged him for
the stuff—

Cupp (interrupting): Ma'am, was he or wasn't he on
imipramine?

Jessica: He was on and off, on and off. That's all I tried
to tell you.

Cupp: No further questions.

Cupp was emotionally drained after the cross-examination.
A local reporter later referred to Jessica as being "hammered
away at."

Usually, when a defendant chooses to testify, there is some
redirect by the defense attorney—to clean things up a bit. It was
extremely significant that Rendell Brown chose not to try to
salvage any damage done to Jessica on cross. He knew that if
he did any redirect, Scott would get another shot at her on recross. By asking no more questions, he was telling the prosecution—and more important, the jury—that he wanted her
off the stand.

After the defense rested, Joe Marx called Corporal Bobbie
Hopper to the witness stand as the prosecution's only rebuttal
witness.

Immediately after she was sworn in, Brown asked to approach the bench, his concern being that the witness had
been at the Schwarz home on the day A.J.'s body was found.
"I don't know what she's going to say."

Marx assured the judge and the defense attorney, "I don't
plan on going into that. I'll keep my questions very narrow."

Corporal Hopper testified that she had been employed
with the sheriff's office for fourteen years.

Marx: Listen to my questions very carefully and just
answer the question. On May 2, 1993, did you have an
opportunity to enter the Schwarz residence?

Hopper: Yes, I did.

Marx: While you were present in the Schwarz residence, did you have an opportunity to go into Andrew's room?
Hopper: Yes, I did.

When Marx prompted her to describe the room, she told him that Andrew's room was a small room off the kitchen area that appeared to be a utility room.

"In the room there was a bed on the far wall; there was a dresser next to it. On top of the dresser were plastic bags and I don't know what was in them. They were all tied up and piled on the dresser. At the foot of the bed, there was a lot more of these plastic bags. There was a pair of sneakers on the dresser and probably a ten-inch plastic police car."

Marx: Was it nicely decorated?
Hopper: Absolutely not. It was . . . it was very depressing.
Marx: Was it barren?
Hopper: There was nothing in there. It was just the bed and a toy.
Marx: Did you have an opportunity to go into the girls' bedrooms? Could you tell me what you saw there?
Hopper: Complete opposite. They had printed bedspreads, matching curtains, TV, Nintendo, toys, games. It was like two opposite ends of the world.
Marx: While you were in the Schwarz residence, did you see pictures on the walls and on the tables of the two girls?
Hopper: There were lots of pictures on the walls and around the residence.
Marx: While you were in the Schwarz residence, did you see one single picture of Andrew Schwarz?
Hopper: No, sir, I did not.

CHAPTER 24

This boy couldn't tell anybody anything. He had nowhere to run—nowhere to go. His whole life was a living hell.

—Joseph Marx

On Thursday, September 1, 1994, Jessica Schwarz, clad in a printed dress topped by a white cardigan sweater, listened sullenly as Joseph Marx gave the closing arguments for the prosecution.

Ilene Logan, who had been kept out of the courtroom because her name appeared on the state's witness list, was allowed to be present for the closing arguments.

David "Bear" Schwarz was on the defense witness list, but he was never called to the stand; in fact, he did not attend the trial at all. As soon as it started, he disappeared. He would later claim that he did not want to testify because he was concerned that the prosecutors would "misrepresent" his real feelings and imply that he was afraid of Jessica.

The prosecution never intended to call him as a witness. Scott Cupp knew that was exactly what Rendell Brown wanted—so he could "lead him by the nose" on cross. David was a wild card for both sides, and a card that neither wanted to play—despite any posturing.

The atmosphere in the packed courtroom was electric and, not surprisingly, the media was present in full force.

When he was interviewed for his job, Joe Marx had been asked what he saw himself doing in five years. He answered, "I see myself giving the closing arguments in the biggest murder case you've got." Ironically, it was five years later—to the day—that he did just that.

As he faced the jury, he felt the pain and anger of his own tragic, personal loss—only months earlier—because of senseless violence. He struggled to push those thoughts and feelings away as he focused on the matter at hand.

"Last night, when I was staying up thinking about what I was going to say—and crumpling up papers—I had a recurring thought and it was this: That in today's society we've come to accept violence as a way of life. We just accept that's the way it is.

"We turn on the TV when we get home and we turn on the news. This person has been shot. This person has been killed. This child has been kidnapped. And we just accept it because we can't do anything about it.

"It's hard to believe that people can be so cruel to one another. Sometimes this thing we call a trial—this search for truth and justice—is an ugly process.

"But the sad part of the story—and what's unfortunate—is that it's true and you can't turn your head and you can't change the channel.

"But you see, there's some good news here. Because this time it's your chance, as citizens and as jurors, that you can do something. It reminds me of an old movie with Faye Dunaway and William Holden called *Network*. And everybody sticks their head out the window and shouts, 'I'm mad as hell and I'm not going to take it anymore!'

"And this is your chance. You send this defendant a message that you're mad as hell and you are not going to take this anymore. You're not! This is your opportunity.

"During the trial, you heard eighteen different people come into this courtroom and tell you that Andrew Schwarz was a loving little boy, a boy starved for love, a boy starved for attention.

"You heard Mrs. Idrissi, a twenty-two-year veteran of the Palm Beach County school system. Mrs. Idrissi is a beautiful woman who cares about children. She got choked up during her testimony. She cared about Andrew Schwarz.

"Several people got choked up during their testimony. The funny thing is, only one person didn't get choked up at all—the defendant, cold and emotionless.

"You see, Andrew Schwarz was desperate to please. Dr. Rahaim told you that. Several witnesses told you that—desperate to please.

"As described by the defendant—this little 'liar' and this little 'thief' came to school during Christmastime . . . and Mrs. Idrissi told you about the Christmas story and that he came to school when all the other kids were excited and happy about buying Christmas presents. . . . And he came to school with no money. So what did she do? She gave him money.

"Now, what did the little 'liar' and 'thief' do? He took the entire amount of money and bought presents for Mrs. Idrissi.

"Emotional abuse—the system of degradation of another— a course of conduct taken by the defendant against Andrew, designed to reduce his self-concept to the point that he considered himself unworthy of friendship, unworthy of love, and unworthy of protection.

"Emotional abuse is just as deliberate as physical abuse.

"'You're stupid.' 'You're a worthless piece of shit.' 'I hate your fucking guts.' She might as well have punched. It's as deliberate as a gunshot. Emotional abuse scars the heart and damages the soul.

"This little boy's spirit was broken. He was ten—ten years old—and his spirit was broken.

"Let's talk about Mr. Brown's defense in this case—or should I say defenses? Let's start with the first one. His client did it—but she didn't know any better. She couldn't help herself. She's a tough woman trucker, educated from a background where she learned discipline.

"Well, is that what we heard? Her own mother took the

stand and told you, 'We taught her right from wrong, she comes from a somewhat privileged background, and she has a high-school education.'

"Now, ladies and gentlemen, you don't need a college education to raise a child. What you need is a heart.

"So, try another one. A.J. was a bad kid, brain-damaged, and uncontrollable. The defense claims that everybody is lying. The only person who is telling you this kid is brain-damaged and uncontrollable is this woman. The only person.

"Eighteen people told you Andrew Schwarz was a good boy—never a discipline problem.

"Back on September 9, 1992, Dr. Zimmern wrote, 'Why is Andrew so cooperative in school—and so rotten at home? Something is wrong here.' There was something wrong. The defendant was lying! The whole world is wrong and Jessica Schwarz is right. Don't buy it. Don't have your intelligence insulted.

"But, most importantly, Dr. Rahaim took the stand. Dr. Rahaim doesn't know anybody, never saw Andrew, doesn't know the defendant—an expert. He told you there's absolutely no evidence in all the stacks of documents and records that he reviewed—no evidence that there was brain damage. None. Zero.

"This whole question of imipramine became comical. It became a joke.

"The defendant couldn't get her story straight. Yes, he was on it. Well, sometimes he was on it—when he wasn't throwing it up. Mr. Cupp got up on cross-examination and said, 'Now, Mrs. Schwarz, isn't it true you couldn't get a prescription?' 'Oh, well, this woman wouldn't give it to me, and Dr. Uttley washed his hands of me. I couldn't get it—but he was on it.'

"'But, ma'am, didn't you tell HRS and Medicaid you wouldn't pay for it, so you couldn't get it?'

"'Well, yes, but I was giving it to him.'

"And then she says she gave it to him, but he threw it up.

That's why he didn't go to school. But the funny thing is, the Vero Beach records show that he was on the imipramine and there was no evidence that he threw up. This is a joke—it's funny.

"On top of all of this—if that isn't enough for you—she tells Dr. Zimmern, 'I'm not giving him the imipramine.'

"Let's assume for a minute that this kid was the worst kid in the world. Let's assume that he was brain-damaged. Let's assume that he was retarded. Let's assume that he was a special child. Assume it.

"Does he deserve to be treated that way? Does he deserve that? Nobody deserves that—and certainly not a ten-year-old boy.

"This boy couldn't tell anybody anything. He had nowhere to run—nowhere to go. His whole life was a living hell.

"Let's try another defense. It's HRS's fault. It's the counselor's fault. It's Dr. Zimmern's fault. It's everybody's fault—but hers.

"So we go to the next defense. This is the best one. She just—flat out—didn't do it.

"The final defense: This is one big conspiracy. People who didn't know each other—veterans of the school system, retired pediatricians, doctors, neighbors that she knew, neighbors that she didn't know, pest control people, friends, enemies—they all got together somewhere over on Triphammer Road. They all got together, got their stories together, and this is all one big conspiracy.

"There's an old saying in the law: 'When the law is on your side, you pound the law. When the facts are on your side, you pound the facts. When neither one is on your side, you pound the table.'

"When this trial started, Mr. Brown walked over and told you, as the defendant sits here, she's innocent—cloaked in this veil of innocence. He was right. She was—absolutely—but after nine days of trial, we slowly removed that veil. And what did we find? A monster. That's what we found—a monster—a person who is manipulative, a bully intimidator, and most of all—a liar. That's what we found.

"She was devoid of any emotion when she spoke about Andrew—a stone.

"When you go back there with the verdict form, it's a hard job that you have to do. You're sitting in judgment of another human being. This is your opportunity to do the right thing. Don't spend one second feeling sorry for this woman. Don't spend one second feeling sorry for Lauren. You're doing her a favor. And don't feel sorry for that defendant because you're not doing anything to her. She did this to herself. She didn't give a crap who was watching. She didn't care. She told you, 'I'm abusive. I'm crude—but I'm not rude.'

"Ladies and gentlemen, when you go back to the jury room, don't think about her. Don't feel sorry for her. You're not doing a thing to her. She did it to herself.

"Thank you."

As Joe Marx sat down, he felt that it had gone well—that he had connected with the jurors and that they would do the right thing. Touched by his powerful and emotional words, many people in the gallery were crying.

After a short break, Rendell Brown gave the closing argument for the defense.

"Mr. Marx said when the law is on your side, you argue the law. When the facts are on your side, you argue the facts, and when neither is on your side, you bang on the table.

"Well, let's extend that a little bit further—there's an extension of that—because of what we've seen in this trial. There's another one that says this: 'When you bring a person into court accused of a crime against a child, the jury is expected to come in with sympathy for the child.'

"So, when you're prosecuting regarding a child, appeal to the emotions of the jury. And that's precisely what the state has sought to do throughout the trial. It's culminated in an argument that went something like, 'If you convict Jessica Schwarz, you'll rid the country of violence on the streets.'

"That's an appeal to nothing that came forward in this case. That's an appeal to your emotions and that is asking you—as jurors—to violate the law.

"Mr. Marx stood here telling you to get mad—show your anger. His Honor is going to instruct you that sympathy, bias, prejudice, have no place in this trial. He will tell you that. Further, he will tell you that the burden of proof is upon the state—not to evoke emotions—not to evoke sympathies—but rather to prove guilt of each and every material element of each and every crime charged, beyond and to the exclusion of every reasonable doubt.

"And when you don't have those proofs . . . when your evidence has failed . . . when your witnesses have obviously failed . . . then you get up here and you say, 'Well, there's a little child involved, feel sorry for him, convict her, evidence be damned.' That's the argument you heard.

"I knew I could represent the truth to you and then stand here proudly, as I do, now knowing that I wouldn't have to argue for you to get emotional. I wouldn't have to ask you to feel sorry for Jessica Schwarz. All I want you to do is look at the evidence and be fair. That's the law and I work within the law.

"We knew it wouldn't be easy. We knew you were going to hear some things that you weren't supposed to hear. And then we were going to ask you to do something that is close to humanly impossible—forget about the fact that there are other proceedings and there are other trials—and focus on the proofs in this case and this case alone.

"Andrew was a young child. That evokes sympathy, but there is no place in this trial for sympathy—that's a violation of that solemn oath you took.

"Most of you admitted that you had—at some point or another—seen news articles or television stories, or whatever, about these allegations. I said to you, ladies and gentlemen, can you do this? It's not going to be easy, but can you do this? Can you sit here; hear the facts—because I know that after you hear the facts, you're going to decide that Jessica Schwarz is not guilty of the crimes charged. But can you hold your head high, square your shoulders, look squarely into the eyes of your husbands and your wives and your friends and your coworkers and your neighbors, and say, 'I found her not guilty because the state failed to prove her guilty'?

"'I found her not guilty because I know the facts. Facts come not from the newspaper—but from this stand—and all of the stuff that you think you know from reading a newspaper just isn't facts. The facts are what I voted on and my conscience is clear. I did the right thing. I sent the lady home to her daughters because she's not guilty of the charges—under the laws of the state of Florida guaranteed to us by the Constitution of the United States—and the state of Florida—as well.'

"And I asked you those questions because, ladies and gentlemen, that's not an easy chore, but you've got to do it—because if you can't make the system work, the system can't work. If you let the system fail, you fail the entire system, the country, everything. It does not avail you in the least to convict an innocent person to satisfy your husbands or your wives or your neighbors or your employees or your coemployees or your employers or anyone else.

"Do the right thing—follow the law. Say to the state of Florida, 'You as representatives of the law are not going to make me break the law by violating my solemn oath and finding a not guilty person guilty.'"

Rendell Brown held up the school picture of A.J. for the jury to see once again.

"The state is very proud of this photograph of this boy. I want you to look at the photograph for what it can help you with. This is a picture taken of Andrew Schwarz at school. I beseech you to show me a mark on this boy or show me there was makeup used to cover a mark. We all know that if a child is brutally beaten and bruised—as these witnesses have said he was—even if the marks heal, the kinds of marks we're talking about will ultimately leave a scar—a permanent scar. Take it back there with you and study it. This is how we test the evidence.

"Ours is not an argument of conspiracy. Things like this can happen when rumors start to run rampant. You've got a bunch of neighbors . . . it's been a hotbed of conversation. I'm not going to trash these kids. I'm going to tell you this way. Children hear rumors, see a playmate on TV. The thought is, that's the way to get some attention: 'I'll go them one better.'

"The [HRS] workers went there—announced at times—unannounced at times. They talked to the child sometimes in Jessica's presence—sometimes out of her presence.

"When you hear the fact that there were various HRS workers—the people who were sent there on unfounded reports . . . I think the evidence says seven or eight occasions—never once founded—never once any real problem. Who do you think those calls were coming from? The same neighbors—whose truth the state seeks to vouch for—kept sending these people there. Police kept going there—can't find a thing there. What in the world is going on?

"So how is it so difficult to understand that they are here lying—if they would lie and tie up these hot lines about abuses that simply weren't going on? Why is that so difficult to understand and to believe?

"Jessica had an obligation to train this child how to function and live in society.

"There's no way in the world Andrew Schwarz—given the problems and situation he had—could have gotten these grades by himself. Jessica Schwarz worked with that child, and I think she did a tremendous job, for him to get these kinds of grades—given the problems and facts of illnesses and the times he missed from school.

"State talked about Jessica Schwarz and, well, she didn't break down and cry—she wasn't emotional. What you see is what you get because that's what she is—and she didn't get up here and try to pretend that she's something that she is not. She was just the way she was because that's Jessica Schwarz—she hurts inwardly, not outwardly.

"Did they prove she was trying to help this child with an education? Or was she trying to maliciously punish? Was she right to punish? She has more than a right. She has an obligation like everybody. If we're going to stop that killing that Mr. Marx talked about, if we're going to stop the kidnappings that he talked about, if we're going to stop all of these ugly things, we're going to start with children Andrew's age and start letting them learn that when you do things—you're going to be punished and not rewarded. That's what Jessica sought to do. She had an obligation to do that. Every parent in society has that obligation and that's what she did—no hatred, no ill will—simply doing what she was taught to do. Get his attention when he does something wrong because society won't tolerate it.

"Can you look at this evidence as presented and decide within your heart and within your soul—beyond and to the exclusion of every reasonable doubt—that it was not done for educational purposes? The things that they did do—making him stay on task—making him go back and do his chores until he got it right . . . if that was malicious and ill will and with hatred, then go ahead and convict if that's what you call that. Go ahead and convict her.

"But if you find what the truth points out here was real—that this lady was trying to do what all of society needs to start trying to do again—then you've got to find her not guilty. She didn't do anything to hurt this child.

"Don't abrogate the law. Don't make a mockery of our laws that our forefathers sat down and thought out to apply to every individual whether it happens to be a tall, slim, attractive, gorgeous lady—or a two-hundred-pound truck driver. Everybody has a right to be presumed innocent until proven guilty by good and competent evidence—and sympathy is not good and competent.

"Untruths and half-truths are not good and competent evidence, and that's what you must determine within yourselves.

"Somehow I'm convinced that you heard what I heard and that your memory is probably far better than mine, and I'm not going to insult your intelligence by going through all of those contradictions and falsehoods and the like.

"You knew it wasn't going to be easy. I knew it wasn't going to be easy, but you vowed to do the right thing. You vowed to do it in spite of whatever others outside this courtroom might feel. You said you understood that the only facts that anybody knows would be the facts that you would hear from this stand and this courtroom and this trial, and that's what His Honor is going to tell you as well.

"If you follow the law and if you do the right thing, you'll have no choice but to find Jessica not guilty. When you do the right thing, justice will have been accomplished in this courtroom, and Jessica Schwarz will have these shackles—that were unlawfully placed upon her—removed from her.

"Thank you."

The hushed courtroom listened intently as Scott Cupp spoke passionately to the jurors in his powerful rebuttal.

"The first thing I want to discuss with you is Dr. Rahaim, HRS, and the Child Protection Team.

"Dr. Rahaim has been treated extremely unfairly—extremely. What you did hear is that on February 23, the first time that Dr. Rahaim—in his capacity as a consultant to the Child Protection Team—had any contact with this situation, he stated in no uncertain terms that this is a target child in this situation. Dr. Rahaim feels that the child is living in exactly the wrong situation.

"Among the recommendations was that HRS, in consultation with the Child Protection Team, determine whether the child is in an appropriate placement with his natural father and his stepmother. And if you remember Dr. Rahaim's testimony, what he was stating is that therapy—family therapy—individual therapy—is not a cure-all. There are times when what you need to do is take the kid out of the home.

"Family therapy?

"All you've heard and all you will hear about David Schwarz is contained in a few signatures, where he signed a few reports. There was no family. This was David. This was Jessica. David was never there. And if any of you think for a minute that if we brought David Schwarz in here, that he would do anything other than do what Jessica Schwarz did . . . I think it's interesting to note that the defense didn't call the defendant's husband. Not even her husband came in.

"What family? It's appalling. It's disgusting that those words—'family,' 'mother,' 'stepmother'—those words shouldn't have even been used in this entire trial because they did not apply. This was not a family. She was no mother—you all know that.

"Mr. Brown mentioned how all that Mrs. Schwarz wanted to do was to train the boy up the right way—to grow up in her home and become a law-abiding member of society. Every once in a while, a trial comes along that teaches us something different. You know what we've all learned? This has been a lesson in what's wrong with our society and this has been '101, How We Train Criminals.'

"Because you know what? In a few short years, Andrew J. Schwarz was going to be a citizen's worst nightmare. He was going to be the accident that came into somebody's house and poured acid on somebody's head—or murdered somebody's spouse while she sat there and watched. And citizens like yourselves would then fill this courtroom, clamoring to me as a prosecutor: 'Nail him, he's sadistic. He's unfeeling. Look at him sitting there. He doesn't care about anybody but himself.' Who trained him?

"That's what trained him! She trained him how to be uncaring about other people, about himself, sadistic. He got a real good course in sadism. Maliciousness. It's sickening.

"I asked you very few questions in jury selection. One of the questions I asked you—because I was concerned about it then and I'm still concerned about it—that one of the biggest difficulties with this case is believing, being open to believe that there are people like that out there among us that can do these sorts of things. And nobody wants you to feel sorry, so I won't even use the word 'child'—that there are people out here that can do this to 'people.'

"We just don't want to have a place for that in our minds. How can anybody do this stuff? And you hear the charges and people are shaking their head and they are going, 'My God, this stuff can't go on. This doesn't go on—it's got to be exaggerated.' But I asked you all, and you all answered affirmatively, 'Would you be open to the possibility that, unfortunately, day in and day out in our community—not other places that you see on CNN—but right here in our communities, this stuff can and does go on?'

"How do Mr. Marx and I show you bruises? This case isn't about bruises. You're not going to hear one charge that A.J. was beaten. His psyche was battered, bruised—ripped to shreds. How do I come in here and show you a picture of this kid's soul? How do I show you a picture of his spirit?

"We did it by bringing people in here. Not a bunch of cops and not a bunch of people that I've got strings on, and certainly not a bunch of people from HRS. Because—make no mistake about it—the system failed this boy horribly. And you did learn—as I warned you in the beginning—to keep your eye on the ball. There are other trials and other cases."

Scott Cupp pointed at Jessica. "This is about that!

"Those are other proceedings—those are other trials. But you did learn that at least one person is under a grand jury indictment—not by Mr. Marx and myself. But from people out of the community who come in—like yourself—but that's not what this case is about.

"In opening, I made a reference to A.J.'s life inside the asylum. I misspoke. In an asylum, there's hope. This was a concentration camp. There was absolutely no hope.

"Thank you."

Before Judge Colbath charged the jury, Joe Marx asked if it would be all right for him to go ahead and leave. When the judge gave his permission, Marx—feeling very strongly that he had done what he came to do—walked out of the courtroom, down the hall, and out of the courthouse.

While the jurors deliberated, Scott Cupp waited—relatively calmly—alone in a hearing room, reading newspapers and "just waiting." After 5½ long hours, word came that they had arrived at their verdicts.

The courtroom was again packed when the clerk read the verdict on count one—that Jessica Schwarz had maliciously punished Andrew Schwarz by forcing him to eat food from a bowl placed next to a cat's litter box. There was a heart-stopping moment when a resounding "not guilty" filled the room.

Cupp would later say that he couldn't describe how he felt at that moment because he was "numb." He stated, "My brain was getting ready to handle a complete acquittal!"

Michael Waites, sitting on a bench in the rear of the courtroom, dropped his face into his hands, his heart sinking.

Jessica Schwarz remained indifferent and unaffected. She stood between her attorneys, devoid of all emotion, as the verdicts were read on the remaining charges.

"Guilty!" Six times. She was found guilty on all the remaining charges—four counts of aggravated child abuse and two counts of felony child abuse—and faced the possibility of seventy years in prison.

Jessica Schwarz merely glanced at Rendell Brown and shook her head, and as she was escorted from the courtroom—handcuffed and flanked by deputies—she averted her eyes and declined to make any comment to the media.

Neighbors of the Schwarz family, on Triphammer Road and the surrounding area, breathed a collective sigh of relief.

Everyone was more at ease—especially the children—knowing that the neighborhood "bully" was safely behind bars.

When Scott Cupp talked to Joe Marx by telephone and told him the news, Marx was "just thrilled out of [my] mind."

On Friday, December 9, 1994, at her sentencing hearing, a very frustrated Jessica Schwarz informed Judge Walter Colbath, "I never did these things. I never hurt him. I never hurt anyone."

Rendell Brown asked the judge not to exceed the nine-year sentence recommended by Florida's sentencing guidelines.

However, Scott Cupp requested that the guidelines be exceeded and a forty-five-year sentence be imposed on Jessica Schwarz.

The judge declared that only a "monumental conspiracy" by A.J.'s friends, neighbors, and teachers would make her story believable, and then sentenced her to thirty years in prison. He also ordered that—after her release from prison—she was to be on probation for fifteen years, and that she pay a $5,000 fine to a child abuse organization.

CHAPTER 25

It's no mystery that she killed A.J. She probably enjoyed it.

—Scott Cupp

In order to get a conviction for second-degree murder, it would not be necessary for the state to prove that Jessica Schwarz intended to cause A.J.'s death. And they only needed to seat a six-member jury, instead of the twelve required for a first-degree murder charge.

Scott Cupp felt that the jury instructions for second-degree murder in this case were quite appropriate:

1. The victim is dead.
2. The death was caused by the criminal act of the defendant.
3. There was an unlawful killing of a victim by an act imminently dangerous to another and demonstrating a depraved mind without regard for human life.

An "act" includes a series of related actions arising from and preformed pursuant to a single design or purpose.

An act is "imminently dangerous to another and demonstrating a depraved mind" if it is an act or series of acts that:

1. a person of ordinary judgment would know is reasonably certain to kill or do serious bodily injury to another;
2. is done from ill will, hatred, or an evil intent;
3. is of such a nature that the act itself indicates an indifference to human life.

A first-degree murder charge would have forced the state to prove premeditation; and all the evidence was circumstantial. Cupp felt that asking a jury to convict on first-degree murder would really be pushing it.

The point became moot, however, when both sides agreed to "waive jury." Defendants have the right to have their cases decided by a jury of their peers, but if a defendant wants to waive that right—and the state agrees—the case is tried by a judge, who then sits as both the finder of fact and decider of law.

Rendell Brown had approached Scott Cupp after the abuse trial and said he may want to waive a jury. He seemed to think that Cupp would automatically not agree to it, but Cupp told him to give him some time to think about it. It had advantages and disadvantage for both sides. The big one for Brown would be that he wouldn't have to worry about not calling Jessica to testify. She had done horribly. Her demeanor alone cried out, "Spite, ill will, and evil intent"—just what the jury instruction on second-degree required.

In a case such as this, the defense runs a huge risk in not having the defendant take the stand and look at the jury and tell them she didn't do it. Judges, however, are trained to make decisions by simply following the law and instructions—regardless of whether or not the defendant testifies. Judges are looking only to whether or not the state proves its case beyond and to the exclusion of every reasonable doubt.

Scott Cupp based his decision to agree to the waiver on who the judge was to be and took a calculated gamble. Karen Martin would be the judge hearing the murder case. New to the circuit bench—having spent time in county court hearing misdemeanor cases and issues of less severity—she had most recently served a rotation in juvenile court. Cupp's concern was that the pressure on her would be tremendous.

A.J.'s murder trial would be her first in "prime time," and she proved to be more than up to the task.

Jessica Schwarz's nonjury trial for murder and witness tampering began on Monday, March 20, 1995. It would seem that her attorneys weren't as concerned about her impressing anyone with her appearance this time around; instead of sundresses, she simply wore her blue jail-issued "uniforms."

The defense chose not to give an opening statement, but Scott Cupp promised—in his opening—to present evidence to the court to show that Jessica was, indeed, responsible for A.J.'s death.

Circuit court judge Karen Martin allowed—over the protests of Rendell Brown—the state to present much of the testimony about Jessica's abuse of A.J., after Joe Marx successfully argued that it showed she had a motive to kill him.

However, the prosecution was not allowed to use the fact that she had rubbed A.J.'s face into his urine-soaked sheets. Or the fact that she kept him home from school as a form of punishment. Or that she forced him to trim the lawn with household scissors.

Ironically—considering that a jury of her peers had already convicted the defendant of the same abuses—Judge Martin considered them to be "inappropriate parenting skills." Judge Walter Colbath had cited the abuses as "barbaric and grotesque."

Many of the witnesses were the same—and their testimony very similar—as those presented at Jessica's trial on the abuse charges. The huge difference now being, of course, that no one had to be careful not to mention the fact A.J. was dead.

The judge heard testimony from several neighbors who said that the young boy was a good swimmer—and that he could easily stand up in the four-foot-deep, aboveground swimming pool.

There was chilling testimony from Catherine Turner, the neighbor who lived behind the Schwarzes, that during the night that A.J. died—between one and two o'clock in the morning—she had heard a young boy cry out, "I won't do it again! I won't do it again!"

Laura Perryman, Serena Perryman's mother, told the judge that Jessica had said to her—at least four times—that she was going to kill A.J.

"She told me she was going to kill A.J. I told her she couldn't really mean it. The more I told her she couldn't mean it, the more cold-bloodedly she said it."

Her voice broke as she tried to describe the tone of Jessica's voice: "It wasn't like anything I'd heard before. She said she just couldn't take it anymore. She told me A.J. was bad."

Laura Perryman had been so troubled by the conversation that she made it a point to avoid Jessica from then on.

Dr. James Benz's testimony for the defense had to be dealt with—and not just neutralized. Scott Cupp knew that Dr. Joseph Burton's opinion had to supercede Benz's.

The prosecution couldn't afford a tie. There's an old baseball axiom that a tie goes to the runner. In a criminal trial, a tie goes to the defendant in the form of a not guilty verdict, so Benz had to be discredited.

Cupp accomplished that by setting it up on cross-examination to be able to call Dr. Philip Colaizzo in rebuttal to show that the nonsense that Benz claimed happened at the infamous meeting in his office after A.J.'s autopsy was just that—nonsense.

Brown saw where the prosecution was going with Benz and tried to stop it by objecting to Cupp asking Benz about the "threats." By then, it was too late.

Scott Cupp would later say, "I would be lying if I didn't admit my personal satisfaction in Judge Martin allowing me to make Benz stand and demonstrate how that name-less, faceless police detective yelled at him during the meeting."

Dr. Colaizzo, of course, had also been present at the meeting with Dr. Benz and had been seated only a few feet from him.

Cupp: At any time during this meeting, did this event take place: Did anyone—in a loud voice, in speaking to Dr. Benz—scream, "Come on, God damn it, you know this woman killed the kid! God damn it, what the hell is wrong with you? You know that!"
Colaizzo: No, it didn't happen.

It came as no surprise that Brown did not call Jessica to the witness stand, claiming later that she wanted to testify, but he didn't think it was "merited," given the state's case.

On Tuesday, April 11, 1995, Judge Karen Martin—after reviewing written arguments—announced the verdicts in the case of the *State of Florida* v. *Jessica Schwarz* to a packed courtroom.

She began with the witness-tampering charge. Florida statutes define witness tampering as knowingly using intimidation or threat to another person with the intent to cause or induce the person to withhold testimony from an official investigation or proceeding, or to testify untruthfully in an official investigation or proceeding.

"In this case, based on the evidence, I find that Jessica Schwarz and her two daughters were waiting in an interview room at the police station while the father was being interviewed about the death of Andrew Schwarz.

"While they were waiting in the interview room, the defendant picked up her four-year-old daughter, held her at face-to-face level, and asked her, 'Do you want Mama to go to jail?' The four-year-old responded, 'No.' And the mother said, 'If you tell them anything, Mama will go to jail.'

"The video shows the mother contradicted the statements

the child is making and telling her, 'Don't tell these people anything. Just say I don't know. You don't talk to nobody anymore.'

"Then on her way out of the police station with the rest of her family, a police officer heard the defendant say again to the two girls, 'I don't want you talking to these people anymore.'

"Later that same day, when the police officer came to the defendant's home with an HRS representative to remove the two daughters from the defendant's custody, the defendant, in the presence of the police officers, said to the two girls, 'Don't tell these fucking assholes anything. They are not your friends.'

"Based on the law and all the evidence regarding witness tampering, I find beyond a reasonable doubt that the defendant, Jessica Schwarz, intended to cause her four-year-old to withhold testimony and testify untruthfully, and that she used intimidation and threat to do so.

"I do find beyond a reasonable doubt that Jessica Schwarz is guilty of witness tampering."

Judge Martin proceeded to give an excellent and detailed synopsis of the case—and of the evidence that she had considered—pertaining to the second-degree murder charge.

A.J. was found dead floating midway between the top and the bottom of a four-foot-deep, aboveground swimming pool in the backyard of his home. He was naked and his body was covered with bruises and scratches—thirty to forty bruises and scratches. Rigor mortis had set in.

The body was autopsied the next day and again four days later. Both medical examiners were very well qualified. They both concluded that the immediate cause of death was drowning. Both made efforts to determine whether the drowning was from natural causes, suicide, accident, or homicide.

Both autopsies revealed bruises and scratches of varying ages on Andrew's body, abrasions on the right side of his nose and the left corner of his mouth. Palpable swelling was above his left ear, three bruises at various other locations were on his scalp.

"And when the scalp was peeled back—called reflected— during the autopsy, it revealed four areas of subcutaneous bruising extending from the skin surface to the galea. There was obvious hemorrhage in the galea."

It went on and on: a crescent-shaped laceration behind each ear, two areas of bruising inside his upper lip, bruises underneath his chin—on each side. A bruise on the right side of his chest, a scratchlike abrasion of the left side of his chest, two bruises on his abdomen. Bruises on his back and multiple bruises on his buttocks, a scratchlike abrasion on his right hip.

"On the arms, the upper left arm at least three bruises within one to two inches of each other with deep acute hemorrhages extending to the underlying musculature; a scratchlike abrasion on the left forearm."

Abrasions and scratches on his left wrist. A scratchlike abrasion on his right forearm and a small bruise on his left elbow.

Large areas of bruising on the back of his right thigh— extending from below the buttocks to his midthigh. Abrasions on his right calf. Bruises on his left thigh. A bruise below his left knee. An abrasion and bruise on his right lower leg and scratchlike abrasions on both his ankles.

"Both doctors concluded, after the autopsy, that Andrew had been physically abused, and both wrestled with the question of whether his injuries were connected with a homicide."

Dr. Benz concluded that he could not state with any degree of medical certainty whether Andrew's death was an accident, a suicide, or a homicide.

Dr. Burton concluded—without any doubt—had A.J.'s body been found in any circumstance other than a pool and water, the case would have been certified a homicide. Because the body was found floating in water, it complicated the issue of determining if A.J.'s death was, in fact, a homicide.

"He reported that the injuries to the scalp were sufficient—in and of themselves—that they could have caused the death in someone of Andrew's age and size."

A.J. did not die from natural causes or suicide.

"Dr. Burton testified there was nothing in any of Andrew's medical history to indicate any natural causes such as blackouts or seizures which might have precipitated such a drowning."

There was no evidence that Andrew committed suicide.

"Dr. Burton testified that committing suicide by drowning oneself in a pool or bathtub is virtually unheard of in children of this age."

That left the remaining question of whether A.J. died as a result of an accident or a homicide.

When A.J. went to bed on May 1, 1993, he seemed to be fine and there were no scratches or abrasions seen on his face. The next morning, he was dead—floating naked in the swimming pool—and there were abrasions on his face.

According to Dr. Burton, "the fingers of a person" caused the crescent-shaped lacerations behind each ear, and a recent scratch on his chest was "fingernaillike."

The bruises on his upper inner thighs were recent.

"As to the bruise on the upper aspect of the left arm, he testified it would have taken a lot of pressure to force that much blood out of the tissues on the left arm.

"And in his autopsy report, Dr. Burton states that the pattern of bruises on the scalp could in no way have been caused by some type of accident. He stated they were multiple—involving all four quadrants of the scalp."

The bruises were approximately the same age—a few minutes to a few hours old.

The abrasions by his mouth, on his nose, behind his ears, and the bruise beneath the left arm were "consistent with someone having held his head with the hand placed behind and possibly another hand across the nose and then being held submerged until he aspirated enough water to become unconscious and die."

The other possibility was that the numerous bruises to the head "could have resulted in unconsciousness and—in an attempt to cover the act—Andrew's body could have been placed in the pool in an unconscious state; he would have aspirated water and drowned."

Dr. Burton indicated there was some swelling of the brain, which could either have been caused by punches or blows to the head—or from the drowning.

"Dr. Burton testified that he had done—I think it was—twenty to forty thousand autopsies and his specialty is working with children.

"Dr. Burton was not able to say with any degree of a reasonable medical certainty that either one of these scenarios was exactly how Andrew came to his death, but the injuries were consistent with either one."

So it became necessary to look at whether any of the recent injuries could have been caused by an accident rather than at the hands of another person. Some of the injuries that A.J. had were definitely older and were not considered.

"The injury to his buttocks could have been caused by a whipping which he supposedly got some days before, a week before.

"The injuries under his chin were consistent with an incident which neighbors observed several weeks prior to his death: Andrew was picked up by the head and neck and swung from side to side with his arms flopping like a rag doll—and was seen to have been picked up by his [step]mother.

"Dr. Burton testified that the injuries to his head could not have been caused by accident. And all of these scratches and bruises could not have been explained by accident.

"Then there's the issue of why was Andrew in the pool in the middle of the night in the first place and why was he naked?"

Had A.J.—as the defense suggested—slipped out of the house to swim alone naked in the middle of the night? Because he was so busy with chores that he didn't have much chance to swim? Was he naked because he didn't want Jessica or David to discover that he had been out swimming in the middle of the night?

"There's no question that this child was constantly made to do chores. But let's examine what was happening the day before the evening that he died."

Jessica and David and the rest of the family had gone to Sunfest and A.J. was left home alone for the day. A neighbor saw him playing in the front yard. If he had chosen to do so, he could have gone swimming at any time that day.

"It makes no sense that he would go out naked in the middle of the night, on a very cold night, in the dark to swim.

"Andrew had never been known to swim naked. And then there's the testimony that nakedness was used as a form of punishment and humiliation in the family.

"Neighbors had seen Andrew forced to run naked down the street. It was obvious that he was embarrassed in trying to cover himself—and crying.

"Then there was the expert testimony of Dr. Rahaim that for a child who had been repeatedly humiliated and punished through nakedness, it would be a terrifying experience to swim naked in the middle of the night.

"So, it is possible? Remotely. Is it reasonable? Not at all.

"So based on the physical evidence alone and the surrounding circumstances, I find beyond a reasonable doubt that the corpus has been proven in this case."

The judge then proceeded to the issue of who had done this and why.

It was obvious from numerous witnesses' testimony that Jessica Schwarz was the disciplinarian in the family. They reported seeing her slap A.J. on the back of the head—and punching him on the head and face. And they testified to seeing her force him—as a form of punishment—to go naked.

"Her motive? The record is replete with testimony that this [step]mother despised this child; that she considered him nothing but trouble."

Laura Perryman had given the chilling and frightening testimony that Jessica had told her that she just couldn't take it anymore—couldn't take A.J. anymore—and that she was going to kill him.

"The neighbor tried to tell her, 'you don't mean that, you cannot mean that,' and the neighbor reported that she became more and more cold-blooded in her insistence that she was going to kill him—as though she had made a business decision. But that happened in December of '91 or [early] '92 and Andrew died in '93.

"Why after a year to a year and a half would Andrew be purposely drowned?

"The record is also replete with evidence that Andrew was becoming a bigger and bigger problem to his step-mother."

At the scene—the morning after the drowning—Bear had been grief-stricken and in tears; he was inconsolable. Jessica's reaction—as described by the police officers—had been "cool and uninvolved."

"It's not in any way reasonable that either one of the [other] children would have committed this offense nor do I find it reasonable that this would have been done by the father.

"At the most—according to the evidence—the father occasionally disciplined the child by spanking him on the behind. He was never known to belittle this child, to punish this child by punching him in the top of the head or on the face, to cause the child to go naked or to humiliate him in any way.

"I find the conclusion that this death was not an accident is inescapable; find that the state has proven beyond a reasonable doubt the elements of this offense:

"That Andrew Schwarz is dead.

"That the death was caused by the criminal agency of Jessica Schwarz.

"And this killing was done by an act imminently dangerous to Andrew and evincing a depraved mind regardless of human life.

"And it makes no difference which of the scenarios of Dr. Burton apply. It's clear that this child was beaten, that this child was either unconscious—perhaps semi-unconscious—when taken to the pool and held underwater. This child did not go into the pool on that night of his own volition.

"So I'm finding you guilty as charged."

Overcome with emotion, Scott Cupp's eyes filled with tears as he laid his head down on the table in front of him. Later—outside the courtroom—he told reporters, "Maybe now, A.J. has some peace."

The proof that the strategy with Dr. Benz had worked was evident in Judge Martin's findings-of-fact. She had barely referred to Benz at all and her verdict was replete with references to—and an almost total reliance on—Dr. Burton's opinions for her conclusions.

Benz's performance in A.J.'s case was the beginning of the end of his career as the chief medical examiner in Palm Beach County.

Scott Cupp would later comment, "In many ways, it was sad to watch over the next several years—but in the end, he did it to himself."

On Friday, July 28, 1995, Judge Martin listened to four hours of testimony at Jessica Schwarz's sentencing hearing for the murder of A.J.

Strangely enough, even though Jessica's parents, Edward and Helen Woods, both claimed that they believed their daughter was innocent, neither one of them asked the judge to show her mercy. Showing very little emotion, they testified that there was no alcoholism or drug abuse in their family and that Jessica had not been an abused child.

According to Mr. Woods, "There is nothing in her past. Nothing reaching a level of such destructive reaction."

Lauren Cross, Jessica's twelve-year-old daughter, cried openly as she told the judge, "If you put my mother away, you'll be locking up an innocent mother and let the real killer run loose."

During almost an hour and a half on the witness stand, Jessica berated her former neighbors, the prosecutors, and even the media for "wrongfully" convicting her.

When Rendell Brown asked her if she had ever cried, she—after thinking about it for several moments—replied, "When my kids were born, when a friend died . . . when A.J. died."

On cross-examination, when Joe Marx questioned her about her abrasive personality, she admitted that she had a "loud mouth," but she claimed she was not violent or threatening.

Marx reminded her of a comment she had made to him during a recess about his wife, Karen Starr Marx, who had been murdered the previous year.

"Do you remember saying, 'Why don't you join your wife? I'll see you out on bond'?"

Jessica Schwarz admitted that she remembered, but she denied that she was threatening him.

She also denied killing A.J. and insisted that she couldn't feel remorse for something she hadn't done.

On Friday, August 4, 1995, Judge Martin imposed the longest prison term possible—under Florida sentencing guidelines—on Jessica Schwarz. A forty-year sentence that would have to be served after she finished her thirty-year prison term for the abuse—seventy years total.

Schwarz's attorney had asked the judge not to sentence her based on her attitude:

"It's easy to understand her indignation because she did not do what she is accused of doing."

Joe Marx—referring to Jessica's daughters—had implored the judge:

"Do them a favor and put her in jail and keep her there as long as possible. Protect these children from her."

EPILOGUE

Many had questioned why no indictment for first degree. Immediately after the trial, I was very sensitive about that question. I guess I was still reeling from the reality that she was actually convicted and would be going off for seventy years on a case that in the beginning was dead in the water. Very few thought she would be convicted!

—Scott Cupp

In April 1997, Scott Cupp, who had been responsible for handling the prosecution of Barbara Black, the HRS worker who had been indicted for threatening Eileen Callahan, announced that Black would not face criminal charges.

The pretrial intervention agreement required only that she perform community service, once a month for six months.

"It sat on the back burner until after Jessica's trials. By that time, it was decided that the point had been made and going after Black may have been overkill and treating her like a scapegoat. I don't know if that was right or not—but that's what we did."

After leaving the Palm Beach State Attorney's Office in 1999, Cupp opened his own practice in LaBelle, Florida—a beautiful little town on the banks of the Caloosahatchee River—twenty miles from Fort Myers. In 2002, he returned to prosecution and is presently chief of felony for the Lee County Office for the Twentieth Judicial Circuit.

(Everyone who was interviewed insisted that the arrest and successful prosecution of Jessica Schwarz was a team effort. However, they all agreed that if Scott Cupp had not insisted on a second complete autopsy, Jessica Schwarz would have gotten away with murder.)

Joseph Marx stayed with the state attorney's office until March 2000, then—after having his own private practice for a few years—he was appointed to a judgeship by Governor Jeb Bush in 2003. On August 1, 2003, he took over as county court judge for the Fifteenth Judicial Circuit in Palm Beach County.

He is married to Judge Krista Marx and has three step-children.

Michael Waites continues in law enforcement as an investigator for the state attorney's office.

Chris Calloway is now a sergeant with the PBSO. Jimmy Restivo has since passed away from a heart attack.

Dr. James Benz continued as the medical examiner for Palm Beach County until 1996. He has since retired and lives in Indiana.

Dr. Joseph Burton has Emeritus status with his office in Georgia and has his own consulting firm.

Near the end of the first trial, David Schwarz surfaced by phone, late one night to one of the investigators. He was alone somewhere in a motel room in another state—drunk and incoherent. That was the last Scott Cupp ever heard of him.

Jessica Schwarz's appeals have run their course. The convictions in both trials were appealed to Florida's Fourth

District Court of Appeals and were upheld, and the Supreme Court of Florida declined to hear them. Her current projected release date is December 3, 2034—subject to review.

As of this writing, she is incarcerated at the Broward Correctional Institution. She is middle-aged with graying hair—and unrepentant.

AFTERTHOUGHTS

by Carol J. Rothgeb

Jessica Schwarz—through intimidation and misguided, twisted loyalty on their part—was able to control her children and her husband. Very much the way William K. Sapp—serial killer and the subject of Hometown Killer—controlled his mentally challenged, and childlike, accomplices.

—Carol J. Rothgeb

Three days before I was asked to join Scott Cupp in this project, I was talking to a dear friend of mine about the possibility of writing another book. We were discussing a case in which a stepfather murdered his two stepchildren. I made the remark that I didn't think I could write one about natural parents killing their child, but maybe I could deal with writing one about a stepparent.

Then I got the phone call. I was hesitant at first. The editor sent me all the information that he had at that time. When I looked through the material, I was immediately touched by this young boy's tragic death, and—even more so—by his tragic life.

There's a young boy about A.J.'s age who catches the school bus across the street on the corner, about one hundred feet from my house. I can see him clearly out my kitchen window in the mornings. For whatever reason, his mother drives him to the bus stop.

She pulls up across the street, and if the weather is nice, the little boy crosses the street to wait for the bus. If the weather is bad or just plain cold, the boy waits in the car until he sees the bus coming down the street, then gets out and crosses over to the bus stop. Either way, his mother waits until the bus comes before pulling away.

So, what I see when I look out my window is a loving mother who cares about her child. For all I know, it is his stepmother, but whoever is driving the car cares what happens to the little boy.

Indeed, a poignant contrast to A.J.'s life.

Only Jessica Schwarz knows the whole story of exactly what happened in the wee hours of Sunday, May 2, 1993, between the times when Ron Pincus Jr. saw A.J. walking his dog and when Bear found his lifeless, bruised body in the aboveground swimming pool.

One can only imagine what the infraction of the rules might have been that so aroused Jessica's anger and rage that she could beat a child nearly to death with her bare hands and fists. And then hold the slender ten-year-old boy's head underwater until he stopped struggling for his very life.

As sad and demeaning as A.J.'s life was—he struggled to survive.

If he would have lived to adulthood—still living under the same miserable circumstances—one can only wonder what would have become of him. It's fairly common to read or hear of murderers—serial killers, especially—who were severely abused as children. Sometimes it's hard not to have compassion—at least for the children they were.

And what if A.J. had been removed from Jessica and David's house and placed in a loving foster home and received the help—and hugs—he so desperately needed? What if just one more neighbor would have called the authorities? So many "what-ifs" and "if onlys" . . .

Most parents worry about what will happen to their children as they venture out into life—into the world. Going to school. Going to play at a friend's house. The mothers and fathers admonish them over and over again not to talk to strangers. Not to accept a ride from someone they don't know.

And then there are the children who have no safe place—whose spirits are damaged or broken—who have no one to turn to for help. Their caregivers—the ones who feed them and clothe them and give them a roof over their heads—are also their tormentors. Surely these children spend their days—and their nights—in the presence of evil.

AFTERWORD

by Scott H. Cupp

I always found it curious that in the aftermath of the convictions and sentences—amid all the many words written and spoken about A.J., Jessica, and HRS, the state agency responsible for his care at the time of his murder—no one other than myself speculated about what A.J. would have been like had he survived to become a young man. No one.

When the proposal for this book made the rounds, the publishers who rejected it sounded a consistent theme. Child abuse is just too painful a subject. Yes, it is. It's the kind of pain that creeps into your dreams. It's the kind of pain that makes you weak. It's the kind of pain we in America persist in refusing to deal with.

Maybe it touches something in us that we lack the courage to think about and to speak about. A.J.'s story not only touches that, it *slaps* it. Maybe what A.J. touches in us are thoughts that, for reasons largely unknown to us, we are ashamed of. Maybe we secretly harbor a relief that he did not survive to become a young, angry man. A man we would certainly have to deal with. That would be easy, though. Then we would be dealing with the behavior, not the person.

Perhaps he touches in us things about our own childhood that are too painful to go back to. Maybe he touches something in us that we fear there have been times in our lives we know we were perilously close to slipping into. The worst of ourselves. And we can't figure out how those times happened. Or what is locked inside us that we can't seem to get to. And then it passes. Maybe it's the same thing I sensed was present during the trial, from being in the presence of Jessica Schwarz.

Ask again—how would A.J. have turned out had he survived the relentless physical and psychological pounding he received? What kind of citizen would he have looked like? A.J., the boy, would have been a prohibitive favorite to become A.J., the man, filled with substance abuse, physically violent to those in his life, and worse. It would not be much of a stretch to see him as a relentless killer.

The child protective system in Florida, as I suspect is the case in most states, has been broken for decades. Children are being murdered and sexually and physically abused by their parents. Children being cared for by the state are being murdered and sexually and physically abused, and this, too, has been so for decades. Nothing is changing.

The court system bends over backward in attempting to keep children in their present placements—even after they have been proved to have been abused. This started many years ago when the focus on "rights" took prevailing importance. It was seen that parents had rights. Rights not only to retain custody of their children after it had been proved that they had burned them with cigarettes or placed them in hot water or engaged in sex acts with them, but they also had the right to expect the state to "teach" them to stop doing those things and become better parents.

They had the right to insist that a court order the state to submit a case plan that would show how—over a period of many months—the state would make it so they could retain custody of the very same children they had abused. If at the time of expiration of the plan there were still problems and the children were still not safe with their parents, the case plans could be extended if the parents could show that the state hadn't provided them enough services or hadn't taught them properly how to be a safe parent.

This continues today. The present trend is called "reasonable efforts." The courts are applying the system of laws laid down by legislatures, which means the people—you and I.

When any adult, including and especially a parent, intentionally and willfully causes the kind of harm previously mentioned, shouldn't they automatically forfeit any "right" they had concerning the child they have abused? Why bother to "teach" someone not to have sex with his child, or not to place a lit cigarette against his child's skin, or allow her boyfriend to have sex with her children? The law's overemphasis on the biological link between parent and child should more easily give way when it is clearly established that parents have abused their children. This will, in the long run, strengthen the concept of family. The law must begin sincerely to apply "the best interest of the child" standard.

When children are finally removed from the people who have harmed them, why are they placed within a system that too often has been shown not able to do much better? The foster care system is broken. Some have suggested that orphanages should again be used. It is clear that far too many children are left in abusive places, and far too many children stagnate in the purgatory of foster care. Centralized schools or homes would allow social services to be given displaced children in an effective and efficient manner. We can and must do better.

My purpose in writing this book is that A.J. helps to begin the debate anew. For everyone who met him—or had to deal with his tragic and senseless death—I can think of no better epitaph.

ABOUT THE AUTHORS

Carol J. Rothgeb is the author of *Hometown Killer*. She lives in Springfield, Ohio.

Scott Cupp has prosecuted many high-profile criminal cases. His articles on child advocacy have appeared in the *South Florida Sun-Sentinel, Palm Beach Post, Miami Herald,* and elsewhere. He lives in LaBelle, Florida.

HORRIFYING TRUE CRIME
FROM PINNACLE BOOKS

Body Count
by Burl Barer   0-7860-1405-9   **$6.50**US/**$8.50**CAN

The Babyface Killer
by Jon Bellini   0-7860-1202-1   **$6.50**US/**$8.50**CAN

Love Me to Death
by Steve Jackson   0-7860-1458-X   **$6.50**US/**$8.50**CAN

The Boston Stranglers
by Susan Kelly   0-7860-1466-0   **$6.50**US/**$8.50**CAN

Body Double
by Don Lasseter   0-7860-1474-1   **$6.50**US/**$8.50**CAN

The Killers Next Door
by Joel Norris   0-7860-1502-0   **$6.50**US/**$8.50**CAN

Available Wherever Books Are Sold!

Visit our website at **www.kensingtonbooks.com.**

MORE MUST-READ TRUE CRIME FROM PINNACLE

Under the Knife   0-7860-1197-1   **$6.50**US/**$8.50**CAN
By Karen Roebuck

Lobster Boy   0-7860-1569-1   **$6.50**US/**$8.50**CAN
By Fred Rosen

Body Dump   0-7860-1133-5   **$6.50**US/**$8.50**CAN
By Fred Rosen

Savage   0-7860-1409-1   **$6.50**US/**$8.50**CAN
By Robert Scott

Innocent Victims   0-7860-1273-0   **$6.50**US/**$8.50**CAN
By Brian J. Karem

The Boy Next Door   0-7860-1459-8   **$6.50**US/**$8.50**CAN
By Gretchen Brinck

Available Wherever Books Are Sold!

Visit our website at **www.kensingtonbooks.com**.

Dear Reader,

It is with bittersweetness that I write Gannon Steele's story because he is the last brother of those "Bad News Steeles." He is the last and the youngest, so you wonder what about his older brothers impressed him the most. Was it their player ways or their ability to recognize when they'd found that special woman who was destined to share their lives forever?

Gannon is in a quandary. Now that he is the last of the "Bad News Steeles," he wants to take it to the limit and enjoy life with women to the fullest. But on the other hand, he doesn't want to miss the opportunity of recognizing that woman who might be his soul mate. Has he met such a woman? Is Delphine Ryland the one? There must be a reason he feels emotions around her that he's never felt for another woman. Or is it a fluke?

From the very beginning, I knew Gannon's story would be special because it would also be the ending of a family of men and women who thought they never wanted to find love but found it anyway.

Join me in giving Gannon his chance to find love. He will either walk away or claim it. Which decision do you think he will make?

Thank you for making the Steeles a very special family. All of them—the Charlotte, North Carolina, Steeles and the Phoenix, Arizona, Steeles—thank you from the bottom of their hearts!

Happy reading!

Brenda Jackson

BRENDA JACKSON

—

CLAIMED BY A STEELE

HARLEQUIN

DESIRE

HARLEQUIN®
DESIRE™

Recycling programs
for this product may
not exist in your area.

ISBN-13: 978-1-335-20907-8

Claimed by a Steele

Copyright © 2020 by Brenda Streater Jackson

This edition published by arrangement with Harlequin Books S.A.

For questions and comments about the quality of this book,
please contact us at CustomerService@Harlequin.com.

Harlequin Enterprises ULC
22 Adelaide St. West, 40th Floor
Toronto, Ontario M5H 4E3, Canada
www.Harlequin.com

Printed in U.S.A.

Brenda Jackson is a *New York Times* bestselling author of more than one hundred romance titles. Brenda lives in Jacksonville, Florida, and divides her time between family, writing and traveling. Email Brenda at authorbrendajackson@gmail.com or visit her on her website at brendajackson.net.

Books by Brenda Jackson

Harlequin Desire

The Westmoreland Legacy

The Rancher Returns
His Secret Son
An Honorable Seduction
His to Claim
Duty or Desire

Forged of Steele

Seduced by a Steele
Claimed by a Steele

Visit her Author Profile page at Harlequin.com, or brendajackson.net, for more titles.

You can also find Brenda Jackson on Facebook, along with other Harlequin Desire authors, at Facebook.com/harlequindesireauthors!

To the love of my life, Gerald Jackson Sr.
My one and only. My forever-hubby.
My everything.

To everyone who enjoys reading about
the Steeles, this one is especially for you.

To the librarians of Mississippi.
Thanks for inviting me to your 2019 conference
in Jackson, Mississippi. It was wonderful and
you guys made it fun! Thanks a million,
and since this is the book that I was working on
in my hotel room, I am dedicating it to you guys.

"With all lowliness and meekness, with
longsuffering, forbearing one another in love."
—*Ephesians* 4:2

Prologue

"You may kiss your bride."

Gannon Steele held back a laugh as he watched his brother Mercury pull the woman he loved into his arms and give her a whopper of a kiss. It was hard to believe that his *I-will-never-fall-in-love-again* brother had done just that. Fallen in love again. Gannon knew no one was happier about it than his mother, Eden Tyson Steele, who adored Mercury's new wife and who'd been ready to see another son married off.

He glanced around at his family. They were probably thinking the same things about Mercury that he was. Sloan Donahue had changed Mercury's mindset about love and Mercury had changed hers about being fiercely independent. Like everyone else, Gannon was convinced Mercury and Sloan were meant for each other.

"Should we think that maybe you're next?"

Gannon glanced over at his oldest brother, Galen. Their parents, Drew and Eden Steele, had given birth to six sons. For years, all six had been known around Phoenix as the Bad News Steeles. Mainly because of their die-hard bachelor ways. Now all those previous die-hard bachelors were married—all except for Gannon.

Unlike his five brothers, Gannon had never wanted to stay single forever. He viewed marriage as a part of his future. However, he was in no hurry to claim a wife, and now that Mercury was married off, that meant more women for Gannon to enjoy. He couldn't wait.

"You all should know that I'm next, Galen, since I'm the last of the Phoenix Steeles. But I intend to have the time of my life before that happens, which I don't foresee happening for another ten years or more."

"Ten years?" Galen asked, raising a doubtful eyebrow.

"You heard me. Ten years at least. Now that I am the last single Steele left standing, I plan to enjoy being the number one player."

"Be careful, baby bro. You'll be singing a different tune if the right woman appears in your life, trust me."

Gannon chuckled, definitely not taking anything his brother said seriously. He was the master of his own mind and his own fate. There was no woman alive who could change him. "Who would have thought?"

Galen gave him a quizzical look. "Thought what?"

"That you would be sounding like Mom in your old age."

Galen frowned. "Be amused all you want, Gannon. Just don't say that I didn't warn you. Do I need to remind you about what happened to me when Brittany appeared in my life? I was the last person anyone expected to fall in love."

Gannon knew that to be true, but then, all one had to do was look at Brittany or any of the women his brothers had married to understand why his brothers had gotten love-whipped. Not only were the women beautiful, but they were also intelligent. However, with his current mind-set, Gannon figured that even if a beautiful, intelligent woman walked into his life right now, he wouldn't bite. Although he had discriminating taste, he still preferred changing bed partners. Now with his brothers out of the way, there would be even more women out there for him. He couldn't see settling down to just one woman anytime soon. He would stick to his ten-year plan.

Deciding to change the subject, he said, "So Zion is having a baby, huh?"

Galen laughed. "No, Celine is pregnant. Zion is strutting around like a damn peacock, like he's the only one who can make a baby. For him to have been the Bachelor in Demand to hold out the longest to get hitched, it's totally hilarious that he's now all in."

Gannon laughed, as well, watching the group of men and their wives standing together. For years those men had been pegged as the Bachelors in Demand. Now they were all married and seemed pretty damn happy about it. And none of them had wasted time getting their wives pregnant.

Gannon wasn't ready for all that.

A short while later, while at the wedding reception, Gannon's cell vibrated. He checked and saw the caller was Delphine Ryland. He frowned. How did he know that name? Why was she listed in his phone contacts? Was she a past bed partner? Although he tried remembering names, he couldn't always do so. Unlike his brothers in their man-whoring days, Gannon didn't have a special phone just for women. If he preferred not talking to one, he just didn't answer.

"When is your interview with *Simply Irresistible*, Gannon?"

He glanced over at his sister-in-law Nikki, who was married to his brother Jonas. The two had announced last week they were expecting a baby. Gannon's brother Tyson and his wife, Hunter, had announced the same thing a few weeks ago. Gannon figured those announcements were another reason his mother was beaming with pride. She'd seen five out of six of her sons married, and by this time next year she would have more grandkids to spoil. Hopefully she would give Mercury and Sloan time to settle into their marriage before waving baby booties in front of them.

"I believe it's this coming week," he said. In all

honesty, with the excitement of the wedding, and all his family and friends arriving in town, he'd completely forgotten about the interview.

Simply Irresistible, a Denver-based magazine, was owned by Chloe Westmoreland, a woman they considered a cousin-in-law. Gannon had felt honored when Chloe contacted him to say the magazine would be doing a series of feature stories on CEOs making a difference within their companies. They wanted him to be one of those they highlighted. In fact, they intended for him to be on the cover.

Over the last forty years, Gannon's father had taken his small trucking company and turned it into a million-dollar business, with routes all over the United States. When Drew retired a few years ago, Gannon had taken over the company as CEO, and he still enjoyed getting behind the steering wheel of a rig himself to make cross-country deliveries and pickups.

He had no problem doing the interview and hoped the feature would help to give more respect to the profession of truckers on the road and their importance to a thriving economy. He figured most people didn't think about how much businesses depended on the trucking industry to deliver their products to consumers.

"When I talked to Chloe last month, she mentioned that Delphine Ryland would be doing the interview with you," Nikki said, breaking into his thoughts.

Delphine Ryland.

At some point Chloe had given him the woman's name and number, and he'd put the contact into his phone list. "Do you know her?"

"Delphine? Yes, I know her."

Gannon shouldn't have been surprised since he knew of Nikki and Chloe's past working relationship and current friendship. Before Nikki's marriage to Jonas, she had freelanced as a photographer for *Simply Irresistible* on occasion. It stood to reason that she would also know some of the people who worked for the magazine.

"I just missed a call from Ms. Ryland."

Nikki nodded. "She was probably calling to remind you about the interview. Making sure you didn't forget since she was to arrive in town this weekend."

"No problem. I'll return her call tomorrow."

"Delphine's a nice person and a great journalist. You're going to like her, Gannon."

He decided not to say anything to that because he was a man who liked all women, and he figured his feelings for Delphine Ryland would be no different.

Glancing at her cell phone, Delphine released a huge sigh. She had placed two calls to Gannon Steele over the weekend and he had yet to get back in touch with her. It was important that she do a good job on this project and Gannon Steele was the last CEO to interview.

So far, she'd done interviews with Ron Paulus, the pizza CEO who often dropped into his stores to make deliveries, Jack Zelle, the owner of a huge manufacturing company who had no problem rolling up his sleeves to help get orders out of his warehouse, and Nathan Beam, who owned a slew of restaurants and often worked as a waiter. All those CEOs had something in common. They believed connecting with their employees was empowering and that the best leadership style was to not ask their employees to do anything that they themselves wouldn't do.

From her research, she knew Gannon Steele was no different. Since taking over at Steele Trucking Company when his father retired close to five years ago, the thirty-three-year-old CEO had transformed the company. Steele Trucking Company was already a multimillion-dollar enterprise, and he'd not only grown the wealth tenfold, but had also made it into a family-oriented business.

Gannon had listened to his employees, and he himself had traveled the routes they'd driven when he'd occasionally left the office to get behind the steering wheel of a rig. Doing so had given him firsthand knowledge of truckers' challenges.

As a result, he had implemented a number of changes that made life better for the truckers and their families whenever the drivers were away. He had opened several schools for the children of his employees and made sure a support system was in place to assist the families when the long-distance truckers were on the road. He'd even offered a tuition-paid program, where his truckers could go back to school to get their GED, professional certifications or even bachelor's degrees. The tuition program extended to the truckers' families, as well, eliminating a big source of stress. Then, on top of everything else, he'd raised the salary for his workers, making them the highest paid in the industry and making Steele Trucking Company one of the most sought-after employers in the state of Arizona. Already Gannon had graced the covers of a number of professional magazines as the boy wonder of the trucking industry.

Simply Irresistible was a magazine that catered to today's up-and-coming woman. The magazine's most popular edition still remained the annual Irresistible Man issue. The feature included a cover shoot and an in-depth story about a man who the magazine felt deserved special recognition because he was simply irresistible in both looks and how he'd made a positive impact on society.

In the past, many notables had graced the cover, including sports figure LeBron James, wealthy rancher Ramsey Westmoreland, professional motorcycle racer Thorn Westmoreland and former movie star turned rancher Walker Rafferty. A few months ago, the board chose Gannon Steele for this year, not only because of his accomplishments, but also because of his sexiness. The staff at *Simply Irresistible* knew the man featured on the cover needed to be thought of by their readers as a fantasy lover.

From the research Delphine had done and all the photographs she'd collected of Gannon Steele, he could definitely be a woman's fantasy lover. He certainly got her vote. The man's green eyes would make any woman drool. So here she was in Phoenix, ready to do the interview, and yet she couldn't get in touch with the guy.

Her boss, Lucia Westmoreland, who knew Gannon personally because of family connections, had given Delphine his cell-phone number and told her that Chloe Westmoreland, the CEO of *Simply Irresistible*, had already given Gannon Delphine's. That made her wonder why he wasn't accepting her calls. Had he changed his mind about doing the interview?

That thought sent nervous chills down her body. The last thing she wanted was to let down Chloe or Lucia when they'd been so good to her. They'd given her a chance because they'd seen the same ambition in her that they'd seen in each other at the start of the magazine. Chloe had launched it right out of college, and when she expanded the business to Colorado, she'd called on her best friend from college, Lucia, to manage the Denver office. Chloe hadn't intended to remain in Denver, but she and Lucia ended up marrying two brothers, and now Lucia mostly ran the business full-time, while Chloe worked from home while raising her family and assisting her husband in his sheep-ranching business. Like Lucia, Chloe also knew Gannon personally because of family connections.

Delphine would always be indebted to both Chloe and Lucia for giving her a job as a journalist. After her breakup with Liddell Bartley, it had been her plan never to return to Denver. She'd been heartbroken when the man she loved—the man she thought loved her in return—had sent her a Dear Jane letter a month before the wedding, letting her know he'd fallen in love with someone else.

But her mother's health made it necessary for Delphine to move back to Denver. She hadn't known just how ill her mother had been until Lucia had written to tell her. Lucia's mother and Delphine's own had been best friends while growing up in Denver. Although Delphine's mother hadn't wanted her daughter to find out just how bad her condition was and had sworn Lucia's mother to secrecy, Lucia hadn't felt that secrecy extended to her. She'd been compelled to let Delphine know the true nature of her mother's health.

No longer caring that returning to Colorado would place her in an awkward position when it came to Liddell, Delphine had quit her job in New York to return to Denver to become her mother's sole caretaker. Knowing the time and attention Delphine would need to give her mother, Chloe and Lucia had offered her a job as a freelance journalist so she could work from home while contributing to the magazine. That was what she'd done for three years.

After her mother passed away last year, Delphine took a full-time position at *Simply Irresistible*. She enjoyed her work and the assignments she'd been given. The thing she liked the most was that her assignments, more often than not, took her away from Denver for weeks at a time. That helped with the grieving process.

The two of them had been close ever since her father had left her mother for another woman and hadn't once looked back. Delphine had been six years old at the time. She honestly didn't know now if he was alive or dead, and frankly, she didn't care. That seemed to be the story of the Ryland women's lives.

The men they loved left them for other women.

The unexpected ringing of her cell phone made Delphine jump. The caller ID indicated it was Gannon Steele, returning her call. "Yes?"

"Ms. Ryland, this is Gannon Steele. I apologize for not returning your calls earlier, but we had a wedding in my family this weekend and I've been quite busy."

She suddenly recalled that Lucia had mentioned there would be a Steele wedding, but Delphine hadn't known it would be happening this particular weekend. "No need to apologize, Mr. Steele. I understand." She inhaled deeply to get past the sound of his voice, a deep, rich baritone that reminded her of Barry White. Unexpected tremors flowed through her.

"So when can we get together?" he asked her.

She knew his question wasn't personal. They had both agreed to meet for the interview. But at that moment the sound of his voice had her imagining other possible scenarios, too. She shook her head, knowing none were realistic. During her research she'd discovered more about Gannon Steele than just his business accomplishments. She also knew he was the last of what the women in Phoenix referred to as the Bad News Steeles. With another brother married off, he was the only single one left. His and his brothers' reputations with women were legendary. Now she wondered if Gannon Steele intended to carry the banner proudly as the last remaining one of the sexy Steeles.

"I'm available whenever you are." Too late, she wondered if her response had come off as unprofessional. Before he could answer, she added, "I'm available to meet with you to discuss the magazine's interview whenever you are, Mr. Steele."

"Okay, what about tonight over dinner."

Dinner? He wanted to meet over dinner? She swallowed deeply, reminding herself that the offer was only business. There was no need to freak out. Too bad he was the first man who'd gotten her attention since her breakup with Liddell five years ago. And he had grabbed her attention just from the photographs she'd seen and the research she'd done. A lot of women considered him a charmer.

"Ms. Ryland?"

Hearing him say her name made her realize she hadn't agreed to meet him for dinner. "Yes, Mr. Steele, just tell me where to meet you and—"

"Sorry, but thanks to my mother, I'm old-fashioned. Business or otherwise, if I invite a woman out, then I'm responsible for making sure she gets there and back. Just tell me the name of your hotel and I'll meet you in the lobby at seven, if that time is acceptable to you."

She also knew all about his mother, the beautiful and vivacious Eden Tyson Steele, a former international model whose face had graced the covers of such magazines as *Vogue*, *Cosmo* and *Elle*. She could see the woman teaching her six sons about the value of respecting women, even if their philandering behavior would tempt them to do otherwise.

"I'm staying at the St. Laurent."

"I know exactly where that is. I will see you at seven, Ms. Ryland."

"Okay. Thanks."

Delphine hung up the phone and wondered what it would be like to sit across from Gannon Steele and talk business. Of course, she would thank him for agreeing to do the interview. She'd heard it was often hard to get their subjects to agree to be on the cover of their Irresistible Man issue. It seemed Gannon Steele hadn't balked at the idea. Instead, according to Lucia, he had even been flattered that she'd asked. That would certainly make Delphine's job of interviewing him easier.

A lot of women considered truckers hot, and Delphine was curious about them, as well. Was it true that a trucker had a girl waiting for him at every truck stop? And that the truck was often used for more than just hauling merchandise? Of course, she wouldn't ask Mr. Steele those specific questions, but she couldn't help wondering.

Glancing at her watch, she saw that she had five hours to kill before he arrived, and she intended to put them to good use. This would be the first time in nearly five years that she'd gone out with a man. Even if the evening was nothing more than a business dinner, she intended to look her best.

Gannon parked his car, quickly got out and headed for the entrance of the hotel. A traffic jam on the interstate had made getting here on time a challenge, but he'd arrived with ten minutes to spare. When he entered the lobby, he recalled that he'd been here a number of times before, with several women. All of whom had known the score and been well aware that he was not looking for a lasting relationship. He was a between-the-sheets sort of guy and the women he slept with knew it. Most weren't looking for anything more serious than he was.

Of course, there were always women with love and marriage on their minds. Those were usually the ones who were one-and-done. Rarely did he repeat an evening with them. Only three that he recalled could make that claim. Gannon knew that when he got married it would be because he was ready to settle down. Like he'd told his brother Galen yesterday, he didn't see that happening anytime soon. He was sticking to his ten-year plan.

According to his watch, he still had five minutes, so he let his mind wander to his upcoming plans. He was looking forward to getting on the road and out of the office for a couple of weeks. He knew his right-hand man, Ozzie Hazouri, would handle things in his absence. Gannon would be heading south to Florida. Once he parked his rig, he would get a rental car and drive to Miami to his beach house. A week there would definitely revitalize him. With this being the end of April, he was two months from the halfway mark of the year. There were still goals he wanted to achieve in his thriving business. He intended to...

"Mr. Steele?"

He blinked, going temporarily speechless when a woman stepped in front of him. Granted, he'd never met Delphine Ryland and hadn't really thought about what to expect, but he definitely hadn't expected the woman standing in front of him. Damn, she looked absolutely, positively beautiful. So beautiful that all he could do was stand there and stare. Or was he gawking?

She had large, expressive eyes that were chestnut brown, shoulder-length curly brown hair with streaks of golden blond, styled to complement her oval face, and strikingly high cheekbones. But what really had him spellbound were lips that looked so indisputably enticing that he was tempted to lean in and give them one hell of a kiss. He was what his brothers often called a "lips" man.

Her lips were perfectly shaped, appealing to everything male within him. Just looking at her mouth made it impossible for him to think straight. Hell, he honestly couldn't think at all.

"Mr. Steele?"

Her repeating his name made him quickly grab control of his senses. No woman had ever captured his attention like this before. "Yes, I'm Gannon Steele. Sorry for staring, but you remind me of someone," he lied, hoping that excuse would cover his initial reaction to seeing her.

"I do?"

At that moment, he appreciated his ability to think on his feet. "Yes, and the resemblance is uncanny." He was satisfied with his response. If she ever caught him staring at her again, she would assume he was thinking of her look-alike, who didn't really exist, instead of being fascinated with her. And he would admit to being fascinated by her, but then, he was a man and, quite frankly, any man would be taken with her.

Even if her looks hadn't captivated him, the outfit she was wearing would have certainly done so. On any other woman the dress would probably have looked okay, but with her small waist, curvy hips and shapely legs, "just okay" wasn't even close. "A vision of mouthwatering lusciousness" would be more appropriate.

He extended his hand to her. "And you're Delphine Ryland, right?"

She smiled, and when she did, it seemed the lights in the hotel's lobby shone brighter. "Yes, I'm Delphine Ryland. I knew who you were the moment I saw your green eyes."

He couldn't help but chuckle. "Thanks to my mom, my brothers and I are easily recognized."

Gannon released her hand even as he thought it felt too good encased in his. "Ready?" he asked her.

"Yes."

"I hope you're hungry. The restaurant I selected serves the best steaks in town."

She chuckled and the sound was warm and inviting. "Yes, I'm hungry. I skipped lunch."

"Well, I didn't skip lunch but I'm still hungry," he said, walking beside her out of the hotel and toward his parked car. "I have quite a hearty appetite. According to my mother, it's because I'm still growing."

Delphine wasn't sure if Gannon Steele was still growing or not, but what she saw now was pretty dang impressive.

She couldn't help giving him a discreet glance as they walked toward the shiny black Tesla. She had to admit, he looked pretty darn good in a pair of black slacks and a white shirt. Almost too good. She had seen photos of him before in different kinds of attire—business suits, jeans, sweats, jogging shorts. She'd even seen him in a pair of swimming trunks when he'd been in one of those male calendars as part of a charity fund-raiser. He'd been Mr. September. She remembered that quite well, since her birthday was in September, and she'd enjoyed seeing him pinned to the wall in her office. However, she was certain that seeing him in the flesh was altogether different. She preferred the real thing.

"Here we are."

She paused as he opened the car door for her and then she slid onto the smooth leather seat. "Thanks."

"You're welcome, Ms. Ryland."

He closed the car door and she watched him walk around the front of the vehicle to get into the driver's side. She noticed he had a manly stroll unlike any she'd seen before. It was a purposeful stride, filled with confidence, but not arrogance. After he backed out of the parking lot, he glanced over at her.

"When did you arrive in Phoenix?" he asked her.

"Friday evening. And again, I want to apologize for disturbing you at your brother's wedding. Lucia had mentioned a wedding in your family, but I thought it was last weekend."

"No harm done. I'm sure my brother Mercury wished it had been a week earlier."

"He was that anxious?"

Gannon Steele laughed. "Yes, he was just that anxious to tie the knot, and I'm happy for him and Sloan. They left immediately after the wedding for a three-week honeymoon to Paris, parts of Germany and Switzerland."

"Sounds nice."

"For them, I'm sure it will be. Now tell me about yourself, Ms. Ryland. And please call me Gannon. If you don't mind, may I call you Delphine?"

"No, I don't mind, and there's not a lot to tell. I've been working for *Simply Irresistible* for a while now."

"Was it your first job out of college? You look rather young."

She shook her head, grinning. "I'm not all that young. I'll be twenty-six in September. After college I got a job with a small publishing house in New York as an editor. I worked there almost a year before my mother became ill. I left New York to move back to Denver to take care of her."

"I hope she got better."

She couldn't hold back the sadness she knew shone in her eyes. "She didn't. Mom had MS and died last May." It was hard to believe the one-year mark was coming up next month. There was never a day that went by that she didn't think of her. Miss her.

"I'm sorry to hear that, Delphine. That had to have been hard on you."

She nodded. "It was. Mom and I were extremely close."

Delphine paused and then said, "Because of the nature of Mom's condition, she needed full-time care and I wanted to be the one to take care of her, along with the visiting nurses who came to check on her every week. Lucky for me, I was hired by *Simply Irresistible* as a freelancer, writing articles from home. I also became a blogger."

He nodded. "What about your father?"

She could understand Gannon asking about him. In the world he'd grown up in, both parents had been present. "My parents divorced when I was six. I never saw him again after the day he left." No need to tell him why her father had divorced her mom, or how both she and her mother had cried themselves to sleep for months after he'd deserted them.

"Do you still live in your mother's house?"

"Yes. It's been in our family for a couple of generations, since it used to be my grandparents' home. I love living there, although I've decided to give it a much-needed face-lift," she said. "While I'm gone, I'm getting my floors redone. Replacing the carpet with wood."

"Who's overseeing the project while you're away?"

"My best friend from high school, Mandy. She likes doing renovation stuff. I trust her to make sure things will be done to my satisfaction and within my budget."

Gannon nodded. "According to Chloe and Lucia, you're a good journalist—one of the best."

Delphine appreciated him changing the subject from her personal life to her professional one. "Oh, I don't know about that, but I appreciate them for thinking so. Lucia's mother and mine were best friends from their high-school days."

She thought about how much support she'd gotten from the Conyers family over the years and added, "During Mom's last days, I don't know how I would have made it without the Conyerses being there for me and for Mom."

He nodded again. "It's always great having good people in your corner when you need them the most."

He brought the car to a stop. "Here we are."

She glanced out the window and saw the restaurant. The Grip. There was one in Denver, although she could never afford to eat there. "Nice restaurant."

"One of my favorites," he said, opening the car door.

Just lovely, she thought. She couldn't afford to eat at The Grip and he considered it one of his favorites, which meant he probably ate here a lot. She tried not to think about the differences in their livelihoods. Instead, she watched him walk around the front of the car to open the door for her. Normally, she wouldn't sit and wait for any man to open her door, but she knew from articles she'd read about him that Gannon had impeccable manners.

When he opened the door, she took the hand he

offered and got out of the car. It had rained earlier and the scent of damp grass and wet soil permeated the air. And then there was his woodsy scent, which suited him. It definitely suited her since she liked the fragrance on him. She thought it made him even more manly.

As they were walking side by side toward the building, he suddenly took hold of her arm to skirt around a couple of puddles. Why did his touch feel so warm and comforting?

When they reached the entrance, he released her arm and stepped back to smile down at her. She was wearing high heels, yet she knew he was at least six-two or six-three. "Welcome to The Grip, Delphine. I hope you enjoy dining here as much as I do."

She couldn't help but return his smile. "Thanks, Gannon. I'm sure that I will."

One

"Now I know why this is one of your favorite places. The food is delicious."

Gannon glanced at Delphine over the rim of his wineglass and smiled. "Glad you're enjoying it."

He liked a woman who didn't mind eating, and was glad Delphine fit into that category. She had suggested that he order for her since everything on the menu looked good. When he'd told her he was a steak-and-potatoes kind of guy, she'd said that was fine since she was a steak-and-potatoes kind of girl.

He had ordered them both juicy rib eyes, baked potatoes and a selection of mixed vegetables. To start things off, their waiter had delivered a basket of delicious bread to their table and a bottle of wine. Gannon had asked her more about herself. She'd obviously assumed he'd wanted to hear more about her work history with *Simply Irresistible* and not anything personal. That was not the case. He was curious about whether or not she was involved with anyone, and if so, were they dating exclusively? Bottom line, there was no way a woman who looked like her wasn't involved with a man.

Why in the hell was he even interested? Did it have to do with the fact that his entire body sizzled each and every time their hands touched, or whenever he looked at her mouth for any length of time? He'd been attracted to women before, but never with this much intensity.

He'd listened while she'd told him about other articles she'd written, as if to assure him that she wasn't a novice. Although that hadn't been the information he'd been looking for, he couldn't help but be impressed with all she'd done. Nor could he not be impressed with how the light from the candle seemed to flicker on her skin, giving it a radiant glow. There was no doubt about it—Delphine Ryland was one hell of a beautiful woman.

"I'm sure I've bored you with all I've told you about myself, so how about sharing information about you," she said, breaking into his thoughts.

He leaned back in his chair. They had ordered dessert, which would be arriving shortly. Both of them had decided on slices of carrot cake. "I'm sure you did your research on me, but I'm not sure how much you know about my family, who I am extremely proud of," he said, smiling, letting her know this interview wasn't his first rodeo.

Journalists had interviewed him before, although he would be the first to admit that none had been as pretty as Delphine. In fact, most of the interviewers had been men, simply because most women weren't interested in writing tractor-trailer-related stories. However, from some of the things she'd mentioned during dinner, she had done her homework regarding rigs and truckers—yet another thing that had impressed him.

Gannon found himself doing something he normally didn't do, which was talk about his family, but for some reason with her, he felt comfortable enough to open up. He told her about his parents and how they met, deciding to leave out his father's former Casanova reputation, and how Gannon and his brothers were convinced they had inherited Drew Steele's philandering genes.

"My brother Galen is the oldest of the six and he's thirty-eight. He's made millions as a video-game creator, something he started while still in college. He's married to Brittany and they have twins, a son and a daughter. My parents' first grandchildren."

He took a sip of his wine and then continued, "My brother Tyson is the doctor in the family, a gifted heart surgeon. He's thirty-seven and married to Hunter. Brother Eli is thirty-six and a prominent attorney in town. He's married to Stacey. Jonas is thirty-five and owns a marketing business, and he's married to Nikki.

Last but not least is Mercury. He's thirty-four and is the one who got married this weekend to Sloan."

A smile spread across her lips and Gannon could feel a tightening in his gut. Why were her lips such a turn-on?

"Nikki loves being married and speaks highly of your brother," Delphine said.

Gannon nodded. "All my brothers are blessed to have married really nice women."

"All six of you are pretty close in age. That means your mother was pregnant practically every year."

He chuckled. "Mom and Dad wanted a big family. She says she doesn't regret being pregnant so often since Dad pampered her."

At that moment the waiter returned with their dessert. After the man placed the plates in front of them and left, Gannon smiled and gestured to their cake. "It's okay to dig in and it wouldn't bother me if you licked your lips."

She threw back her head and laughed. "Is that your way of letting me know this carrot cake is that good?"

"Yes, I guess it is." In truth, he wanted to see her lick those lips. It would be torture watching her, but he was convinced it would be well worth it.

"Thanks for a wonderful evening, Gannon," Delphine said, as he walked her back inside the hotel a couple of hours later. She had truly enjoyed his company.

"Glad you enjoyed it. We covered a lot of topics,

but we didn't get down to the specifics of the interview, did we?"

No, they hadn't, even though that had been the intent of meeting for dinner. However, she had to admit she'd rather liked their unorthodox meal. It had seemed more like a get-to-know-you date than a business meeting. She knew from his schedule that he would be leaving on Friday for Florida. It would be one of those trips where he became a trucker behind the rig.

She could just imagine him removing his suit and tie for a pair of jeans, a T-shirt and trucker boots. She wondered if she could talk Nikki into taking some photos of him in that attire for the magazine's cover. Nikki was a great photographer and still did freelance work on occasion for *Simply Irresistible*. There was no doubt in Delphine's mind that seeing him as a trucker instead of a businessman on the magazine's cover would make it one hot issue. She would suggest it to Lucia the next time they talked.

"What time should I expect you in the office tomorrow?"

She glanced up at him. "When would be a good time to come?"

He shrugged. "On Mondays I usually get in around nine. It's usually my day to meet with my department heads to see how things are going."

She nodded. In addition to the interview, he'd agreed to let her shadow him around the office. "I can't wait to see how things are done. I hope you know that your way of doing things has made people take a different look at the trucking industry as a whole."

They stopped walking when they reached the spot in the lobby where they'd met earlier. "There are a lot of different ways to operate a trucking business. Mine is just one. My dad ran the company for years and made it successful. The people who worked for him thought the world of him, and he of them. However, I took over at a time when I knew the industry was changing. I established focus groups to determine what was important to the drivers, especially those who spent a lot of time away from home. One of the studies showed a high divorce rate among those truckers and that bothered me."

"And you were determined to do something about it?" she asked him.

"I was determined to try. I figured happy employees make better employees." He glanced at his watch. "I've bored you enough for one day. Besides, everything I'm telling you can wait until tomorrow. Good night, Delphine. I'll see you at nine in the morning."

"I'll be there. Good night, Gannon." She stepped on the elevator and noted he stood watching her until the door closed between them. That was when she released a deep sigh. She had enjoyed being with him tonight and she'd taken note of the times she'd caught him staring at her. She understood; she reminded him of someone. Delphine figured the woman must have meant something to him at one time. Was he pining for this woman? If so, he should resolve his issues with her before moving on. What if he got seriously involved with someone, but ended up returning to that other woman? The one she reminded him of. That wouldn't be fair, but then, when were men fair? She and her mom had certainly been the recipients of their unfairness. In her experience, men had no qualms about tossing aside a woman like yesterday's garbage.

She sighed deeply, refusing to let any resentment toward the male species ruin what had been a nice evening getting to know Gannon. What he did, or with whom, was his business, she thought, stepping off the elevator when it reached her floor.

A little later, Delphine had taken off her clothes, showered and was ready to call it a night when her cell phone rang. She smiled when she saw the caller was Nikki. "Hello, Nikki."

"Hello, back at you. Welcome to Phoenix. I understand you've been here a couple of days."

"Yes. How did you know?"

"Gannon. At the wedding he saw he'd missed a call from you," Nikki said.

"I forgot about the wedding and apologized about bothering him."

"The two of you did connect?"

Delphine eased into the wingback chair in the room. "Yes. In fact, we had dinner tonight." She thought she should clarify, so she added, "It was a business dinner."

"I understand. How did it go?"

"Okay, I guess. It was one of those getting-to-know-you kind of meetings, to sort of break the ice before tomorrow. That's when I start the interview process, by shadowing him and asking him questions."

"Well, the reason I called is because I'd like to invite you to dinner. Jonas is looking forward to meeting you. Is Tuesday okay?"

"Yes. What time?"

"How about six?"

"Six is fine. I'll just need the address. I have a rental car with GPS, so I shouldn't get lost."

Delphine and Nikki talked for another ten minutes, then ended the call. Getting up from the wingback chair, Delphine glanced over at the clock on the nightstand next to the bed. It was past ten already. She would get a good night's sleep and be ready to meet with Gannon again tomorrow.

And she couldn't deny she was eager to see him again.

Gannon entered his condo, went straight to the bar and poured a shot of brandy. He needed it. Being in Delphine Ryland's company had challenged his libido to no end. Each and every time she licked her lips, his erection would throb. And when she'd excused herself to go to the ladies' room, his gaze, along with several other men's gazes in the restaurant, had followed that perfect walk, that good-looking ass and those legs in stilettos.

He was glad that by the time they'd been ready to leave the restaurant, he had regained a semblance of control. Otherwise, she would have known the effect she had on him. Hell, anyone who'd seen him would have known and that would not have been good.

Gannon put down the shot glass and rubbed his

hand down his face. The last thing he needed right now was for any one woman to hold his interest the way Delphine Ryland was doing. Like his brothers before him, he enjoyed women. He relished one-night stands. What he didn't do was allow his thoughts to linger on any one woman, like they were doing now. What was it about Delphine that affected him like this?

He had looked forward to the day when his five brothers would no longer be competition. And that time was now. He could have any woman he desired without wondering if she was using him to work her way up to one of his brothers. Of course, the Steele brothers never, ever shared women. But that didn't stop some women from trying.

Gannon figured the reason he was so taken with Delphine tonight was because he hadn't expected her to be so gorgeous. In all honesty, he wasn't sure just what he'd expected, but it hadn't been to gaze into her eyes, and then shift his gaze to her lips, and feel such an intense attraction—one that he had to work to control. Being attracted to a woman was nothing new, but there was something about his fascination with Delphine Ryland that was different. He just couldn't put a finger on what that difference was.

Gannon hoped like hell that his imagination was merely running wild at the thought that with all his brothers off the market, he was the last one standing. In fact, he couldn't wait until he visited his cousins in Charlotte over the summer to check out all the beautiful women there.

Feeling better that his mind was back on track, and his libido in check, he headed toward his bedroom to call it a night, certain that when he saw Delphine Ryland in the morning, he would be his old self again.

Two

"Well, Delphine, what do you think so far?" Gannon asked, as if he really wanted her opinion.

To say she was impressed was an understatement. She had arrived on the Steele Trucking Company lot at eight, determined to get there early, only to discover he'd already arrived. Not only was he there, but he had also gotten her through the security process in what she figured to be half the time, probably quicker than that.

He had given her a tour of his office before they'd taken a short walk to the company's cafeteria, where everyone was served a complimentary hot breakfast before the start of the day. He had introduced her to the cooks, the husband-and-wife team of Ms. Pearl and Mr. Sam. They were excellent at their jobs and breakfast had been to die for.

Before returning to his office, via a golf cart, he had taken her on a short ride around the lot to a huge mechanic shop where repairs were done. Then there was the terminal garage, where it seemed as if over a thousand or so trailers were stored. He had explained that some of their shippers used their own trailers and some did not. Then there was another huge lot where the cabs were parked. He said he would continue the tour after their next meeting.

She switched her mind back to his question. "So far, I think everything is overwhelming. The next time I pass a tractor trailer on the interstate, I will do so with a lot more respect."

And she meant it. She hadn't realized just how tightly the trucking industry was regulated. She would admit a lot of the laws were to protect both the truckers and regular drivers on the road. But there were some that were all political, and they varied from state to state. That meant the truckers needed to know the rules and laws of several states.

Gannon smiled. "Good answer. Now how about lunch?"

She rubbed her stomach and laughed. "Are you kidding me? Who can eat lunch after a breakfast like the one we had this morning?"

"I can. Remember what I told you yesterday. My mom claims I'm still growing."

Either that or he had a high metabolism. He also had a fantastic-looking body. All muscle and no fat.

It was obvious he also used the gym he had installed on the premises for his truckers. She would admit to seeing quite a few nice-looking male bodies walking around. That dispelled the myth that most truckers had beer bellies. At least, not on Gannon Steele's watch. When she asked him about the state-of-the-art gym, he told her it was important to keep his drivers healthy.

Another thing she'd discovered was that there were quite a few female drivers. Gannon told her that he was constantly looking for ways to accommodate their needs while on the road. He also employed a number of team drivers that included husbands and wives.

When he asked her again to join him for lunch, she agreed, figuring it would give her a chance to ask him more questions. By the time they'd left the lot to go to a café a few miles away, she had pretty much covered everything on her list for today. She would use the rest of the day to shadow him.

It was obvious that, for a man of thirty-three, he was well respected by the people who worked for him, both young and old. "Has it always been this way, Gannon?"

He glanced over at her when he parked the car. "Has it always been what way?"

"Your employees. They like you a lot. Was it easy taking over for your dad?"

He shook his head and laughed. "Heck, no. Those who worked here twenty years or more thought Dad walked on water and didn't like him turning the company over to his wet-behind-the-ears son. You wouldn't believe the rumors that went around even before I took over. Some believed I would fire everyone over fifty, or that I would merge with another company, and some even thought they would come in the day after Dad retired to find I had shut down the place and hired all new people."

She nodded. "How did you win them over?"

"By being myself and giving them a chance to tell me how they felt. I also included them in my focus groups. I convinced them I was here to make the company better and not to get rid of it. I persuaded them to trust me and believe in me just like they had with Dad, because, after all, I was his son."

"That worked?"

"It worked."

When he opened the car door for her, they walked side by side toward the entrance of the café. They were about to enter the building when a very attractive woman came out. The moment she saw Gannon, she threw herself into his arms, nearly knocking Delphine out of the way in the process.

"Gannon! It's so good seeing you. I missed you at the ball game this weekend."

He politely removed the woman's arms from around his neck. "Hey, Trish. Mercury got married this weekend."

"Oh, yeah, that's right." That was when the woman turned to Delphine. "Oh, hi."

"Hello." Delphine returned the greeting, ignoring the woman's daggered expression. Delphine had seen such looks before, mainly from Liddell's wife, Agatha, whenever Delphine would run into them at the grocery store. It amazed Delphine that the woman could even think she'd ever want Liddell back after the way he'd humiliated her by calling off their wedding.

"Trish, I'd like you to meet Delphine," Gannon said.

The woman's eyes narrowed. "You're new to town?"

Delphine was tempted to tell Trish to pull back her claws because she had no designs on Gannon. In fact, she was surprised during the introduction that Gannon hadn't explained the nature of their relationship and let the woman know it was strictly business and nothing more.

Delphine was curious about something. If there was as much to the woman's relationship with Gannon as this Trish evidently wanted Delphine to assume, then why hadn't Trish been invited to his brother's wedding? Delphine quickly concluded that Trish was just one of a number of women who were vying for a top spot on Gannon's "keepers" list.

"I'm in town for only a short while," Delphine said.

"Oh? Did you come for the wedding?" Trish asked.

Before Delphine could answer, Gannon said, "That's none of your business, Trish. Now if you don't mind, Delphine and I would like to enjoy lunch."

Without waiting to see if Trish minded or not, Gannon took Delphine's hand, opened the café's door and escorted her inside. He glanced around, and when he spotted a vacant table in the back, still holding firmly to her hand, he led her to it.

"Gannon?"

He looked over at her. "Yes?"

"Maybe sharing lunch isn't a good idea."

He lifted an eyebrow. "Why?"

"I don't want to cause problems for you with anyone." Namely, she didn't want to cause problems with him and that woman named Trish.

"You're not causing any problems, trust me," he said, pulling out a chair for her. Before taking his own seat, he handed her a menu out of the rack on the table. "There's an assortment of great choices here."

She figured he meant it to be the end of that discussion when he added, "You're going to love their ribs."

Did the man honestly have room in that flat stomach for ribs? As he had yesterday, he was wearing a pair of slacks and a dress shirt. Also, like yesterday, the moment she'd seen him her nerves had jumped into overdrive, and had made goose bumps form on her arms. He definitely had an effect on women, and whenever he would level those green eyes on her, she wanted to melt right on the spot.

"I'll just have a salad. A small one."

He shrugged. "Just wait until you see my plate. I bet you'll ask to try one."

Instead of saying whether she would or wouldn't, Delphine glanced around. The place was crowded with the lunchtime crowd. She looked at the table next to theirs, where a waitress was delivering a plate of ribs to the couple sitting there. She leaned across the table and asked Gannon, "That plate of ribs is for two, right?"

He followed her gaze and a soft chuckle escaped his lips. "No, it's for one."

The ribs, oozing with barbecue sauce, were stacked so high on the plate that they nearly covered all the French fries and hush puppies. "Please don't tell me you plan to order something the size of that one."

He chuckled again. "Okay, I won't tell you. But before you have a panic attack, I'll level with you. I'll only eat some of it here. The rest goes home with me for dinner."

Delphine thought that made sense, but still...eating that many ribs in one day couldn't be healthy. She decided to keep those thoughts to herself.

The waitress came to take their order. Gannon ordered the rib plate and Delphine ordered a small salad. When the woman walked off, he said, "I need to apologize for Trish's rudeness."

She shrugged. "You think she was rude?"

"Don't you?"

She shrugged again. "She's just a woman who wanted to mark her territory."

"She has no territory when it comes to me. No woman has. I don't operate that way."

She wondered what way he operated, and then decided it wasn't any of her business. She was a journalist who'd been sent here to do an exclusive interview with him and nothing more. What he did in his spare time didn't concern her. But still, she couldn't help but wonder if he was one of those men like Liddell, who didn't give a crap when it came to breaking a woman's heart because they truly didn't value the concept of what a serious relationship was about.

She'd known her mother had never liked Liddell even when they'd dated in high school. Her mother thought they'd made the right decision in going to separate universities. It had always been Delphine and Liddell's plan to marry as soon as they finished college. He'd even encouraged her to begin planning their wedding when they'd both reached their junior year.

A month before graduation everything had been set. Even the invitations had been sent. They were to marry two weeks after his graduation, since hers was slated a week before his. His parents had even offered them the use of an empty apartment over the garage until they got on their feet. Both their mothers had worked together to make sure their wedding day would be one they would always remember. Then out of the blue, Delphine got the Dear Jane letter, and her world as she'd known it hadn't ever been the same.

"Delphine?"

She looked at Gannon when she heard her name. Had he been talking to her when she'd taken a stroll down memory lane, reliving those memories that still pained her to think about? Their broken engagement had become the talk among those who knew them—neighbors, classmates, friends and church members. It didn't take long for everyone to find out that there would still be a wedding. She just wouldn't be the bride. For her that had been the humiliating part.

She forced herself back to this conversation. "Yes, Gannon?"

"I asked what you plan to do for dinner tonight."

"I'm going to dine in that restaurant in the hotel. I understand the food is good. Then before going to bed I'll enter my interview notes onto my laptop. It will save time for me later."

The waitress arrived with glasses of water. When she left, Delphine glanced over at him to find he'd been staring at her. That wasn't the first time today she'd caught him doing that very thing. In the meeting this morning, when his dispatcher was covering all the things her job entailed, Delphine had felt someone looking at her and had glanced over at him to find his gaze intently on her. Again, she couldn't help but wonder about the woman she resembled who could cause such a reaction from him.

After taking a sip of the water the waitress had placed on the table before leaving, she said, "I understand you're taking a load down to Florida over the weekend. Tell me about it."

Gannon noted Delphine hadn't pulled out that little brown notepad or her cell phone to record. Did that mean she was asking because she was interested? Or had she merely asked about his on-the-road trip to change the subject? And he knew she'd caught him staring at her more than once today. Was she wondering about that? Or was she used to men being mesmerized by her beauty?

Today she was wearing a pair of chocolate-colored slacks and a pretty beige blouse. He'd glanced up this morning and seen her walking across the parking lot toward the main building, where his office was located. A number of his truckers, who were heading out with that day's load, had seen her, as well, and had stopped to watch. Married or not, they could appreciate feminine beauty, so he couldn't rightly blame them for ogling her. She had a confident stride and her outfit revealed what a curvaceous body she had. For a quick moment he had envied whatever man claimed her as his. What a damn lucky bastard.

"Gannon?"

He blinked as he realized that while he'd been sitting there staring at her like a nitwit yet again, she'd been waiting for a response from him. "Sorry, my mind was elsewhere," he said, hoping she would accept that and not question his sanity. "Yes, I have a load of merchandise to deliver to this huge clothing warehouse in Jacksonville, Florida."

"Do you do that often? Get behind the steering wheel of a rig?"

Although she didn't have her notepad or recorder, he could tell she was still in her interviewer mode. He had no problem telling her what she wanted to know. Talking would help him keep his mind on the questions and not on her. "I do it often enough. Not only does it give me a chance to get out of the office, but it also gives me firsthand knowledge of the challenges my drivers face."

"Such as?"

"Regulations, for one. Each state is different and if my drivers cross state lines they need to be aware of that particular state's laws. The Department of Transportation shows no mercy on violators, whether the violations are intentional or not. For instance, to get to Florida I have to travel through Texas, Louisiana, Mississippi and Alabama. Before hitting the road, I need to familiarize myself with their laws."

"Any reason you're doing this particular delivery?"

He nodded. "In addition to all I've said, I have a beach house in Miami Beach. After delivering the load in Jacksonville, I plan to drive to Miami for a short vacation. I figure a week at my beach house will be nice. I love the Atlantic Ocean."

She smiled. "That sounds nice. I've seen the Pacific Ocean, but never the Atlantic."

"It's beautiful."

At that moment the waitress returned with their lunch. They had to move aside some of the condiments to make room for his huge plate of ribs. "Are you sure you don't want to share these with me?"

"Positive. My salad is all I can handle. Besides, you're going to take the leftovers home for dinner, remember?"

He grinned. "Yes, I remember."

At the end of the workday, when Gannon entered his home, he was still remembering. In fact, he was remembering a lot of things. Going straight to the kitchen, he placed the package of leftovers on the counter. He wasn't hungry just now since he had eaten a lot of the meal at lunch…while trying not to openly stare at Delphine with every bite he took.

He had managed to get her to talking again after she'd asked several more interview questions. He had no problem with the interview because he'd never been shy about talking about his work. She had told him about her college days and her first job with that New York publisher. Then she proceeded to tell him about all the interviews she'd done since starting to work for *Simply Irresistible* on a full-time basis and how much traveling the interviews entailed.

He had used that as the perfect opening to ask her how the man in her life dealt with her being away from home so often. She had, without preamble or pause, told him that after spending three years taking care of her mother, she'd been ready to include adventure in her life. She'd always wanted to travel, and being an on-the-road journalist for *Simply Irresistible* took care of her wanderlust cravings. With the issue of the man in her life, she stated that she chose not to date and didn't provide a reason why.

Gannon could understand a woman who traveled a lot not engaging in a serious relationship, just like he understood a man like himself who preferred one-night stands. But to say you didn't date at all was a bit much, especially for someone who looked like her.

Unfortunately, he didn't get a chance to ask *why* she chose not to date because he'd had to end their lunch to head back to the office for an important conference call. The call had lasted longer than he'd expected, and by the time it had ended, so had the workday. When he'd asked his administrative assistant about Delphine, he'd been told she had left for the day with a message that she would see him tomorrow.

Yes, he would see her again tomorrow. In fact, it would be her final day with him. In a way, that was good, since he wasn't sure how much longer he could control himself when in such close proximity. And he still had that fascination with her lips. Each and every time she'd smiled at him today, he'd thought of all the things he would love doing to her mouth.

He was about to leave the kitchen when his phone rang. Checking caller ID, he saw it was his sister-in-law Nikki. He picked up and said, "Yes, Nikki, what's going on?"

"Not much. I'll be glad when the morning-sickness part of my pregnancy is over, though."

"I bet you will be." Jonas had mentioned how bad Nikki was feeling in the mornings.

"The reason I'm calling is that I invited Delphine to dinner tomorrow night and thought that since it's her last day here, you'd like to come, as well."

He leaned back against the counter, thinking that he'd spent the better part of the day with Delphine Ryland and she hadn't mentioned anything about dinner at Nikki's tomorrow. But then, it wasn't as if he needed to be privy to her every move.

Blowing out a deep breath, he knew what his an-

swer would be. What it *had* to be. It was bad enough
not acting like himself around her while being interviewed, but the last thing he needed was for that
behavior to extend past his work hours. There had
not been a single moment in her presence today that
his entire body hadn't been on high alert.

"Thanks for the invite but I have something planned
already," he said.

"You sure?" she jokingly asked. "I've never known
you to turn down a meal."

He smiled. His family knew of his hearty appetite. "I'm positive."

"Okay. If you change your mind, just drop by. As
always, there will be plenty."

"Thanks, Nikki."

Delphine stepped out of the shower to dry off,
thinking the interview with Gannon that day had
gone well.

In her line of work, she'd discovered that some
people, when being interviewed, placed a high importance on themselves. She categorized those as the
"me" people. It was all about them and they didn't
believe in giving credit to anyone. Then there were
others, like Gannon, who preferred acknowledging
everyone but themselves.

It was easy to see that Gannon admired his father
and credited him with not only starting the business,
but also working hard to make it into a financial em-
pire to pass on to his sons. Gannon had shared with
her that, initially, Drew Steele had assumed all six

of his sons would one day work the family business. When it became apparent that five had other plans, he was grateful when his youngest son had shown interest.

According to Gannon, his love of tractor trailers began at an early age. One year, Drew Steele needed to deliver a load of supplies to Texas on his birthday. A young Gannon had been determined not to let his father be alone on his birthday and had done what his mother had done years ago—stowed away on his father's truck. By the time his father had found him it had been too late to return him home, so Gannon had continued the route to Texas with his father and had the time of his life. From that day on, Gannon had looked forward to summers when he could take road trips with his father.

When the time came for college, Gannon made the decision to attend a university in Phoenix to be available to help out his father on the weekends. No one was surprised that Gannon had majored in transportation management and logistics and later acquired an MBA.

She could just envision a twelve-year-old Gannon hiding in the back of his father's truck just to make sure his father wasn't alone on his birthday. He'd told her birthdays were important to him. As a result, he implemented a policy at the company where no one worked on their birthday. They got it off with pay. Now she understood why the Steele Trucking Company was such a sought-after employer.

She also understood why Gannon Steele was a

sought-after man with the ladies. Trish hadn't been the only woman vying for his attention at the café. Others had stopped by their table just to tell him hello. Several times his phone had rung, and without answering it, he would press the decline button.

Being around him for the past two days had reminded her that she was a woman who could appreciate a sexy man when she saw one, and he was definitely sexy. While being her mother's caretaker, she'd pretty much lived a secluded life. Lucia and her mother had tried encouraging Delphine to get out and enjoy life, and they would volunteer to look after her mother while she did so. She soon discovered that most of the single guys in town preferred not hooking up with a woman who had a sick mother; very few men asked her out. However, she would be the first to admit she hadn't often made herself available to be asked.

After her mother died, that was when the guys began calling. First they'd give her their condolences, and then in the next breath they'd offer to help her get over her loss. Most tried convincing her that a night in their bed would do it. She had no problem letting them know she wasn't interested. And she'd even told a few to lose her number.

She wondered what Gannon had thought when she'd told him she was not dating. Had he assumed constant traveling was the reason, or did he think there was more to it than that? There was no way for him to know that, thanks to a man name Liddell

Bartley, she was a woman who was scared of giving a man her heart again.

She tried pushing thoughts of Liddell from her mind, and instead, she thought about her beautiful, sweet mother. Till the end, June Ryland had been concerned about her only child. Delphine had known her mother assumed the reason Delphine had refused to date was because she hadn't gotten over Liddell. June hadn't been happy with the idea of that. Her mother had wanted Delphine to move on with her life, find someone to make her happy so she wouldn't be alone. Delphine hadn't been able to convince her mother that being alone worked well for her. Even now, she could recall the last coherent conversation the two of them had. She would never forget how her mother had pleaded with her not to let Liddell win by never loving again. Breaking one's heart did not necessarily mean destroying it. June believed there was a man out there worthy of her daughter's love, and that when she found him, that man would give Delphine unconditional devotion and be true to her. Only her.

Delphine had not spoken to her mother about the skepticism she'd felt. Nor had she pointed out that her mother was asking her to believe in something that June hadn't believed in for herself. Her mother had been a beautiful woman, yet when Theodore Ryland up and left her for someone else, she hadn't picked up the pieces of her life and moved on. At no time had Delphine recalled her mother going out on a date. Instead, her mother became part of singles group at church, preferring group activities.

Deciding to think of other things after slipping into her gown, she turned her thoughts back to Gannon. Things were different with Gannon compared to other interviews she'd conducted. He didn't act as if she was a bother, or like this was free publicity and nothing more. At no time had he made her feel that she was disrupting his day, or that her questions had been intrusive. That had definitely made things less stressful for her and more relaxing.

Tomorrow was her last day with him and she was beginning to feel a sense of… She wasn't sure what. She was certain these mixed emotions were due to the fact that Gannon had never made her feel like he was the superior being and she the lowly person sent to interview him. Instead, he had taken her out to dinner, shared breakfast with her this morning and taken her to what he said was his favorite place for lunch.

Not feeling the least bit sleepy, she moved across the room to sit on the love seat and grabbed the remote off the table before folding her legs beneath her in a comfortable position. All during her shower she had thought about Gannon. It was unusual for her to think about any man. But how could she not think of him, when he was so good-looking? But she knew his good looks were just part of what made Gannon Steele an irresistible man, worthy of gracing the magazine's cover.

She was about to find a news channel to watch when her cell phone rang. Leaning over, she picked it up off the table. Her heart began beating fast when she saw the caller was Gannon.

"Gannon?" she said, after clicking on.

"Delphine, I'm sorry to bother you. I know we're supposed to meet in my office first thing in the morning, but I just got a call from one of my shippers and I need to go meet with them. I should be at the office around ten. I look forward to seeing you then."

He looked forward to seeing her then? Although she was certain he hadn't meant for his comment to be anything but professional, for just a quick second she pretended it wasn't. That he did look forward to seeing her and that his response didn't have anything to do with the interview. That was stupid for her to even pretend because *everything* had to do with the interview. That was the reason she was here and she must not lose sight of that.

She wished she could respond by saying that she looked forward to seeing him, as well, but she knew saying such a thing would not be appropriate. She figured the reason she was acting so unlike herself was because this was the most time she'd spent in a man's presence for nearly five years. Five years alone was beginning to take its toll, especially when being around a hottie like Gannon.

"Okay, Gannon, I will see you tomorrow."

When she ended the call, she reminded herself that after tomorrow, the chances were she wouldn't be seeing Gannon again. She would have to be content with the photos of him.

Three

Gannon listened to what the owner of Murdock Mart was saying, and he had to agree that the man's concerns were legitimate. For the past two months one of Gannon's trucks was routinely late to its destination. This wasn't the first time Gannon had received complaints about Lester Oakwood. The driver had been placed on probation twice and had been counseled several times. Gannon knew he couldn't put off any longer what needed to be done. He could not give Oakwood any more chances.

A divorce last year had nearly ruined the man's life and he hadn't gotten over it. Instead, he was spending way too much time at the truck stops and Gannon knew why. He'd gotten reports on that, as well. "Thanks for bringing it to my attention, Mr. Murdock. I will take care of it."

The older man nodded. "I know you will, son. And I know you hate to do so. Oakwood has been around a long time. He started years ago with your daddy. One of his first drivers."

And that was why Gannon figured the man should probably want to go ahead and retire. However, Gannon was aware that the man's wife had left him in a financial bind when she'd wiped clean his bank account. Then she'd broken Oakwood's heart because the two had been married over thirty years and she'd left him for another man.

Anticipating what this morning's meeting with Murdock would be about, Gannon had already spoken with his father for advice. Drew had left the decision to Gannon as to how to handle it. Oakwood would be turning sixty-seven this year and was eligible for a darn good pension, but Gannon knew the man needed more than that. Driving trucks was Oakwood's life and had been for close to fifty years.

Not wanting to think about what he had to do when he returned to the office, Gannon instead thought about the person he would see when he got there. Delphine. There had been no reason for him to call her last night to tell her about the change in plans for this morning. His secretary could have given her the information when Delphine arrived at the office this morning. But for some reason, he had wanted to hear her voice one last time before going to bed.

He wasn't sure that had been a good thing because after hearing it, he hadn't been able to go to sleep. Instead, he had thought about, or rather fantasized about, Delphine the rest of the night. He thought back to how she'd looked at dinner Sunday night in that killer dress and how she'd looked yesterday in her slacks and blouse. He'd even gone further and imagined how she would look in a pair of Daisy Dukes, or just a bra and a pair of panties, and then with nothing at all. In other words, he'd imagined her as naked as the day she'd been born. Those fantasies had been what put him to sleep, although for the life of him he couldn't remember when he had finally dozed off.

It honestly didn't matter. What did matter was that whatever was happening to him because of Delphine had to stop. After tomorrow, she would be gone and there would be no reason for their paths to ever cross again…unless he decided to visit with his friends the Westmorelands. But just because he visited Denver didn't mean he would run into her. Denver was a big city and the Westmorelands had their own area on the outskirts of the town known as Westmoreland Country. To see her, he would have to intentionally look her up.

He shook his head, deciding not to be taken in by a beautiful face, a gorgeous body and a pair of lips that hit him hard whenever he thought about them. He wasn't supposed to be so attracted to her. So why was he? Maybe it was just a phase he was going through, because his five brothers were now happily married. The last thing he should be doing

was feeling curious as to whether there was a perfect woman out there somewhere for him. It was too
soon. He had ten years to worry about such a thing.
So why on earth was he wondering if perhaps that
woman could be Delphine?

Not liking the way his thoughts were going, he
decided to call and talk to the one brother who'd
always kept it real—Eli Steele. Although Gannon
hadn't imagined any of his brothers getting married before forty, Eli had been the biggest shocker.
Namely because Eli had been the one most resistant
to the idea of wedded bliss. However, he'd ended up
being the second one to succumb to love when he'd
married Stacey.

Pressing the button on his car's steering wheel,
Gannon instructed, "Call Eli Steele."

Moments later his brother's voice came on the
line. "What do you want, kid?"

Gannon shook his head. It used to annoy him
whenever his brothers would call him that. He soon
decided not to let it bother him. He was the youngest, and he figured no matter how old he got, his
five older brothers would see him as the kid.

"When did you know you had a thing for Stacey?"
Gannon decided to come right out with his question. There was no reason to beat around the bush.
Besides, the attorney in Eli wouldn't let Gannon do
such a thing, anyway.

There was hesitation on his brother's end of the
phone. Then Eli asked, "Why do you want to know?"

The attorney in Eli also often drove him to counter-question.

"Just answer, Eli."

Gannon could picture his brother rubbing his chin, trying to decide what to tell him and how much. "It wasn't love at first sight."

"I didn't say it was," Gannon responded.

Eli chuckled. "Stacey grew on me. Remember, she was Cohen's sister and I was in no hurry to get my ass kicked. We had womanizing reputations and Cohen was overprotective."

Cohen was their brother Tyson's best friend, so Gannon definitely understood the ass-kicking part. "How long did it take for her to grow on you?"

"Growth started from day one. I detected it but couldn't do a damn thing about it. I knew I was in big trouble when my desire for other women began fading. In fact, it started fading the moment I met Stacey."

Gannon didn't say anything. Had his desire for other women dwindled away? It'd only been two days, but he'd gone longer without thinking about women, if he was busy enough. He didn't need to be in a woman's bed every night. But he would admit that when he'd seen Trish yesterday, he hadn't felt anything but annoyance. And Trish had made it to his "keepers" list—the women he slept with more than once or twice.

Over the years, only three women had made the cut, and Trish knew she was one of them. Delphine had picked up on Trish trying to be territorial, so maybe it was time Trish was removed from his list. However, as it related to what Eli had said, Gannon hadn't desired another woman since meeting Delphine. No other woman had even crossed his mind.

"Whether you tell me why you're asking these questions doesn't matter. The fact that you are means something."

Gannon frowned. "Means what?"

"You've met a woman who has undoubtedly blown your mind."

Gannon's jaw twitched. He didn't like what his brother said. "I wouldn't go that far."

"I would. One thing I discovered in talking to Galen, Tyson, Jonas and Mercury is that we should have suspected something was up. We should have known our wives were our soul mates when we began doing things we didn't normally do. We definitely should have been forewarned when we treated them differently from the way we'd treated other women. We didn't pick up on the changes right away, but when we did, we were smart enough to know what to do to seal our fates. The last thing you want is to lose the one woman who is meant for you."

Frustration swept through Gannon. He'd heard enough. "I'll talk to you later, Eli."

"So when will we get to meet her?"

Gannon lifted an eyebrow. "Who?"

"The woman who got you calling me in the middle of the day asking questions," Eli said, sounding amused, which only frustrated Gannon even more.

"There's no such woman."

"If you say so. When you discover there is, let me know. I can't wait to meet the woman who made you rethink your ten-year plan. Goodbye."

Gannon cursed under his breath. Eli was crazy. There was no woman alive who could make him do that. Not a single one.

"Mr. Steele has arrived, Ms. Ryland, and he's ready to see you."

Delphine smiled over at Gannon's secretary, not sure if she was ready to see him. "Thanks."

In reality, she'd already seen him. From where she sat in the lobby, she had a good view of the parking lot. She had known the exact moment Gannon had parked his car in his designated CEO spot, and later entered the building through a side door.

She had sat there fascinated by seeing him wearing a dark suit and could barely keep her heart from racing. The man looked good no matter what he wore. Drawing in a deep breath, she stood and headed down the long corridor to his office. When she reached the closed door bearing his name in huge print, she inhaled and then exhaled before knocking.

"Come in, Ms. Ryland."

He'd called her "Ms. Ryland" instead of "Delphine." Did that mean they were back to being formal again? Was that how it was supposed to work when he was in more businesslike attire? she wondered. She would find out soon enough and decided to follow his lead.

When she opened the door, their gazes connected.

For a second, Delphine felt weak in the knees. He stood when she walked in and she immediately noticed that he had removed his jacket and loosened the tie around his neck. And, of course, she didn't miss the one button at the top of his white dress shirt that was undone. Why did seeing him so relaxed have an effect on her?

But then, she could say the same for him. He was staring at her the same way she was staring at him. She knew she was fully dressed and the last time she checked her hair was in place. What was going on here?

She knew the answer. Lust. Something she definitely wasn't used to. It was kicking both their butts. Lustful vibes had been strong yesterday, but they were even stronger today.

That wasn't good. Whenever he looked at her, she got overheated. Today his look was almost setting her on fire. This was her last day and she needed to take control of the situation or burn to a crisp right in front of him.

Clearing her throat, she said, "I hope things went well at the meeting you had this morning with your shipper."

As if the sound of her voice broke whatever spell he'd been in, he blinked and then said, "Yes, they did." Then, shoving his hands into his pockets, he added, "However, there's a matter I need to handle."

She nodded. "I understand. I can come back—"

"No. Let's wrap things up with the interview now because I'll be busy for the rest of the day."

Was that his way of letting her know he was tired of this process? Tired of her doing the interview? More than anything, she wanted to believe his change in attitude had nothing to do with her, but was connected somehow to that meeting he'd had earlier.

"I'll be quick," she said, taking the chair in front of his desk. The same one she'd sat in yesterday. "I just have a few more questions."

"Fine," he said, moving to sit down at his desk. "Ask away."

While fighting to keep his concentration on the questions he was being asked, Gannon noted that Delphine never failed to bring out the sexual beast in him. He tried keeping his focus on her eyes, but his gaze would slip to her lips time and time again. If she'd noticed, she wasn't letting on. In fact, she was acting like the professional in the room. He was the one sitting there getting more aroused by the minute.

And he didn't like it one damn bit.

He didn't like that she had this pull on him. When she had walked into his office, he'd stared at her, trying to get his breathing under control. The mere sight of her had done something to him, made him feel things, want things and need things. She had to have felt the sexual tension between them because it had sparked all over the place. She had held his gaze with as much intensity as he'd held hers. At least the attraction wasn't one-sided.

At least, he wanted to believe that it wasn't.

Beginning to feel annoyed again that she could so easily get next to him, he tossed his pen on the desk.

"Are you about through with your questions?" He'd thought she'd said she only had a few. Well, she'd asked more than that. It wasn't the questions that annoyed him since they were typical interview questions—it was just the fact that she was the one asking them. He wanted to do more with their time together than answering questions. He didn't like that she was ignoring what he knew was going on between them, when he was about ready to climb the walls.

"I can end the questions now if you'd like."

It was on the tip of his tongue to tell her exactly what he would like—first would be her sitting in his lap; then he'd taste her delectable-looking lips. "No, you can finish your questions."

The only reason he told her that was because he knew that when she asked the final question, there would be no reason for her to hang around. He knew from Lucia and Chloe that she wasn't leaving town until Thursday, but asking the last question would truly be the end for them. Unless he made a special attempt to do so, he wouldn't be seeing her again. He wasn't ready for that to happen. So when she asked two more questions, he took his time answering, in an attempt to keep her there a little longer.

"Well, that's it, Mr. Steele," she said, standing.

He wished his gaze hadn't followed the movement, but it had. His breath hitched at the way her hair fell to her shoulders. The perfect fit of her breasts against her blouse.

Damn, he had it bad.

"Why are you calling me 'Mr. Steele'?"

She then had the nerve to shrug her shoulders—shoulders she'd bared with the dress she'd worn Sunday. Shoulders he knew were sexy as hell. "I was just following your lead," she said.

He lifted an eyebrow. "My lead?"

"Yes. When I knocked on the door you addressed me as 'Ms. Ryland.' I figured that meant we were no longer on a first-name basis. I thought that's what you wanted."

Had he called her that? He didn't remember if he had and he certainly hadn't meant to change anything between them...although there really wasn't anything between them. He forced his gaze to lock on her eyes and not drift to her lips. "Then I apologize. That's not what I wanted."

Now was a good time to tell her exactly what he wanted. But he couldn't when he didn't know what he wanted himself. Other than to kiss her, and he knew that was a line he dared not cross. No telling what might happen if he did. He'd never been addicted to any woman, but he could see himself becoming addicted to her.

"Thanks for everything, Gannon," she said, extending her hand out to him. "You've been nothing but kind and I appreciate it."

Gannon stood and took her hand in his. Immediately he felt a flare of response in his chest. He figured it was twofold. One for wanting her as much as he did, and the other for knowing when she walked out his door that it was done.

Did she realize they were standing there staring at each other like two people who knew what they had to do but didn't want to do it? He knew he should drop his gaze from hers and release her hand, but he couldn't. Not now.

The sound of a door slamming somewhere in the building made them jump, and he immediately released her hand. Too late. If she hadn't noticed anything oozing between them before, there was no way she could ignore it now. The heat of touching her was still evident in his hand.

"I have to go," she said as she backed up a few steps, then turned around to quickly head for the door.

"I'll walk you to your car."

She stopped and turned back to him. She shook her head. "No, you don't have to. Besides, I need to say goodbye to a few people before I leave."

"Oh, I see."

He felt warmth spread through his body as he watched her head for the door. When she reached it, he willed her to turn and look at him one last time. She didn't. He watched her open the door, quickly step out and slide the door closed behind her.

Delphine entered her hotel room with her heart still pounding in her chest. What had happened in Gannon's office? She might not have dated in over five years, but she could detect attraction...couldn't she? Had it been there all the time and she'd just picked up on it? Or was her mind playing tricks on her?

After placing her purse on the table, she slid into the wing chair. She needed to think, something she hadn't been able to do on the drive from Gannon's company. Her mind stayed stuck on that handshake. She had felt something. If she was totally honest with herself, she had felt something as soon as she'd entered his office. Things seemed to skyrocket from the moment their gazes locked.

Never in her twenty-five years had she felt desire claw at her the way it had done today. Gannon's large hand had encircled her wrist and held on tight, yet it had felt gentle. Intense heat had spread through her like butter melting on bread. Standing, she checked her watch. She would be dining with Nikki and her husband tonight, and since she'd ended her interview early with Gannon, she had time for a nap before leaving.

She was about to head toward the bathroom to strip down to her bra and panties when her cell phone rang. Recognizing the ringtone, she quickly picked up the call. "Hey, Mandy, what's up?"

"You might want to extend your time away from Denver for another week, girlfriend."

Delphine lifted an eyebrow. "Why?"

"The company doing your floors suspects asbestos."

"Oh, great," Delphine said, a little agitated, although

she knew she really shouldn't be. After all, she did have an older home. "What's next?"

"A building inspector will be coming out today to obtain samples, and it will be a couple of days before the results are known. In the meantime, all the work on the floors must stop until we know the results. If asbestos is found, then it will be removed. I got this, and there's nothing you can do for now. If you return home, you won't be able to stay in your house, so you might as well enjoy yourself in Phoenix for another week."

Delphine knew that was easier said than done, especially if it meant running into Gannon while she was here. Even though he worked close by, there was no reason she would run into him when he lived on the other side of town. "Not sure my staying in Phoenix is a good idea."

"Why not?"

Delphine nibbled on her bottom lip, not ready to share any of the details about her confusion over Gannon with anyone, even her best friend. And she *was* confused. She had felt something toward Gannon that she hadn't felt for a man in years. And the depth of her attraction to him was confusing.

"I was ready to come home."

"Why?"

She knew why her best friend was asking. With her mother gone, there was nothing in Denver for Delphine to rush back home to. It wasn't like she had a boyfriend, and she knew if she asked, *Simply Irresistible* would give her any time off she needed, since over the past year she hadn't taken any of her vacation days. "I just was."

"I thought you wanted to do as much traveling as you could."

"I do."

"Then do it, Del. If you don't want to stay in Phoenix, then you can really be adventurous and make the drive from Phoenix to Vegas. You'll get to travel through the desert and Navajo land."

"I'll think about it. Either way, I won't come home Thursday as planned after all."

"Fine, just let me know. And like I said, don't worry about things here—I've got this."

"So, there you have it, Dad," Gannon said. "I was able to talk Lester Oakwood into retiring."

Drew Steele nodded. "I'm glad. Had he been fired, which you had every right to do, considering Lester's work habits lately, he would have lost all his benefits and his pension. I'm glad Lester did what you suggested."

"I'm glad, too. I think that deep down he knows he's messed up more than a few times and there was no way I could give him any more chances."

Gannon had come straight here when the office closed. Although his father had retired, Gannon still consulted with him whenever he needed advice. As far as he was concerned, nothing could top Andrew Steele's experience and expertise.

He glanced around. "Where's Mom?"

"Out shopping with friends. I expect her back any

minute so we can go out to dinner. By the way, how did your interview go this week?"

His father bringing up the interview made Gannon think about Delphine. Not that he hadn't been thinking about her anyway. Although he knew it was for the best, considering how attracted he was to her, it still bothered him that he wouldn't be seeing her again. Unless…

He shook his head, refusing to go there, namely Jonas and Nikki's place. Gannon knew Delphine was joining them for dinner tonight. He'd been invited but had turned down Nikki's invitation. At the time he'd figured it was for the best. But now…

"Gannon?"

He glanced at his dad. "Yes?"

"I asked how the interview with that magazine reporter went this week. I guess your mind was a thousand miles away."

He wished it *was* a thousand miles away, but it was right here in Phoenix and on a certain woman. "The interview went fine. We finished up today."

"I was hoping we'd get to meet her," Drew said.

"Who?"

"The woman who interviewed you."

Gannon studied his father, then asked, "Delphine Ryland? Why would you have wanted to meet her?"

"No special reason other than she interviewed you and you seem quite taken with her."

His father's words surprised Gannon. "What makes you think I was quite taken with her?" He knew for a fact he hadn't mentioned one thing about

Delphine to his parents, or any of his brothers except Eli. And of all his brothers, Eli, being the attorney and used to confidentiality, was the one who could be depended upon to keep his lips sealed. And Gannon figured Nikki had no reason to suspect anything.

"The obvious."

The obvious? "Which was?" he asked.

"You mentioned to me and your mom on Sunday that you felt bad about not returning her calls and that you intended to invite her out to dinner as a way to atone, and to get to know her before the interviews began yesterday."

"Yes, and…?" he prompted, certain there was more, but he couldn't figure out what.

"And that's it. I talked to you last night and not once did you mention anything about her or the interview. The only reason we're talking about her now is because I asked."

Gannon stared at his father. Everything he'd said was true, and for any normal person, none of it would mean a thing. But he had to remember he wasn't dealing with just any normal person; he was dealing with Drew Steele, the man who'd been the original Bad News Steele.

In Drew's younger days he'd been so much of a womanizer that he'd been run out of Charlotte by a bunch of women out for blood—namely Drew's. He had fled from North Carolina, where most of the Steele family lived, and made his way to Phoenix.

That was where he'd eventually met and fallen in love with Gannon's mother.

"I never talk about any of the women I date," he reminded his father.

"No, but you and Ms. Ryland aren't dating, are you?"

"No."

"In that case, you had no reason not to bring her up. If nothing else, I'd expect you to mention how the interview was going."

Gannon shook his head. There could have been a number of reasons why he hadn't mentioned anything about Delphine to his folks, and none of them would have had to do with his attraction to her.

He was about to say that, but his father's next words stopped him. "I know my sons. More specifically, Gannon, I know you."

Gannon released a deep breath, knowing his father was right. Drew was close to all his sons, so he knew them all well. But when it came to Drew and Gannon, there had always been a special relationship, a tighter-than-normal bond. Gannon was the one who'd worked alongside his father for years at the trucking company. As a teen, he had been his father's traveling partner when Drew would make his deliveries across the country. They had rolled up their sleeves together to tackle problems related to the company. And when he had begun dating, initially it had been his dad who'd answered his questions about girls rather than his brothers.

So, yes, his father did know him. "It's confusing, Dad. I only met her three days ago. Yet…"

"Yet what?" Drew asked.

"She is confusing me."

Drew nodded. "Three days is more than enough time for a woman to confuse a man. However, I'm sure you will eventually figure things out."

In truth, Gannon wasn't sure exactly what he was supposed to figure out. But just in case his father was alluding to there being more to Gannon and Delphine's relationship than was really there, he said, "I have a ten-year plan."

His dad chuckled. "That's right. You don't intend to settle down for another ten years."

"Right."

Drew leaned back in his chair. "I had a twenty-year plan, and the woman who threw that plan right smack out the window just walked in the door."

Gannon knew whom his father meant when he heard his mother enter the house. Gannon stood, deciding he would leave before Eden Tyson Steele had a chance to grill him about anything. While growing up, he'd discovered his parents often thought alike. "I'm leaving now. However, we'll talk again before I hit the road Friday."

"Okay."

"Gannon. How are you doing, baby?"

He turned at the sound of his mother's voice. While growing up, he'd thought his mother was beautiful. She still was. "Hi, Mom. I'm doing fine.

Glad you arrived when you did because I was just about to leave."

Crossing the room, he gave his mother a kiss on the cheek before quickly heading for the door.

Four

"Thanks for inviting me to dinner, Nikki," Delphine said, handing the bottle of wine to her friend and then giving her a hug.

Delphine had met Nikki the first year Delphine had begun working at *Simply Irresistible*. She knew Nikki had started out with Chloe years earlier, when she started the magazine in Florida, as a freelance photographer. When Chloe opened the Phoenix office, Nikki had been the one to do that magazine's inside photos and covers.

Although Delphine had been working remotely, and only part-time, she had written several articles for the magazine, and Nikki had taken the corresponding photos. Her shots were always right on point. After Nikki got married, she did less freelance work for the magazine so she could work more closely with her husband's marketing company.

"No thanks needed and welcome to our home," Nikki said, holding the wine bottle in one hand and hooking arms with Delphine. She led Delphine toward the living room. "And thanks for the wine."

"You're welcome. You have a beautiful home."

"Thanks."

"And congratulations on your pregnancy. I know you and your husband must be very happy."

"Yes, we are," a deep, masculine voice said behind them.

Delphine turned toward the sound then sucked in a deep breath. The smiling man walking toward her resembled Gannon. His green eyes were a dead giveaway that they were brothers. His were the same shape and shade as Gannon's. Both men were also tall, although she figured Gannon was an inch or two taller, but even their build was about the same.

"Delphine, this is my husband, Jonas."

"You favor Gannon," Delphine said, taking the hand the man extended.

Jonas chuckled. "Since I'm older, Gannon favors me. My brothers and I consider ourselves the perfect blend of our parents. The six of us have our mother's green eyes, our skin tone is a combination of the two, and the rest of our features are strictly our father's."

Jonas turned to his wife. "Dinner is ready, sweetheart."

"You cook?" Delphine asked him in surprise.

He gave her a smile that looked identical to Gannon's. "Yes. In our bachelor days, my brother Mercury and I took a cooking class. Every once in a while, I enjoy getting in the kitchen and putting what I learned to good use."

"Let's be honest, Jonas. You like putting it to good use more than every once in a while, and I definitely appreciate it. He's a fantastic cook, Delphine."

"Thanks, gorgeous," he said, leaning over to kiss his wife on the lips.

They seemed to be comfortable being affectionate in front of others. Delphine wasn't used to that. Since there had only been Delphine and her mother living together, the only married couple she'd known well while growing up had been Lucia's parents, the Converses. Since the Converses had had a long marriage, Delphine figured they were affectionate toward each other without openly displaying that affection, like Nikki and Jonas.

"Since the chef says dinner is ready, I'll take you to where you can wash up."

"All right."

Before they could head that way, the doorbell sounded.

"I'll get that," Jonas said. "That's probably my brother Tyson. He's a doctor and works at the hospital a few blocks away. His wife, Hunter, is out of town, so he's probably just getting off work and figuring he can drop by to get a free meal," Jonas added, heading toward the door.

A few minutes later, after having followed the directions Nikki had given her, Delphine made her way back toward the living room from the bathroom, thinking just how huge this house was. She could sit hers in this one several times. What she liked most were the double spiral staircases and how they joined at the landing.

Delphine walked into the living room and saw Nikki and Jonas talking to a man whose back was to her. She figured it was another Steele brother, the one who was the doctor. When Nikki saw her, she smiled and said, "Look who decided to join us, Delphine."

The man who turned around to face her was Gannon.

Gannon saw the surprised look on Delphine's face and knew why she'd reacted that way. He hadn't mentioned anything to her about coming here this evening. Hell, he hadn't known that he would come here himself until he'd gotten home and taken a shower. That was when he'd decided to come see what Jonas had cooked for dinner.

Gannon drew in a deep breath. Who was he kidding? Definitely not himself. The reason he'd come here tonight was because he had known Delphine would be here and he had wanted to see her again. He hadn't been ready for the goodbye they'd shared earlier.

"Gannon, I didn't know you were coming," Delphine said.

His gaze roamed over her. She was wearing a pair of jeans and a pretty pink blouse. This was the most casual he'd seen her. But then, she could say the same for him, since he was wearing jeans, too.

Jonas cleared his throat, making Gannon realize

he hadn't yet responded to what Delphine had said. "I hadn't planned on coming. When Nikki invited me yesterday, I had already made plans, but those plans changed."

"Well, I'm glad they did," Nikki said, smiling brightly as she hugged her brother-in-law. "Now go wash up and join us in the dining room."

He grinned down at Nikki. "Will do."

Gannon knew where the bathroom was and headed in that direction. He wondered if Delphine had been aware of the way her gaze had bored into him just now. The intensity of it had messed with his senses and made him even more aware of her not just as a woman, but as a woman he wanted. He hoped he hadn't made a mistake in coming here. Nikki might be clueless about his motives, but Jonas wouldn't be. A Steele male understood another Steele male, and there was no doubt in Gannon's mind that his brother had recognized his male interest in Delphine.

At this point, Gannon really didn't care what Jonas did or did not recognize. He was too wound up to care and he honestly didn't know why. That was what he was determined to find out. Mainly, why a woman he'd just met three days ago could have him tied in knots in a way that kept him from pursuing his freedom. And yet he wanted to be free. He wasn't a serious-relationship sort of guy. He didn't want to commit to any woman. He was supposed to be having the time of his life with plenty of them. As long as he was selective and up-front with whatever woman he was with, the sky was the limit.

Then why had he declined six calls already today and four yesterday? What was there about Delphine Ryland that had him not thinking straight or not thinking at all? Knowing he wouldn't find any answers here in the bathroom, he left and headed toward the dining room, where voices could be heard.

"For a minute there I thought you'd gotten lost," Jonas said jokingly as he placed platters on the table.

Gannon didn't say anything as he slid into the seat across from Delphine. He could have taken the seat beside her, but he wanted to look into her beautiful face and study those delectable lips.

"I hope you're hungry, Gannon," Nikki said.

"He's always hungry," Jonas added.

He saw the way Delphine's lips curved into a smile. She wouldn't be so amused if she knew what else he was hungry for. Namely her. He would love to spread her on this table and make her his treat. He would undress them both and then he would spread her legs and sink into her and—

"Gannon!"

He jerked his head in Jonas's direction. "What?"

"I asked if you'd spoken to the folks today."

He wondered why his brother wanted to know. "I talk to them every day."

Jonas laughed. "See, didn't I tell you, Delphine. He's the good son."

Gannon wondered when Jonas had told her that. How much conversation had been going on around him, about him, while he'd been sitting there staring at Delphine, imagining doing all kinds of wicked things to her?

"It's a habit."

"And a good habit," Nikki said, as if coming to his defense. "I think it's wonderful that he talks to them every day."

"Only because he didn't have to worry about Mom drilling him about marriage every time he called. He was the youngest and she started from the top. Mercury and Gannon got reprieves for a while."

Gannon thought Jonas was talking too much, although he didn't mind the ribbing. He heard it on occasion from all his brothers because he was the youngest. He had lived at home the longest and he had a close relationship with his parents. He had no problem talking to them every day and enjoyed doing so. He knew his father liked knowing how well the truckers were doing and his mom liked keeping up with him, period. He knew how much to tell her and how much not to tell her. He and Eden had a system. There was no need for her to put pressure on him because he intended to stick to his ten-year plan regardless.

He was piling mashed potatoes onto his plate when Nikki asked Delphine, "You're still leaving on Thursday?"

He glanced over at Delphine when she nodded. "Yes, but I won't be returning home as planned."

"Where will you be going?" he asked, as if he had every right to know.

"Not sure yet. All I know is I can't go home. I

was having work done on my house and the workers found asbestos. The inspector stopped work until it's all removed. There's no reason to return home until that's completed."

"So where will you go?" Jonas asked.

Delphine sighed deeply, then added, "I thought about driving to Vegas from here. I heard it's a scenic drive."

"It is," Nikki said. "But I don't know if you should do it by yourself."

Delphine smiled at Nikki. "I'll be fine."

Although Gannon didn't say anything, he agreed with Nikki. He wasn't sure it was a trip she should take by herself. He recalled her telling him about the work she was having done on her home. He also recalled her telling him about how she enjoyed traveling and wanting a life filled with adventure.

"So how did the interview go?" Jonas asked.

Delphine smiled again. "I thought it went great. Gannon was an intriguing subject."

"Nah, it went well because you're a good interviewer. You made things easy."

She smiled over at him. "I merely asked questions about you that I figured the readers would want to know."

"And like I said, you did an awesome job. You can interview me again anytime, Delphine."

"Thanks, Gannon."

Gannon was about to take a bite of his meat loaf when he glanced over at Jonas and noticed his brother staring at him. He recognized Jonas's look. Whether

Gannon wanted it or not, he knew Jonas would be talking to him later. He didn't have to wonder what the conversation would be about.

He found it downright amusing that Jonas, who was once pegged by the society tabloids as being the city's number one womanizer, was giving Gannon the eye. Of course, at one point or another, all of his brothers had worn that title. And none of them had seemed ashamed of it. So why Jonas felt the need to talk to him about anything was beyond Gannon's comprehension. Just like Jonas had once lived the good life while he was single, Gannon felt it was his time to do the same.

During dinner it was hard to keep his eyes off Delphine and, frankly, he didn't care who noticed. He was beyond caring. It was what it was. He was attracted to Delphine and would finally admit that he hadn't desired another woman since meeting her. Granted, it had only been three days, but still, for him to be this into a woman had to mean something. Didn't it? Even if it meant he needed to get laid in a bad way.

The good thing was that there were no longer any business dealings between them. Not that it mattered, since he'd never been one to separate business from pleasure. When opportunity knocked, a man took advantage of it. Just as long as he stayed in control of the situation and both parties understood the limits.

"Dinner is great, Jonas and Nikki. Thanks for inviting me," Delphine said.

"You're welcome," Nikki said, smiling broadly.

"And I ditto what Delphine said. Thanks for having me over, guys," Gannon added.

"You know you're welcome anytime, Gannon," Nikki said.

"Yeah, Gannon, with you around we never have to worry about leftovers," Jonas said, chuckling.

Gannon grinned and glanced over at Delphine. She was grinning, as well. She knew about his voracious appetite. At least, she knew about one of his appetites. Before she left Phoenix it might be a good idea to introduce her to the other one.

Delphine finished off the last of her dinner while trying to ignore the intensity of Gannon's gaze. His stare was making her feel things she'd never felt before, even with Liddell. They'd been sexually active since their senior year of high school. When they'd gone to separate colleges, they'd only hooked up when they returned home for the holidays.

Delphine now realized how the infrequency of their lovemaking could have made Liddell an easy target for someone like Agatha...not that it excused his infidelity. Delphine had been faithful to him for those four years while attending the University of Wyoming. Liddell had attended a university on the East Coast and sworn he would be faithful to her, as well. He'd even promised to invite her to visit him in Virginia, saying he would show her the Atlantic Ocean. He never did.

Refusing to think about Liddell's unfaithfulness any longer, she glanced over at Gannon. He was staring at her, and when their gazes connected, she again felt a strong stirring in the pit of her stomach. She quickly broke eye contact and took a sip of her iced tea. She didn't know just how much longer she could handle the feelings she was experiencing around the very handsome and sexy man sitting across the table from her. Maybe she should head out for Vegas tomorrow instead of Thursday, since there was nothing holding her here. She figured she could use the extra day to begin writing her article on Gannon from her hotel room. A hotel room in Vegas would work just as well as one here. She'd been to Vegas before and wouldn't be lured by the excitement of walking the Strip.

"I hope everyone is ready for dessert," Nikki said, grabbing Delphine's attention. "And it's my contribution to the evening's meal. A key-lime cheesecake."

"That sounds good," Delphine said, smiling over at Nikki.

Again, she thought about how happy Nikki was. Delphine couldn't help but feel a little envious that at one time she'd wanted the same situation for herself—a husband who loved her and to be pregnant with his child.

A short while later, she was pushing herself away from the table. The cake had been delicious. "I'm full," she said, grinning.

"I'm not," Gannon said.

She glanced over at him. She'd noticed his slice had been double the size of hers and he'd eaten all of his dinner. Where did the man put it all and how did he keep his body stacked so nicely? This was the first time she'd seen him in jeans and he looked fine, with the best-shaped tush she'd ever laid eyes on. And then there were those sinewy thighs and firm hips... He could be in a western-wear ad easily.

"Well, I'm glad everyone enjoyed dessert. I couldn't have you think Jonas did all the cooking while I didn't contribute at all," Nikki said, laughing.

Jonas stood. "And this is the part she never volunteers for," he said, smiling over at his wife. "The cleaning up. But that's okay since Gannon is going to help me."

Delphine saw Gannon switch his gaze to his brother. "I am?"

"You are. Seems only fair since you ate most of the food."

"I'm a growing boy, what can I say?" Gannon said, standing and following Jonas's lead as he began clearing off the table.

"If you guys need additional—"

"Don't you dare volunteer for kitchen duty," Nikki interrupted Delphine with a huge grin on her face. "The guys can handle things. Besides, I can't wait to tell you about the decorating plans I have for the baby's nursery."

Gannon helped Jonas load the dishwasher and then tackle the pots. Although he did use his own kitchen on occasion, he never had as many pots and pans to clean as Jonas did whenever he cooked. He recalled when Jonas and Mercury had taken that cooking class. That had been in Jonas's before-Nikki days.

Gannon knew that neither Mercury nor Jonas had really been interested in learning how to cook. Their main interest had been the single women they figured they would meet in the class. For months the two had bragged about all the invitations they'd gotten for free home-cooked meals and no-strings-attached sex.

"What's going on with you and Delphine, Gannon?"

He'd wondered how long it would take for Jonas to get around to asking. His brothers usually had an agreement of don't ask, don't tell. At least, the five oldest ones did. For some reason they hadn't included Gannon in that agreement. Since he was the youngest, they felt it was their God-given right to know what he was doing at all times and with whom. Of course, he never told.

They claimed if they didn't watch out for him, their parents would never forgive them. There were times they seemed to forget that, at thirty-three, he was a grown-ass man who could take care of himself.

"What makes you think something is going on?" he asked, not bothering to glance at his brother while drying another pot.

His brothers always said they could look in his eyes and tell if he was truthful or not. This time it didn't matter. He was being truthful. There was nothing going on between him and Delphine. Had Jonas asked what he would *like* to be going on, then he would have given his brother an entirely different answer.

"I've seen the way you've been looking at her."

Jonas was right—he had been looking at her and hadn't tried hiding it. "So what of it?"

"It can only mean one thing."

He glanced over at Jonas. "What?"

"I've noticed how you stare at other women, but this was different. You want Delphine bad."

Gannon wished his brother would tell him something he didn't already know. "And?"

"I think you need to find out why."

"I already know why. She's a good-looking woman, intelligent and has a nice body. All the things I look for."

"She's also all the things you're not looking for."

Gannon lifted an eyebrow. "Such as?"

"She's a woman a man should consider marrying."

The pan Jonas was handing Gannon nearly slipped from his hand. He had to act quickly to stop it from hitting the floor. "Marrying? Are you crazy? I'm not marrying anyone until after my forty-third birthday."

"Then you should mark Delphine off your to-do list."

After drying the pan and placing it aside, Gannon leaned against the kitchen counter to stare over at his brother. "You just met Delphine today. What makes you so protective of her?"

"Because she's Nikki's friend and I know her story."

"What story?" Gannon asked.

"The one about how she's been hurt before by a man, and how she spent three years taking care of her sick mother and how she's just getting her feet wet in the dating scene. The last thing she needs is to get entangled with a guy like you, who means her no good."

Gannon crossed his arms over his chest. "By no good, you mean a man who isn't interested in settling down?"

"Yes."

Gannon didn't say anything for a minute and then walked over to the window and glanced out before turning back to his brother. "What did the guy do to hurt her?"

"That's for me to know and for you to find out. If she wants you to know she will tell you."

Gannon frowned, not liking that Jonas was trying to be all secretive, like Eli. "Well, I'm glad you've let me know where her head is. If it's in marriage, then it's definitely not where my head is." Although he would admit that since meeting her he had thought a lot about their heads joining on the same pillow. He guessed that wouldn't be happening now since the word *marriage* had slipped into the mix.

"Can I share something with you, Gannon?"

He wondered why Jonas was even asking. If it was something he wanted to say, Jonas would say it, regardless of whether or not Gannon wanted to hear it. "Go ahead."

"I've watched you with other women and I think there's something about Delphine that has gotten to you."

Gannon shrugged. "And what if it has?"

"Then I think you'd be making a huge mistake if you don't find out why."

"I already know why," Gannon said.

"Do you really? Did I ever tell you that one day Nikki and I shared an innocent kiss? We had gotten caught up in my getting this big deal, and the next thing I knew, we were kissing. Before then, our relationship had been strictly business."

"And?"

"I felt something in that single kiss with Nikki that I'd never felt in a kiss before with a woman. It scared the shit out of me."

Interested in what his brother was saying, Gannon asked, "What did you do?"

"I did what I thought was best for my peace of mind and my survival."

"Which was?"

"To put distance between us. When I left her office that day, I intentionally stayed away from her for eighteen months. A whole damn year and a half, Gannon. I was determined not to let any one woman interfere with the way I wanted to live my life, which was a life that would include plenty of women. For eighteen months I went through other women to get my desire for Nikki out of my system. I had convinced myself that what I'd felt that day while kissing her had been a fluke, and that I would eventually feel the same way if I kissed other women. It never happened."

Jonas didn't say anything for a moment and then added, "I think you owe it to yourself to find out why Delphine gets next to you in a way no other woman can. Otherwise, ten years from now when you're ready to settle down, you might realize the woman intended to be Mrs. Gannon Steele will have gotten away and married someone else, with kids that should have been yours. And all because of that ten-year plan of yours. Take it from someone who's been out there, doing women and thinking the next will be better than the last, only to discover the woman destined to be mine could have been lost to me forever had I not come to my senses when I did."

A short while later, after he and Jonas joined Nikki and Delphine on the back patio, Gannon wished he could put Jonas's spiel out of his mind, but he couldn't. Hell, his brother had talked about the lasting effect of kissing Nikki, and Gannon hadn't even gotten that close to Delphine. As far as he was concerned, he didn't need to kiss her to wonder what it would do to him if he ever did. Just looking at her lips stirred his guts. If he ever tasted her—sinking his mouth into hers, ravishing her tongue with his, without any restraint or control—he would definitely be a goner.

What Jonas evidently hadn't figured out yet was that Gannon was a step ahead of him. There was a reason he'd shown up unexpectedly here tonight— mainly because the thought of not seeing Delphine again bothered him. That in itself spoke volumes. And now he intended on taking it from there. He wasn't sure *where* he was taking it, but he knew it had to happen within the next twenty-four hours because she was leaving town on Thursday.

He honestly didn't like the thought of her driving from Phoenix to Vegas alone, but he couldn't say that when she was a grown woman who could take care of herself. Hadn't she been doing so for twenty-five years already? And what information did Jonas know about Delphine's ex-boyfriend? What had the bastard done to her? She'd told Gannon she wasn't dating and he had suspected there was more to the story. Now he knew that there was.

When the doorbell sounded, Jonas grinned and said, "I bet that's Tyson. I figured he would drop by, so I packed him a to-go container."

It was Tyson, still wearing his medical attire. He met Delphine and she remarked how much Tyson, Jonas and Gannon looked alike. Tyson stayed to converse for a little while before grabbing his to-go bag and leaving. As he was walking out the door, Tyson gave Gannon a look that indicated they would talk. As far as Gannon was concerned, they didn't have to talk. Since marrying, his brothers had become saints, conveniently forgetting the times when they'd given the name Bad News Steeles special meaning.

"Thanks again for everything, Nikki and Jonas. I really enjoyed myself, and thanks for giving me an extra slice of cake. And it was good seeing you again, Gannon."

He blinked. He had been staring at her the entire time, but he hadn't been keeping up with the conversation between her, Jonas and Nikki. She was standing, clutching the bag he knew contained the slice of cake Nikki had given to her. Did that mean she was leaving?

He stood up, too. "Same here, Delphine, and since I'm leaving, as well, I'll walk you to your car." He knew what he said sounded ridiculous since her car was parked right out front in his brother's circular driveway and not off in a parking lot somewhere.

"You don't have to do that, Gannon," she said, looking at him.

"I want to." He really meant that. "Besides, I want to talk to you about something."

"Oh, okay."

He watched as she gave both Jonas and Nikki hugs, and then they walked her to the door. He followed. After thanking his brother and sister-in-law for dinner, he and Delphine went outside. Although it was still light out, the sun had gone down and dusk was arriving.

"What do you want to talk to me about, Gannon?" she asked, as they walked side by side.

He gazed down at her. "How would you like to see the view of the city from the Black Mountains tonight?"

Five

Not for the first time, Delphine thought the green eyes staring at her were as sexy as sin. She'd gotten so caught up in them that she nearly missed what he'd said. "The Black Mountains? Tonight?"

"Yes, tonight. I figured I could follow you back to the hotel and we can go in my car. There's a small section of the mountains on my brother Galen's property. That's the only way you can get to it, so it's considered private."

Delphine thought about what he was saying. He was basically asking her to go parking with him. She hadn't gone parking with a guy since Liddell in high school and she knew what parking with a guy often entailed. "Why?"

They had reached her rental car and she leaned against it.

"Why what?"

"Why would you want me to go to the Black Mountains with you?"

He smiled and she felt her legs nearly turn to jelly. "I thought you would enjoy the view."

Yeah, right, she thought. But had she really expected him to give her the same answer Liddell would have given her had she asked him why they would be parking up on one of Denver's mountains? Liddell would have told her in five words or less exactly what they would be going up there to do. But then, Liddell had been her boyfriend and they'd been sexually active. Gannon was just a man she'd been sent here to interview for the magazine she worked for. A man she'd only known three days.

Delphine was very much aware that times had changed since her high-school days, but was she ready to drive to an isolated mountain location with someone she barely knew? Did he assume she was open to such a thing now that the business part of their relationship had ended?

"To just enjoy the view?" she asked him, doubting that was all he wanted.

"And I figured it could be a place where we could also talk privately."

She lifted an eyebrow. "Talk privately about what?"

"I'd rather not discuss it here."

Delphine nibbled her bottom lip. Although she hadn't known Gannon long, interviewing him had revealed a lot. Namely, his integrity. She honestly didn't think she had to worry about him taking her up there to the mountain and then forcing her to do anything against her will. Besides, why would he when there were women like Trish just willing and waiting to get into his pants?

Then there was something else she should take into consideration. Could she trust *herself* with him? There was chemistry between them and plenty of it. If there had been any doubt in her mind before tonight, it had been squashed. Every time she'd glanced at him across the table, heat had flooded her insides. Parts of her were even tingling now from him standing so close. What if he kept his hands off her but she couldn't keep her hands off him? What if—

"Will you go, Delphine?"

Tilting her head back, she held his gaze and felt the heat slither through her already hot body. At that moment, her entire body stirred with an emotion that until now had been foreign to her. But she recognized it for what it was. Sexual hunger. She never would have thought she had it in her to feel such intense lust until Gannon.

Hadn't she said that with her newfound independence she wanted to be adventurous? Granted, a sexual adventure wasn't what she'd had in mind, but maybe she should consider it.

"Yes, I will go with you," she said, before she could change her mind.

Gannon sat in his parked car and waited for Delphine to come out of the hotel. She'd gone in to take the cake Nikki had given her up to her hotel room. He had watched her walk inside, admiring the sway of her hips and trying to deal with the throb of his erection with every step she'd taken.

For the first time in his life, he didn't have a plan when it came to spending time with a woman. Usually he knew exactly how he intended the night to end, and he and the woman would be on the same page. But tonight, he was entering uncharted waters, and he wasn't sure if he would sink or swim. No woman had ever placed him in such a predicament before.

Drawing in a deep breath, he picked up his phone and punched in Galen's number. "You caught me at a bad time. What do you want, Gannon?"

He smiled, wondering if he had interrupted anything between his brother and his sister-in-law Brittany. If he had, it wouldn't be the first time he'd done so. They claimed that with twins under three they had to sneak in passionate moments whenever they could.

"I'll be on your property tonight, going up to the Black Mountains. Just wanted you to know so you wouldn't think it was trespassers."

"And why would you be going up to the mountains at night, Gannon? On second thought, don't answer. Maybe it's best I not know."

"Not that you were getting information out of me anyway. And don't use your telescope tonight." They all knew about Galen's powerful telescope.

"Um, I'm not making you any promises about that."

"Do me a favor and try real hard. Good night, Galen, and give Brittany my love."

"She doesn't need yours when she gets enough of mine. 'Bye."

Gannon chuckled when his brother clicked off. He then glanced back at the hotel's entrance to see Delphine walking through the revolving doors. When a jolt of sexual need rocked him to the bone, he gripped the steering wheel to steady himself.

Moments later, Gannon got out of the car so he could open the door for her. She smiled up at him. "You didn't have to do that, Gannon."

"Yes, I did," he responded as he gave her time to slide onto the leather seat before closing the door. He would offer to snap her seat belt in place, but figured he wouldn't last long enough to do so. Her scent alone would render him mindless.

As he walked back around the car to get inside, he refused to question his sanity in asking her to go to the Black Mountains with him. But he was too far gone now. He got in the car, closed the door and then buckled his own seat belt before glancing over at her. She seemed nervous and he figured he needed to reassure her that she was safe with him. "I don't bite, you know."

She met his gaze and a smile touched her lips. "I would not be going anywhere with you if I thought you did, Gannon."

Their gazes held for a moment and he knew there was no way she didn't feel the strong sensual vibes flowing between them. The passion. The need. The desire. Sexual awareness seemed to thicken the air between them.

When a low moan slipped from her lips, he knew she was as far gone as he was. Gannon was aware of everything about her—her nearness, her scent and the look in her eyes. Heaven help him. He didn't understand what was happening, but he figured she didn't, either.

A primitive force he couldn't combat had him reaching out to trace the tip of his finger around her lips. Lips he wanted to kiss.

"Don't know what's happening between us, Delphine, but it's worth exploring, don't you think?"

In all honesty, Delphine couldn't think.

In fact, she could barely handle Gannon's closeness and his touch. Intense desire clawed at her and they hadn't left the hotel's parking lot yet. She was tempted to tell Gannon to forget about the drive up the mountains, and ask him inside her hotel room instead. When had she gotten so bold to even think of doing such a thing?

What she should do was tell him she had changed her mind about going anywhere with him and bid him goodbye. But something was keeping her from doing that. She hadn't been with a man in over five years, and until Gannon had come along, she could have gone without one for another five. But he had made doing such a thing difficult, nearly impossible.

"Are you sure that you still want to go with me up the mountains, Delphine?"

His question, spoken in a deep, throaty voice, sent spiraling sensations to her very core. Yes, she wanted to go up to the mountains with him, although she knew she shouldn't.

When she didn't respond right away, he said, "I promise not to do anything that you object to."

If he thought that would make her feel better, he was wrong, because she might not object to anything. "I believe you."

He reached out toward the console and soft music began playing. It was relaxing, definitely something she needed to hear. She'd never pegged him for a symphony type, but as the sounds of Mozart, Dvořák and Beethoven flowed in the car's interior as they made their way up the mountain, she concluded that evidently he was. Her mother had loved symphony music, so Delphine was familiar with it. She saw this as just another side of Gannon she was getting to know.

They had done enough talking for now, and she was satisfied to just relax and listen to the music.

"We're here, Delphine."

He knew she hadn't been asleep, although her eyes had been closed. The sound of a symphony could do that. He'd read somewhere that it could decrease a person's stress level, as well as stimulate the regeneration of brain cells. And then, according to his brother Tyson, the renowned heart surgeon, music could also decrease blood pressure and improve a person's memory.

Gannon had brought the car to a stop and shut off

the ignition. Releasing his seat belt, he watched as she sat up and looked around. He wasn't surprised by her gasp of surprise. Down below you could see the scattered lights of a number of households, as well as a good view of downtown Phoenix, although they were miles away from it.

"Oh, it's beautiful up here, Gannon."

He'd known it would be since he'd been here with his brothers, cousins and selected friends. They had gathered up here to celebrate Galen's pending marriage to Brittany, Eli's to Stacey, Tyson's to Hunter, Jonas's to Nikki and, most recently, Mercury's to Sloan. It had been a guys' night with their favorite bottles of liquor. This was the first time Gannon had been up here with a woman.

"I think so, too. If you look to the left, at that place surrounded by so many lights that it actually looks like a lit Christmas tree, that's where my oldest brother, Galen, lives."

She leaned forward to look out the windshield. "His house seems isolated from all the others."

"It is, intentionally so. He likes his privacy, so he bought all the land surrounding him, which includes this private road up the mountains. He won't hesitate to report trespassers, trust me."

She glanced over at him. "Does he know we're here?"

"Yes, he knows," he said, sliding back his car seat to stretch out his long legs.

She didn't say anything for a moment and then

glanced over at him. "Earlier you mentioned wanting to talk to me about something."

Yes, he had told her that. He had thought about what he wanted to discuss with her before leaving Jonas's house. "I'm leaving Friday on a road trip," he said.

She nodded. "Yes, I know. What about it?"

He opened his mouth to respond, when suddenly she nervously swiped her tongue across her bottom lip. The action caused a spike of heat to catch in the lower part of his gut. It would not have been so bad if he hadn't been thinking about them, dreaming about them, fantasizing about those same lips since meeting her, but he had. And if that wasn't torture enough, he was sitting close enough to breathe in her luscious scent.

Seemingly with a will not his own, he leaned in toward her and tilted his face close to hers. As if drawn to him, she tilted her head to move closer, as well. And when he reached out and took the pad of his thumb and angled her mouth even closer to his, she didn't resist. A part of him was glad they were on the same page, because he honestly didn't know what he would do if she denied him this kiss. He wanted the sweet taste of her mouth and a chance to devour those delectable lips.

His gaze shifted from her eyes to her lips and an intense arousal surged within him. Desire didn't just claw at him; it ripped him open, laid him bare to a need of the most intense kind.

Not able to resist temptation any longer, he closed

his eyes on a groan and hungrily covered her mouth with his. He released another groan, this one of deep longing and satisfaction, while burying his fingers into the thick curls on her head, as if doing so would bring her mouth closer and lock it tight with his.

His tongue took possession of hers, claiming it like he had every right to do so, with a hunger he felt through his bones. The pounding of need in his groin made him groan again in raw male appreciation. His body was making demands and they were all for her. He felt like he was burning from the inside out.

His hands left her head and he wrapped his arms around her to pull her across the seat to him. From the very beginning, her lips had presented a temptation that made him question his sanity, while at the same time testing the bounds of his endurance. Never had the taste of any woman lit him up this way, overwhelming him to the point where raw male satisfaction was humming all the way to his soul. His body was throbbing while a hard shot of lust rushed through his veins.

Gannon knew if he didn't pull back from the kiss now, he would strip off her clothes and be inside her in a matter of minutes. But he didn't want that. He refused to treat her as a one-night stand when he had a gut feeling she was meant to be more than that.

And it was up to him to find out why he felt that way.

What Jonas had said to him had hit a nerve, rattled him. What if ten years from now he did discover that she had been the one, and he'd let her get away? He had to know for certain before beginning his life for the next ten years as the ultimate man-whore. Was she the woman destined to be claimed by a Steele? Namely, claimed by *him*? On the other hand, was he ready to walk away from all those other sinfully erotic women's beds just for a possibility?

He knew the answer the moment he adjusted his mouth to deepen the kiss. How could he think of Delphine as a mere possibility, when at this moment he was feasting on the most scrumptious lips ever tasted by a man? Definitely the most enchanting ones he'd had the pleasure of kissing. Their mouths were perfect for each other, as if they belonged together, were meant to be connected this way. Not just for tonight, but for always.

For always?

The sound of a wolf's howl pierced the night and Gannon reluctantly released Delphine's mouth, but not before giving her lips a sweep with his tongue. Never had he felt such primal desire for any woman. Never.

"Gannon…"

She said his name on what sounded like a breathless moan and he braced his forehead against hers. Now he knew how it felt to have his common sense hammered by passion. He was one short sentence away from suggesting they crawl into the back seat, strip naked and have crazy, mind-blowing sex.

"I've never been kissed like that before," she whispered, as if saying the words sucked up oxygen she desperately needed.

He heard the words and was moved by them. If that was true, some man hadn't been taking care of business like he should have. That made him even more determined to find out what part, if any, she could play in his life. Or was he just getting caught up in a very sexual moment with her?

She then tilted her head to look at him, to stare deeply into his eyes. As if she needed to regain control of her senses, too. Then she asked, "What did you want to discuss with me, Gannon?"

Her question heightened the beating of his heart, which he was convinced had skipped a beat or two while kissing her. "It's my road trip."

Her gaze roamed over his face before returning to his eyes. "What about it?"

He was tempted to lean in and kiss her again, but he knew he needed to answer her question. "I want to take you with me."

She stared at him with a beautiful pair of wide eyes. "You want to take me with you on the road trip?" she asked, as if she needed to make sure she'd heard him correctly.

"Yes."

And Gannon knew at that moment, there was no way he could leave her behind.

Six

Delphine moved away from Gannon to ease back into her seat. She didn't say anything, just stared out into the darkness, and then beyond to the lights of the houses below. Just a few moments ago she had melted in his arms, had allowed her mouth to be ravished by his kiss. And for a few moments she had thought…

What exactly had she thought?

That for once in her life a man had appreciated her for being her, and not for what he could get from her? That was the story she knew all the other single women were bitching about, and rightly so. Men weren't interested in love and forever after. They wanted the here and now. To leave their mark and move on.

But then, did she really want forever after? She'd honestly believed she'd had that with Liddell, but he had proved her wrong in the most hurtful way. Could she really risk her heart on another man? She honestly knew she couldn't. It would be a cold day in hell before she would think about getting back into a serious relationship. If that was her story and she was sticking to it, why did the thought of a man like Gannon, known for changing bed partners so often he had a problem keeping up with names, bother her?

"Delphine?"

She pulled herself together, considering the man she was dealing with. His business mind was brilliant. His sense of duty to his employees was remarkable. The only time they'd covered his personal life was when he'd gone on record to say he was a single man and intended to stay that way for a long time. She figured that was his way of letting any single female readers of the magazine know what to expect.

When he said her name again, she slowly turned to look at him. Green eyes were searching hers and she couldn't help but remember how much she had enjoyed the passion they hadn't been able to keep in check.

"Why, Gannon? Why do you want me to go with you?" She knew the answer but wanted to hear him say it. To put things in perspective. To tell her outright that she meant nothing to him, but was just another woman to add to his list of many.

"I enjoy your company and figured you coming

with me would be our way of getting to know each other better."

His response hadn't been good enough. She needed more. "Why would you want to get to know me better?"

He didn't say anything for a minute, and she watched his expression closely. He was thinking hard, as if what he said was important. Why? He was the ultimate player, who should have his lines down pat. Why did it seem as if he was searching for words?

"I've never met a woman quite like you before, Delphine."

She didn't say anything. To keep the promise she'd made to her mother about giving love another try, and to prepare herself for dating, she'd purchased a book entitled *Be Aware of Pick-Up Lines Men Use*. She wasn't surprised that the one he'd just used had made the list.

"Keep living because you will undoubtedly meet others," she said, looking away from him.

"I doubt that very seriously. I don't think you understand."

She looked back at him. "Then make me understand, Gannon."

He broke eye contact with her, and she wondered if it was because he was trying to come up with a new line. She was about to tell him to forget it, and that he honestly didn't need to answer because she wouldn't be going anywhere with him regardless, when he glanced back at her.

She wasn't always good at reading people, but at the moment a part of her felt that every emotion known to man was expressed in Gannon's eyes. Why she thought that, she wasn't sure. All she knew was that the man she'd interviewed for two days had been confident, self-assured, even a little arrogant. However, the green eyes staring at her were filled with uncertainty.

"I need to make sure that you aren't the woman meant for me, Delphine. The one woman in life I'm supposed to claim. The woman who is my destiny. If I don't make sure, then it will be a missed opportunity and you will be lost to me forever."

Delphine's jaw dropped slightly, because those particular lines hadn't made the list.

Gannon doubted Delphine was aware that the words he'd just said were the most serious he'd spoken to any woman. They had been heartfelt, sincere and truthful because he knew of no other way to be with her. Whether she realized it or accepted it, something was going on between them. Something powerful. He couldn't stop it and doubted neither could she.

"That's the most ridiculous thing I've ever heard."

Her words hit a nerve. Ridiculous? His jaw twitched in anger. "Do you honestly think I want to feel that way? That I want to believe there's a woman somewhere who exists for me? A woman for me to claim? Then let me set the record straight. I've never been into claiming women, just enjoying sex with them.

But for some reason, you're different. You make me feel things, want things, need things, and I don't like it. I liked the path my life was taking before you came along just fine."

Gannon watched Delphine angrily cross her arms over her chest. "Then why change it?" she snapped.

"Because of you. Can you honestly say you can't feel the vibes we generate? That you don't think something strong is happening between us?"

He watched as she nibbled her lips and his gut clenched. At least he had her thinking.

"All I'm asking is a chance for us to determine why we are drawn together like we are. I'm not asking you to go with me on the road for a sexathon. I want you to go because I truly want you with me, to share that side of myself with you. Namely, my love for the road. It has nothing to do with the interview, but with me. I've never wanted to share myself that way with any woman."

"I think you're just confused, Gannon."

"Then unconfuse me. I honestly meant what I said about needing to make sure that you aren't the woman meant to be in my future."

"Trust me, I'm not."

"Then prove it, Delphine. While we are together, I don't plan to pressure you into doing anything you don't want to do. Any ground rules or limitations you set I will abide by."

He knew he could say that because the force of passion between them was so strong, there was no way they could spend time together and not share

"One Minute" Survey

You get up to **FOUR books** <u>and</u> TWO Mystery Gifts...

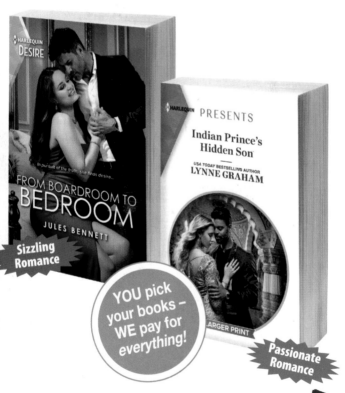

Sizzling Romance

YOU pick your books – WE pay for everything!

Passionate Romance

See inside for details.

YOU pick your books –
WE pay for everything.
You get up to FOUR new books and TWO Mystery Gifts.
absolutely FREE!
Total retail value: Over $20!

Dear Reader,

Your opinions are important to us. So if you'll participate in our fast and free "One Minute" Survey, **YOU** can pick up to four wonderful books that **WE** pay for!

As a leading publisher of women's fiction, we'd love to hear from you. That's why we promise to reward you for completing our survey.

IMPORTANT: Please complete the survey and return it. We'll send your Free Books and Free Mystery Gifts right away. **And we pay for shipping and handling too!** *We pay for EVERYTHING!*

Try **Harlequin® Desire** books featuring the worlds of the American elite with juicy plot twists, delicious sensuality and intriguing scandal.

Try **Harlequin Presents® Larger-Print** books featuring the glamourous lives of royals and billionaires in a world of exotic locations, where passion knows no bounds.

Or TRY BOTH!

Thank you again for participating in our "One Minute" Survey. It really takes just a minute (or less) to complete the survey… and your free books and gifts will be well worth it!

Sincerely,

Pam Powers

Pam Powers
for Reader Service

www.ReaderService.com

"One Minute" Survey

GET YOUR FREE BOOKS AND FREE GIFTS!

✓ Complete this Survey   ✓ Return this survey

1 Do you try to find time to read every day?

☐ YES   ☐ NO

2 Do you prefer stories with happy endings?

☐ YES   ☐ NO

3 Do you enjoy having books delivered to your home?

☐ YES   ☐ NO

4 Do you find a Larger Print size easier on your eyes?

☐ YES   ☐ NO

YES! I have completed the above "One Minute" Survey. Please send me my Free Books and Free Mystery Gifts (worth over $20 retail). I understand that I am under no obligation to buy anything, as explained on the back of this card.

☐ I prefer Harlequin® Desire 225/326 HDL GNWS

☐ I prefer Harlequin Presents® Larger Print 176 /376 HDL GNWS

☐ I prefer BOTH 225/326 & 176/376 HDL GNW4

FIRST NAME

LAST NAME

ADDRESS

APT.#

CITY

STATE/PROV.

ZIP/POSTAL CODE

intimacy. According to his now married brothers, intimacy was one of the purest displays of love between a couple.

Love...

He swallowed deeply, wondering how and when that one single word had entered the equation. But he couldn't worry about that now. Gannon saw from the bemused expression in her eyes that he needed to make her understand and he would use a new angle to do so.

"Didn't you say that you couldn't return home just yet?"

She nodded. "Yes."

"And didn't you say you wanted to experience different things? Adventure? To tap into your wanderlust side?"

She hesitated a second, then said, "Yes, I said that, too."

"Didn't you also tell me that you'd never seen the Atlantic Ocean and that it's always been your dream to one day see it?"

She broke eye contact with him for a second before relocking her gaze with his. "Yes, I said that."

"Then let me share those things with you, Delphine. Going on the road with me will be an adventure— I can promise you that. It will satisfy your wanderlust since we will be crossing several states—Texas, Louisiana, Mississippi and Alabama—and end up in Florida. And I want to show you the Atlantic Ocean."

What he wouldn't spring on her just yet was that he intended to invite her to spend a week with him at his beach house in Miami. That was an invitation he'd never issued to a woman and he wasn't sure why it was important that he invite her, but for him it was.

He studied her features, namely her eyes, when she said softly, "Someone else promised to do that once."

"Do what?" he asked her.

"Show me the Atlantic Ocean."

He saw the pain in her gaze and had a feeling that someone was the same guy who'd broken her heart. The one Jonas refused to tell Gannon anything about. "I'm not that person and I intend to keep my promise."

Their gazes continued to hold as Gannon drove home another point. "You were going to leave here and go to Vegas anyway, so why not share the road with me instead?"

Already thinking of the excuse she would use next, he said, "The cab of my truck is internet-ready, with everything you need to continue working on your article. Plus, I'll be there in case you discover there's something you should have asked me but didn't."

His goal was to make it nearly impossible for her to say no. She looked away again and licked her lips. "I need to think about it, Gannon."

"All right. Can I have your answer by noon tomorrow?"

She glanced back over at him. "Yes, I'll have an answer for you by noon tomorrow."

"Think about it? Honestly, Del, what's there to think about when a hunk like Gannon Steele invites you on a road trip? If it was me, I would jump at the offer in a heartbeat."

Delphine heard what her best friend was saying, but still, they were two different people. "Of course you would, Mandy. You've always been the self-confident one." Mandy had married a guy she'd met in college and they had two sons. Mandy, Roger and the kids were the perfect family.

"And so were you until Liddell did what he did. The woman who returned to Denver after that was timid, with less self-esteem. I told you that."

Yes, her best friend had. But how was Delphine supposed to be confident when the man she'd loved had dumped her and the entire town knew why? "Yes, but—"

"But nothing. Why do you continue to let Liddell win?"

"I don't know what you're talking about."

"Don't you?" Then there was a pause before Mandy said, "Then maybe you don't."

"What do you mean?"

"What I mean is that Liddell Bartley is an asshole. He is not the nice guy we knew in high school. He went to that college on the East Coast and someone must have convinced him he was God's gift to women. Even Jerome can't stand him anymore."

Jerome Applegate used to be Liddell's best friend while growing up. "Why?"

"Because of the lies he's telling his wife. Do you know that to keep her in line, he's telling her that he can leave her for you anytime and that you would take him back?"

"He definitely lied to her if he told her that. No wonder she gives me daggered looks whenever she sees me."

"And you aren't helping the situation."

Delphine frowned. "What do you mean I'm not helping the situation? I have nothing to do with Liddell. We don't even speak."

"Yes, but because you aren't involved with anyone, he's giving people, especially his wife, the impression that you're pining for him. Hell, I honestly think he believes it himself."

"That's not true and you know it, Mandy."

"Of course I know it isn't true, but others may not. I think everyone understood why you didn't date while your mom was ill, but they're probably wondering what's your excuse now, Delphine. I know guys have asked you out, but you've turned them down. You're making it easy for everyone to think that maybe you are carrying a torch for Liddell and hoping he will dump Agatha and come back to you. A lot of people remember how much you loved him."

Delphine's head was spinning. How could anyone think she could still love Liddell after what he'd done to her? If they did think that, that meant they must also think she was pathetic. "I'm rarely in Denver. I travel a lot."

"Yes, but you're here enough, and when you are, you don't date. How do you think that looks?" Mandy asked her.

"Like I'm not interested in the guys who asked me out. I have that right."

"Yes, you do, and it's nobody's damn business. But as your best friend, I thought you should know what Liddell is saying. I know how much he hurt you, but I wouldn't give him the pleasure of thinking he's ruined you for another man."

"He hasn't!"

"You sure? If he hasn't, then we wouldn't be having this conversation, Del. You would already have your bags packed for that road trip with Gannon Steele. The mere idea that you need to think about it means something."

"Yes, it means that I know what kind of women Gannon is used to."

"And we both know you're different. Evidently he knows that, too, if you're the first one he's asked to go on a road trip with him. I think Gannon sees something in you that Liddell ignored, which will forever be his loss."

Mandy's argument made Delphine remember what Gannon had said earlier tonight. She recalled his exact words… *I need to make sure that you aren't the woman meant for me, Delphine. The one woman in life I'm supposed to claim. The woman who is my destiny. If I don't make sure, then it will be a missed opportunity and you will be lost to me forever...*

With nothing else to be discussed, Gannon had returned her to the hotel. It was obvious that he intended to kiss her good-night, but she had opened her own car door and rushed inside the hotel without looking back. She had called Mandy the moment she'd returned to her hotel room.

"This is just a new thing for Gannon—it won't mean anything."

"Then let it be a new thing for you, as well. Do you plan on giving your heart to this guy?"

"Of course not!"

"Then go have some fun. Stop living in the past and begin embracing the present. And there's nothing wrong with sleeping with him if that's what you want to do, on your terms and not his."

"I'm not promiscuous, Mandy."

"No, you're not, but you have urges just like the rest of us, sweetheart, and please don't deny that you do. There's nothing wrong with satisfying those urges once in a while. The desire to do so doesn't make you promiscuous."

Deep down Delphine knew that to be true, and for the first time, she saw what she was doing. She was fishing for anything to legitimize her fear of being hurt again. "I still have to think about it, Mandy."

"Then do so, if you must. In the end I believe you will make the best decision for you."

Later that night when she went to bed, Delphine replayed in her mind everything about Gannon, from the time they'd officially met in the hotel lobby on Sunday night until tonight. How could three single days be so impactful on her life? Could she handle seven days in close quarters with him?

She closed her eyes when sleep overtook her with that question on her mind.

* * *

Gannon glanced at the clock on the wall in his office. Today was the day Delphine would give him her decision. He'd tried to keep busy, but every so often his mind would replay every single detail of last night in the Black Mountains…especially their kiss.

How could one kiss be so powerful? Leave a lasting impression on every part of his body? The more time he spent with Delphine, the more he was beginning to think…

No, he wouldn't go there.

He refused to do so. But then, it hadn't helped matters when Tyson had called this morning. According to Dr. Tyson Steele, who barely missed seeing a thing, he couldn't help but notice the way Gannon kept staring at Delphine last night. Tyson said it was a way he'd never seen Gannon stare at another woman. His brother felt it was obvious that Gannon was taken with her, and like Jonas, Tyson felt Gannon should find out why.

Evidently, Tyson had shared that opinion with Galen and Eli because Gannon had gotten calls from them, as well. That was just great, Gannon thought, annoyed that they felt the need to call to give him advice, as if he couldn't handle his business.

His cell phone rang, and his heart began pounding when he picked it up and saw the caller was Delphine. Swallowing deeply, he clicked on and said, "Good morning, Delphine."

"Good morning, Gannon. I'm calling to let you know I've made my decision."

He breathed in deeply, knowing her decision could either make or break him. He hadn't realized just how much he wanted her to travel on the road with him until after he'd asked her. "And what have you decided?"

There was a pause. Or was it a hesitation?

He swallowed deeply again and waited.

To him it seemed an eternity before she said, "I've decided to take you up on your offer and go on the road trip with you."

At that moment, Gannon couldn't stop the smile that spread across his lips.

Seven

Early Friday morning at seven, Delphine arrived on the lot of the Steele Trucking Company to find Gannon standing in front of a huge tractor-trailer rig. Over the past forty-eight hours she had constantly asked herself if she'd made the right decision. Now just seeing Gannon standing there made her believe that she had.

Even if she never again became involved with a man, seriously or otherwise, she would have memories of this trip with him. Mandy was right. It was time to start living in the present and not hang back in the past. And it was time to have fun...on her terms, of course.

But what were her terms when she'd never gone out of town with a guy before? Not even with Liddell.

She refused to dwell on that now. Instead, she much preferred putting all her concentration on the man whose gaze had been on her from the moment she'd parked her car and gotten out of it with her carry-on in tow. The man whose gaze was still on her as she walked toward him, and he acted as if he never intended to break eye contact.

Delphine wished that thoughts of the kiss they'd shared weren't weighing so heavily on her mind. Memories of it were still having an effect on her. She was inflamed with intoxicating yearnings. It was as if she could still taste him on her tongue, as if his scent was in her nostrils, as if his touch would now be impossible to resist. But she would try.

He was wearing a pair of jeans and a T-shirt that said Living for the Moment. Was that supposed to be a reminder of his philosophy? Or was that an invitation for her to think the same way? She wasn't certain which it was, but she decided not to sweat the small stuff right now. Instead, she tried to focus her attention on the ultrahandsome man whose company she would be sharing for an entire week.

"Good morning, Gannon," she said, coming to a stop in front of him.

"Good morning." He glanced down at her luggage and smiled. "That's all you have?"

Delphine couldn't help but smile back, especially when she saw the mischievous sparkle in the depths of his green eyes. "That's not enough?"

"Not if you were Eden Tyson Steele," he said,

chuckling. "Whenever Mom went on a road trip with Dad, he had to make room for all her luggage."

She nodded. "Since I travel a lot, I've learned to pack light. Besides, I've heard that a number of the truck stops have Laundromats."

"They do. You would be surprised at what all they have." He glanced at the clipboard in his hand. "I've got our orders and I'm ready to hit the road if you are."

"I'm ready." Delphine hoped that she truly was, because just being near Gannon was causing an incredible warmth to spread through her.

"Then follow me so we can get this show on the road."

She followed him toward the cab, which didn't have a trailer attached. She knew the trip from Phoenix to Jacksonville, Florida, would cover two thousand miles. The road trip would take thirty hours if they drove straight through. However, she knew it would take longer due to federal legislation requiring rest for drivers.

"Where's the rest of the truck?" she asked Gannon.

"At the shipper's dock, being loaded. Most of the time that's how it's done. My drivers are drivers— the shipper and the recipient of the goods have people in place at the starting point and destination to load and unload."

When they reached the cab, he used the key fob to unlock it. She also saw the way the steps seemed to appear miraculously by the door. "Hideaway steps. Nice touch," she said.

"It was a suggestion we got from our employees' opinion surveys. Because the truck is so high off the ground, climbing up into the cab isn't always easy, especially for shorter and older drivers."

"Definitely a good idea and a considerate implementation," she said.

"Thanks."

He offered his hand to help her get into the truck. Delphine had glanced inside a cab before, but now she was getting a full view. It was roomier than she'd expected, especially the area behind the curtain. That was more than just a bunk area—in fact, there were several compartments and cubbyholes where they could store clothes and other miscellaneous items. He showed her how the bunk bed could convert to a desk and table with a laptop and miniature television. There was also a small refrigerator and microwave. Everything was neat and tidy, and the space was utilized efficiently.

"As you can see, there's no bathroom facilities, so let me know when you need to go. I have no problem stopping," Gannon told her after placing her carry-on bag in one of the cubbyholes.

"Okay, and drivers actually sleep in the truck?"

"Most of them do, which is why I try to make things as comfortable and easy as possible. A lot of the truck stops are connected to hotels. That makes things convenient."

"I just bet it does," she said. She knew a lot of truckers indulged in affairs on the road. Since Gannon didn't ask what she meant, she decided not to expound on it. Besides, she was pretty sure he'd gotten her meaning. "What's the time frame for us to get where we're going?" she asked.

"The dispatcher will provide all that to us. Right now, the route we're taking and the states we're covering require at least a thirty-minute break after eight hours on the road. After the break we can do three more hours."

"And then?" she asked, buckling her seat belt.

"And then we have to rest for eleven hours."

That was a lot of time and Delphine wondered what they would do during their rest times. She glanced around the truck at the first-aid kit, map, GPS and all the other gadgets. "What do drivers do to keep themselves company?" she asked him.

He shrugged. "Listen to music, some make use of CB radios, books on tape, talking on their cell phones, as long as it's not handheld. Definitely no texting. Would you like some coffee?"

She saw the huge thermos. "Yes, thanks." He poured them cups of hot, steaming coffee.

"And I got a box of snacks if you get the munchies later."

"Thanks, Gannon."

He took a sip of coffee and then slid on his aviator-style sunglasses. Smiling over at her, he said, "Let the fun begin."

"This coffee is so good, Gannon."

He took a quick glance at her as he pulled the truck out of the lot. "Thanks. I made it myself. I discovered long ago that if you did a road trip with Drew Steele, you had to learn to make good coffee. He taught me. When it comes to making coffee for my dad, you have to be on top of your game."

Mixed with the scent of the coffee, already the truck smelled like her. He didn't mind since he definitely liked her scent. In fact, he liked everything about her. Today she was wearing a pair of jeans and a button-up olive green shirt. Her hair was pulled back, away from her face, and clamped on both sides to keep it that way. A cute pair of navy blue sneakers were on her feet.

He had watched her from the moment she'd gotten out of the car and had immediately known his testosterone level would be at an all-time high around her, but he would manage.

"Do you really talk to your parents every day?"

He had brought the cab to a stop at a railroad crossing to let a train pass. He glanced over at her and knew she was referring to a comment Jonas had made at dinner the other day.

It was a beautiful day, the last one in April. The sun was shining bright and seemed to highlight the golden streaks in her hair. He liked that. In fact, he had accepted from that very first night that he liked everything about Delphine Ryland.

"Yes, we either talk or text. Lately, we text. I lived at home longer than my brothers. After they left, I saw no reason to leave, even during college, since I went to a local university. My parents traveled a lot, so I had the entire place to myself a lot of the time." No need to tell her that taking a woman to a hotel for the night had been fine with him since he'd preferred one-night stands anyway.

He took another sip of his coffee and then said, "And when Mom and Dad were home, they still gave me space, even though I enjoy their company."

Being around his parents, he'd observed just how in love they were because they were both openly affectionate. Gannon knew he wanted that same kind of forever love in his life one day. However, he also knew it would be a while before he would be ready to make such a commitment. His father had enjoyed his bachelor days before marrying Eden, and Gannon wanted to follow in his father's footsteps and do the same.

"I agree with Nikki. I think it's wonderful. My mom and I also had a close relationship since it was just the two of us."

He recalled her telling him that her parents had divorced when she'd been six and that her father hadn't maintained a relationship with her. He wondered how many parents could disconnect from their child that way. How had she handled such a rejection? And that was how he saw it. Not only had the man rejected her, but he'd also obviously rejected the responsibilities of being a father.

"I'm sure you miss her a lot," he said.

"Yes, especially with Mother's Day coming up. It will be my first without her. And the first anniversary of her death will fall on Mother's Day this year, so that day will be especially difficult."

Gannon understood how it would be. He could

hear the sadness in her voice. Although he hadn't told her yet, it was his plan for her to be with him on that day. He didn't want her to be alone. He couldn't ever remember a day when he and his brothers had not spent Mother's Day with their own mom, but he'd already told his mother of his plans and why. She had understood and felt he'd made the right decision.

A short while later, he was glad to pull the cab into the parking lot of the shipper. For the next thirty minutes, he noticed she was attentive to how the trailer was connected to the cab. He also noticed how other truckers were trying not to be obvious in watching Delphine with deep male interest, which he understood. But still, he didn't like it. That was another first for him, since he'd never been jealous when it came to a woman. But he grudgingly accepted that he was now.

"Time to hit the road again," he said, once the hitching had been done and they'd returned to the truck.

"I'm excited about the route we are taking." She looked at the map he'd handed her.

He glanced at her before putting his sunglasses back on. "Interstate Ten is a good one to take while traveling from Phoenix to Jacksonville, Florida, where the interstate ends."

She didn't ask what would happen after that and he decided not to say. He wanted her to get to know him better and feel comfortable with being with him before broaching the subject of her spending even more time with him in Miami.

"Tell me about some of your other assignments, Delphine."

She began talking and he loved hearing her voice. It was smooth, soft and seductive. He could tell she was excited about what she did and the people she got to meet. A couple of her stories had him chuckling and laughing out loud. He, in turn, told her some of his road stories and loved hearing her laugh as much as he liked hearing her talk.

Usually he preferred being alone on his road trips, but her presence was rewarding. He enjoyed having her with him. During their conversation, he got a call and declined it when he saw who it was: Trish. It was time to tell her to lose his number. Galen had mentioned that he'd run into Trish at the grocery store and she'd all but insinuated that she and Gannon were in a serious relationship. Now, that was BS.

He glanced over at Delphine and saw she'd fallen asleep. She looked as beautiful asleep as she did awake, and he wondered what time she'd gotten up this morning. His gaze landed on her mouth. He'd finally tasted it and he had not been disappointed. He could clearly recall the moment their lips had touched, when hers had parted for his tongue to slide inside. And the moment her tongue had touched his, a jolt of sexual energy had rocketed through every part of his body. Later that night, in his bed, he had decided that no woman's mouth should taste that delicious.

Knowing that thinking about her lips could get him into trouble if he wasn't careful, he checked his watch and saw he'd driven for nearly four hours now. In two hours, he would stop at a café in El Paso for lunch. Once on the road again he would drive another two hours before taking a second thirty-minute break. Then he would drive into Fort Stockton to hunker down for the night. There was a nice truck stop there with all the comforts.

She moaned and he glanced over at her again when there was a backup on the interstate, and every vehicle was at a standstill. He hoped the traffic jam wouldn't mess with their schedule too much. Even if it did, he, like other drivers, was smart enough to build in reserve time to use if needed.

"Gannon..."

She had mumbled his name in her sleep. Was she thinking about him? Dreaming of him? If so, what thoughts were going through her mind? Were they similar to those he'd had of her last night? The ones that had been so intense they had awakened him with one hell of a hard-on?

She mumbled his name again and the throbbing of his erection got even worse. And then she moaned again. Then his name again. Hell, the sounds were getting to him.

The sound of a police cruiser trying to get through the throng of vehicles was blasting loud. Like all the other vehicles, he moved to the right to let the emergency vehicles through.

"What happened?"

He glanced over at Delphine and watched as she wiped sleep from her eyes. His body ached even more with arousal. "I think there's an accident up ahead."

"Oh."

The truck came to a stop again and he watched her stretch, saw how her breasts pressed against her blouse. He would give just about anything to see those breasts. To touch them. Taste them...

"Sorry I passed out on you."

"Don't apologize. You evidently were tired."

"I was. I didn't get in bed till late and then got up early." She glanced out the truck's huge window. "Where are we, anyway?"

"Near El Paso. I figured we could stop there for lunch. I know a café that's known for its Mexican food."

"Great! I love tacos."

He chuckled. "So do I. If you get hungry don't forget I have snacks in the bunk area."

"Thanks for reminding me."

Traffic began moving again, slow at first and then a little faster. When they got farther down the interstate, they saw there had been an accident. A fender bender. Thankfully, no one seemed hurt.

"I downloaded a few movies on my phone last night. I think I'll watch one now."

"Sounds like a good idea. What's the movie?"

When she told him, he chuckled. "That's a romance. I think my mom has seen it a couple of times."

"I don't doubt that since I've seen it a couple of times myself."

He chuckled. "My mom would love you."

Too late, he realized what he'd said. But then, he knew what he'd said was true. Eden *would* love her. Gannon glanced over at her. She seemed not to have been fazed by his words. It was obvious that she'd gotten wrapped up in the movie on the phone screen. Maybe it was wishful thinking on his part, but he was looking forward to getting all wrapped up with her.

"You're right, Gannon. These tacos are the best," Delphine said, taking another bite. Her movie had ended just seconds before they'd arrived at the café. She thought that was perfect timing.

He flashed a smile that sent all kinds of sensations through her. "Glad you like them. This establishment has been here for years. When I used to take road trips with Dad as a kid, we would always make a stop here. The original owners have passed away and their sons are now running things. I'm glad they got the family recipe for the sauce. That's what makes the tacos unique."

Delphine would have to agree with that. She had eaten a lot of tacos in her day, but had to say the ones she'd just had were the tastiest. More than once during their meal, Gannon's phone had rung. He would check the caller ID and then decline the call. She tried not to let the thought that he was in such high demand by the female population bother her. They were not in an exclusive relationship. In fact, they weren't even in a relationship. He had invited her to come along and she had said yes. As far as she was concerned, there were no expectations beyond that for either of them.

Gannon had told her they would drive for another two hours after lunch, then take another break, and would eventually reach Fort Stockton after that. So far, the trip had been rewarding for her. She wasn't sure how he felt about it since she'd gone to sleep on him and then watched a movie. He might see that as her not being much company.

"Gannon?"

He glanced over at her as he wiped his mouth after finishing off the last of his meal. "Yes?"

"Do you regret asking me to join you? I haven't been much company."

"I disagree. You've been a lot of company." He reached across the table and took her hand. "Your presence alone means a lot to me. I enjoy having you here, even if you never say a single word. Just knowing you are with me means everything."

She held his gaze, wanting so much to know why he felt that way. Despite how much she wanted to know, she didn't want to ask. She couldn't risk his answer being one that would make her fall for him even more. And, yes, she was falling for him, even when deep down she knew she should not. But she wasn't sure she could stop herself.

Just like he claimed he enjoyed being here with her, she definitely enjoyed being here with him. When she'd first arrived in Phoenix, she figured it would take two days to complete the interview and another two days in her hotel room to write it up. She hadn't counted on this road trip with him, or him getting to her like he had. He'd turned around all her plans.

A short while later they were headed back to their truck for the next few hours of road travel. He had parked his rig in the far back of the restaurant, and when they reached it, he touched her arm before she went to her door. "What is it, Gannon?"

Instead of answering her, she saw his gaze shift from her eyes to her lips. She immediately felt heat infuse her mouth. She swallowed, knowing he'd looked the same way when he had kissed her the other night.

"Is anything wrong?" The heat from her mouth was slowly spreading through other parts of her body.

"Nothing is wrong, Delphine. I just need this," he said, lowering his mouth to hers.

A part of Delphine was screaming that she should take a step back. But she couldn't. She didn't want to.

What she did was meet him head-on when he slanted his mouth over hers. She couldn't do anything but surrender, allowing him to devour her with the passion he'd introduced her to a couple of nights ago. There was no way she could resist the fact that this was what she wanted and needed.

She had gone nearly five years without being in any man's arms, without being tasted by one. Lord knew when she arrived in Phoenix, she hadn't expected this. But her plans didn't matter. She would take this, and when she returned to Denver, she would have memories to take with her.

When the kiss ended, he pulled her into his arms and held her for a moment. She scanned the parking lot, grateful that he had parked the truck in a way that gave them privacy. Had he done so intentionally, knowing he would be kissing her? A thrill of excitement rushed through her at the thought. Were there any more plans in store for her?

"Thanks. I needed that, Delphine. Now I'm good to go for the next few hours."

Was he giving her a heads-up that he would be kissing her on a regular basis on this road trip? If he was, he would get a "yes, please" from her. "Glad I could be of service," she said, smiling.

He chuckled before leaning in and placing a quick kiss to her lips. "Damn, I've never seen a more gorgeous pair of lips before. I like them. I like them a lot."

Did he honestly believe that, or were those just words? She began to think that maybe there was truth to his words when he licked her lips in earnest, like they were a piece of candy he enjoyed. Goose bumps formed on her arms and heat filled her stomach. When she suddenly felt weak in the knees, she grabbed hold of his shoulders to stay balanced.

"I guess I better stop, or we'll be late arriving in Fort Stockton," he murmured against her lips, before lifting his head to stare at her. Then, smiling as if seeing how wet he'd made her lips had pleased him, he said, "I've given you fair warning about my fetish with your lips, Delphine."

Yes, he most certainly had, and in a most delicious way.

Eight

"Tell me about him, Delphine. The man who broke your heart."

They were less than twenty miles to the truck stop in Fort Stockton and already the sun had gone down. Conversation between them had been steady, interesting and, to his way of thinking, pretty darn enlightening. They had shared information about each other, their likes, dislikes and parts of their pasts.

He'd told her about living in the spotlight as one of Eden Tyson Steele's sons, the strength of his parents' marriage and his close relationship with his brothers. And he'd talked about his grandparents and how he'd never met his maternal grandmother because she'd died before he was born, but how he had spent time with his maternal grandfather.

Delphine had told him that she'd been a cheerleader in high school and how she'd taken piano lessons for a while. She'd shared her love for Denver and how she'd missed it while away at college. She'd told him about her college days in Wyoming and all the groups and activities she'd been a part of. It was obvious she'd been an outgoing person who loved having fun. He didn't quite see her as that sociable person now.

Granted, she was friendly enough, and he knew the employees who'd met her this week had liked her on the spot. However, she was nothing like the gregarious person she'd described. He'd been around enough women to tell when one was not only protecting herself from heartbreak, but also doing so by withdrawing from the happy-go-lucky life she'd once lived.

"What makes you think some man has broken my heart? I don't recall giving you that impression."

He could tell by her tone of voice that she hadn't liked his question and, as a result, she was copping an attitude. That didn't bother him because she had that right. However, he refused to back down in asking what he had. This was a woman who affected him in so many ways he couldn't even count them, and the more time he spent with her, the greater the impact. So the bottom line was that he wanted to find out every single thing about her.

They had come to a stop at one of the weigh stations and he had turned around in his seat to look at her, to stare into her eyes. Feast his attention on her lips. "No, you didn't give me that impression. In fact, you haven't given me any impressions, one way or the other. You're deliberately staying clear of mentioning any involvement with a man. Do you want me to believe there has never been a man in your life? A special man?"

"You didn't mention any involvement with a woman, Gannon. Do you want me to think there weren't any for you, either?"

"You interviewed me, Delphine. I won't believe that you didn't research my life before you did so. I know what the magazines and papers have printed, and most of it I won't deny. I'm a single, heterosexual male who likes spending time with women. There have been plenty of them in my life. That's not a secret. However, none of my affairs have been serious and the women knew it."

She didn't say anything for a minute and then said, "My past isn't a secret, either. I just choose not to talk about it."

"Okay."

He decided he would back off for now. He didn't want her to feel cornered. They'd enjoyed each other's company for the past eleven hours and he had no intention of changing that. Besides, he was more determined than ever to build a relationship with her, whether it was as a friend, lover or both.

The inspector gave him the okay to move his truck back onto the interstate to continue on his route. It was hard keeping his eyes on the road when he wanted to glance over at her.

"Are you mad at me, Delphine?" he finally asked her when he'd driven a mile and she hadn't said anything.

"Should I be?"

"Nope. I asked because I care," he said.

"And why should you care?"

Gannon waited a moment before answering. Not because he didn't have an answer, but because he needed to make sure he worded it so she fully understood what he was saying. "You know why I asked you to come with me on this road trip."

"To make sure I'm not *the* one," she said with a little mockery.

He ignored her tone. "Or to make sure you are."

"That's not possible."

"I figure the reason you might feel that way is because of something in your past involving a man," he stated.

"Not necessarily. It could be because I live in a more realistic world than you do," she responded.

He chuckled. "Well, at least you didn't call me crazy."

"I would never do that."

"And I appreciate you for not doing so because I am totally sane. I just want to get to know you."

Maybe it was something he said, or maybe it was something he didn't say. Either way, she began talking, telling him what he wanted to know.

"His name is Liddell Bartley. His family moved to Denver in my junior year of high school and we began dating in our senior year."

Delphine said nothing for a while, and he was certain she'd told him all she intended to tell him, when she surprised him as she added, "After high school we decided to attend separate colleges, not because we wanted to, but because our parents convinced us that was the right thing to do. They felt we were too into each other's pockets in high school and the four-year separation would do us some good."

She paused again. "They felt if we truly loved each other, everything would work out fine and the separation wouldn't matter. As far as I knew, it didn't. We would see each other whenever we came home for the holidays and we spent all our spring breaks together on the beach in Galveston, where his parents owned a time-share condo. We were to marry a week after graduation. Everything was set. Invitations were sent."

He heard the way her voice trembled, either from anger, pain or both. "What happened?"

"I got a letter from him a month before our wedding day letting me know he was marrying someone else because she was pregnant with his child."

Gannon said nothing. The thought that this Liddell guy had been committed to her and yet got another woman pregnant fueled his anger. "Was she really pregnant?" He knew the game some women played to get a man to the altar.

"No, but he didn't find out until after the wedding that she wasn't. She claims she honestly thought she was, and her parents demanded that he marry her."

"Are they still married?"

"Yes, and are living in Denver."

He figured that had to be pretty damn uncomfortable for Delphine. "You're better off without him."

"I know that. But still, not in a million years would I have thought he would have betrayed me that way. That just goes to show that you never know who you can truly trust."

He had pulled the truck into the huge lot of Truckers Bay, the largest chain of truck stops in the United States. When he brought the truck into Park, he glanced over at her. "I guess you could look at it that way or you could look at it another way entirely, Delphine."

"And what way is that?"

"That it was never meant for the two of you to be together in the first place. He was never your destiny."

He was never your destiny...

Although Delphine hadn't responded, his words hadn't been lost on her. He was into this destiny kick, so she'd decided to pretend to ignore what he'd said. In truth, he hadn't said anything her mother hadn't said, as well as those friends who knew her well.

One of the reasons she hadn't returned to Denver after college was because she hadn't wanted to see pity in anyone's eyes. That was why she'd taken the job in New York. Then when she heard Liddell and his new wife would make Denver their home, she'd known her visits back to see her mother would be less frequent. At least, that had been the plan until her mother had gotten ill.

For the most part, since Denver was a big city, her path hadn't crossed much with Liddell's, and she was grateful for that. But once she wasn't confined to the house as much, she saw him more frequently. The first couple of times had been awkward, but the more she saw Liddell, the more she accepted that she had been his loss and not the other way around. In a way, she knew what Gannon had said was true. Liddell hadn't been her destiny, obviously. She was convinced no man was.

"Do you want to go jogging with me in the morning?"

Gannon had parked the truck and they'd climbed out of it. "Jogging?"

"Yes. This place has a gym with an indoor track."

Although she had yet to take a tour of the facility, she would admit she'd never seen a truck stop as spacious or with as many amenities as Gannon said it contained. In addition to a restaurant, there was a Laundromat, gym, arcade and a number of other conveniences. Across the lot there was even a hotel, where Gannon said they would be spending the night. Although he hadn't specifically said so, she expected they would each have a room.

Knowing they would end up in Florida, she had brought along a pair of shorts and a T-shirt that she could jog in tomorrow. "Yes, I'll go jogging with you in the morning."

"Good. Is five o'clock okay?"

"Five in the morning? You're kidding, right?"

He flashed her a smile. "No kidding. The best time to use the facility is when others are still sleeping. That means we'll be finished before they arrive."

"That's fine."

"You're tired?" he asked, reaching out to tuck a strand of hair away from her face.

She wasn't sure why he was asking, but, yes, she was tired. Yet not in the way he assumed. Her body was exhausted from combating the urges she felt from being around him. And him standing so close to her, messing with her hair, letting her inhale his scent, wasn't helping matters.

"Yes, I am kind of tired," she said, faking a yawn. "When I check into my hotel room, I don't plan to come out."

"What about dinner?" he asked her.

"I'll pass. I normally don't eat after seven anyway. Besides, those tacos we had earlier filled me up pretty good." There was no reason to ask if he would be eating again because she knew he would. Gannon loved to eat.

"If you change your mind and get hungry later, I'll be glad to bring you something."

"I won't change my mind, but thanks." Backing up a step, she said, "I'll see you in the morning. We can meet in the hotel's lobby and stroll over to the truck stop's gym." She knew she needed to get away from him as soon as she could, before she was tempted to do something stupid like inviting him to her hotel room.

"Okay. Sleep well. Tomorrow is a long day. My goal is to make it to San Antonio by dinnertime. That's where we'll spend the night."

Spend the night...

His words caused a sizzle of heat to spread through her. It was definitely time to part ways with him. "I'll see you in the morning, Gannon."

She quickly turned and headed toward the breezeway where her room was located, not caring that she was walking as if fire was at her heels.

Despite the fact that it wasn't quite daybreak and was still dark outside, Gannon saw Delphine the moment she stepped out of her hotel room. He wasn't a fan of breezeway-type hotel rooms that faced the outdoors, but he knew this style was a favorite with other truckers. They didn't want to be confined in a building without having quick access to their trucks if needed.

For that reason, he'd known that if Delphine was to meet him at five this morning as planned, she would be crossing the parking lot to the hotel's lobby in the dark, by herself, and he didn't plan for that to happen. There had been no reason to tell her he would be coming to her hotel room to escort her over to the truck stop because she would have argued about it. He hadn't wanted to argue. At least, not last night.

As far as he was concerned, yesterday had been perfect. It had started on a high note and he'd wanted it to end the same way. The only time he figured he'd somewhat gotten on her nerves was when he'd questioned her about that asshole who had hurt her. She'd finally told him what he wanted to know, but that still raised even more questions. Namely, was she still carrying a torch for the dude? Was this Liddell the reason she hadn't invited another man into her life, even though she'd said he wasn't? Even though she'd admitted she was better off without him in her life? Knowing it and accepting it were two different things.

He could recall the woman who'd broken Mercury's heart back in college. It had taken his brother a long time to get over the hurt, the anguish and the betrayal. Then he'd met Sloan and allowed himself to fall in love again.

Gannon's attention perked up when Delphine began walking away from her door. He knew this particular hotel was usually safe. There were video cameras and policemen periodically cruising the parking lot, but still, he had decided to hang back in the shadows to make sure she was okay. He discovered doing so was worth his time and effort as she strode into a lit area and he could clearly see the sway of her hips with every step she took. In her shorts and top, he could see that she definitely had nice hips and thighs. Now he was glad he was following her, even if she didn't know he was there.

After she'd left him to turn in for the night instead of going to his room, he'd had dinner with a couple of his drivers who were on this same route. That was one of the things he appreciated about these road trips—maintaining the various relationships he had with his employees. One team consisted of a husband and wife who'd been working with him for around five years now. They worked well together and always made their deliveries on time.

Even after a lively dinner and spending eleven hours behind the steering wheel of his rig, he'd had difficulty getting to sleep. Horniness had overwhelmed any exhaustion he should have felt. Every time he closed his eyes, he remembered their kiss. The second one they'd shared. It had been even better than the first, and he'd thought nothing could top that one.

Deciding that if he continued walking behind her, the enticing motion of her ass would be his downfall for the rest of the day, he called out, "Delphine. Wait up."

She turned and her expression indicated she was surprised to see him. "Gannon? Where did you come from?"

"My room." That wasn't a lie. No need to tell her that his room was only a few doors down from hers and that he'd been standing beneath the stairs waiting for her to come out.

"Oh. Did you sleep well last night?"

"I did." At least, he had once he'd finally drifted off with thoughts of her on his mind. "What about you?"

"After my shower I thought I'd get a little work done on the article. At some point I called it a night and climbed into bed. Not sure when or how. I woke up this morning still lying on top of the covers."

Gannon wondered if she realized she'd painted a pretty good picture in his mind of that entire scenario. He would have loved to have climbed in that bed right along with her, and if he had, there was no way she would not have remembered when and how. And she would not have awakened this morning still lying on top of the covers. If anything, she would have still been lying on top of him.

"Ready to jog this morning?" she asked as they began walking together side by side.

"Yes. Are you?"

She shrugged her shoulders. "I guess. I'm not really a jogger or even a walker, for that matter."

"Then how do you stay in shape?" he asked as they passed the hotel's lobby.

She chuckled. "Who says I'm in shape?"

"I do." And he would say it again if he had to. If she wasn't into physical fitness, he couldn't tell it. She looked sexy as sin in jeans, slacks, a pair of shorts or a dress. He'd seen her in all of them. Now he wanted to see her in none of them. More specifically, he would love to see her naked.

"Thanks for being sweet by saying that, but I could use a membership at the gym. But..."

When she stopped talking, he glanced over at her. "But what?"

She hesitated, as if trying to decide whether to

give him an answer. Looking up, she met his gaze. "There's a gym not far from my house, but Liddell's wife is a member, so I choose not to go there. The next closest is on the other side of town."

"Oh, I see." And he honestly didn't like what he saw. Her decision not to go to a gym convenient to where she lived was because of her ex-fiancé's wife. He wondered what else she avoided for that reason.

They reached the truck stop and there were a couple of guys hanging around inside. Truckers who'd just parked and were on their way to the shower room. Gannon led her in the opposite direction, to where the gym was located.

"Wow. This is nice," she said, when they entered the huge room that contained several pieces of exercise equipment.

"It is. That's one of the reasons I make sure this place is on my drivers' routes. Sitting behind the wheel of a truck for twelve hours and then not moving muscles isn't good for your body. Leg cramps aren't a joke."

When they reached the jogging track, she glanced up at him. "We don't have to jog together. I plan to go at my own pace. And it will be a slow one."

He chuckled. "Okay. Will an hour work for you?"

"Heck, no," she said, grinning. "I was thinking more like thirty minutes. I would do half of that if I thought you would let me get away with it."

"I won't. Like I said, leg cramps aren't a joke. If

you finish up before I do, there are other pieces of equipment you might want to try out."

He smiled when she gave him a look that all but said not to press his luck. "We'll see, Gannon. We'll see."

Nine

"Ready to roll again?"

Delphine glanced over at Gannon as she snapped her seat belt in place. "Yes, I'm ready." And she would admit she was looking forward to today's adventure. She'd visited San Antonio a couple of times with her mother and had always loved the River Walk.

Earlier that morning, after she had taken her thirty-minute jog, she had strolled another thirty minutes to keep Gannon company. Not that she felt she needed to, since he would happily jog by her. He had walked her back to the hotel room to shower, and they'd met back up again twenty minutes later to head over to the café for breakfast.

Now they were in the truck and ready to ride.

She watched Gannon as he backed the truck out of the parking spot with ease, admiring his ability to handle the huge rig. "Who taught you how to drive one of these?"

He glanced over at her and smiled. "My dad. I also went to truckers' school to get my necessary licenses."

"You like this, don't you?"

He glanced over at her. "Like what?"

"Getting out of the office and out on the road."

He gave a slight shrug. "I like running things at the office, as well. I guess you can say I have the best of both worlds."

Yes, she could imagine him thinking that. The look that had shone in his eyes during her interview with him whenever he talked about his work had touched her. He had the ability not only to put people to work, but also to change lives. He did both.

She decided to stay awake today after he'd told her of the different sites they would pass along the way. Besides, she wanted to be better company for him. They talked about a lot of stuff, some she'd learned during the interview, like how involved he was in several charity organizations in Phoenix.

"All my brothers are," he told her. "You can't be one of Eden Tyson Steele's sons and not be," he added.

For a short while they listened to his classical music, and he suggested she check out the bunk area. She did and saw how roomy it was for her to sit on the bunk and use her laptop on the small desk. She edited most of her work before she pushed back the curtain to go back up front.

Later, after they had stopped for lunch, they re-entered the truck to head out on the three-hour drive to San Antonio. He glanced over at her. "We're going to eventually have to find a place to hole up for an hour or so."

"Why?"

"Word just came from dispatch. There's a bad thunderstorm up ahead. It came out of nowhere on a practically sunny day. Regardless of how good your tires are, you have to be concerned with traction. We'll ride through it for a while and then we'll head toward a truck stop nearby. It's not as big as the other truck stops, but it will work to wait out the storm."

They hadn't gotten too far before the rain began. She leaned forward to stare out the windshield and could barely see outside. She did see other trucks pulling off the interstate and wasn't surprised when Gannon did, too.

The words of the dispatcher were slightly choppy, but Delphine understood them just the same. A tornado was in the area. "We're making it to the truck stop instead of remaining out here in the open," Gannon told her.

She nodded, knowing Gannon was better equipped to deal with the situation than she was. He drove the truck at a slow rate of speed with his caution lights on, then exited the interstate a short while later.

The rain had let up some, but the wind was howling something fierce. When they reached the truck stop, he parked on the lot and unbuckled his seat belt. "For safety reasons we need to get away from these windows. Let's get behind the curtain in the bunk area."

He evidently saw the frightened look on her face. She had never been a fan of thunderstorms and had a feeling her fear was showing.

He reached out and undid her seat belt before taking hold of her hand. "Come on."

She followed him to the bunk area, and then he put the curtain back in place so she wouldn't see what was taking place outside. Rain—so much rain— pounded hard on the truck. The thunder was so loud it seemed as if the ground shook from the sound. He sat her on the bunk and placed a quick kiss on her forehead. "You're safe with me, Delphine. Usually these sudden storms pass as quickly as they come up," he said, sitting down beside her.

Delphine wanted to believe that, but when the sound of thunder hit again, even louder, and seemingly lit up the entire truck, she pressed her face into his chest. He wrapped his arms around her and gently rubbed her back. At that moment, a comforting warmth spread through her body and she did believe what he'd told her. She was safe with him.

He pulled back slightly, his concerned green eyes staring down at her. "You okay?"

She could barely hear his question for the sound of the torrential rain beating all around them. She was grateful for him closing the curtain so she wouldn't see it. Hearing it was bad enough. She nodded. "Yes, I'm fine."

She wanted to add...*since you're here with me, I feel safe and protected.*

He placed another kiss on her cheek and she glanced up at him. Was she imagining things or were the depths of his green eyes getting darker and darker? Was that heat she was feeling flowing from him to her?

Delphine began nibbling on her lower lip and he watched her. Then she remembered what he'd told her about her lips and his fetish for them. Suddenly, she felt hot all over and she couldn't stop her gaze from moving over Gannon's very handsome face.

"Like what you see, Delphine?"

The question was asked in a deep, throaty voice, causing more heat to suffuse her. She decided to be both honest and bold. "Yes. What about you, Gannon? Do you like what you see?"

A sensuous smile lifted both corners of his lips. "Yes. Most definitely. And do you know what I yearn to do? Right now?"

"No. Tell me." Then, deciding to go up another notch in boldness, she said, "Show me."

He leaned in and lowered his mouth to hers. The exact moment he did, she felt not only the warmth of his kiss, but also the intensity of it. When he slid his tongue inside her mouth, she became so caught up in what he was doing and how he was doing it that she forgot the sound of the fierce rain outside, and the loud clapping of thunder.

Instead, she wholly concentrated on how he was taking her mouth with an expertise she felt in every part of her body. And when he deepened the kiss, she moaned into his mouth and wrapped her arms around his neck. He began doing creative things to her mouth, making her moan even more. Even louder. She felt the hard pounding of her heart with every bold sweep of his tongue. He'd told her how much he loved her lips and he was showing her just how much he did.

She wasn't sure how long they kissed, but when they finally tore their mouths apart, their breathing was erratic. Her eyebrows drew together in a question. Why had he stopped? She would not have minded if they'd continued. Gannon had the ability to bring out desires in her that she hadn't known existed.

"I think we better stop, don't you?"

Did she? No, not really. She wanted more. She wanted what she'd denied herself for close to five years. What she'd gone without since Liddell. Gannon had awakened feelings in her that she thought were essentially out of sight and out of mind. He'd proved that theory wrong.

She wanted him.

As if he read what she wasn't saying, he leaned in and said, "You know you're welcome to join me in my bed at any time."

Was that the invitation he issued to all the women who wanted him? The thought didn't freak her out as much as it should have. Heck, it honestly didn't bother her because she was the one woman, by his own admission, who had him thinking there could possibly be more between them. Even if it wasn't true, which she was convinced it wasn't, the notion that she had gotten his attention in a way no other woman had made her feel good inside.

"I'll keep that in mind, Gannon." It was obvious her response surprised him by the way his eyebrows drew together. Good. Let him feel as off-kilter as his kisses were making her feel.

"Sounds like the rain has stopped now," he said.

Had it? She listened and discovered he was right. But little did he know he had essentially awakened a quiet storm within her, and she had a feeling after this road trip with him that her life would never be the same.

It was time for her to begin enjoying life. Her mother had died before her fiftieth birthday and the last three years of her life had been full of agony and pain. But, according to her mother, she had not had any regrets. June Ryland often told her daughter that even with the humiliating ways her father had treated her, she never regretted falling in love and marrying him because they had produced Delphine.

Maybe it was time Delphine had that kind of attitude. No regrets. Live for the moment.

By the time Gannon stood, Delphine's mind was made up. Whether he decided she was his destiny or not, that didn't matter. She honestly knew she wasn't, anyway. What mattered to her was that she thought of him as her knight in shining armor. He had helped her get through the storm and now it was time for him to show her how to dance in the rain.

Ten

Gannon heard the knocking on the door, glanced at his watch and figured it was Housekeeping bringing him another coffeepot since the one in his room wasn't working. He and Delphine had arrived at the truck stop in San Antonio a couple of hours ago. This stop wasn't as big as the one in Fort Stockton, but he liked this hotel a lot better since it wasn't the style with hotel rooms opening out to a breezeway. He'd taken a shower, changed clothes and lain across the bed to watch television until it was time to leave to meet Delphine. He'd told her he would be coming to her room at seven to walk her to dinner.

They would be heading out early in the morning. He figured they were making good time and would be in Jacksonville as planned on Monday, barring any more bad weather. But he would be the first to admit that being held up with Delphine had been rewarding. When they'd gotten on the road again, she'd told him of her fear of storms since she'd been a little girl and how even now, whenever a bad storm hit, she would close all the curtains in her home, darken the house and go to bed and cover her head until it was over. Storms had never bothered him and the thought that they made her afraid had brought out a protective instinct in him.

Using the remote to lower the volume on the television, he eased off the bed, strolled to the door and looked out the peephole. It wasn't Housekeeping. It was Delphine, and she was holding several bags in her hands. He quickly opened the door.

"What's going on here?" he asked her, relieving her of the bags. The aroma flowing from them was a dead giveaway. Food.

"And just what do we have here?" he asked as she entered.

"I noticed how crowded the restaurant was and thought it would be nice if I ordered the food and we ate in. I hope you don't mind."

"No, I don't mind," he said, taking the bags over to the desk. "Something smells good."

"I hope you like everything I ordered, and I think they were generous with the portions."

He chuckled as he began removing containers. "Most truck-stop restaurants are. They know how hungry truckers can get."

He glanced up from the food to see Delphine look-

ing around the room. He figured his was identical to
hers and wondered why the interest. Instead of asking her, he said, "I'm ready to dig in. What about
you?"

She laughed. "If your brothers had your hearty
appetite while growing up, I don't envy your parents one bit."

He chuckled. "All six of us love to eat and we were
lucky that Mom loved to cook. That's why we have
Thursday nights at her house."

"Thursday nights?"

"Yes," he said, pulling a couple of chairs closer
to the desk. "When everyone left home, Mom didn't
want to feel out of touch with her sons, so she implemented Thursday nights at my parents' house. She
cooks dinner and expects everyone to show up so she
can see all her sons together in one place. Namely,
under her roof."

He watched Delphine slide into her chair before
he took his. Like him, she had showered and changed
clothes. He liked the tan-colored top and slacks she
was wearing. But then, he'd liked the jeans she'd
worn earlier, as well.

"Everyone usually shows up?"

"Anyone in their right mind knows not to miss
it. She figures if you miss one that means she needs
to spend extra time with you. Trust me, Eden Tyson
Steele has no qualms about showing up at your place
unannounced at the worst possible time."

Delphine laughed and he liked the sound. "You're
kidding, right?"

"Nope. Several of my brothers have received Mom's unexpected visits when they were entertaining lady friends."

Gannon liked the choices she'd ordered for them. Pork chops smothered in delicious gravy, wild rice, an assortment of mixed vegetables and what looked like the best-tasting corn bread ever.

"I hope you enjoy all the food," she said.

He smiled over at her. "Don't think for one minute that I won't."

As they ate, more than once, he complimented her on the meal.

"It's not like I cooked it, Gannon."

"No, but you were thoughtful enough to think it would be better to eat here instead of the restaurant. I like it."

She tilted her head to look at him. "And why do you like it?"

He decided to be honest with her. "Because I like sharing private space with you."

Gannon truly meant that. She was the best traveling partner a trucker could have. They'd covered a lot of topics during their conversations, but he knew she still kept parts of her life away from him. Even so, he knew the important parts, namely about her ex and the pain the man had caused her.

A short while after they'd finished eating, there was a knock at the door. "That's probably Housekeeping bringing me another coffeepot," he said, heading for the door. "I called for one when I couldn't get this one to work."

He opened the door and a woman from House-keeping walked in. She looked to be in her early twenties and gave him a flirtatious smile, although he was certain she'd seen Delphine sitting at the desk. "Where would you like me to place this?" she asked him.

"You can grab the old one and replace it."

He'd never had a problem with flirtatious women before, but he'd discovered that lately he found them pretty damn annoying. Like Trish, this woman was attractive, and as she crossed the room to the coffeepot, she was deliberately swaying her hips with every step. He'd also noticed the top two buttons of her blouse were undone.

He wasn't biting.

Not one stir of desire flowed through his groin. The only woman he wanted with a passion was the one sitting at the desk pretending not to notice the other woman's bold antics. However, Delphine had to be very much aware of the not-so-subtle message the housekeeper was giving him.

"Will there be anything else?" the woman asked in a sultry voice while raking him up and down with her eyes.

If there was anything else, did she think he would disrespect Delphine by inviting her to come back to his room later? "No, there's nothing else, and there's no need for you to return."

After the housekeeper left, Delphine stood and began placing all the empty containers back in the bags. "It's time for me to go," she said, not looking at him.

He leaned back against the closed hotel-room door and crossed his arms over his chest. "Why do you do that?"

"Do what?" she asked, looking at him now.

"Feel the need to retreat whenever it comes to other women?"

She lifted her chin. "I don't know what you mean."

"Don't you? I noticed it that day with Trish. After meeting her, you thought that maybe we shouldn't eat lunch together. You've also admitted how you avoided going to that gym close to where you live because the wife of your ex-fiancé goes there, like you should care. Then just now, that woman came on to me, which I handled, yet now you want to leave. Retreat."

She shrugged. "I don't want to cause problems."

He didn't say anything for a minute. Dropping his arms to his sides, he crossed the room. "When it comes to me, you could never cause problems, Delphine. You're here because I want you here. Always remember that. And I also hope you're here because you want to be here."

He reached out, took the bags from her hands and placed them back on the desk. Taking a step closer to her, he wrapped his arms around her waist and felt her quiver from his touch. "Do you want to be here with me, Delphine?"

She didn't answer at first, and then she reached up to place her hands on his chest, gently rubbing against the cotton of his T-shirt with the tips of her fingers. She met his gaze. "Yes, I want to be here with you."

He figured it had taken a lot for her to admit that. "Convince me. Convince me you want to be here with me."

Delphine licked her lips and he felt a stirring in his groin. "And how am I supposed to do that?"

He continued to stare into her eyes, hoping they were encouraging her to be as bold as she could be. "Any damn way you want will be fine with me."

She hesitated and then she leaned into him. Her arms shifted away from his chest to loop around his neck. Then she stood on tiptoe. Deciding to meet her the rest of the way, Gannon lowered his head to join his lips with hers. He wanted her to take control and moaned when she slid her tongue into his mouth. Then she began maneuvering it, like he'd done when they'd kissed earlier, and the other times. He could only take so much before his control broke and he began devouring her mouth greedily, enjoying the sweetness of her taste and the feel of her warm body plastered to his.

Lifting his mouth from hers, he tightened his arms around her waist while gazing into her eyes. "Convince me some more, Delphine," he said, leaning in, zeroing in on her lips to lick around the corners. "Convince me some more."

Delphine had never convinced a man of anything and wasn't even sure she knew how. But she was determined to try.

She had to. Because at that moment her body was filled with desire for Gannon. He hadn't made any promises to her and she hadn't made any to him. She'd learned the hard way that when it came to love, promises could easily be broken. She much preferred things this way. Simple. Easy. No commitments. Gannon wasn't beholden to her and she wasn't beholden to him. They could walk away at any time, and no matter what he thought about her having a possible place in his future, they would separate at the end of their trip. She would be flying out of Jacksonville and heading back to Denver in a few days.

That was why she needed this. A chance to show him just how much she enjoyed being here with him. How much she wanted to be here. She hoped she could pull it off because the desire shining in the depths of his green eyes could not be ignored. He wanted her as much as she wanted him. And she did want him. More than she'd ever wanted another man.

She stepped out of his hold and tugged her blouse over her head, knowing he was watching her every move. Then she placed her hands on her waist to slide down her slacks.

"Let me help with those."

His husky voice had her watching as he moved toward her. He got on bended knees to tug the fabric all the way down her legs. She stepped out of her shoes and then her slacks, leaving her wearing only her bra and panties.

He leaned back on his haunches and glanced up at her. "We're almost there," he said.

She swallowed and then took a deep breath as she removed her bra and tossed it on the chair. Her hands went to her panties and Gannon said, "Let me. I want to help with those, too."

She nodded. It was obvious he liked undressing her below the waist. When he leaned in to tug her panties down her legs, the desire she saw in the depths of his eyes seemed to increase tenfold. Standing there completely naked, she stared down at him. He again leaned back on his haunches while his gaze raked heatedly over her body.

Then he met her eyes. "You're beautiful, Delphine."

Although she wished they hadn't, his words stirred something within her that made every bone in her body turn to mush. She could barely stand under the heat of his gaze.

"What about your clothes?" she finally asked him.

"What about them?" he asked, standing back up.

"Aren't you going to take them off?"

He shook his head. "No, but you can if you want."

Yes, she wanted, so she moved toward him. His T-shirt came off easily, but she figured his jeans would be a little more challenging, especially when it was quite obvious that he was aroused.

"Need my help, Delphine?"

She glanced from his midsection up to his face. "Yes, if you don't mind."

"I don't mind at all."

She watched as he unzipped his pants and then tugged both his jeans and briefs down his legs. When he stood before her, it was just like she'd figured. Gannon Steele was beautifully made. Tight abs, wide shoulders, broad chest, taut thighs. Her gaze moved from the soles of his bare feet all the way up to the top of his head. Of course, she'd allowed her gaze to linger on certain places. Just looking at that part of him had her heart beating fast and furious against her rib cage. This was the second man she'd ever seen naked and he looked more impressive, definitely more powerful, than the first one had. She hated to compare the two, but Gannon gave her no choice.

"Let me know when you've gotten your fill."

She looked up into his eyes and saw the twinkle in the green depths. He was teasing her, but all she wanted to do was get it on with him. The sooner, the better. She hadn't wanted a man this bad, ever. "I don't think that's possible. For me to get my fill."

Gannon chuckled. "Glad to hear you say that because I doubt that I can get my fill of you, either, Delphine."

Now he was scrutinizing her body again, which made her nervously nibble her lips. He was in perfect shape, but her, not so much. However, he didn't seem to mind that her breasts weren't as big as some women's and that she had more curves than she thought she needed.

"You look perfect."

She would accept his comment and appreciate that he'd made it. "Thank you."

And then he swept her into his arms and carried her to the bed.

* * *

She was light as a feather, Gannon thought, as he moved across the room, carrying a nude Delphine. Her naked flesh rubbed against his, sending even more desire racing through him. After placing her on the bed, he stood back, needing to look at her nakedness some more.

He felt eager at the thought of making love to her. Easing inside of her, rocking her with hard, deep strokes and hearing her moan his name. Pleasure pulsed through his veins at the thought of all he wanted to do to her. All that he intended to do.

After sheathing himself with a condom, he crawled on the bed with her, straddled her body and slid between her legs. But first he needed to taste her. He began kissing her breasts, thinking they were a perfect size and shape. He loved the way the nipple fit in his mouth, and wrapped his tongue around it. Then his mouth moved lower as he licked her stomach, while his fingers massaged her breasts. He liked licking her navel almost as much as he liked her nipples.

Intent on going lower still, he began licking his way downward. He could feel her squirm beneath his mouth. He placed a kiss on her womanly folds before lifting his head to meet her gaze. "Easy, baby. I love all kinds of lips. Even these."

"I can't take much more," she whispered as she dug her fingers into his shoulders.

Gannon smiled before burying his head between her legs and sliding his tongue inside of her. His tongue swirled. Then he nipped at her clit and tasted her with ferocious intent.

"Gannon… Gannon…" She whispered his name over and over while rubbing the back of his head. He knew when her body became even more aroused. It made heat flare through his groin. Desire for her heightened even more and his lips and tongue were wet from her juices. Then she screamed and he quickly rushed up to her mouth to drown out the sound.

There was a raw sensuality about her that brought out everything male within him. He knew the moment the spasms had subsided, and it was then that savage lust took over his mind and body.

Moving back between her legs, he eased inside of her, loving the tightness, the perfect fit, the connection. His desire to mate with her this way, filling her with all of him, could no longer be denied. He glanced down at her, appreciating her beauty. His brothers' warnings had been right. The flame of desire that had kindled between them from the first had been lit for a reason. A powerful male force passed through him and he began moving with a need that had been building inside of him since the first day he'd laid eyes on her.

As he thrust hard into her, with every stroke he claimed her. Hearing her chant his name over and over was driving him past the edge. Each time he would quickly snatch himself back, needing more and more from her.

Their mating was in perfect unison. He wanted to give her all he had because he knew she was the only woman with the ability to do this to him. The only one. Every thrust was shared pleasure that he wanted to last forever. Suddenly, he felt an explosion, and when she screamed his name again, he couldn't silence her because he was hollering out his pleasure, as well.

He leaned down and captured her mouth, needing her kiss, her taste. Their mouths mated in a way he was convinced was meant to be.

He pulled away and, with their lips just inches apart, she asked, "Did I convince you?"

A smile touched his mouth from corner to corner when he said, "Yes, baby, you convinced me."

Delphine cuddled in Gannon's arms, completely sated and depleted of energy. She'd never felt a sense of satisfaction like this before. All she had to do was close her eyes to remember orgasm after orgasm while he'd thrust into her, rocked his hips hard against hers and been gripped in the throes of passion. Her body had shuddered, and the more it had, the harder he'd thrust. The hotel room was quiet. She heard only the sounds of their breathing mingling with the low hum of whatever he'd been watching on television.

"Are you okay?"

If only he knew just how okay she was. He had kissed her all over, tasted her, made love to her in the most erotic ways, and then they had lain there, absorbing the sensuous aftermath before doing it all over again. She had screamed his name and he had hollered hers. Yes, she was okay, because to-night she'd experienced all that was Gannon Andrew Steele.

She shifted in his arms to stare up at him. "Yes, I'm fine. What about you?"

"I feel great. Now we need to get some sleep. Tomorrow is a long driving day. We need to make it to Baton Rouge by evening. Make up for the couple of hours we lost during the storm. Now go to sleep."

Sleep? He hadn't asked that she get dressed and go to her own room. "You want me to stay?"

He'd closed his eyes, but he reopened them to stare at her. "Of course I want you to stay. I love having you here with me." He then leaned in to kiss her forehead. "In fact, I'd like to ask you something."

"What?"

"I had mentioned to you that after I reach Jacksonville and unload the cargo, I plan to show you the Atlantic Ocean before I head to my beach house in Miami for a week. I'd like to invite you to go with me."

Delphine felt a deep pounding in her chest. She recalled him mentioning his plans. "You're inviting me to go with you to Miami?"

"Yes. You said you didn't have to rush back to Denver, right?"

"Yes, that's right."

"And I want to show you the Atlantic from Miami instead of Jacksonville."

"Miami?"

"Yes. I'd like to take you with me to Miami. That

way I can do more than show you the Atlantic Ocean. I want to spend time with you in the water. I want to share that with you, Delphine."

That he wanted to do that for her filled her with a degree of happiness she hadn't felt in a long time. "Are you sure you aren't tired of my company?" she asked him, nearly overwhelmed with joy.

"Trust me, I'm positive. Like I said, I love having you with me. So will you go to Miami and stay on the beach with me?"

Delphine smiled. She knew she shouldn't let what he'd said get to her this way, but it had. Gannon wanted to spend even more time with her, and what was so amazing was that she wanted to spend more time with him, as well.

"Yes, I'll go to Miami with you."

Eleven

Two days later, Gannon pulled his truck into the lot of the Duval Clothing Warehouse in Jacksonville. The dispatcher had notified him that a crew would be there to unload the truck. Glancing over at Delphine, he saw she was still asleep, and had been since they'd left Pensacola a few hours ago. He knew she needed her rest since he'd been keeping her up at night and he couldn't help smiling when he remembered how. Those nights had had an impact on him, and he hoped they'd had an impact on her, as well.

Leaning over, he gently shook her awake, then watched her eyes slowly open and meet his. The smile that touched her lips appeared as one of contentment, but the smile he returned was one of total admiration. He'd decided that Delphine Ryland was every man's fantasy come true. She was certainly his.

"We're here?" she asked in a groggy voice, but it sounded pretty damn sensuous to his ears.

"Yes, we're here." Not able to help himself, he leaned in and placed a kiss on those lips he loved. Over the past two days he'd given her numerous demonstrations of just how much he loved them. He got hard just thinking about it.

Straightening back up in his seat, he knew he had to get control of the situation or he would be putty in her hands. And speaking of...it didn't take much to recall just how she had used her hands on him, along with that mouth.

Forcing those erotic memories from his mind, he grabbed the clipboard from overhead. They had come to the final leg of their journey and he would admit he had enjoyed every mile of it because of her. As soon as he finalized things here, they would take the five-hour drive to Miami. He had called ahead and everything would be ready when they got there. He intended to make the time special for her.

He glanced over at her. "I've ordered a car to be delivered to us and I think that's it over there. I'll help get everything out of the cab and loaded into the car in a few."

He got out of the truck to take care of the final part of his business. A few moments later, he returned and unloaded their stuff from the cab into the trunk of the car.

"Are you sure you feel like driving to Miami after just arriving here?"

"I'm positive," he said before slipping behind the wheel. "I figure we can stop for something to eat in Daytona. Unless you're hungry now."

"Are you kidding? After all we ate for breakfast?"

They had eaten breakfast at a café in Pensacola and he was convinced they'd been the best pancakes he'd ever eaten. He had eaten more than he should have, and for once he'd noted she'd cleaned her plate, too. He glanced over at her and smiled. "I will admit that for once I'm full."

"Really?"

He chuckled. "Yes, really."

He had driven away from the warehouse and headed toward the interstate, feeling content in a way he'd never felt before. Being in a serious relationship with a woman was something he'd always avoided and now he thought doing so wouldn't be so bad if the woman was Delphine. They connected on all levels, both in the bedroom and out.

"And you're sure you don't want me to drive for a change?"

He glanced over at her. Warmth spread through him in a way it had never done before when he'd been with a woman. "Yes, I'm positive. I just want you well rested for tonight."

She chuckled. "Um, have you thought that maybe I want you well rested, as well?"

He laughed. "If you think for one minute I'm not on

top of my game, then you're wrong. I intend to prove just how wrong you are over the next several days."

A huge smile lit her face. "We'll see."

"You said, 'you'll see.' Have you seen yet?"

Instead of answering him, Delphine looped her arm around his neck and stood on tiptoe to place a kiss on his lips. "This is simply beautiful, Gannon," she said, looking into his eyes and then switching her gaze back to the ocean.

Upon arriving in Miami, Gannon had driven straight to his beach house on the ocean. It wasn't just a beach house. It was a masterpiece. He'd told her on the drive to Miami that his parents had owned it, and when they'd decided to sell it, he was the only sibling interested in buying it. The five others had loved their summers here while growing up, but wanted to try other locations for a change. He had not. He'd told her how this place held special memories for him of his childhood summers and he'd wanted to keep the house to share with the kids he would have one day.

That had been the first time he had mentioned settling down, marrying and having a family. Of course, he had mentioned it when he'd given his spiel about why he wanted her to come with him on this road trip, claiming that a part of him believed she was his future, but she'd never really believed that. She figured he had wanted her with him and would have said anything that sounded convincing to get her here. That thought didn't bother her because she didn't regret coming.

Being here with him was helping her on a number of levels. It was showing her that she could share a relationship with a man, even when she knew it wasn't headed anywhere. She'd seriously doubted that she could, but she felt good in knowing it was possible. She would never give her love, heart or dedication to a man again. Liddell and her father had shown her men didn't know the meaning of loyalty to one woman. In accepting that fact, she knew what she needed to learn was how not to enter into a relationship blindly, or love so quickly, or give her heart so easily.

"I love it here, Gannon. Now I know why you wanted to come here to stay a week."

He smiled down at her. "Did you enjoy walking on the beach with me?"

She had. In fact, that was the first thing they'd done when they got here. He had laughed when she'd raced toward the water and gotten her toes wet. This part of the beach was private, and they didn't have to worry about others sharing their space. "I can see why you bought this place from your parents. I can't believe they gave it up."

He chuckled. "Only because they purchased something bigger a few miles from here. They said the new place was an investment in their future. They figured their sons would one day marry and have kids of their own, and they wanted to own a place that would accommodate everyone. It's been a long-standing tradition in the Steele family to spend the Fourth of July together with the folks, and it's usually here in Miami at their beach house."

She nodded. "What about your brothers? Did they tire of a place on the beach?"

He wrapped his arms around her waist as they stood on the patio and looked out at the Atlantic together. "No. They just wanted a different beach for a change. Galen and Tyson own beach houses on Hilton Head, Mercury likes the Gulf and bought a place on the beach in Destin, Florida, Eli couldn't make up his mind and bought a beach house in California and also one in the Keys, and Jonas also got a place on the beach in Destin."

He leaned down and nuzzled her neck. "I thought we would go out tonight, if you aren't tired. We have the rest of the week to fend for ourselves. I don't cook much but I do like to grill."

She smiled up at him. "Sounds like fun."

They ended up going to a restaurant within walking distance of the beach house. Gannon had to put up a good argument to get her to walk with him, but he'd been very persuasive. It was obvious the owner of the establishment, Mr. Tyler, knew Gannon and gave him special treatment. They ate in a private room that overlooked the Atlantic with soft classical music playing in the background.

Gannon had told her the restaurant had been in the Tyler family for years and that it was the place his family would visit often while spending those summers on the beach. They had grown up with Mr.

Tyler's two sons and three daughters, who were now partners in the restaurant business. They'd met one of the daughters earlier when they'd arrived.

"How is the food?" Gannon asked.

"Great. In fact, I feel stuffed. Walking back to the beach house probably is the best idea."

He grinned. "That's one of the reasons I suggested it."

On the walk back, he kept her close to his side with his arms wrapped around her waist. She liked the way they fit together and how they seemed to stroll in unison. It wasn't lost on her that every so often Gannon's hand would dip lower and purposely squeeze her butt. That didn't bother her, since over the last three days he'd done more to it than that. She didn't want to think of the passion marks probably covering it.

When they reached his beach house, he opened the door and quickly ushered her inside. She soon knew why when he said, "Watching you eat your food almost drove me crazy. The way you tackled those oysters was a total turn-on."

Delphine had discovered that practically everything was a turn-on for Gannon when it came to her. It seemed just breathing turned him on. She had no complaints and rather liked it. In fact, she liked it a lot, although she refused to let it go to her head.

"What do you intend to do about it?" she asked him, knowing the last thing she should do was encourage him or taunt him when she knew where it would lead. In the three days since first sharing his bed, she had discovered a lot about herself. She enjoyed making love with a man. More specifically, she enjoyed making love with Gannon.

"You should have learned your lesson about doing that," he said, backing her up against the closed door.

"In doing what?" she asked innocently.

"In making me want to show you anything. What usually happens is I end up showing you a lot. Some of the things I wonder if you're ready for."

She would be the first to admit Gannon was a man of various ideas when it came to lovemaking. So far, nothing he'd done had turned her off. In fact, without a doubt, everything they'd tried had turned her on. "I'm ready for anything and everything from you, Gannon."

Delphine meant what she said, wanting him to know the effect he had on her. He had managed to tap into her passionate side, and she couldn't stop her body from responding to him even if she'd wanted it to.

"In that case…" he said, before easing her up and then propping her back against the door.

"What do you think you're doing?" she asked breathlessly. Her heart was beating fast and the area between her legs was pounding just as furiously. Gannon was hot-blooded and he was bringing out the hot-bloodedness in her, as well.

He had managed to pull down her shorts and underwear, as well as tug down his own. She wanted to say they were behaving like a pair of horny teenagers, but she couldn't say that when she and Liddell had never acted this way. Somehow, even in their positions against the door, Gannon managed to remove her top and her breasts sprang free.

"Well, well, what do we have here?" Gannon said, and she heard the huskiness in his voice.

"Like you didn't know I wasn't wearing a bra," she said, and then moaned when he began licking his lips.

"Damn right I knew," he said before sliding a nipple into his mouth.

She released another deep moan and he began sucking hard. When the sucking motion became more demanding, she felt every nerve ending in her body electrify.

"Gannon…"

"Hmm?"

She couldn't say anything, not when he'd moved to the second nipple and was giving it just as much torture as he'd done the first. All that pleasure had made her wet.

"Did you want something?" he asked, when he finally let go of her breasts to look at her. The green eyes staring deep into hers were intense and held promises of more to come.

Before she could say if she wanted anything or not, he lifted her hips a little higher, tilted her toward him and drove hard into her while still gazing into her eyes. She saw how the intensity in the green depths transformed into lust of the richest form.

She wanted to close her eyes, but she couldn't. It was as if his gaze demanded that she continue to look at him while feeling him deep inside of her. She was transfixed, thoroughly captivated, by the beauty of the man making love to her.

Delphine was convinced she felt him all the way to her womb. And while their gazes remained connected, he continued to thrust hard into her, with a vigor and fierceness that had her quivering all over.

"You have no idea what you do to me, Delphine," he murmured. "You have no idea." His voice was thick with emotion.

He was right; she honestly didn't. Had he determined if she was truly any different from all the others he'd done this with, or had that been just a line he told every woman he'd wanted? That they were his destiny? She pushed the question to the back of her mind, refusing to let anything dim the pleasure he was making her feel. She wanted this. She needed this.

Although she wasn't new to sex, she was new to Gannon Steele's brand of sex. He had introduced her to a degree of passion she'd only thought could be found in romance novels. She'd figured it was all make-believe, the work of an imaginative author. However, she'd found Gannon had the ability to bring all that passion from the pages of a romance novel right into his bedroom.

He broke eye contact with her when he lowered his head to take the lips he claimed he loved, and like always, he was demonstrating just how much he loved them. How could he multitask this way, and kiss her while steadily thrusting hard into her?

Suddenly a shiver of intense pleasure took over her entire body, rocking it back and forth. She began squeezing her inner muscles together when the throb between her legs strengthened and the ache increased. "Gannon, please…"

He knew what she wanted. Suddenly, he broke off the kiss, threw back his head and hollered her name. The sound triggered every passionate cell in her body to react, and she was thrust into an orgasm of gigantic proportions. She tightened her legs around him when she felt him explode inside of her. Immediately, she realized they were making love for the first time without him using a condom. She knew the moment he realized it, as well. He opened his eyes to look at her, and when she murmured that she was on the pill, he lowered his head and kissed her.

And he kept on kissing her, long after the last of the spasms had ended. It was as if they needed their mouths to be joined this way, while a surge of passionate warmth joined their bodies.

When he finally slid her body down his and her feet touched the floor again, he stared at her with a serious expression on his face. "I know what you said about being on the pill, but nothing is one hundred percent. If anything happens you will let me know, right?"

The intense look on his face gave her pause. Or was it a worried look at the thought he might have gotten a woman pregnant?

"Nothing will happen, Gannon," she said to reassure him. And then she placed a kiss on his lips.

* * *

Gannon glanced over at Delphine and saw she was asleep. Ignoring the twitch in his penis from wanting more of her, he slowly disengaged their bodies and eased out of bed. After returning from the bathroom, he grabbed his shorts off the chair and slid them on. Glancing over at Delphine again, he was tempted to crawl back in bed with her, but knew he couldn't. He had to think.

Opening the French door, he stepped outside and noticed there was a full moon in the sky that appeared to touch the ocean water. The scent of the salty sea filled his nostrils, but nothing could clear his mind of what had happened earlier. For the first time ever, he'd made love to a woman without using a condom.

Protection had always been his strictest rule, no matter what form of birth control the woman claimed she was using. And he didn't use just any type of condom. He used ones that were custom-made for their fit, as well as their performance effectiveness.

He hadn't wanted any woman to ever claim he was her baby's daddy. To that end, the last thing he'd ever wanted to encounter was a condom malfunction. His brothers used to tease him about being so particular, but that was the way he was.

Yet tonight he had gotten so caught up in making love to Delphine, so caught up in the passion, the desire, the pleasure, that he'd done just what he'd sworn he would never do. And he had liked it. Damn, he had liked the feel of exploding inside of her a whole hell of a lot. He had liked it to the point that when he had swept her off her feet to carry her into the bedroom, he had made love to her again the same way—without a condom. What would make him toss caution to the wind that way?

He eased down on the lounge chair and stared out at the ocean. Everything about Delphine got to him. Her beauty, the way she would look at him when he wasn't supposed to know she was looking. Her scent, the way her body would take his into hers, and those sexy moans that flowed from her delectable lips right before she came.

He liked touching her, sharing his beach with her, and his home. And he definitely liked the way she would wrap her legs around his waist whenever he would slide inside her to make love. That was when her inner muscles would clamp down on him hard, while her body arched into his so the connection would be deeper, each thrust more meaningful.

"Gannon?"

He turned at the sound of her voice. She was standing in the doorway naked. His gaze roamed over her, lingered on her pert breasts and flat stomach before lowering to the juncture of her thighs. He was about to explode just seeing that part of her that had pleasured him so much over the past few days.

"Gannon?"

He swallowed deeply. "Yes, Delphine?"

"I woke up and you were gone. I just want you to know you were missed."

"That can easily be remedied," he said, and slowly

moved toward her. He swept her into his arms to take her back inside, knowing he was about to toss caution to the wind yet again.

Twelve

Delphine ran faster knowing Gannon was right on her heels, intent on catching her to toss her into the water. For the past three days, they'd taken a walk on the beach every afternoon, but he'd yet to convince her to go swimming with him. Today he'd decided that would change and began chasing after her.

She refused to look over her shoulder for fear that would slow her down and he would catch her for sure. So she kept on running, even if she was running in circles. Hopefully, he would tire out before she did. But then, all she had to do was remember all their lovemaking sessions and how he had the stamina of a bull and…

"Got you!"

They tumbled to the sand and she inwardly admitted that, yes, he had her. But then, he'd been having her for the past few days now. Not that she was complaining. Now she was flat on her back—nothing new there, either. When Gannon just continued to stare at her, she said, "I hope you know I'm getting sand all in my hair."

He lowered his head toward her lips and said, "I'll help you wash it out."

"Will you?"

"Of course I will."

Gannon's mouth came closer and his lips touched hers and she knew she was a goner for certain. But she didn't mind. She never minded when it came to him. It could be because she had gone and done the one thing she'd sworn she'd never do again.

She'd fallen in love.

She felt his hands glide beneath her T-shirt to touch her breasts. At the moment, she truly appreciated that they were on a private beach. She knew what he was about to do to her and she knew she would let him. Gannon had a way of breaking down her defenses and robbing her of all common sense. How else could she have fallen in love with him when she'd known better? When she had known that regardless of what he claimed, she was not his destiny. She was certain that by now he knew it, as well.

She figured he was just waiting for the perfect time to tell her that although he'd enjoyed her company, both in and out of bed, she was no different from all the others he'd dated. The sexual chemistry between them might be strong, but that was all it was—strong sexual chemistry. Nothing more. Too bad it had taken him a whole road trip with her to find that out.

While it might end up being too bad for him, she would always consider it one of the best weeks of her life. She had needed it, and she appreciated him giving it to her. She would leave here on Monday knowing that although she loved him, he didn't love her. But for one week, they'd been together.

"I want to make love to you, Delphine. Here. Now. On my beach. So whenever I come back here, I'll remember."

Whenever *he* came back here. Not whenever *they* came back here... Was that his way of letting her know that there wouldn't be a *they* in his future? That she wouldn't be coming back here with him? She got it. She wasn't his forever girl after all, like she'd suspected. That meant all she would ever have was this and she would take it.

Gannon made beautiful love to her under a magnificent blue sky on his beach. Afterward, he picked her up in his arms and carried her inside the house so they could take a shower together. True to his word, he helped wash her hair. He also washed her body and then he made love to her again.

He held her while she slept. For some reason, she'd tossed and turned most of the night, to the point where he'd awakened her to ask if she was okay. How could she tell him that, no, she wasn't okay? She knew that at some point before Monday he would be letting her know where they stood. Instead of telling him anything, though, she'd asked that he make love to her again, and he had.

"You okay, Delphine?" he asked her the next morning before either of them got out of bed. It was close to ten already and they'd decided to make today a lazy day and sleep in.

"I'm fine. I just have a lot on my mind," she said. "No worries." After placing a kiss on his lips, she eased out of bed to go to the bathroom. That was when she heard the ringing of his phone. She quickly noted the ringtone was different from any of the previous calls he'd gotten. It was to the tune of a flirty love song.

Instead of declining the call, like he'd done with all the others he'd been receiving, he clicked on and she heard him say, "Hello, beautiful. If you're calling to see if I miss you, the answer is yes, and I can't wait to return to Phoenix to see you."

At that moment, Delphine's heart crumbled. She'd known he would be telling her at some point that she wasn't his destiny, but she hadn't expected him to already be planning to get together with another woman. Why couldn't he at least wait until after she left to make those plans? They only had three more days together.

She took several deep breaths as she entered the bathroom and closed the door behind her, fighting back her tears. She leaned against the vanity as her heart broke in a million pieces. She then recalled something she had conveniently forgotten.

He'd told her the first night they'd met that she

had reminded him of someone. Was that the person who was calling him? Had he been with Delphine, but in the back of his mind he'd been fantasizing about that other woman?

The last thing Delphine intended to do was to say anything to him about the phone call she'd overheard. What had he told her just a few days ago when they'd been on the road together? He'd pretty much accused her of feeling the need to retreat whenever it came to other women. He was probably right. She had learned her lesson. She refused to let a man decide she wasn't worthy by selecting someone else over her.

"Are you sure you're okay, Delphine?" Gannon asked.

He was concerned about her. She hadn't slept much last night for tossing and turning, and today she'd seemed withdrawn. He kept asking her what was wrong, but she refused to tell him what was bothering her. However, he knew something was. The first anniversary of her mother's death was Sunday, which was also Mother's Day. Maybe that was it.

"I'm fine, Gannon, but there's something I need to tell you," she said, looking across the table at him. He'd grilled steaks and they had decided to eat outside on the patio.

"What do you need to tell me?"

"I'm leaving tomorrow."

He frowned, certain he hadn't heard her correctly. "Excuse me? Did you just say you're leaving tomorrow?"

"Yes," she answered simply. Just "yes" and nothing more. And what bothered him more than anything was that she was looking at the food on her plate instead of him.

"I thought you agreed to stay until Monday."

"Nothing was definite," she responded.

The hell it wasn't, he thought angrily. How could she not know he assumed they would be leaving together on Monday…but not before he told her how he felt.

That he had fallen in love with her.

"Why, Delphine? Why are you leaving?"

She lifted her head to look at him. "It's time for me to go home."

He held her gaze. "Is your house ready for you to move into?"

"No."

"Are you needed back in Denver for some reason?"

She shook her head. "No."

"Then why do you want to leave?"

"I just do."

As far as he was concerned, that answer wasn't good enough. "Does it have to do with your mother?"

"My mother?"

"Yes. I know the anniversary of her death is Sunday. Is that it? Is that what's bothering you?"

Delphine said nothing for the longest moment and then she broke eye contact with him. He waited. Then she looked back at him and said, "Yes, it has something to do with my mother."

Reaching across the table, he took her hand in his. "Then let me help you get through this, Delphine. Let me—"

"No. I don't want you to help me, Gannon. I want to handle this alone. I don't need your help."

Her words should not have been such a blow to him, but they were. Why was she acting this way? He was trying to be understanding, but he couldn't help her if she didn't want his help. Granted, he'd never been around someone still grieving the loss of a loved one, but why couldn't she see he wanted to be there for her? Why was she shutting him out?

"And you don't have to take me to the airport in the morning. I've scheduled an Uber already. The car will arrive around eight."

He stared at her, trying to hold back his anger. He could understand her being upset because of her mother. He could even understand her wanting to be alone. But there was something called being considerate. She hadn't been considerate enough to let him know of her change in plans ahead of time, and now she was informing him that not only was she leaving, but she'd also scheduled an Uber?

"I'm taking a walk on the beach," he said, standing up. Normally they would walk together, but he needed time to himself. It seemed she was deliberately pushing him away. He couldn't understand why. He wanted to be with her, do what he could to help her weather this difficult time in her life, but she was refusing to let him.

Maybe it was time to tell her that he'd fallen in

love with her. He wanted to hold her in his arms, tell her how much he loved her and assure her that she would never have to be alone again because he knew she was his destiny. The one woman he was meant to claim, to share his life.

"In fact, I think it would be best if I left tonight."

He glanced over at her, shocked at what she'd said. "Tonight?"

"Yes. There's no need to wait until morning. I can stay at a hotel that's closer to the airport and—"

"What the hell is going on here, Delphine? Why are you in such a rush to leave? I thought you'd want to—"

"To what? Make love one last time for the road? I'd rather not."

He heard the venom in her tone and didn't understand why it was there. He knew women could be moody at times, but she was being downright difficult. "Talk to me, Delphine. What's going on? Why are you shutting me out? I'll even go to Denver with you and—"

"No," she said, and stood, too. "I don't need or want you to do anything for me, Gannon. Nothing at all. I enjoyed my time with you, but the bottom line is that it's over and I want to go home."

"Fine, suit yourself. I'm going walking," he snapped.

He walked the beach an hour longer than he usually did, trying to figure out what was going on with Delphine. If it had to do with her not being able to deal with the anniversary of her mother's death, he wanted to be there for her. He would not accept her shutting him out like this. He would not.

He headed back toward the beach house, intent that he and Delphine talk. He would tell her he needed to be with her during this time because she was his destiny, the woman meant to share his life. She was the woman he loved and he would always be there for her. No matter what.

He knew something was wrong the moment he walked into the house. He entered the bedroom and saw the note she'd placed on the pillow.

Thanks for everything, Gannon, but it's time for me to go. I wish you the best. Delphine.

Gannon crushed the note in his hand as anger flared through him. She wished him the best… She couldn't even wait for him to return so he could say goodbye? What kind of crap was that?

Deciding to go for a swim, he grabbed a pair of swimming trunks from the drawer, intent on swimming away his troubles.

Thirteen

"So there you have it, Mandy," Delphine said to her best friend. "I left without telling him goodbye. At least, not in person. I left a note."

"Coward."

"Think what you want. There was no way I could have stayed and told him goodbye without crying a river of tears, and I refused to cry over another man."

"Yet it's been a week and you're still crying, and don't say you're not, because I can hear it in your voice. You should have called me."

"I told you why I didn't call you. I needed time to myself." Once she'd arrived back in Denver, knowing her house wasn't ready for her, she had checked into a hotel downtown and hadn't told anyone she was back. She had needed time to try to pull herself together. Instead, for the past seven days, all she'd done was cry even more.

She had gone to the cemetery on Mother's Day, the one-year anniversary of her mom's death, to place flowers on her grave. At least she'd kept the promise she'd made to her mother about giving love another try. She had fallen in love again, but, unfortunately, the man she loved didn't love her back.

"It doesn't matter that I'm crying or how long I've been crying, as long as Gannon never knows," Delphine said, sniffing. "I refuse to let another man know how deeply he's broken my heart."

Mandy was quiet for a minute. "Maybe you should have confronted him about the phone call you overheard, Del."

"It would not have mattered. Gannon had a right to talk to whomever he wanted to talk to. I didn't have dibs on him." Delphine drew in a deep breath. Gannon hadn't called her, but she really hadn't expected him to. He had wanted to get back to Phoenix, to the woman who'd called him. He probably didn't remember Delphine existed now that he was back with her, whoever she was. For all Delphine knew, it could have very well been the woman named Trish.

The one thing Delphine decided not to share with Mandy was that her period was late. Now, on top of everything else, she had to wonder if perhaps she was pregnant. She was on the pill, so hopefully it was a false alarm, but what if it wasn't? What if she was pregnant with Gannon's child? It was too soon to tell, and she honestly didn't want to consider that possibility.

"Do you need me to come over, Del?"

"No, I'll be okay." Wanting to change the subject, she said, "And the house looks great, by the way. Thanks for taking care of everything for me."

"What are your plans today?"

"I don't have any. I am going to just lounge around and enjoy my new floors."

A short while later, after ending the call with Mandy, Delphine wiped her eyes. She'd gotten over Liddell and she intended to get over Gannon, too.

"I hear you've been in a bad mood."

Gannon glanced over at Mercury. He and his wife, Sloan, had returned from their honeymoon a couple of days ago. It was Thursday evening and, as usual, everyone had shown up to his parents' home for dinner. The women were in the kitchen helping his mom, and his brothers, those with the good sense to leave Gannon alone, were in their father's man cave watching a baseball game with Drew. His brothers had informed Mercury correctly. Gannon wasn't in a good mood and hadn't been for almost two weeks. That was why he'd come outside to sit in his mother's courtyard, which contained every type of flower imaginable.

"What of it?" Gannon asked.

"You want to talk about it?"

"Nope." Gannon's response was quick and simple.

"I think you should."

Gannon rubbed his chin and stared at his brother. "You've been married all of three weeks and you think you're an expert on relationships now?"

"No, but what I do know is that if it hadn't been for your visit to my office that day suggesting that I make some decisions regarding Sloan, I might not have had three of the best weeks of my life. I never thanked you for that and I don't want you to make the mistake I almost made, Gannon."

Gannon didn't say anything as he took a sip of his beer. He then looked over at his brother and said, "It might be too late for me, Mercury."

"What did you do?"

Gannon shrugged. "As far as I know, I didn't do anything. At least, she didn't say I did anything." He then told Mercury what he remembered. Delphine's sleepless night, the way she'd suddenly begun withdrawing from him and her sudden rush to leave.

"And you think it's all related to the anniversary of her mother's death?" Mercury asked.

"I think so. This was the first year of her mother's passing and it happened to fall on Mother's Day."

Mercury shook his head. "That's a sad situation for her to be in this year. But why shut you out when you wanted to be there for her? You told her that you'd reached the conclusion that she was your soul mate? Your destiny, right?"

Gannon rubbed a hand down his face. "No, I hadn't gotten around to it. She left before I had the chance."

Mercury stared at him for a moment. "Let me

get this straight. You convinced a woman to take a road trip with you, to get to know her better, because there was a chance that she was your soul mate. And when you realized that she was, you didn't tell her?"

"Like I said, she left before I got a chance."

Mercury glared at him. "It's been almost two weeks, right? So what are you waiting for? You know your way to Denver."

"Yes, I know my way to Denver, smart-ass, but—"

"But what?"

Gannon took another sip of his beer, then said, "She left. What if she doesn't feel the same way about me that I feel about her? What if she—"

"Does it matter?" Mercury interrupted. "She's the woman you want to claim, right? The woman you love?"

"Yes, I love her." Gannon hadn't realized just how much he loved Delphine until he'd spoken his feelings out loud. He truly loved her.

"Stop fearing rejection, something you've never had to deal with before, and go after her. Do you think any of our wives made things easy for us? Once we determined who we wanted, that was the end of it, for them and for us. If you think she doesn't love you now, then use that Steele charm you're known for. If she's truly meant for you, then it will all work out. If I were you, I would let her know how you feel."

"You're pregnant?"

Delphine sat on the edge of her bed. The pregnancy test she'd just taken had confirmed her suspicion. "Yes, Mandy, I'm pregnant," she said, filled with all sorts of emotions. Both happiness and fear topped the list. "I suspected I was two weeks ago, but wanted to wait to take the test."

"Are you going to contact Gannon Steele and let him know?"

Delphine nibbled on her bottom lip. Was she? Other than knowing she was having a baby, she wasn't sure about anything right now. She felt so overwhelmed. However, she couldn't help but remember what Gannon had told her when the possibility of a pregnancy had been discussed. He wanted her to let him know.

"He has a right to know and I will tell him. I just don't know when."

And speaking of when, she'd racked her brain wondering how the pregnancy had happened when she was on the pill. Gannon had warned her that nothing was 100 percent. He'd been right.

"Well, I am happy for you, and I know you will make a wonderful mother."

Delphine intended to be that. She wanted to be the best mother to her child, just like her mother had been to her. "Thanks, Mandy. And you will make a great godmother."

Her best friend's scream nearly pierced her ears. Delphine laughed. "Come on, Man. Did you think I was going to let you off the hook? With two kids already, for which I am a proud godmother, you're the one with all the experience."

Later that day, after preparing more food than she

could ever eat in a week, Delphine took a shower. She had a tendency to cook a lot when she was overwhelmed. Knowing she was having Gannon's baby had definitely overwhelmed her. She tried to think positively about the situation. Her mother had been a single mother and had done a great job raising Delphine. She would do the same for her child.

After her shower she had changed into a pair of shorts and a top. Grabbing a book off the table to read, she had settled into what had been her mother's favorite chair when the doorbell rang. She glanced at the grandfather clock on the wall and saw it was six. It was dinnertime for most people, and she wondered who would be paying her a visit.

After crossing the room to the door, she glanced out of the peephole and immediately caught her breath. Gannon was standing on her porch directly under the light. And as if he knew she was staring at him, he stared back.

She quickly backed away from the door. What was Gannon doing here? How did he know where she lived? Why had he shown up when she hadn't heard anything from him in nearly three weeks? Although she honestly hadn't expected him to contact her. There had been no reason for him to do so. There was no way he knew about her pregnancy, since she'd just found out herself today. But what if he suspected it? What if...?

He knocked again and she jumped at the sound. Drawing in a deep breath, she opened the door. For the longest time they stood there staring at each other. If things were different between them, she would have rushed into his arms because she needed a hug. She needed his kiss.

But things weren't different.

One thing was the same. He looked good. He was wearing a pair of jeans and a white shirt. And he smelled good, as well. "What are you doing here, Gannon?"

"I think the reason for my being here is obvious, Delphine."

She frowned. If he thought so, then he was wrong. Since there was no way he could know she was pregnant, she said, "Well, your presence here is not obvious and how did you know where I live?"

He shrugged. "Finding you wasn't hard. Were you trying to hide?"

"Of course not."

"Then will you invite me in? There are a few things I want to say to you."

She wondered just what he had to say to her. She started to ask, but decided to let him say his piece. Besides, she could see Miss Anna's curtain moving, which meant the old lady across the street was curious about the car parked in Delphine's yard and the man standing at her door, whom she hadn't invited in yet.

"Come in, Gannon." She moved to let him inside.

Gannon thought Delphine looked beautiful. If he'd had any doubt in his mind that he loved her, it was erased now. But then, there had not been any doubt.

The more he thought about how he felt, the more he was convinced he had fallen in love with her that day in the lobby of the hotel, when he'd seen her for the first time.

She smelled good, too. He'd picked up on her scent the moment she'd opened the door. It was the same scent he'd remembered waking up to, making love to. He had missed her and he hadn't realized how much until now.

He hadn't wanted to rush her. He'd given her three weeks. That had been time enough to deal with whatever she'd been going through without him. That would be her last time to go through it without him, because from this day forward, they would be dealing with things together. It was time she knew that.

After closing the door behind him, she turned to face him. "So what do you have to say?"

"A lot," he said, crossing his arms over his chest. "But first of all, I want you to know you aren't getting rid of me so easily."

She lifted an eyebrow. "What are you talking about?"

"I'm talking about the way you deliberately shut me out and didn't let me be there to help you deal with the anniversary of your mother's death. I wanted to be there for you."

"Yeah, right."

He stared at her, certain he hadn't really heard her flippant remark. "Are you saying you don't believe me?"

"Why should I? Let's be completely honest with

each other, Gannon. You got what you wanted from me. I know you lied about thinking I was your destiny. That was just a line you came up with to get me to go on the road with you. You did say the first night we met that I reminded you of someone. You probably took me with you to Florida to pretend I was her."

What in the heck was she talking about?

He had no idea, so he asked her. "What are you talking about? Who are you supposed to remind me of?"

"I have no idea. The first night we met you said I reminded you of someone."

Gannon dropped his arms to his sides, remembering the excuse he'd come up with when he'd been caught staring at her beauty. He would address that later. Right now, he was focused on the other thing she'd accused him of. Lying about her being his destiny. "Would you care to tell me why you think I lied?"

"I overheard that phone call you got, Gannon. I heard what you told her."

Gannon frowned. *Her? Her who?* He searched his brain for what phone call he might have gotten. He knew for certain that although women had called him during the time he'd been with Delphine, not once had he answered a call from any of them. He had declined every single one.

"Women might have called me, but not once did I answer their calls."

"Yes, you did," she said, crossing her own arms over her chest and lifting her chin.

"No, I did not." He searched her face and saw the intensity in the depths of her eyes. He also saw something else. Pain. "I think we need to talk, Delphine."

"We are talking."

"No, you are accusing me of doing something I didn't do."

She glared at him. "I heard you."

It was beginning to dawn on him that the reason she'd acted the way she had, the reason she had left, hadn't had anything to do with the anniversary of her mother's death after all. "What exactly did you hear, Delphine?"

For a minute he wasn't sure she would tell him. Then she said, "You thought I'd made it to the bathroom, but I hadn't. I heard your phone ring. First thing I noticed was that she had a different ringtone than the other calls you'd been getting. Then when you clicked on, you called her 'beautiful' and told her you missed her and couldn't wait to return to Phoenix to see her."

Gannon stared at her, saw the pain in her features as she retold what she'd heard. "You actually think I was with you, yet making plans to hook up with another woman when I returned to Phoenix?"

She lifted her chin. "Yes. I know what I heard, Gannon."

"You only know what you think you heard, Delphine. I'm trying real hard right now not to turn and walk out that door because of your accusations, but I won't."

While she watched, he took his phone out of his back pocket and made a single click. Then he said, "Please call me back." He then clicked off.

Within seconds his phone rang with that same ringtone Delphine was talking about. He clicked on and placed the caller on speaker. "Thanks for calling me back."

"No problem, baby. What's this about?"

Delphine frowned, wondering what point Gannon was trying to make. It had been the same ringtone she'd heard that night and it was a woman. A woman who had what Delphine thought was a very sexy voice.

Delphine was about to ask Gannon to leave when his next words stopped her. "This is about me being in Denver with the woman I've fallen in love with. However, there seems to be a problem caused by your ringtone, Mom."

Mom? Had he just called the woman with the sexy voice *Mom*? Delphine was certain she'd heard him wrong. And had he admitted to loving her?

He obviously knew what she was thinking because he then said to her, "You heard me right, Delphine."

"Hi, Delphine," the woman—Gannon's mother—said.

Delphine swallowed hard before returning the

greeting. She dropped her arms to her sides. "Hello, Mrs. Steele."

"Gannon has told me and his father all about you and we're looking forward to meeting you. Soon, we hope." Then she asked, "So what problem did my ringtone cause?"

Still holding her gaze with intensity in his green eyes, Gannon said to his mother, "I'm sure it's nothing Delphine and I can't work out."

"I certainly hope so," Eden Tyson Steele said.

"'Bye, Mom."

"'Bye, baby. 'Bye, Delphine."

"Goodbye, Mrs. Steele."

Gannon clicked off the phone and put it back in his jeans. He then looked over at Delphine. "What do you have to say now, Delphine?"

"But the ringtone…"

He shrugged. "It was Mom's choice. She assigned each of her sons a different ringtone. That particular one is mine because I am the youngest and she thinks I will always be her baby."

"Oh." Delphine then said, "You called her 'beautiful.' Who calls their mother 'beautiful'?"

He shoved his hands in the pockets of his jeans. "I do because she is beautiful. And I told her I missed her because I did miss her, and I looked forward to returning to Phoenix to see her."

Delphine threw her hands up in the air, as if frustrated. "Well, how was I to know the caller was your mother?"

"If the phone call bothered you, then you should

have asked me about it instead of assuming anything. I recall pointing out to you before that you have a tendency to retreat whenever you feel somewhat threatened by another woman. This time the woman was my mother, but I have a feeling there is more to this retreating thing with you than I understand. So will you explain it to me?"

Delphine's head began spinning, and before she could answer his question, she knew she needed him to clarify what he'd said earlier. "You really love me?"

He took a couple of steps to stand directly in front of her. "Yes, I really love you. I also told you the truth about the reason I wanted you to go on the road with me. It wasn't a line or a lie."

"But what about the woman I remind you of?"

"You don't remind me of anyone. I just made that up the night I saw you to cover why I was so taken by you. Why I'd gone into a daze. The sight of you had overwhelmed me. Let me go on record now and say that you don't remind me of anyone but yourself. The woman I'm in love with."

Tears formed in her eyes. "But you didn't tell me that you loved me."

"I had planned to tell you, Delphine. I had decided on my walk on the beach that I would, but when I got back to the beach house, you had left. Without bothering to tell me goodbye."

She swiped at the tears she couldn't stop from falling. "I couldn't hang around to tell you goodbye."

He reached out and wiped away a tear that she'd missed. "And why couldn't you?"

"Because I really didn't want to leave since I had fallen in love with you, too," she said brokenly.

"Oh, sweetheart." Gannon swept her into his arms and carried her over to the sofa. He sat down with her cradled in his lap. He captured her mouth and began kissing her in ways that she had missed. Ways she thought she would never experience again. Ways that had her heart pounding in her chest. Then when he deepened the kiss, blood rushed through her veins and her pulse felt like it was on fire.

He released her mouth and held her in his arms. She could feel his warmth through his clothing. He looked down at her and touched her chin. "I love you, Delphine."

"And I love you, Gannon."

He was kissing her again, more passionately than all those other times, and then she felt him standing. "Which way, sweetheart?"

She knew why he was asking for directions. She had no problem giving them to him. "Down the hall to your right."

Gannon placed Delphine on the bed fully clothed, and he joined her there. They still needed to talk. Coming here, telling her that he loved her and accepting that she loved him, as well, were all firsts for him, and she needed to know that.

He pulled her into his arms. "Tell me, Delphine.

Why do you allow yourself to be threatened by other women? If a man tells a woman he loves her, then—"

"He can change his mind," she said, looking into his eyes. "Liddell told me that he loved me and asked me to marry him. I believed he did and agreed to marry him. I told you what happened."

Yes, she had, Gannon thought.

"And then my father left my mother for another woman and we haven't heard from him since. I don't know if he's alive or dead."

"And because of those two situations you think if I asked you to marry me that I would eventually call it off or leave you?"

She looked away. "I don't want to think that."

He reached out and touched her chin to bring her gaze back to his. "Then don't. Believe what I'm telling you, Delphine. I am asking you to not compare me to your ex-fiancé or your father. There is no excuse for what they did. I love you. I want you for my wife, as the mother of my babies, as my partner in all things. Will you marry me? If you say yes, I intend to make all those things happen."

She leaned against him and stared into his eyes. "One of those things you mentioned is already in the works."

He lifted an eyebrow. "What do you mean?"

She slipped out of his arms and scampered off the bed. "I need to show you something."

Before Gannon could ask what she had to show him, she had rushed out of the room. He glanced around, checking out her bedroom for the first time. He liked the way it was decorated, in yellow and green.

"I think you need to see this," she said, handing him a box.

He read it and then looked at her. "A pregnancy test kit?" When she nodded, he said, "Does this mean…?"

She nodded again as a huge smile appeared on his face.

"We're having a baby?"

She smiled, as well. "Yes. I don't know why the pill didn't work."

"It wasn't supposed to that time, for us." He couldn't contain the happiness and excitement in his voice.

She nodded for the third time and he pulled her back into his arms. "Will you marry me, Delphine, and believe that I will make a good father for our child and will love you forever? Will you trust me to do that?"

She smiled. "Yes, I will marry you and I trust you."

And then he pulled her down to him for another kiss.

Epilogue

Delphine smiled as she danced with her husband of two hours. It was their first dance together as a married couple and she had a feeling it wouldn't be their last. She was happy, and Gannon had told her several times today that he was happy and she believed him.

She had a wonderful husband and she was marrying into a wonderful family. She'd not only met all his brothers and his parents weeks ago, but today, she'd also met his cousins from Charlotte, North Carolina. And pieced together the puzzle of how the Steeles and the Westmorelands were semi-related. It had all started when Quade Westmoreland married Gannon's cousin Cheyenne Steele…

It seemed everyone was at the wedding, which was held at her church in Denver. The reception was in the ballroom of one of the city's largest hotels. Another reception would be held in Phoenix next month.

"Did I tell you how beautiful you look today, Mrs. Steele?"

Delphine smiled up at Gannon. "Yes, several times, but I appreciate every compliment."

If his family was curious as to why they'd wanted to get married right away, no one had asked. Gannon and Delphine decided they would announce the news about the baby to everyone when they returned from their honeymoon in two weeks. They would be leaving tonight for Barcelona, Spain, and she couldn't wait.

They would make Phoenix their permanent home and Delphine would continue to be a freelance journalist for *Simply Irresistible*. Everyone was excited about the issue containing the interview with Gannon that was coming out in September, on Delphine's birthday. She'd seen samples of the cover and thought the same thing everyone would think when they saw it—Gannon Steele was a very handsome man. She hoped everyone would enjoy her article, as well. The interview revealed just what a wonderful man she had fallen in love with and married.

"Happy?" Gannon asked her as they continued to dance.

"Extremely," she said, tightening her arms around his neck.

He smiled down at her. "There is another extremely happy person today, too. My mom. She has all of her sons married off and she is walking around with a huge smile on her face. And just so you know, now that you're mine, your life will never be the same."

"Um, more road trips?"

He chuckled as he brought her close. "More of everything. This I promise you."

Not caring that over three hundred people were probably watching them, he pulled her into his arms and kissed her. There was no doubt in anyone's mind that she was officially being claimed by a Steele.

* * * * *

*Read all the Forged of Steele
novels from*
New York Times *bestselling author
Brenda Jackson!*

COMING NEXT MONTH FROM

DESIRE

Available June 2, 2020

#2737 THE PRICE OF PASSION
Texas Cattleman's Club: Rags to Riches • by Maureen Child
Rancher Camden Guthrie is back in Royal, Texas, looking to rebuild his life as a member of the Texas Cattleman's Club. The one person who can help him? Beth Wingate, his ex. Their reunion is red-hot, but startling revelations threaten their future.

#2738 FORBIDDEN LUST
Dynasties: Seven Sins • by Karen Booth
Allison Randall has long desired playboy Zane Patterson. The problem? He's her brother's best friend, and Zane won't betray that bond, no matter how much he wants her. Stranded in paradise, sparks fly, but Allison has a secret that could tear them apart...

#2739 UPSTAIRS DOWNSTAIRS TEMPTATION
The Men of Stone River • by Janice Maynard
Working in an isolated mansion, wealthy widower Farrell Stone needs a live-in housekeeper. Ivy Danby is desperate for a job to support her baby. Their simmering attraction for one another is evident, but are their differences too steep a hurdle to create a future together?

#2740 HOT NASHVILLE NIGHTS
Daughters of Country • by Sheri WhiteFeather
Brooding songwriter Spencer Riggs is ready to reinvent himself. His ex, Alice McKenzie, is the perfect stylist for the job. Years after their wild and passionate romance, Alice finally has her life on track, but will their sizzling attraction burn them both again?

#2741 SCANDALOUS ENGAGEMENT
Lockwood Lightning • by Jules Bennett
To protect her from a relentless ex, restauranteur Reese Conrad proposes to his best friend, Josie Coleman. But their fake engagement reveals real feelings, and Josie sees Reese in a whole new way. And just as things heat up, a shocking revelation changes everything!

#2742 BACK IN HIS EX'S BED
Murphy International • by Joss Wood
Art historian Finn Murphy has a wild, impulsive side. It's what his ex-wife, Beah Jenkinson, found so attractive—and what burned down their white-hot marriage. Now, reunited to plan a friend's wedding, the chemistry is still there... and so are the problems that broke them apart.

YOU CAN FIND MORE INFORMATION ON UPCOMING HARLEQUIN TITLES, FREE EXCERPTS AND MORE AT HARLEQUIN.COM.

HDCNM0520

*To protect her from a relentless ex, restaurateur Reese
Conrad proposes to his best friend, Josie Coleman.
But their fake engagement reveals real feelings, and
Josie sees Reese in a whole new way. And just as things
heat up, a shocking revelation changes everything!*

Read on for a sneak peek at
Scandalous Engagement
by USA TODAY *bestselling author Jules Bennett.*

"What's that smile for?" he asked.

She circled the island and placed a hand over his heart. "You're
just remarkable. I mean, I've always known, but lately you're just
proving yourself more and more."

He released the wine bottle and covered her hand with his…and
that's when she remembered the kiss. She shouldn't have touched
him—she should've kept her distance because there was that look
in his eyes again. Where had this come from? When did he start
looking at her like he wanted to rip her clothes off and have his
naughty way with her?

"We need to talk about it," he murmured.

It. As if saying the word *kiss* would somehow make this situation
weirder. And as if she hadn't thought of anything else since *it* had
happened.

"Nothing to talk about," she told him, trying to ignore the warmth
and strength between his hand and his chest.

"You can't say you weren't affected."

"I didn't say that."

He tipped his head, somehow making that penetrating stare even
more potent. "It felt like more than a friend kiss."

Way to state the obvious.

"And more than just a practice," he added.

Josie's heart kicked up. They were too close, talking about things that were too intimate. No matter what she felt, what she thought she wanted, this wasn't right. She couldn't ache for her best friend in such a physical way. If that kiss changed things, she couldn't imagine how anything more would affect this relationship.

"We can't go there again," she told him. "I mean, you're a good kisser—"

"Good? That kiss was a hell of a lot better than just good."

She smiled. "Fine. It was pretty incredible. Still, we can't get caught up in this whole fake-engagement thing and lose sight of who we really are."

His free hand came up and brushed her hair away from her face. "I haven't lost sight of anything. And I'm well aware of who we are…and what I want."

Why did that sound so menacing in the most delicious of ways? Why was her body tingling so much from such simple touches when she'd firmly told herself to not get carried away?

Wait. Was he leaning in closer?

"Reese, what are you doing?" she whispered.

"Testing a theory."

His mouth grazed hers like a feather. Her knees literally weakened as she leaned against him for support. Reese continued to hold her hand against his chest, but he wrapped the other arm around her waist, urging her closer.

There was no denying the sizzle or spark or whatever the hell was vibrating between them. She'd always thought those cheesy expressions were so silly, but there was no perfect way to describe such an experience.

And kissing her best friend was quite an experience…

Don't miss what happens next in…
Scandalous Engagement
by USA TODAY bestselling author Jules Bennett.

Available June 2020 wherever
Harlequin Desire books and ebooks are sold.

Harlequin.com

Love Harlequin romance?

DISCOVER.

Be the first to find out about promotions,
news and exclusive content!

Facebook.com/HarlequinBooks

Twitter.com/HarlequinBooks

Instagram.com/HarlequinBooks

Pinterest.com/HarlequinBooks

ReaderService.com

EXPLORE.

Sign up for the Harlequin e-newsletter and
download a free book from any series at
TryHarlequin.com

CONNECT.

Join our Harlequin community to
share your thoughts and connect
with other romance readers!
Facebook.com/groups/HarlequinConnection

MORE MUST-READ TRUE CRIME
FROM PINNACLE

BOOK YOUR PLACE ON OUR WEBSITE AND MAKE THE READING CONNECTION!

We've created a customized website just for our very special readers, where you can get the inside scoop on everything that's going on with Zebra, Pinnacle and Kensington books.

When you come online, you'll have the exciting opportunity to:

- View covers of upcoming books

- Read sample chapters

- Learn about our future publishing schedule (listed by publication month *and author*)

- Find out when your favorite authors will be visiting a city near you

- Search for and order backlist books from our online catalog

- Check out author bios and background information

- Send e-mail to your favorite authors

- Meet the Kensington staff online

- Join us in weekly chats with authors, readers and other guests

- Get writing guidelines

- AND MUCH MORE!

**Visit our website at
http://www.kensingtonbooks.com**